1982

AN INTRODUCTION
TO GUIDANCE

AN INTRODUCTION TO GUIDANCE

E. L. TOLBERT
University of Florida

LITTLE, BROWN AND COMPANY
Boston   Toronto

Library of Congress Catalog Card No. 77–88041

First Printing

Published simultaneously in Canada
by Little, Brown & Company (Canada) Limited

Printed in the United States of America

ACKNOWLEDGMENTS

The table on page 14 is from *Career Education* by Sidney Marland, p. 11. Copyright © 1974 by McGraw-Hill, Inc. Used by permission of McGraw-Hill Book Company.

The table on page 15 is adapted from D. J. Prediger, J. D. Roth, and R. J. Noeth, *Nationwide Survey of Student Career Development: Summary of Results*, A. C. T. Research Report No. 61, pp. 9–10. Used by permission of American College Testing Program, Iowa City, Iowa.

On page 93, the summary of material from *Developmental Tasks and Education*, third edition, by Robert J. Havighurst, pp. 1–98, is used by permission of Longman, Inc. Copyright 1948 by the University of Chicago, copyright 1950 by Robert J. Havighurst, copyright 1950, © 1972 by David McKay Company, copyright © 1977 by Longman, Inc.

The table on page 138 is adapted from S. R. Baker and J. C. Hansen, "School Counselor Attitudes on a Status Quo-Change Agent Measurement Scale," *School Counselor* 19, no. 4, p. 246. Copyright 1972 by the American Personnel and Guidance Association. Used by permission.

The table on page 174 is from J. C. Hansen, T. M. Niland, and L. P. Zani, "Model Reinforcement in Group Counseling with Elementary School Children," *Personnel and Guidance Journal* 47, no. 8, p. 743. Copyright 1969 by the American Personnel and Guidance Association. Used by permission.

The table on page 189 is taken in part from Thomas J. Jacobson et al., "A Study of Career Centers in the State of California, Final Report (1975)," p. 75. Reprinted by permission of the author.

The data on page 198 is taken from a table in P. J. Lauver, R. H. Gastellum, and M. Sheehey, "Bias in *Occupational Outlook Handbook* Illustrations," *Vocational Guidance Quarterly* 23, no. 4, p. 337. Copyright 1975 by the American Personnel and Guidance Association. Used by permission.

(Continued on page 451)

TO FRANCES, JANE, YVES, AND MARGARET

PREFACE

This book is designed to help students learn about the guidance profession and to explore its suitability as a career—two particularly important goals for an introductory course. In the first guidance course, students need a forward-looking, practical introduction to the field, providing basic information and facilitating career planning. Suitable for one-quarter or one-semester introductory courses in counselor preparation, this text can also be used in other courses for teachers and administrators. Workshops, in-service education, and similar programs can use selected chapters. Emphasis on the basic aspects of counseling and guidance in school and non-school settings will make the book suitable for anyone planning to enter one of the many specialized programs now established.

Counseling and guidance are expanding in terms of the ages of those served, their problems, and the variety of programs to meet their needs. In addition, the needs of the handicapped, family groups, minorities, and women are receiving increased attention. To successfully meet the new challenges in the field, a counselor must be professional, well-prepared, and capable of carrying out the task of helping others.

A student who wants to be such a counselor should begin by surveying all aspects of guidance: the need for services, current practices, the history of the field, existing programs, specific functions, professional requirements, opportunities for practice, evaluation of effectiveness, and future prospects. At this early stage in preparation, it is also important for the student to understand the process of helping others grow, develop, and fulfill their potential. The student needs to begin to build a professional identity that will give him or her direction and purpose in career planning. This book is organized to cover these important areas logically and comprehensively, benefitting not only beginning students but also practitioners who wish to update their knowledge.

The sixteen chapters are presented in an order that enables the reader to gain an overall view of guidance and counseling, examine practices, explore dimensions of the role, and learn how to assess results. Throughout the entire text, many examples of actual guidance situations illustrate the current practice of guidance and the direction of the field.

Chapter 1 highlights needs and problems faced by individuals and the society and reviews major guidance themes as they relate to these conditions. Guidance programs K through 12 are shown in action in Chapters 2 and 3. Chapter 4 reviews the development of guidance, emphasizes the value of history in understanding the present, and describes factors which enable one to predict the future. The philosophical and scientific bases that provide the values, research, and theory for professional practice are explained in Chapter 5. Chapter 6 describes program models and emphasizes how recent developments in conceptualizing and designing systems facilitate the effective planning, implementation, and evaluation of programs. In addition, guidance roles are described, and the importance of the teacher is recognized. Chapter 7 deals with the critical task of individual counseling and summarizes theories that provide bases for face-to-face approaches. Chapter 8 reviews the major types of group work and identifies a number of special populations with whom the counselor will be concerned. Chapter 9 covers the increasingly complex information service and explains how modern technology can practically eliminate the time-consuming drudgery of compiling and disseminating information. Chapter 10 presents the consulting function, a new strategy that greatly enhances the spread of guidance by enlisting teachers, parents, and other significant persons in the helping process. Chapter 11 analyzes the pros and cons of assessment and describes how problems often result from the misuse or lack of understanding of tests and other instruments. Chapter 12 discusses the use of support personnel to carry out specific responsibilities under supervision and describes how they can extend the scope of services and allow counselors to use professional skills where they are most needed. The use of peer counselors is viewed as a way of expanding help to pupils as well as giving the peer counselors a valuable learning experience. New and innovative educational programs and institutions are discussed in Chapter 13; counselor participation in planning these programs is needed because guidance has much to offer and lack of involvement can lead to isolation and loss of effectiveness. Chapter 14 covers ethical standards, preparation guidelines, requirements for certification and licensure, legal responsibilities, and professional organizations. In addition, the roles of colleagues in this country and abroad are discussed, and suggestions are made for keeping abreast of new developments. Chapter 15 reviews problems and opportunities resulting from the growing emphasis on accountability and suggests ways for the counselor to turn this new requirement into an advantage. Finally, Chapter 16 looks into the future.

This book contains a number of special features designed to facilitate and extend learning. Goals at the beginning of chapters provide a framework for reading. Objectives with answers at the end of each section help review major points and assess the students' changes in understanding and attitude. Experience activities for individual or group use are included within each chapter. These activities emphasize affective elements to help the reader explore attitudes about guidance and counseling and gain a deeper understanding of the topics covered. Key research material is set apart in prominent boxes to highlight recent findings. Annotated references for each chapter indicate valuable additional readings to expand the students' understanding of topics and facilitate the development of a broader perspective on problems, issues, and trends. A glossary defines terms that students will frequently encounter in the preparation program. Five appendixes contain preparation standards, ethical standards, licensure guidelines, and a listing of professional organizations. An instructor's manual provides suggestions for class procedures, additional experience activities, multiple-choice and essay questions, and materials for duplication and distribution to students.

Many persons have contributed to this book. Leaders in the field have generously provided materials and suggestions. Colleagues and students have reacted to concepts and activities. Special mention should be made of the invaluable assistance provided by the staff of the American Personnel and Guidance Association in obtaining materials needed for the book. The author is indebted to Milbrey L. Jones of the Department of Health, Education and Welfare for her expertise in resolving difficulties concerning information retrieval. Perceptive suggestions and invaluable editorial assistance were given by Mylan Jaixen, Betsy Foote, and Jan Beatty of Little, Brown. My appreciation also extends to Robert Read, Northeastern University, Boston; Frank L. O'Dell, Cleveland State University; and Janet C. Heddesheimer, George Washington University who read the manuscript and made helpful suggestions. Margaret Tolbert, with little help from those of us who lack visual perception, prepared the vivid and imaginative illustrations that highlight key concepts in the book. All of these persons made the task of writing this book more stimulating and enjoyable than it had a right to be.

—E. L. Tolbert

CONTENTS

CHAPTER FOURTEEN
GUIDANCE AS A PROFESSION   279

CHAPTER FIFTEEN
EVALUATION, RESEARCH, AND ACCOUNTABILITY   310

CHAPTER SIXTEEN
THE FUTURE: ISSUES, TRENDS, AND PROSPECTS   340

APPENDIX A

APPENDIX B

APPENDIX C

APPENDIX D

APPENDIX E

EXPERIENTIAL ACTIVITIES AND RESEARCH DATA

To highlight discussions in the text, we have included two types of enrichment material, which are set off from the text in bold type. Experiential activities are situations designed to assess your feelings about guidance as a profession; research data demonstrate the ways in which problems in the field are investigated and provide support for points in the text. The introductory and closing chapters (1 and 16) are the only ones that do not include these special activities and data.

CHAPTER SEVEN
FACE-TO-FACE COUNSELING FOR INDIVIDUALS

CHAPTER EIGHT
ADAPTING GUIDANCE TO SPECIFIC NEEDS

CHAPTER NINE
PROVIDING INFORMATION: THE COUNSELOR'S ROLE

CHAPTER TEN
CONSULTATION: EFFECTING SYSTEM-WIDE CHANGE

CHAPTER ELEVEN
THE NEED TO ASSESS

CHAPTER TWELVE
SUPPORT PERSONNEL AND EXPANDED SERVICE

CHAPTER THIRTEEN
NEW EDUCATIONAL MODELS

CHAPTER FOURTEEN
GUIDANCE AS A PROFESSION

CHAPTER FIFTEEN
EVALUATION, RESEARCH, AND ACCOUNTABILITY

AN INTRODUCTION
TO GUIDANCE

CHAPTER ONE
GUIDANCE:
SCOPE
AND CHALLENGE

The occupation you choose determines how you will spend a major portion of your waking hours and, more importantly, profoundly affects your life-style. In the ideal situation, occupation and life-style suit each other — each enhances the other to create an ongoing pattern of productive and stimulating harmony.

To achieve such a match of work and life-style, you must choose your occupation with a realistic understanding both of the work and of your attitudes towards all it involves. Only then is your decision likely to lead to an engrossing and personally meaningful career.

This book is designed to familiarize you with the guidance and counseling profession and to help you explore your own values and attitudes towards the work. A soundly based decision to enter the field depends on personal preferences combined with a good insight into a process whereby you can help others plan for themselves.

An overview of negative conditions in contemporary society gives a vivid account of the kind of problem anyone who plans to be a helper will have to face.

GOALS

1. To become aware of needs and problems of individuals and society.
2. To appreciate the conditions and trends that require a helping service.
3. To understand the extent and nature of guidance services.

CONTEMPORARY SOCIETY: NEEDS AND TRENDS

Surveying the faults and conflicts in society obscures many strengths and advantages and seems to put undue stress on the negative. But these are the factors that must be highlighted. There are shortcomings that demand immediate and comprehensive remedies. Guidance and counseling obviously cannot solve everything alone, but they can play a major role. Guidance workers can reach individuals who need assistance, help modify conditions that call for improvement, change institutions that are failing in their missions, and take steps to reverse destructive trends.

Problems and needs in society are nothing new, but today they seem to be proliferating at an unprecedented rate. Problems once hidden have become visible; new ones arise. All are given extensive coverage by media. No area of life is taboo. But rapid and unexpected local, national, and international changes give rise to needs and challenges qualitatively and quantitatively different from those of the past.

THE CHANGING FAMILY   On nothing has there been so great an impact as on the family. A recent feature article in *Newsweek* raises the question, "Who . . . is raising today's children?" and cogently points out that parents lack time and commitment to serve as models for their children. But these are not the only family problems. The home, once regarded as the ideal setting for bringing up children, is being disrupted by divorce and separation. The institution of the family is being attacked by critics who decry its deficiencies and suggest alternative life-styles. Working parents face hectic schedules. Another *Newsweek* article concludes that "the emotional demands in a two-career family are profound."

Geographic mobility, changing housing patterns, and the establishment of retirement communities have contributed to the erosion of the extended family. Far fewer grandparents and other relatives live in the home or nearby and now baby-sitters and day centers give children the personal attention once provided by relatives.

CITIES IN UPHEAVAL   The plight of cities is becoming commonplace. Financial pressures are accelerating the decline of the quality of life in large urban areas.

Cities were once favorable environments for education and personal development, but social conflict, economic crises, loss of family ownership of property, street crime, and deteriorating neighborhoods have spoiled many of them. Vandalism in schools has increased, and in some areas teachers and pupils alike are assaulted by youth gangs. The inner city has been hit hardest, but crime has also been moving to the suburbs. In many regions, the stabilizing effects of work are missing; unemployment rates are high, particularly among minority youths.

Family and community life exert a reciprocal influence on each other; as the neighborhood deteriorates, the positive contribution of the family diminishes. Even though efforts are being made to rehabilitate blighted communities, many families move out, thus accelerating the negative trend.

CONFLICTS IN VALUES, ATTITUDES, AND MORALS   The unprecedented spread of therapies points to a widespread sense of life as meaningless and deep conflicts of values. Psychiatry has been called the new religion.

Much of the present unease and uncertainty began in the 60s, a decade in which traditional morals, ethics, and values were profoundly challenged. The 70s is a period of searching for meaning and purpose, and is marked by a new media-wide openness about changing patterns of values. The cover of *Time* shows a sergeant in the Air Force saying "I'm a homosexual . . ." A few years ago, the topic could not have been discussed in the general press. This new frankness reveals issues that must be faced, and confronts young people with complexities once relatively unknown.

There are other equally striking examples. The daily newspapers carry frequent reports on the behavior of government officials that would have been called sensationalized, improbable fictions only a few years ago. Stories about cheating scandals on college campuses appear with almost monotonous regularity. Drinking has increased among the young— studies reveal that one out of every four 13-year-olds is a "moderate" drinker. Cohabitation is a widely accepted life-style for many college students. Many high school students drop out because of unwanted pregnancies.

But traditional values have strong supporters. In the search for ways to build moral awareness, schools and professional colleges are introducing new courses in ethics. Secondary schools stressing traditional standards of discipline, dress, and manners have waiting lists. A well-known psychologist has advanced the point of view that the ethical and moral values that have evolved in human societies have a scientific basis.

THE NEW CYNICISM ABOUT POLITICS   Distrust of politicians and the political system is not new, but in the previous and current decades they have reached unprecedented intensity.

The Vietnam War threw the issue of credibility into sharp relief. In this decade Watergate, revelations about CIA and FBI intrigues, and invasions of privacy have multiplied the questions. Lurid sex episodes have surfaced about members of Congress. National government, however, has not been alone in provoking distrust. Governors, judges, and legislators have been convicted of minor and major violations of the law.

People have grown doubtful and cynical about the sincerity of the government's concern for the welfare of the individual. Social services, education, and programs for those in need have been cut back. Moreover, the public is convinced that the government is more keenly aware of the problems and needs than at any time in the past and that ignorance is not the reason for neglect. As a result, many feel overlooked and powerless to take action in matters that deeply affect their lives.

ECONOMIC FACTORS   Much of what constitutes the "good life" is tied to the state of the economy. Inflation erodes resources for education, travel, and improved living conditions. Unemployment and underemployment caused by economic slowdowns wreak havoc on family life, particularly for women, minority group members, and young people who are just catching up in the job market.

The very economic conditions that aggravate social problems also necessitate reductions in services to those most severely affected. An enormous burden rests on helping agencies and educational institutions, which must cope with long waiting lists and overcrowded classrooms.

The most destructive effects, however, are psychological—the feelings of apprehension, uselessness, and selfishness generated by depressed economic conditions. Capable people with much to offer give up looking for work. Students spoil each other's experiments to improve their own chances of getting into highly competitive medical schools. Only a few businesses and industries agree to reduce wages so that no one will be laid off.

THE CHANGING ROLE OF WORK   Many young people are uncertain and confused by the conflicting attitudes about work. They hear that the work ethic is disappearing, that most jobs are demeaning and destructive, that technology will replace large numbers of workers, and that in many specialties a flooded market will cause unprecedented unemployment. But they also hear the unemployed asking for a chance to work, that work is the path to equality for minorities, and that you have to develop salable skills to meet the demands of a technological society.

Many young people worry about the future. Realistic and accurate occupational information is lacking and rumors of shortages and overcrowding proliferate. Career plans can change in a day. In case after case, individuals who have spent years preparing for a specific occupation suddenly

Doctor, lawyer, Indian chief . . . or cowboy? A counselor can offer information to help a person choose.

realize they must find employment in an unrelated field. Many programs are restricted to avoid projected worker surpluses. Freedom of choice dwindles.

Automation and technological advances have reduced the number of low-skill entry jobs, and have also lessened the worker's pride in his share in producing a finished article. Efforts to establish new procedures to give employees more status and control have met with limited success.

NEW PRESSURE AND DEMANDS ON SCHOOLS   Problems, issues, and trends in public education figure prominently in this book. They are in fact often the same as those in guidance and counseling. The most pressing are listed below; others will be covered later. The list touches on aspects of all the problems previously mentioned; school problems reflect the problems of society.

1. Writing skills and achievement in science are declining.
2. The quality of preparation of entering college students is declining.
3. New workers can expect considerable difficulty in finding jobs.
4. There is a growing concern about pupils' moral development.
5. The rights of pupils are being violated.
6. School vandalism is costing taxpayers over half a million dollars a year.
7. Violence in schools is increasing.
8. Lack of discipline is considered a major school problem; many parents would prefer stricter schools.
9. Schools have taken over responsibility after responsibility and raised unrealistic expectations in the minds of the public.
10. Questions are raised about the value of increased funds for schools.
11. Schools do not provide an effective learning environment. As much as 95 percent of current educational practice is of questionable value.
12. Schools need to be dejuvenilized. Break down the isolation of the school subculture, treat pupils more like adults, and make the educational institution more integral a part of life.

PROBLEMS OF YOUNG PEOPLE   Difficulties for school-age youth and young adults are inherent in the conditions already described. But some particularly pressing ones need to be emphasized. Social and academic pressures on youth have caused increased drug use, running away from home, emotional disturbance, and suicide. Lack of involvement and commitment to meaningful work, education, and social activities leads to isolation and alienation. Difficulties in role identity arise, as typified by expressions like "I don't know who I am"; "I've got to find myself." Family mobility generates feelings of rootlessness and lack of community identification among the young, some of whom seek a sense of belonging in allegiance to strange or destructive cults and groups. By the end of high school, the typical teenager has watched 15,000 hours of TV, and TV is acknowledged to breed a fascination with violence and a craving for instant success.

Changing sex roles pose problems for all ages, but particularly for the young experiencing conflicts about work, sexual freedom, and family responsibilities. For example, the girl or boy who has learned the traditional sex roles with respect to careers may, because of both personal values and societal pressures, find it difficult to choose a nontraditional occupation.

The increasing average age of the population will also affect the young. More concern is being expressed for problems and needs of older Americans. Major changes in social, economic, and political policy that will touch young people include, for example, increased taxes for services. The proportionally fewer young persons will wield less influence and therefore receive, for example, less attention from consumer markets.

This is only a sampling. Other changes could be listed; and it is likely that even more pressing ones are just over the horizon.

GUIDANCE TODAY

A report on the contemporary status of guidance coming after a review of societies' needs might seem to suggest that the profession will supply all answers. But although the guidance profession is a powerful force, its focus must necessarily be limited to appropriate high-priority targets. Trying to do everything for everybody will result in frustrations for workers, gaps in coverage, and thin or invisible effects. The following description of guidance today will help identify priorities and outline the most important factors to weigh when considering the occupation and the lifestyle it involves.

The prospective counselor should be aware that counseling is at a crossroads. Demands of the people served and developments within the profession have led to differences of opinion about strategies, needs, roles, priorities within the population, work certification, and degree of support. Each issue is complex; all defy a brief summarization. In chapters that follow, they will be examined in depth, but at this point it is important to note a handful that have major implications for opportunities and limitations in the field. First, there is the issue of serving as an agent of change—how actively should the counselor be involved in altering customs, laws, and established patterns of society? Some want to help the individual adjust to what exists; others want to take an active role to alter prevalent conditions, for example, current attitudes toward minority groups. Second, there is a trend towards developing large-scale programs and strategies; one-to-one and one-to-small-group counseling is being replaced by training and preventive activities (Ivey 1976). Third, new standards for preparation are emerging (Moore 1977). Finally, among other issues and dilemmas, two related matters stand out—accountability and the limitation of resources. Counselors, like other educators, are being required to demonstrate the difference they make in the lives of others; even though financial support may not match needs. There is a definite trend to require services for all sorts to prove their effectiveness; support is based on evidence. Moreover, counselors will be expected to produce more without increased support or to prove that higher levels of support will result in measurable and desirable change.

Still, it is apparent that counseling and guidance are well established in public educational institutions, community agencies, colleges, and universities. An impressive number of practitioners are currently employed in public schools. In 1970–71 there were more than 40,000 counselors in more than 90 percent of the schools. This is up from a little over 2,000 in the 1930s (Odell 1973). The mission of providing developmental and remedial help to all pupils during the critical formative years is ambitious. The profession has enjoyed a position of prestige and status in time of critical national needs; its services are sought when human resources must be developed, social conflicts eased, and destructive behavior eliminated. Relatively new on the helping scene, it has matured to the point where hundreds of graduate preparation programs are offered; standards, ethics, and local guidelines have been developed; and strong national organizations have emerged with an impressive, stimulating array of professional publications.

Guidance is longest-established and most prevalent in secondary schools. At latest count, nine out of ten school counselors were working at this level. Development at the elementary-school level has been more recent, but expansion has been rapid. From 1967 to 1971, the number of counselors more than doubled, reaching almost 8,000 in 1971. Growth in the middle/junior high school, post high school, community, and rehabilitation settings has also been substantial.

Guidance and counseling, grades K through 12, are characterized by common major themes. Among them are concern for the total person, the importance of collaborative work, similarities in helping procedures in all settings, and emphasis on development.

The chief theme is the importance of looking at the total person, rather than fragmenting services as if each need existed independently. Help is provided for educational, career, and personal development; thus the work of the counselor extends to all aspects of school, home, and community life. Emphasis varies with grade level. Parents play a larger role during the elementary years, but increasingly counselors in all grades are extending services to include work with the pupils' whole environment and with other significant persons in their lives. Help must be more comprehensive than that provided by individual conferences; consultation, coordination, and training are being added to the direct, face-to-face assistance of counseling.

A second theme of guidance is the use of a team approach. Counselors in elementary, middle, and high schools participate with a team of teachers, social workers, psychologists, and medical personnel to provide a comprehensive help system. Even so, counselors are unique members and occupy a key position. Being school-based, they can maintain close contact with teachers, pupils, and administrators and emphasize a truly developmental approach. The counselor is the logical person to coordinate the work of all team members (Gibson, Mitchell, and Higgins 1973, pp. 47–48; Hill 1974, pp. 102–103).

A third theme is establishing a common core of helping approaches and rationales applicable on all educational levels. There are differences due to pupils' ages, but theoretical concepts, human relations, skills, and other helping procedures are being developed and tested to build a body of professional knowledge of use to all guidance workers. A degree of specialization is needed, but the bases of guidance at different educational levels are more alike than not.

A fourth major theme, emphasis on development, is visible in the effort to facilitate pupil development rather than concentrating on remediation, and by the trend to link services at all educational levels. It has, for example, recently been recognized that the choice of an occupation is not a single event that takes place at the end of school or college—preparatory decisions are made as early as the first years of school, and each year confronts pupils with related new decisions and tasks. The developmental view has given rise to a sequential approach to guidance. The total K–12 program is integrated rather than broken down into elementary, middle/junior, and senior high school.

In addition to these four themes, a trend toward increased work with pupils with special needs has been set off by recent state and federal legislation. The new responsibility is mostly diagnostic and could have the long-range effect of blending the roles of the school counselor and the school psychologist.

Within the fields of guidance and counseling there is an ever-increasing professionalization. Statements by guidance organizations articulate roles and responsibilities. Ethical codes are formulated and put into effect. Preparation standards are upgraded to guarantee quality services. Licensure issues have recently arisen, and guidance organizations are striving to insure that counseling is represented in the formation of school policy. Taking over the destiny of the profession is an uphill battle, but leaders are making substantial progress. Much more needs to be done, but there is no doubt that guidance has established itself as a major helping profession.

ADDITIONAL READINGS

Cook, David R., ed. *Guidance for Education in Revolution*. Boston: Allyn and Bacon, 1971.

A number of chapters speak to issues, problems, and trends in guidance and education. Section I on this historical and philosophical context is a good starting place.

Goethals, George W., and Klos, Dennis S. *Experiencing Youth*. Boston: Little, Brown, 1976.

A book of vivid and engrossing first person case reports. While the individuals who tell their stories are beyond high-school age, their accounts of adolescent goals, conflicts, achievements and frustrations give insight into the emotional lives with which the school counselor is concerned.

Hill, George E. *Management and Improvement of Guidance*. Englewood Cliffs, N.J.: Prentice-Hall, 1974.

Chapter 2, "The Need for and Purposes of Guidance in Schools" explains convincingly why guidance is needed and summarizes major issues in the field.

Shaw, Merville C. *School Guidance Systems*. Boston: Houghton Mifflin, 1973.

Shaw gives a succinct statement about the bases of need for guidance services on pages 5–10, and includes a helpful definition of guidance.

Shertzer, Bruce and Stone, Shelley C. *Fundamentals of Guidance*, 3rd ed. Boston: Houghton Mifflin, 1976.

Chapter 1, "The Adolescent in Today's Society" gives an excellent review of problems and needs of young people that support the position that guidance services are needed in schools. The discussion of adolescents in the 70s is particularly helpful.

Tolbert, E. L. *Introduction to Counseling*, 2nd ed. New York: McGraw-Hill, 1972.

Chapter 1, "Need for Counseling," gives the author's views on the contribution of this specific part of the guidance program, and defines counseling and other terms used in pupil personnel work.

Wrenn, C. Gilbert. *The Counselor in a Changing World*. Washington, D.C.: American Personnel and Guidance Association, 1962.

This book is a landmark publication of the 60s, and much is still relevant and extremely useful for the counselor. Chapter 2, "New Directions in American Society," is a good place to start.

———. *The World of the Contemporary Counselor*. Boston: Houghton Mifflin, 1973.

This book in some ways updates the previous one by the same author and gives a vivid account of present-day challenges for the counselor. Any section is useful in connection with this chapter, but "Facts and Trends in three vital areas in American Life," pp. 182–209, is especially helpful.

CHAPTER TWO
SECONDARY SCHOOL
GUIDANCE IN ACTION

This chapter is about school guidance in action. It describes a school, a community, staff members, and pupils, and identifies critical needs and problems. Counselors discuss their accomplishments and frustrations. The situation is not ideal; it has its negative as well as positive features, and much needs to be done to make helping more effective. But it is a slice of life that shows what school counseling is all about.

GOALS

1. To gain an understanding of a typical secondary school guidance program.
2. To experience the rewards and frustrations of working in a secondary school setting.
3. To develop sensitivity to problems and needs in school and community.
4. To become aware of how school and community are interdependent.

THE JAMES CITY COMMUNITY

Formerly a small rural agricultural community, James City has expanded rapidly in the past two decades and now has a population of approximately 100,000. The increase has resulted largely from growth in the city's three educational institutions in the city: a large private university, a community college, and a vocational-technical institute. James City has the typical small factories, retail and wholesale businesses, and similar establishments, but no very large organizations. Growth has involved a heterogeneous influx from other areas, including a substantial number of South Americans and more recently some refugees from Southeast Asia. The black-white ratio has remained at about 20 : 80 over the years, with blacks forming by far the largest minority group. While the racial balance has not changed, the expectations of blacks have changed radically in recent years. Although race relations have been quite good, several confrontations have occurred, mainly over educational and housing discrimination. Biracial community groups are actively studying the causes of conflict, but many citizens ignore problems, hoping they will just go away.

Economic conditions are quite similar to those in other sections of the country. Unemployment is at about the national average, with school dropouts having the most difficulty finding work. The educational institutions, nonseasonal businesses and industries, and agricultural enterprises give the area economic stability, but not all young people can find work locally. Many employers who have job openings complain that job hunters lack a sound basic education and good work habits and attitudes.

James City has the typical community employment, rehabilitation, mental health agencies, as well as special government programs for education and employment like CETA (Comprehensive Employment and Training Act) and Job Corps. There is little help, however, for the many people out of work who make daily trips to the employment office. Some have even given up looking. Services are scarcely coordinated at all, and many of the most needy are overlooked.

The public school system, not including the community college and the voc-tech institute, is administered by an elected school board and an appointed superintendent. The superintendent has been quite effective in anticipating major community trends and exercises considerable control over the board. He understands the community power structure and endeavors to keep on its good side. Consequently, he is authoritarian with school personnel. He has delegated some responsibility to school principals, but if they do not carry out his policies, they face removal. A recently announced policy, brought about partly in response to parents' complaints, is to improve high school guidance services.

Desegregating and achieving racial balance in schools has been an emotionally charged process. Some racial conflicts took place at the outset, partly because the one black institution was closed and students were scattered around the city in schools where they were obviously not welcome and where they had little chance to participate in activities. Tensions increased as black pupils realized that many expected them to cause a decrease in academic and moral standards and an increase in crime and disorder. Feelings have cooled down considerably in recent years. However, there is still an undercurrent of resentment among blacks about

RESEARCH

EDUCATIONAL POWER STRUCTURE

The superintendent, like many other educators in similar positions, cannot make major decisions on his own about matters such as guidance services or school busing. His decisions and those of the school board are controlled largely by an informal group of a few community leaders at the top of a pyramid of power. Professional educators as well as government officials are likely to act in accordance with this local power structure (Innaccone and Lutz 1970, pp. 33–40).

Kimbrough (1964, p. 33) points out that a few powerful individuals hold a monopoly on policy decisions and major projects, and that those further down on the scale have little influence. Not all informal power structures are monopolistic, however. Competitive systems exist, involving two or more groups striving to control local policy (pp. 105–106).

---

perceived differential treatment on disciplinary problems, grades, assignments to special education and social adjustment classes, and suspensions; whites get the best treatment by far.

Programs in the university, community college, voc-tech center, and the public school system give the residents of James City a number of educational opportunities. Besides the typical programs of these institutions there are adult classes in all three systems and an embryonic community education program. Even with all that is available, few members of the disadvantaged group choose to enjoy this privilege.

The problems, needs, and strengths of the community exert a powerful influence on George Miller High School. The institution is in many respects a reflection of the community.

GEORGE MILLER HIGH SCHOOL

Near the center of town, George Miller High School is the city's oldest school and, with an enrollment of approximately 2,000, its largest. The other two high schools, Eastern and Western, each have student bodies of approximately 1,500. About 20 percent of the pupils are black and come from all over the city, while most of the others are from the sections the school served originally. The school population used to be made up of middle-class, college-bound pupils, but now represents the total spectrum

RESEARCH

THE DROPOUT PROBLEM

George Miller High School's dropout rate is not very different from those reported nationally in general programs that prepare neither for a career nor further education. Marland (1974, p. 11) summarizes these trends in the period from 1970 to 1973.

	Annually
High school dropouts	850,000
General curriculum high school graduates	800,000
Dropouts from post-high-school education (e.g., college)	900,000

These people do not have the credentials (diplomas, certificates) or the salable skills to cope in our technological society. Figuring education costs at $1,000 per year per pupil, he estimates the investment for these persons' development as follows:

	Billions
Dropouts with 10 years of public schooling	$ 8.5
Graduates from a high school *general* curriculum	$10.4
Dropouts from post-high-school education programs	$12.6
	$31.5

The National Center for Educational Statistics (Grant 1975, back cover) reports that about three fourths of the young people in school graduate while about one fourth, or one million, drop out. Some who do not graduate will complete their formal education by equivalent certificates or other means.

with respect to socioeconomic and intellectual background and motivation, and their number greatly exceeds the 1,600 for which the facilities were designed. Nine years ago, before integration, about 80 percent went on to college; the figure today is nearer 30 percent. Another 20 percent do some work at the community college or voc-tech center. Usually about 80 percent of a class entering George Miller choose the college preparatory program and state career goals in high prestige and professional areas. About 40 percent end up, after several program changes, in the general curriculum. Girls tend to name the traditional female occupations as career goals.

The dropout rate prior to graduation is about 30 percent of the entering ninth graders. A number of other pupils might be classed as potential dropouts—they are frequently late or absent, very deficient in one or more subjects, and do little more than go through the motions of doing their school work. Some staff members refer to the dropouts as "pushouts," because many who leave are subtly urged to by teachers and administration. Having them go is an accepted solution for academic and behavior problems.

To the casual observer, the pupils appear enthusiastic, interested, and friendly toward each other, teachers, and administration. But closer scrutiny reveals many conflicts and tensions just below the surface.

RESEARCH

PUPIL PROBLEMS

The problems at George Miller are common in other schools. A well-designed, large-scale study of 32,000 eighth, ninth, and eleventh grade pupils (Prediger, Roth, and Noeth 1973) indicates that pupils want help with problems but feel they receive very little assistance. Findings are as follows:

Help Pupils Say They Need	Percentage of Students, Grade 11
Improving study skills	65
Discussing personal concerns	30
Making career plans	78

Career Planning Help Pupils Say They Receive from School	Percentage of Students, Grade 11
Little, none	49
Some	37
A lot	13

Three percent of the pupils said they did not have a guidance counselor. Forty-three percent said they could see a counselor whenever they wanted, and 41 percent said they usually could. Availability of counselors does not seem to be the cause of the problem.

Black-white problems are neither admitted nor dealt with. Drug use seems to be increasing, but no one knows to what extent. Recently several gay pupils have "come out," and there are sharply divided opinions among pupils, staff, and the community about whether they should be expelled, counseled, arrested, or accepted. Sexual problems such as venereal disease and pregnancies among unmarried girls have increased; the community is in conflict over whether the school should provide sex education. Recently some parents have been checking school texts and library books and have turned up material they consider pornographic or otherwise harmful. Many pupils lack direction and goals and see no reason for attending school, and several girls feel pressure from parents and staff to elect traditional careers. "In-group" members assert that they should have free rule over school activities; outsiders resent the tight control of the elite few. Pupil-teacher conflicts increase the number of program changes each term.

The principal and a small proportion of the staff of George Miller are relatively new, but the great majority of the teachers have been there for ten years or more. The new principal, following the model of the superintendent, has adopted a firm policy and keeps tight control of all school programs and activities. He is a firm believer in the three R's. He wants counselors to insure that all pupils are in the "right" courses, to be available to meet parents at all times, and to see every pupil at least once a term. To fulfill the first requirement, the principal wants counselors actually to schedule pupils' classes. The major portion of the guidance staff's time, therefore, is devoted to scheduling, meeting briefly with all pupils each term, intervening in teacher-pupil conflicts, making program changes to resolve them, and being in their offices in case parents call or come by.

RESEARCH

PRINCIPALS' EXPECTATIONS OF COUNSELORS

Principals and other administrators have similar expectations of counselors. Hart and Prince (1970) questioned Utah secondary school principals on counselors' responsibilities and compared responses with opinions of counselor educators. The results showed complete disagreement at the .05 significant level[a] even for principals who had taken counseling courses or worked as counselors.

[a] The .05 level of significance means that the difference between principals' and counselors' attitudes found in the study could have happened by chance only five times out of one hundred. The sample was from a specific and limited population, and its findings cannot be used as a basis for generalization.

Principals felt that counselors should:

— Be involved in discipline (mainly the principals without counseling courses or experience).
— Carry out clerical duties.
— Give little emphasis to help with personal-emotional problems.
— Share confidential information.
— Be given many duties not related to counseling.

Other studies support these findings of discrepancies between counselors' roles and principals' expectations (Boller 1973; Buckner 1975). But agreement exists on certain specific duties. Maser (1971) found substantial accord on many counseling functions, e.g., helping the potential dropout and assisting pupils to assess strengths and limitations. Most evidence points to administrators' emphasis on clerical, disciplinary, and nonguidance functions.

EXPERIENCE

SCHOOL CLIMATE

Visit a secondary school. Get permission from the administration to spend some time there. Five types of observations are suggested.

1. Walk along the hall when classes are changing.
2. Walk through the halls when classes are in session.
3. Spend some time in the administrative offices.
4. Observe the traffic in the guidance offices.
5. Walk around the recreational area while pupils are engaged in sports or other activities.

What are your feelings about the pupils you observe? What can you infer about their attitudes toward each other? the school? Would you enjoy working with them?

Give five words to describe your reactions toward each observation. Would they be the same for your school?

George Miller has supportive psychological, social work, and medical pupil personnel services at the district level. There is a guidance director who moves very cautiously. He advises school counselors, "Do the scheduling, even if it gets in the way. You have to start where the people are." Counselors don't agree but have followed the advice, hoping for eventual policy changes. A new director of career education has been appointed to set up new programs in the city's schools; his major efforts have been directed at teachers as he feels, with some justification, that counselors are less than enthusiastic about career guidance.

OBJECTIVES

(It is suggested that you cover the answer and formulate your own response. Then compare it with the one given.)

1. To be able to identify community conditions that affect school programs. Name three community conditions that have a positive effect and three that have a negative effect.

Positive	*Negative*
— Variety of educational opportunities.	— Lack of jobs for those leaving school.
— Rapid growth bringing in new groups.	— Housing segregation for minority groups.
— Large number of community service agencies.	— Lack of coordination among community agencies.

There are others, but these illustrate how community factors can help or hinder the effectiveness of the school program.

2. To understand the forces in the community and school that shape guidance and other educational programs. Briefly summarize the meaning of the term "power structure."

Communities tend to have a small but highly influential group of persons who exercise power through informal avenues rather than through the visible lines of governmental action. This power elite is so influential that school boards, superintendents, and principals tend to reflect its desires. Obviously educators have a great deal of leeway. But if a conflict arises between the local power structure and the school board, evidence suggests that the school board will lose.

3. To understand the adequacy of career plans of entering high school students. Give two pertinent descriptive statements.

Some typical ones:

Many seem to be unrealistic. For example, about 60 percent elect the college preparatory program, while about 30 percent actually attend.

Female pupils choose traditional career roles.

4. To be aware of the role and function problems faced by high school counselors. List four such problems in rank order.

Ranking depends upon your point of view. The author gives most weight to factors that limit effective use of all resources, e.g., lack of program goals. You may consider other factors more significant. In any case, the elimination or reduction of counselors' problems should result in more effective help to pupils. The author's ranking is as follows:

1. Lack of a clear understanding of pupil needs.
2. A tendency to encourage the principal to establish goals and functions for counselors.
3. Faulty perceptions of counselors' functions on the part of the pupils.
4. Lack of specific objectives to serve as useful guidelines for counselor efforts.

THE GUIDANCE STAFF

The guidance staff is balanced according to sex and race, a point the principal refers to with pride when affirmative action is brought up. Furthermore, the staff represents a wide range in age, type of preparation, and approach to helping.

Sam Jones, senior in age and experience, has a long history of teaching, administrative work, coaching, and counseling. Certified in guidance through summer college work some years earlier, he feels that he keeps up to date by reading journals, attending local meetings and workshops, and taking occasional evening courses at the university. He has the title of *Coordinator*, which has never been defined and which does not require him to coordinate anything. His approach to guidance and counseling emphasizes one-to-one contact, and he considers himself a good listener who knows how to use the current expressions to communicate. "Kids just let it all hang out with me." "I don't know how I do it, but they rap with me like I'm one of them." "I know where they're coming from."

Mrs. Jayne Joyner also arrived at counseling via a circuitous route, including home economics, teaching, home-demonstration work, and elementary school teaching. She moved into the job through two NDEA (National Defense Education Act) summer institutes where enrollees, supported with generous stipends, devoted their full time to the study of guidance. Her approach could be best described as "come on strong"; she thinks of herself as a positive person. She gives pep talks to pupils, keeps in close contact with parents and teachers, and is on the go all day. This is how she describes her point of view: "Action guidance. That's the way I do it. Go where the kids are. Keep in touch."

Pat Smith and Will Sharp represent youth and modern trends. Pat, a white female, has had no previous work experience of any kind. Will, the young black male counselor, has just completed an intensive preparation program, after a variety of the typical low-level jobs open to minority persons. Like Pat, he has had no teaching experience. Will's Afro, Pat's long hair, and what is interpreted as a permissive attitude toward drugs, sex, gays, dress, and pupil demonstrations have resulted in mild suspicion on the part of older teachers and some parents. They realize that in the two years they have been at the school they have become more like the teaching and administrative staff. This bothers them, but pleases the principal and most of the teachers.

Pat and Will need not worry too much about turning into teaching or administrative types; they have the support of other professionals in maintaining guidance roles.

Two paraprofessionals and a secretary complete the guidance staff. Mary Carter, one of the two paraprofessionals, moved into her job from a secretarial desk in the principal's office.

"I want to help people, not browbeat them. You have to be a hatchet man to be in the principal's office as his secretary."

She has had no specific preparation for the work and is counting on the counselors to help her develop skills. So far, however, her responsibilities have been record keeping, filing, and filling in forms.

The other paraprofessional, Donald Biggs, a middle-aged black, came into guidance through a two-year community college preparation program for aides in schools and community agencies. He was employed so the school would have another minority group member to work with pupils and to help with job placement in the career-education program. He spends a great deal of his time contacting potential dropouts, searching for job openings for those leaving school, and following up those placed.

Physical facilities consist of a classroom partitioned into four small offices and a conference room. The offices are well furnished and attrac-

RESEARCH

EFFECTS OF COUNSELOR ISOLATION

At George Miller the counselors can be supportive of each other. In a school with a single counselor, there can be a problem in maintaining identity. Wasson and Strowig (1965) studied attitudes of isolated counselors, counselors in schools with a counseling team, and teachers and administrators.

Results showed that isolated counselors had attitudes more similar to those of teachers and administrators than to those of counselors in multiple-counseling situations or of highly committed counselors. While the authors point out limitations of their research (small numbers of subjects and a nonrandom sampling of schools), the results suggest that counselors need the support of colleagues.

Pupils' needs should be a factor in determining the services a counselor provides — up to a point.

tive, and the reception room is large enough for displays of guidance information, a table for magazines and brochures, and bulletin boards.

A mimeographed description of the George Miller Guidance Program includes philosophy and goals with which it would be hard to disagree. For example, it says that the program will "help pupils to develop meaningful goals," and "will build a positive community climate at George Miller High School." It asserts further that "each person is valued as an individual" and that "each individual is motivated to achieve and develop," and expresses various positive, optimistic beliefs about the nature of man. Nothing indicates what guidance staff members actually do or how they assess the effectiveness of their work.

The program itself is not specifically related to philosophy or goals but consists of a list of techniques and services that were prompted more or less by school policies. Each counselor is assigned about 500 pupils by an alphabetical division of the roll. Pupils are to be seen at registration, and the assigned counselor is expected to help with any type of problem. Counselors are also allotted some specific responsibilities. Mrs. Joyner has charge of the College and Career Days in October and March, and Mr. Jones is responsible for school administration of the state and district testing programs. Beyond these assignments, all share equally in guidance for college, work, personal problems, and orientation. About 10 percent of their time is devoted to face-to-face help (not including the brief registration conferences), but counselors say that at least 50 percent should be devoted to this type of direct assistance.

RESEARCH

PERCEPTIONS OF THE COUNSELOR'S JOB

Counselors at George Miller High School share role problems with colleagues in other schools. Stinzi and Hutcheson (1972) report that counselors described the two major ones as:

1. Being assigned tasks unrelated to counseling, e.g., attendance reports, discipline.
2. Lack of authority, i.e., no voice in the district to promote counseling.

School administrators in the Stinzi and Hutcheson study, somewhat in contrast to the principal of George Miller, emphasized their preference for counselors' freedom from administrative tasks, concentration on counseling, and availability to meet with parents.

Pupils wanted vocational information, help with social and personal problems, and separation of services from disciplines.

Teachers, however, took a position sharply contrasting with counselors' preferences. They felt:

1. Counselors should support them.
2. Counselors should help teachers with discipline problems, and even administer discipline.
3. Counselors should help with scheduling.

Other research cites lack of agreement over appropriate roles (Riese and Stoner 1969), lack of opportunity to perform counseling functions (Trotzer and Kassera 1971), and lack of counselors' understanding of their roles (Buckner 1975) as causes of counselor problems.

Two recent developments herald improvement in the guidance program. One has already been mentioned—the superintendent's stated policy to give high priority to improving secondary school guidance. A second is a growing concern among counselors about a number of old and new problems that have recently become more visible: lack of communication in the school, racial incidents, use of drugs, sexual permissiveness, gays coming out, poor achievement, dropouts, and lack of career plans. Teachers have become more vocal with suggestions that guidance workers do something about these problems, and have also been referring pupils more frequently and requesting help with problems. Comments such as "Something needs to be done," and "Guidance counselors don't know what we're up against," are being heard more often.

Specifically, the superintendent has insisted on setting up a district-wide series of monthly meetings to upgrade guidance services. The first, focusing on the question of accountability, was held during the preschool workshop. This meeting made clear that there was only fragmentary information about problems and needs; the superintendent concluded that the first order of business should be a needs survey, a recently popular procedure in his administrative circles. The counselors saw this as a threat rather than as an essential step, but because it was required, plans to conduct the needs survey were developed during the preschool workshop.

THE NEEDS SURVEY

After a review of surveys by other schools, the guidance staff decided to contact teachers, pupils, parents, and other people in the community. They also agreed to keep a record of how they spent their time and to inventory school facilities and resources.

Those surveyed were to be asked to list problems and to specify types of help they wanted from guidance. Later, the staff agreed unanimously that the open-ended approach had been a mistake; comments, while interesting and often colorful, were extremely time-consuming to classify and summarize. Furthermore, since counselors had felt that only anonymity would guarantee freedom of expression, there was no way to identify and follow up those who did not respond.

The needs survey was completed by the end of October. Counselors' logs were adequate, but the responses from others did not meet expectations. Community members, parents, and employers did best with about 75 percent returns. Pupils were next with about 70 percent. Teachers were lowest with about 60 percent. The survey of guidance activities and resources in the school was incomplete; few understood what they were supposed to report.

COUNSELORS' LOGS

How Time Was Spent	Percentage of Time
Conferences with pupils for registration	50
Paperwork on scheduling	20
Orientation	10
Group counseling with pupils	2
Consulting with teachers	2
Conferences with parents	2
Individual counseling	8
Other	4

The results surprised and disappointed the staff. They had felt sure that much more time was devoted to counseling.

RESEARCH

HOW COUNSELORS SPEND THEIR TIME

The way the guidance staff of George Miller spend their time is not very different from what is seen in many high schools. A well-designed study in the Mesa, Arizona, school system (Mesa Public Schools, n.d., b) used a sample of pupils (grades 6, 9, and 12), school staff, and parents. The analysis of how high school counselors used their time revealed the following:

Activities	Percentage of Time
Interpersonal counseling — helping students get along better with others	5
Academic-learning counseling — helping students to learn better in school and elsewhere; helping them improve study skills and habits	5
Intrapersonal counseling — helping students feel better about themselves	5
Educational-vocational counseling — helping students plan better for their current and future schooling and work	20
Registration, schedule changing, and orientation	66
Attendance	5
In-service	3
Clubs	1

RESULTS OF SURVEY OF PUPILS' PROBLEMS AND ATTITUDES   The needs survey asked pupils to list problems, specify the type of help desired from the guidance programs, and give their attitudes about the program. Results were as follows:

1. Parents don't understand me—50%
2. Plans for the future—40%
3. Lack of confidence—35%

Other problems expressed by many included getting along with others, "not understanding myself," not being popular, failing in school work, and feeling worried about drugs. The totals astonished the counselors; they realized that they would never be able to contact more than a small percentage either for individual or even small-group assistance. They wondered if the results were deliberately inflated by pupils or if their school had more than its share of pupils with problems.

RESEARCH

PUPIL PROBLEMS

The George Miller pupils were probably quite honest and open in their responses. The Mesa survey referred to above revealed an extensive number of problems; the following brief listing includes only one or two high-frequency items from each of the major categories (pp. 25–26):

— "I need to improve my memory."
— "I need to understand my abilities, interests, and other characteristics."
— "I need to get along better with my parents."
— "I need to be more satisfied with my life, my achievements, and myself."
— "I need to make plans for developing the abilities in my career choice."

Another study, this one in the southwestern part of the country, shows similar findings. A survey of 1,800 pupils (Redfering and Anderson 1975) ages 14 through 18, listed the following top problem areas:

1. Concern about the future
2. Boy-girl relationships
3. Personal appearance
4. Money, job
5. Health
6. Social adjustment and responsibility

Pupils wanted guidance services to provide personal contact, someone to talk to about plans for the future, things that bother them, problems with parents, problems with teachers. Many seemed to feel the guidance service was for those with severe emotional problems and referred to counselors as "shrinks." The psychotherapy role disturbed the staff, who considered themselves to be helpers for everyone, particularly the average or normal pupil who needed developmental assistance or aid for mild emotional problems.

RESEARCH

HOW PUPILS SEE COUNSELORS

Pupils' attitudes and perceptions about guidance would surprise many counselors. Heilfron's study (1960), carried out some years ago, gives results and methodology which are still valid. A group of 107 high school students were given a series of brief case studies describing pupils with various problems and needs and asked to indicate the amount of counseling, including outside referrals, they would consider appropriate. This is a sample case:

"Athlete. A natural athlete. Even at this grade level is the star of all athletic events held in the school. Has average intellectual ability and grades are generally average also. Has pleasing personality."

A total of 14 brief case descriptions were used, including such types as "bright," "failing," and "gauche."

The results indicated that pupils see counseling as a service for the odd and obviously maladjusted, and that no one whose social performance is adequate needs it.

Project Talent data were used to analyze other facets of pupil utilization of counselors. Shapiro and Asher (1972) studied the assistance high school pupils received in planning. Results showed that:

— Pupils from higher income families are likelier to see counselors.
— Less than half the pupils of both sexes discussed plans with a counselor.
— Girls planning to marry early are less likely to discuss plans with a counselor, even if academic achievement is high.
— Counselors spend little time with counselees from backgrounds unlike their own, e.g., those of low socioeconomic status, the non-college-bound, and those with difficulty in communication.

The staff was quite disappointed with the response to questions about help received from guidance and counseling. A large number of pupils said that they did not know there was a guidance service or they had no idea of its purpose. A few stated that talking to a counselor had been a great help, but many more complained that they had not been helped at all.

TEACHERS' ATTITUDES   Teachers were asked about services they would like from the guidance program, attitudes toward the service, and ratings of its effectiveness. The preponderance of responses were of the "stop something" variety—stop behavior problems, vandalism, drug abuse, absenteeism, or indifference toward school work. Attitudes were somewhat negative. Teachers indicated resentment over having pupils called out of classes, paperwork for guidance, and the liberal and permissive approach of the guidance staff. Some comments, however, were quite positive, particularly from teachers who had had extensive personal contact with counselors.

ATTITUDES OF PARENTS AND OTHERS   Opinions of parents, other people in the community, and employers on what they would like guidance services to do were more numerous and detailed. Most of the comments focused on the quality of preparation for work, college, and adult life. Parents emphasized the need for help in selecting a college, while employers stressed the need to improve work attitudes and basic academic skills. Some responses indicated either by implication or by flat statement that the individual did not know guidance services existed. A few warned against sensitivity-type group activities.

The guidance staff had trouble boiling the masses of data down into a summary that could be a useful basis for future plans. Eventually they presented the principal and the staff with compilations to be used for setting goals and priorities. No plans have since been made for work groups to translate needs into actual goals, and no decisions have been reached about who will approve the new accountability statements of the guidance service. These are future steps in the process of improving the guidance program.

SUCCESSES AND FAILURES   In addition to the needs survey, the guidance staff has made an informal evaluation of successes and failures. They feel that registration conferences have helped many pupils think about life plans and given pupils the sense that at least one person in the school takes a personal interest. They believe they have helped many pupils *avoid* drug problems, dropping out, and becoming entangled in other difficulties. While they readily admit having had extensive personal contact only with a few of the 500 assigned to each counselor, they are convinced that there is a spread of effect from the ones they have seen to others, for example in reducing racial conflicts. They realize that many of these results cannot be documented to demonstrate their effectiveness.

Counselors feel their greatest failures to have been with pupils to whom they could not devote enough time, particularly those who wanted to talk about conflicts at home, career plans, feelings of loneliness, dropping out, and trouble getting along with others. In addition, there were groups of pupils who wanted to improve their ability to communicate, develop self-confidence, or master effective social behavior. Most of these pupils were never reached.

EXPERIENCE

THE COUNSELOR'S PERSONAL PERCEPTION OF HELPING

In a small group, have one member role play one of the counselors of your school dealing with a pupil problem brought by either a teacher, parents, or pupil. Other group members guess which counselor is being portrayed and explain choices. Ask the role player to describe personal feelings during the episode.

EXPERIENCE

A NEEDS SURVEY

Do a mini-needs-survey. Without trying to get a representative sample, ask four or five high school pupils to list five things that they would like to improve about themselves. Summarize the results. (Use fellow students if high school pupils are not available.) If possible, ask several the same question about other pupils. Compare perceptions of needs.

The needs survey reveals a great deal about problems, but going beyond the responses on the survey forms and meeting the pupils, one can gain more insight into why they respond as they do. Will Frisbe and Ralph Parker are examples. If they bothered to fill in the needs survey questionnaires, they no doubt gave negative answers. Will, passive and parent-dominated, sees the guidance staff as an extension of his parents' authority, especially since the day when he was referred because his mother and father said he needed help in getting interested in school and keeping out of trouble with girls.

Ralph Parker, a black regarded by his teachers as militant, is about to transfer to the alternative school for pupils with serious behavior problems. He sees counselors as members of the establishment who want to "keep him in his place," and is particularly hostile toward the black counselor for failing to side with him in clashes with teachers and administration.

Mary Thornton, however, praises guidance highly. Mrs. Joyner helped her, a National Merit finalist, choose a college and get a large scholarship. She considers the guidance service one of the school's best features, but wonders if pupils headed for work after graduation benefit as she did. She has friends in the work-study program who expect to continue their present part-time positions, but others have no job connections and no idea how to find work.

Susie Jones and Hal Wright, two of the VIP's on campus, say they never heard of the guidance service but wouldn't go to a "psychologist" for help even if they knew one were available. Both are performing poorly in classes and spend their time running for offices, directing school social affairs, and in sports. They think anyone who needs help is odd.

The list could be continued indefinitely, but the basic pattern is clear from this sample. The role of guidance is not generally understood; contact with counselors is scanty; communications are poor. Pupils who could profit from guidance scoff at it, and the rating of guidance is low.

EXPERIENCE

THE PUPIL'S VIEW OF GUIDANCE

Imagine that you are a 12th grader in George Miller High School and about to graduate. You have been asked to suggest improvements in the school guidance program, no holds barred. Think back over your high school years. Imagine going through a typical day. See how much of a fantasy trip you can take into George Miller High School.

Then give your top three suggestions.

It may be helpful to do this exercise with several other students.

OBJECTIVES

1. To understand the importance of a needs survey in guidance programs. Name three sources of needs that should be used in determining guidance objectives.

In this chapter the needs survey has been described as an essential step in program planning. Pupils themselves are perhaps the major source for articulating needs.

2. To be aware of the necessity of looking below the surface to detect guidance problems and needs. List five problems that could easily be missed by a superficial glance at a school.

Using George Miller High School as an example, some below-the-surface problems are:

— Lack of trust in the guidance service on the part of many pupils who view it, for example, as an extension of disciplinary procedures.
— Racial tension resulting from covering problems up.
— Lack of goals on the part of many pupils.
— Unrealistic or sexually stereotyped occupational plans.
— Covert distrust on the part of some teachers toward young members of the guidance staff.

3. To be aware of your feelings about a career in guidance. Identify three negative and three positive factors.

There are no right or wrong answers in this item. While the George Miller guidance situation is far from ideal, it can help you begin to test your attitudes. The important point is that you can pick out factors that are positive or negative for you. Some typical ones are as follows:

Positive

— Opportunity to help (service to others).
— Personal relationship with pupils (close personal contacts).
— Chance, to some extent, to establish own priorities (some independence).

Negative

— Responsibility for too many pupils (frustration).
— Counselors' purposes not understood (lack of well-defined identity in work setting).
— Difficult to judge accomplishments (little chance to see results of efforts).

4. To be aware of how you feel about tackling the challenges of a guidance position. Express how you feel about applying for a job at a high school (or George Miller High School).

There is, of course, no right or wrong response. You would no doubt have both positive and negative feelings. These are some that might be expected:

— "It's a great challenge. I'm needed."
— "The situation is too bad to help. I'd be swamped."

— "Attitudes about guidance could change, and that would open the way to a whole new approach."

5. To have at least a tentative idea of how a career fits in with the life-style you prefer. List five words that describe your life-style. Check the ones that reflect feelings about guidance work.

Words like *independent, full of variety, challenging, secure, placid, exciting, significant* are some that could be used to describe life-styles. Any of these could be checked to reflect feeling about guidance work.

ADDITIONAL READINGS

Hays, Donald G., and Linn, Joan K. *Needs Assessment: Who Needs It?* Washington, D.C.: American School Counselor Association, 1977.

A clear and interesting explanation of the whys and hows of needs assessment, with useful instruments to adapt for local use, and a list of institutions from which the reader can obtain information on ongoing projects.

Heilfron, Marilyn. "The Function of Counseling as Perceived by High School Students." *Personnel and Guidance Journal* 39, no. 2 (1960), pp. 133–136.

Both results and techniques are of interest to contemporary counselors. A brief comment on this study appears in this chapter, but the report as a whole makes valuable reading.

Morgan, Lewis B. *A Casebook for School Counselors.* Washington, D.C.: APGA Press, 1974.

The book vividly describes a wide array of the problems of pupils, teachers, and parents. Brief cases give a sense of the situations the counselor faces on the job.

Prediger, Dale J.; Roth, John D.; and Noeth, Richard J. "Career Development of Youth: A Nationwide Study." *Personnel and Guidance Journal* 53, no. 2 (1974), pp. 97–104.

This brief summary of ACT Research Report no. 61, *Nationwide Study of Student Career Development: Summary of Results,* presents a striking picture of guidance needs and effectiveness of current services. Emphasis is on career guidance, broadly defined, and pupil problems of all types are included.

Stinzi, Vernon L., and Hutcheson, William R. "We Have a Counselor Problem — Can You Help Us?" *School Counselor* 19, no. 5 (1972), pp. 329–334.

The study is reviewed briefly in this chapter; it is worth reading in its entirety, particularly for the counselors' recommendations for improvement.

CHAPTER THREE
ELEMENTARY
AND MIDDLE/JUNIOR HIGH
SCHOOL GUIDANCE

Guidance programs in elementary schools have been in existence a relatively short time compared with those in secondary schools, but have shown substantial progress in only a few years. This chapter points out some of the rewards and problems a counselor faces as a new program gets underway. A discussion of work in junior high and middle schools reviews guidance in the middle years of school. Of the two types of program for early adolescents, the junior-high-school type is older and better known. But over the years it has come under fire for imitating senior-high-school programs, and guidance services have been subjected to similar criticism. The middle school, designed to replace the junior high school, is structuring guidance services that follow the trend from a former vocational-education emphasis to a new balanced program of psychological-personal-guidance and career education (McGlasson 1973, p. 26). More similar to programs on the elementary than the secondary level, the middle school program is developing its own identity.

GOALS

1. To understand guidance programs in elementary, middle, and junior high schools.
2. To experience some of the rewards and frustrations of work at these levels.
3. To understand the interrelationships of problems in the school and in the community.
4. To develop sensitivity in recognizing problems and needs at these school levels.

WEST END ELEMENTARY SCHOOL

The community of Columbus (population 50,000) is served by ten elementary schools. West End, one of the newest, was built five years ago to accommodate population increases. Pupils include children from middle-class-professional families in the immediate area, inner-city children who are bused in, and rural children brought in from the outlying areas. Its composition resembles that of other elementary schools in the city, showing a cross section of socioeconomic levels and about the same proportion of minority students.

THE COMMUNITY   Columbus is a smaller community than James City, described in Chapter 2, and while similar in many ways has not seen the rapid growth of that high school setting. Its diversified economy includes agriculture, small factories, the typical stores and businesses, and several educational institutions. This variety has provided stable employment, and the area does not feel the full impact of changing economic conditions. The unemployment rate is well below the national average except in building trades and semiskilled production; in these occupations, unemployment is at about the same level as throughout the country.

Education is one of the community's major industries. A medium-sized private university, offering a wide variety of undergraduate and master's level graduate programs, is largely residential, but a substantial number of students commute. A vocational-technical center prepares both high-school and post-high-school students for careers in business, trade, technical, and service occupations. A third institution, a new community college, is just getting underway and provides both transfer and terminal two-year programs.

The community has been involved in a relatively mild controversy over integration for several years. Blacks make up approximately 20 percent of the population, and schools have used various procedures such as busing and redistricting to achieve racial balance. These adjustments have caused little difficulty, but there has been a continuing struggle between various parents groups and the school board to eliminate all or most of the busing for younger pupils. The children themselves have had no real difficulty and typically get along rather well. Even so, several private schools, which are in rather precarious financial status, have sprung up for pupils whose parents oppose the public school plans.

SCHOOL, ADMINISTRATION, AND STAFF   West End Elementary School, with a pupil population of 900, is housed in a modern building with ample recreational facilities. The staff consists of 30 teachers, the principal, and an assistant principal. Before the new counselor was employed, there was no specific person designated for guidance. The school has had the services of the county school psychologist and social worker, and several paraprofessionals have been employed as teacher aides. Open-classroom approaches and team teaching have been discussed, but although facilities are suitable, nothing has actually been set up.

Academic and behavior problems are a major concern. Tests have indicated that the reading level is low, and a remedial program has been instituted. There is a class for behavior problems, called the "social development" class. A special education teacher works with pupils who have severe difficulty with the regular program. (There is considerable disparity in the educational achievement of various social groups, with rural and minority pupils scoring lowest.) Many of the teachers are younger persons with recent preparation including special emphasis on working with minority groups, but they are experiencing considerable frustration over behavior problems and the wide range of achievement in each classroom.

The district testing-program has become a focal point for criticism of the school. An organization of black parents has protested the use of psychological tests and inventories, and presented evidence from research suggesting that these instruments are unfair to minorities. The issue is still under study by the school board. No decision has been made about the use of results of the county and state testing-programs.

THE SCHOOL STAFF   The principal has been at the school for two years and is relatively new to the system. He prides himself on his awareness of new developments in elementary education and wants to make the school as orderly and efficient as possible, partly because he is very professional about his work and partly because he sees the principalship as a stepping-stone to a more important job in school administration. He has developed a high level of morale in the school and is regarded as a good administrator. He sets up guidelines and policies cooperatively, placing responsibility on teachers for carrying out duties, without a great deal of checking.

The principal welcomed the opportunity to have West End be one of the first schools in the district to have an elementary school guidance program. His enthusiasm, however, did not neutralize some teacher resentment about the source of funds for the new position. The counselor's salary was taken from the school budget for staff, and since the total number of positions is based on attendance, teachers felt another teacher could have been employed to lighten class loads.

About one third of the teaching staff are older both in years and attitude, and are not particularly interested in new educational concepts like guidance and counseling. The attitude prevalent among them is that guidance and counseling are mainly therapy for pupils with serious problems; the counselor is supposed to "cure" the difficulty and return the pupil to the classroom completely changed. Some teachers have had experience with a school psychologist and see the counselor's primary role as administering individual intelligence tests to prospects for special education.

The younger teachers, particularly those just out of preparation programs, have heard about guidance and tend to feel better about it, but have no real understanding of the help it is supposed to provide. Even they have a feeling that counselors represent an outside threat and that asking the counselor for help implies a lack of competence to manage classroom problems. Still, they are more aware of the need for specialized help and are more sensitive to pupil problems, realizing, for example, that withdrawn pupils are not model pupils and that active, noisy individuals do not necessarily have emotional problems.

RESEARCH

POLITICAL POWER AND GUIDANCE

It would be of value to find out why the superintendent supported the elementary-school guidance-program. In view of research findings about local power structures as described in Chapter 1, it is likely that influential community support arose, because the move has a definite impact on the school budget. But another source of support has been effective at this level. Counselors and others who support guidance programs have organized lobbying groups to contact state legislators. Bluhm and Anderson (1976) describe a six-step program involving cooperative action by the Utah Congress of Parents and Teachers and the Association of Pupil Personnel Directors. The program began with building a data bank and eventually involved appearances before legislative committees. The efforts succeeded in obtaining funds for improving elementary school guidance in all 40 school districts.

OBJECTIVES

1. To be able to identify community conditions that affect school programs. Name three with positive effects and three with negative effects.

Some samples are as follows:

Positive	*Negative*
— Heterogeneous population.	— Many private schools that tend
— Diversified economy.	to isolate groups.
— Variety of educational	— Protesting parent groups that
institutions.	stimulate conflicts among
	pupils.
	— Great variations in educational
	achievement.

2. To understand some aspects of the differing backgrounds of elementary school pupils. Give three descriptive statements about the diversity.
The major points brought out in this chapter are:

— Achievement differences.
— Differences in employment and educational opportunities.
— Ethnic differences.

3. To be aware of the importance of looking below the surface to detect guidance problems. List five problems that could easily be missed by a casual observer.
Some brought out in the chapter are:

— Attitudes of parents on busing, integration, and ethnic differences.
— Teachers' concern that employment of a counselor increases their teaching load.
— Pupils' poor reading ability.
— Inequality of referrals on racial basis for discipline and special education.
— Problems faced by transfers.

THE NEW COUNSELOR

Carolyn Schwartz recently graduated from a counselor education program with an elementary counseling option. Her preparation featured practicums in both elementary and high schools and a one-semester full-time internship in an inner-city elementary school. After graduation, she worked for a year in an elementary school in a large city. Her training and first job were thus in established programs where roles and procedures were already fully developed. She applied for the position in the Columbus School System, expecting that in initiating a new program she would have the opportunity to establish a service to suit her own preferences. She felt competent and experienced, but somewhat apprehensive about entering into a completely new situation. Carolyn arrived at West End Elementary School several weeks before the beginning of the school year, and a few days before preschool workshops.

FIRST STEPS   The first contact with the school staff was not as Carolyn would have preferred. The principal insisted that she take over one or two pre-school workshop sessions to describe her role and the kinds of services she would offer teachers and pupils. From previous experience she knew that her large group presentations were not very effective in conveying roles and functions. She would rather have made a brief group presentation and then met with teachers individually. Nevertheless, she discussed her major goals and in a brief exercise or two with volunteer teachers demon-strated ways she might work with small and class-sized groups of pupils, for example, discussing feelings.

Reactions were mixed, but predominantly favorable. Carolyn's empha-sis on consulting with teachers and parents and working with groups of pupils obviously disappointed teachers who expected her to do more indi-vidual work with problem cases. Others, however, were impressed by the strategy of working with teachers to help reduce problems in the settings where they occur—the classroom. The principal was pleased to hear that the counselor had a definite concept of what was to be done, and was particularly impressed with the emphasis on working with parents. Keenly aware of the importance of parents' attitudes, he felt it was neces-sary to meet them more than halfway as problems emerged. He was not pleased with Carolyn's explanation of the need for confidentiality; he had assumed that she would keep him informed about anything discussed with pupils or parents that might bear on the school.

During the preschool workshop meeting, the new counselor outlined her plans for carrying out her responsibilities. The first priority would be to determine needs. For this, she would meet with all the teachers indi-vidually to discuss services and get their perceptions of problems, and gather additional information from samples of parents and pupils. Results would be pulled together and presented to principal and faculty, along with a set of high-priority objectives based on needs.

The counselor said she would prepare a weekly schedule of what she would be doing, when, and where. The teachers and principal liked this plan, which sounded efficient and organized. They did not realize that this systematic planning would make the counselor unavailable for a host of other things like cafeteria and bus duty, clerical work, and substituting for absent teachers.

Activities the counselor had not brought up at the meeting were family counseling and work with handicapped pupils. She was still formulating her role in these two areas and felt it best to wait until she had a more

According to some administrators and teachers, counselors do all those things teachers don't have time for.

crystallized statement to make. A first step will be to meet the school psychologist to develop cooperative working-relationships for services to the handicapped. At the same time, she will review several approaches used in family counseling and select the one that seems most suited to the local situation.

The counselor is aware of the increasing need to work with the handicapped and pupils in special education (DeBlassie and Cowan, 1976). This trend is visible both in new legislation and a growing awareness of services counselors can provide, particularly at critical points like school entry and the onset of adolescence (p. 247). The new emphasis brought about by Public Law 94–142 will require an effective cooperative relationship between the counselor and the school psychologist as their roles will begin to overlap. PL 94–142, which gives the school the responsibility for educating the handicapped, is of major concern to school counselors at all levels. Counselors will be involved in helping to make the classroom situation as profitable as possible for the handicapped who can be accommodated, in diagnostic and referral services, in planning parent-approved individual special education programs, and in other related duties.

When school started, the counselor began immediately to put her plans into effect. By the end of the second month, she had accumulated enough data to suggest that some of the major problems were as follows:

Pupil Problems
— Don't like teachers. Teachers too strict.
— Don't have any friends here. This is an unfriendly school.
— Don't like this school. Wish I were back at my old school. (those who transferred from other schools)
— Don't understand lessons. Failing in courses.
— Some people pick on you. Some people make you afraid.
— Feel left out of everything. Lonely.
— Some pupils are teachers' pets.

There were, of course, many positive comments, and the counselor emphasized them at the start of her summary to the school staff.

Problems Stated by Teachers
— Pupils easily upset and emotionally unstable.
— Pupils who disrupt the classroom and are constantly out of their seats.
— Children mistreated or deprived at home. Come to school without adequate meals and/or signs of physical mistreatment.
— Hostility. Some children pick on others all the time. Make scapegoats of one or two pupils.
— Bad language. Use of profanity and obscenities.
— Pupils who do not know how to make friends or how to keep them. Some are lonely and isolated pupils.
— Some are very deficient in learning skills, particularly reading. May actually be unable to read or communicate with others verbally.

Problems as Viewed by Parents
— Children do not seem to be learning very much. They don't have any homework.
— Teachers pick on certain pupils, particularly those from minority groups and those from the lower socioeconomic sections of town.
— Racial conflicts. Apprehension about violence by minority group members.
— Classrooms are too rowdy and unruly. Children say they cannot learn in classrooms because of disturbances.

— Teachers do not insist on good-quality work.
— Teachers insist on too high a quality of work and make many feel stupid.
— Difficult to talk with teachers, or teachers are mainly critical of pupils when conversations are held. Difficult for a parent to get information from the teacher or principal.

In presenting the report to the school staff, the counselor pointed out that this was how various groups *perceived* the situation, and not proof that things were this way.

RESEARCH

SCHOOL PROBLEMS

Current publications on elementary school counseling name the same needs the counselor found in her survey. Long (1971) describes school phobia and suggests remedial steps a counselor can take, pointing out that the condition is difficult to deal with because it is often reinforced by actions of parents and others.

The abuse of pupils by parents and guardians is another widespread problem. According to Forrer (1975), at least 700 children die every year from mistreatment and abuse by parents or guardians; approximately 60,000 cases of abuse were reported in 1974. Forrer concludes that while the danger of death or serious injury decreases as pupils grow older, the possibility of psychological damage is great.

The counselor's needs survey reflected special problems of minority pupils similar to those in other elementary schools. Christensen (1975) comments on the tendency to lump various minority groups together as if all had the same needs and stresses the importance of knowing the unique background of each group to counsel effectively. As an example, he describes Puerto Ricans' open demonstration of love, tolerance of children, and gregariousness. This group makes up a sizable minority; there are currently approximately 2 million Puerto Ricans living in the U.S. Cross and Maldonado (1971) review the problems of Mexican Americans and describe how their values might differ from the counselor's own. The authors underline the importance of accepting individuals as unique and recognizing their cultural values and characteristics.

Smith, Barnes, and Scales (1974) enumerate problems that arise in counseling blacks. Blacks seek greater identification with each other, they are developing an awareness of their rich and colorful heritage, and communicate a great deal nonverbally. The authors illustrate the difficulties that blacks face in a predominantly white-oriented system.

The elementary-school counselor's attention is coming to focus on children from disrupted families. Concern has been expressed in the past for the effects of stressful family conditions on children, but recent emphasis is more systematic and productive. A special issue of *Elementary School Guidance and Counseling* shows this involvement. Helping the pupil understand and accept the death of a family member is one example (Ryerson 1977). Dealing with the child of an incarcerated parent is another (Chaney, Linkenhoker, and Horne, 1977). Counselors are developing new approaches for helping abused children (Griggs and Gale 1977), children of alcoholic parents (Hecht 1977), children of divorced parents (Wilkinson and Bleck 1977), foster children (Bard 1977), those who move frequently (Splete and Rasmussen 1977), and children from homes where a different language is spoken and a different culture is dominant (Inniss, 1977).

SUCCESSES AND FAILURES For the first several months since the start of the year, the counselor sums up successes as follows:

— Contact has been made with all the teachers in the school. The counselor feels that she has communicated what she is trying to do. She realizes that some of the teachers are not really enthusiastic and that they will cooperate no more than minimally.
— The needs survey has sensitized many people—parents, teachers, pupils, administrators—to pressing problems in the school. Previously they had had only vague and uncomfortable feelings that something was wrong and that something needed to be done.
— Some successful cases have been worked out in the classroom using planned reinforcement-type activities.

The counselor would be the first to point out certain shortcomings. She does not regard the lack of complete acceptance by teachers as a failure; it is a typical situation and it would be unrealistic to expect 100 percent acceptance, at least this early. She plans much more work in this area in the future, but is realistic enough to accept the fact that she may never find enthusiastic support from all of the teachers in the school.

Other problem areas are as follows:

— The public relations function. There has not been enough time to communicate the purposes of the counseling service to parents. (Public relations also includes work with teachers and pupils.) Very little has been done to contact and work with groups of parents and to let the community know more about the counseling program. This is a high-priority item for the rest of the year.

— The peer counseling program is at a standstill. The counselor had hoped to get it started early in the year, but teacher apathy and lack of time have prevented any progress.

— Guidance and counseling demonstrations in the classroom have not been failures, but they have not advanced very far. Most teachers are positive, but so far few visits have been made. This is the counselor's highest-priority item; she intends to set up a schedule of visits and try to get to each classroom or talk with each teacher at least once a month for the rest of the year.

— Accountability is a high priority even though there is currently very little pressure to set up objectives. The administration and teachers do not seem to be especially interested in identifying objectives, but the counselor is certain that by the end of the year questions will arise as to what has been accomplished. She is, therefore, developing a procedure to involve teachers and parents in establishing objectives and in deciding on how to assess progress.

— Counseling with parents is also an area that the counselor plans to develop. Tentative goals are to help parents in small groups bring out problems, learn how to communicate with children, and build productive strategies for positive discipline. Models such as Parent Study Groups (Dinkmeyer and McKay 1974) and Parent Effectiveness Training, P.E.T., (Gordon 1970) will be used. The counselor is particularly impressed with Dinkmeyer's STEP program, Systematic Training for Effective Parenting, (Dinkmeyer and McKay 1976) which the school has recently acquired, and plans to put it to use.

RESEARCH

WORKING WITH TEACHERS

The counselor has been promoting techniques to demonstrate results in the classroom, partly to develop good working relationships with teachers and partly to deal directly with pressing problems. Disruptive behavior is one of the concerns of most teachers, so this area has been her focus. Her choice is good; she knows effective techniques that yield observable results. Mitchell and Crowell (1973) used behavior modification to reduce disruptive behavior in art classes. Randolph and Saba (1973) describe procedures to change behavior through modeling and consulting, in which teachers reinforced desired performance. Briskin and Anderson

(1973) illustrate how pupils can be used as contingency managers. Six boys in sixth grade were recruited to reduce disruptive behavior of third graders and were trained in six half-hour sessions to administer *time-out procedure* and to give positive reinforcement for appropriate behavior. (The time-out procedure involved removing pupils from the class when their behavior was disruptive.) The pupil was reinforced if not sent for time-out. Others, including the teacher and principal, provided support and encouragement for the work of the sixth graders. The contingency management approach resulted in a sharp decrease in disruptive behavior.

RESEARCH

PEER COUNSELING

Bringing peers into the counseling program is an effective strategy. Pupils learn helping skills, derive personal benefits, and help spread the effects of counseling (McCann 1975; Richardson 1976; Gumaer 1973). McCann illustrates the potential in a study done with eight sixth-graders in Driden Central School, New York. The pupils learned helping skills in eight training sessions covering topics such as definition of a peer counselor; qualities of a helping person; how to listen; and how to reflect. After these training sessions, at least one peer counselor was on duty during the two periods each week when the drop-in center was open to sixth graders. The study points to several positive effects of the program; students learned helping skills, positive attitudes were developed toward receiving help, and students began to feel that a peer was often able to help.

EXPERIENCE

PERCEPTIONS OF THE COUNSELING ROLE

In a small group, have one member play a counselor (elementary or middle school) explaining the counseling role to a pupil, parents, or teachers. Other group members play the people receiving information.

At the end of the presentation, ask group members to comment on how clearly the role was communicated. Ask the "counselor" to describe how the role play felt.

EXPERIENCE

FEELINGS ABOUT PUPILS' PROBLEMS AND NEEDS

One person or a small group can do this exercise. In a classroom of twelve or more students, subgroups of three or four may be used.

The previous section identifies a number of types of pupils with problems or needs. Choose the two types you would most like to work with and the two you would least prefer. Then take turns explaining why you feel the way you do, as if you were talking to a pupil in one of these groups. Have the others comment on what your statements convey about your work preferences.

Does the experience give you new insights about yourself? Share them with others. (If the exercise is done alone, think through the explanation in your head, but write your new insights down.)

OBJECTIVES

1. To understand the importance of a needs survey in building effective guidance programs. Name three groups whose perceptions of needs should be used in establishing guidance objectives.

Pupils, teachers, and parents.

2. To understand how classroom conditions affect the school counselor's work. Identify three positive and three negative conditions.

Among the teacher attitudes that might be identified are:

Positive	*Negative*
— Interest in new developments.	— Lack of interest in new developments.
— Sensitivity to personal problems of pupils.	— Preference for the submissive, quiet type of pupil.
— Awareness of the importance of ethnic differences.	— Negative views on ethnic differences.

NEEDS AND PROBLEMS To understand guidance at West End Elementary School, one must know something about the pupils and their problems. Some examples will show the kinds of pupil the counselor encounters and the wide variety of socioeconomic levels and types of homes they come from. All are coping with developmental problems typical of the elementary-school age and practically all could use assistance in areas such as learning to get along with others, feeling good about themselves, developing abilities and skills, and establishing rewarding relationships with teachers and parents. Some need more help than others and are trying to deal with problems already well advanced.

Mary Beasley, a third grader who has just transferred to West End Elementary School from another town, lives with grandparents because her parents are separated. She is withdrawn, anxious, and feels very ill at ease in the new school. Any attention from the teacher upsets her, and other pupils have either ignored or teased her as an outsider.

Billy Browning presents the teacher and counselor with a different type of challenge. He is bright, active, and assertive, and insists on telling other pupils how everything should be done. His manner has earned him the intense dislike of most of the other pupils, and he is left out of activities or admitted grudgingly by hostile peers.

Frances Malone, a black pupil, is in continual trouble. She is large for her grade, often belligerent, and tries to intimidate other pupils. Her parents are of little help and have told her to take up for herself and "don't let any of those people put anything over on you." Her teacher declares she cannot keep her in the classroom any longer.

Susie Newell, a second grader, is an only child with a rather cold and unloving home life. She is constantly seeking attention and reassurance. Her parents, socially active and influential in the town, are quick to criticize the school for all of Susie's shortcomings.

Luis Alvarez has been in the United States only a year and is still having trouble with English. He is caught between the social patterns of his family and the customs and attitudes of his classmates and finds it hard to maintain an identity and still fit in with the school group. So far, most teachers have told him to adapt to the American way and forget about his national characteristics.

Louis Denning, a black fifth grader, is bright and capable. In subtle ways he has been given to understand that black students are not expected to achieve very highly, and that he is unrealistic in hoping to get top grades. He is becoming discouraged and resentful without knowing why.

There are several cliques and in-groups in the school; one of the more active ones, the "Chargers," is made up of fifth-grade girls. They exercise considerable power on the playground and in the halls and attempt to control many school activities. Membership in the group is highly valued, and most girls are not accepted. The Chargers have prestige among peers and are looked up to by pupils in the lower grades.

The school has a number of other problems, such as absenteeism, dislike of school, school phobia, stealing, and vandalism. Those who are frequently absent and have extremely resistant attitudes toward attending school are usually handled by the district office. A concentrated effort to find out who steals lunch money and school supplies has so far met with little success. Vandalism takes place both during and after school and has become a serious problem; the cost of repairs has soared. The principal is pushing the development of an educational program to cope with the problem and insists that staff members search for evidence and inform him of any clues that will help identify the culprits. The efforts so far have not met with success.

The pupils described present crisis-type problems, but most of the others also need help for development. Harry O'Neal is an example. He is making adequate progress in all of his classes, gets along well with fellow students at his grade level, and is active in sports. But he has difficulty in reading and studying and is performing well below the expected level. Furthermore, he is apprehensive about talking in class and impresses his teachers as indifferent and unprepared. He has only a few friends and his greatest desire is to become more popular.

HOW PUPILS VIEW GUIDANCE   Pupils in West End Elementary School have had no prior experience with counselors and have no preconceptions about the counseling and guidance service. Since school started, however, they have gotten to know the counselor, and had a chance to participate in guidance activities and compare reactions.

There have been some positive changes in attitudes. Before, when someone in the administration contacted a pupil, it was for wrongdoing or deficiency. The counselor's appearance in the classroom has done much to allay students' fear of the administration, and classroom guidance activities have convinced many pupils that the counselor is willing to listen to them and help them express their feelings. Those who have participated in small groups have been very excited and pleased, although a few have felt threatened when expected to talk freely about themselves. Mary Beasley, for example, the timid, withdrawn third grader, is quite apprehensive about seeing the counselor individually or taking part in groups. She has not learned to trust anyone at school and feels that whatever she says will be used to criticize or tease her. Frances Malone has not come around to talk to the counselor whom she views with suspicion as part of the school administration.

These are some of the pupils the new elementary school counselor will have to cope with. She is not surprised to find a great need for counseling and guidance services, but now faces the problem of setting up priorities; she sees clearly that she will not be able to attend to each individual problem. She prefers a developmental and preventive approach, and this will be the major focus of her program. She knows too that some crises demand immediate attention.

EXPERIENCE

A NEEDS SURVEY

Do a mini-survey of needs. Without trying to get a representative sample, ask several pupils and teachers to list the three most important areas in which they need help. Summarize the results. See how stimulating you would find it to help pupils and teachers meet these needs.

GUIDANCE IN THE MIDDLE/JUNIOR HIGH SCHOOL

A discussion of guidance in school years 6 through 9 could very well constitute a separate chapter—work at this level presents unique challenges unlike those in elementary and high school and merits specific attention. This is particularly true for the middle school but also applies for the junior high school. Unfortunately junior high schools have in some cases tended to follow practices of the senior high school. The middle school guidance program, on the other hand, tends to resemble elementary school services and emphasizes group work, parent contacts, work with teachers to help them improve classroom climate and promote exploration of self and environment. But the middle school does need its own strategies and approaches.

The evolving role of the middle school counselor reflects the needs and problems of pupils at this stage, but not all professional issues are resolved. As Tindall says (referring also to the junior high school): "Many . . . counselors feel they do not have a special identity and place. They often feel they are [in] a smaller high school or a bigger elementary school and feel frustrated with the lack of training and information to perform a good job at the junior high/middle school level" (1976 p. 5). But there is a visible trend to strive for continuity from grades K to 12, giving the middle school the responsibility to promote the development of social, emotional, and physical growth, and assisting with educational planning and career development (Hill 1974, pp. 78–79). Specific goals and objectives need to be developed for this stage. Functions must be expanded beyond traditional individual and small-group assistance to include teaching teachers guidance techniques to help them understand and facilitate the growth of individuals in their classes, and preparing pupils to help their peers (Tindall p. 5).

THE MIDDLE/JUNIOR HIGH SCHOOL   The intermediate school years used to be considered grades 7, 8, and 9, which make up the typical junior high school. More recently the middle-school concept has emerged, covering grades 5, 6, and 7 or 6, 7, and 8. The elementary school may thus run from grades 1 to 4 or 1 to 5. In more traditional junior high school organizations, the 6 : 3 : 3 system includes 6 years of elementary school, 3 of junior high school, and 3 of senior high.

Both educational plans are aimed at meeting the needs of early adolescents. Research does not strongly support one over the other, but there are a number of reasons why the middle-school concept has caught on and why it is beginning to replace the junior high school. It provides a program specifically aimed at the 10–14-year age group, and is characterized by flexibility and exploratory emphasis rather than the specialization typical of high school. Even the term "middle school" gives the new-type institution an identity of its own (Howard and Stoumbis 1970, p. 205), distinguishing it clearly from the high school. Methods and curriculum content take into account characteristics of the students' developmental stage. Pupils take responsibility for learning (Kohut 1976, p. 8). There is a widening of interests, and individuals are ready, with the security of adult guidance and supervision, to assume more self-direction and self-management (Hansen and Hearn 1971, p. 20). Whether or not the middle school replaces the junior high school and constitutes, as some claim, the major educational development of our times (Howard and Stoumbis 1970, p. 216), it does have features designed to make the transition from elementary to high school a period of growth.

DON C. ALLEN MIDDLE SCHOOL   This school is in a small city with a population of about 200,000. Recently there has been a change from the older 6 : 3 : 3 plan, partly because of a new building program and partly because of financing. It was felt that it would be economical to have grades 6, 7, and 8 together on the same campus without the ninth grade. The new middle school has about 1,000 students and is considered to be a model institution for its age group.

The school has a number of innovative features. Pupils are divided into groups of about 100, each with a team of four teachers. Modular scheduling is used to break down groups according to pupil needs and to provide flexibility. The procedure has not been an unqualified success; teachers complain that it is difficult to keep up with pupils. Some problems have arisen with the learning center for individual, self-initiated work. Some pupils seem unable to accept responsibility for individual study.

Guidance is organized around teaching teams. A counselor is assigned half time to each team, with a full-time guidance coordinator supervising the program. Major activities of the counselors consist of work with individuals and small groups, consulting with parents, and guidance sessions in classrooms on topics like values clarification, career education, personal development, and exploration of feelings classes. The guidance program is new to counselors as well as teachers, and opinions vary as to just what it should accomplish. On the whole, however, the program has made an acknowledged and distinct contribution, helping the school to facilitate physical, intellectual, and personal growth of pupils (Gatewood and Dilg 1975, pp. 6–17).

The counselors have no difficulty convincing others that guidance is an essential part of the middle school program; the position is widely accepted. They have used the role statement published by the American School Counselor Association (*Elementary School Guidance and Counseling*, March 1974, pp. 216–218), which emphasizes group work and consultation to keep problems from developing. Role suggestions include:

— Individual, group, and peer counseling to help students develop an identity and understand themselves.
— Consulting with teachers to help them become aware of the needs of early adolescents.
— Providing pupil data to teachers.
— Assisting the administrator in evaluating the curriculum and in providing a positive approach to discipline.
— Working with parents on an individual or group basis.
— Identifying, and building ties with referral resources.
— Publicizing the program in school and community. Building wide support.
— Helping pupils with preparation for the next step (moving to high school).
— Participating in activities to promote pupils' career development in school.
— Participating with teachers in planning and carrying out experiences that take into account the uniqueness of early adolescence and promote self-understanding and self-direction in each pupil.

RESEARCH

PROBLEMS AND GUIDANCE METHODS FOR MIDDLE SCHOOL COUNSELORS

Middle and junior high school pupils present the counselor with a wide range of problems and needs. Typical ones are test anxiety, difficulties in career planning, ineffective communication, low achievement, and poor parent relations. Some small-scale studies should be replicated before generalizations are made, but they illustrate potentially effective approaches for typical needs and difficulties. Hillman and Shields (1975) report that the use of consultation and positive reinforcement increased a seventh-grade boy's attending behavior and achievement. There is evidence pupils well-adjusted to school also communicate better with their parents (Sporakowski and Eubanks 1976). Communication effectiveness appears to be enhanced by group peer-counseling preparation (Gray and Tindall 1974). Studies of occupational values of junior high pupils indicate the importance of assessing needs and values at this level to plan guidance interventions (Perrone 1973). Systematic programs can facilitate career exploration and planning (Perrone and Kyle 1975; R. Harris 1974).

In a total of seven small group meetings, Deffenbacher and Kemper (1974) used desensitization to reduce test anxiety with a group of eleven boys and eleven girls in sixth grade. Changes in GPA provided the measure of success. The counseling-group grades improved an average of .42, significant at the .001 level, and the increase was slightly greater for those who were failing prior to counseling. Though a limited study, it does indicate that counseling can reduce test anxiety, and illustrates a procedure the teacher or counselor can learn in a relatively short time.

An earlier study by the same authors (Deffenbacher and Kemper 1974) applied the techniques successfully to 28 test-anxious junior-high-school students, grades 7–9. Differences found between pre-counseling and post-counseling grades were significant at the .001 level. No significant difference was found between male and female. Failing students improved to the same degree.

EXPERIENCE

PREFERENCES FOR WORK SETTING

Designate parts of the room for elementary school counselors, middle school counselors, and secondary school counselors. Ask students to choose one of the areas and move to it, and then discuss why they made the choices. Ask each group to report the one most positive and the one most negative feature of the work setting as they have emerged in the discussion.

Review similarities and differences brought out.

EXPERIENCE

CONSUMER REACTIONS

Invite several pupils in the middle/junior high school to participate in a panel discussion about their "ideal counselor." Ask each to take two or three minutes to describe an "ideal." The audience should be ready with questions to explore their preferences. For example, if a pupil says that the "counselor understands me," ask what the counselor does that shows understanding or how it feels to be understood.

Follow up the presentation with a discussion of what the pupils' comments told students about their own suitability for work as a counselor.

OBJECTIVES

1. To be aware of the problems counselors face. List five problems for each of the two school levels covered.

Elementary

— New pupils adapting to public school.
— Developing good working relations with pupils and teachers.
— Helping transfer pupils adapt to the school.
— Promoting good race relations among pupils.
— Dealing with cultural differences of first-generation-American families.
— Helping plan experiences for low-achieving pupils.

Middle

— Pupils moving from one educational level to the next.
— Developing good working relations with pupils and teachers, with more emphasis on teamwork.
— (same as for elementary) Promoting good race relations among pupils.
— (same as for elementary) Dealing with cultural differences of first-generation-American families.
— (same as for elementary) Helping plan experiences for low-achieving pupils.

2. To understand the major functions of the elementary school counselor and the middle school counselor. List key concepts for each level.

The key terms are as follows:

Elementary   *Middle*

— Counseling, individual and group.   — (same)
— Consulting.   — (same)
— Coordinating.   — (same)

3. To be aware of your feelings about a career in guidance at the elementary or junior high school level. Identify three factors that evoke positive feelings, and three that evoke negative feelings.

These will be unique for you; the following are illustrations:

Positive   *Negative*

— Setting up your own program.   — Colleagues (teachers) not
— Dealing with critical needs.   cooperative.
— Close relationships with others.   — Too much to do.
                                                — Cannot change pupils' de-
                                                  structive environments.

4. To be aware of how you feel undertaking the challenges of a guidance position. Express your feelings about the idea of applying for a job at West End Elementary School or Don C. Allen Middle School.

Responses may be like those for Objective 3, but the emphasis here is on *applying.* Think about talking to the principal, explaining the contribution you could make to the program, and describing the working conditions you would like.

5. To be aware of how a career in guidance fits with the life-style you would like. List five words that describe your life-style. Check the ones that reflect your feelings about guidance work.

Think in terms that fit you, for example, "helping," "independent," "high status," "dislike routine," "stability."

ADDITIONAL READINGS

Agati, Giacomo, J., and Lovino, James W. "Implementation of a Parent Counseling Program." *The School Counselor* 22, no. 2 (1974), pp. 126–129.

An interesting description of a program for parents of pupils in grades 1–8, set up to provide help in understanding and promoting growth. Evaluation showed several positive results, including a much better understanding on the parents' part of the role of the counselors.

Morgan, Lewis B. *A Casebook for School Counselors.* Washington, D.C.: APGA Press, 1974.

The cases, involving elementary, middle, and junior high school pupils, make interesting reading and help give an understanding of situations counselors confront. Problems include working with parents, teachers, and pupils and cover the whole range of counselor functions.

Peters, Herman J., and Shertzer, Bruce. *Guidance Program Development and Management.* 3rd ed. Columbus, Ohio: Charles E. Merrill, 1974.

The description on pages 551–563 gives an excellent picture of an elementary school program.

Poppen, William A. "Idea Exchange Column." *Elementary School Guidance and Counseling.*

These columns appear as a regular feature in this journal. The problems described and the ways counselors deal with them give a feel of the work of the elementary school counselor.

Ryan, Mary K., ed. "Middle/Junior High School Counselors' Corner." *Elementary School Guidance and Counseling.*

This column runs in most issues. The contributors describe problems counselors face and explain strategies for solutions.

Spielbichler, Otto, and Spielbichler, Vivian. "The Open Space School and the Counselor." *The School Counselor* 22, no. 1 (1974), pp. 31–35.

A description of the Argyle Junior High School in Montgomery County, Md., which incorporates new concepts for the middle years. The article explains how counselors can develop relations with large numbers of pupils and work as team members. It is a good example of counselors devising new ways to work with modern school programs.

Stamm, Martin L., and Nissman, Blossom S. "The Counselor's View of the Middle School Student." *The School Counselor* 21, no. 1 (1973), pp. 34–38.

The authors compare growth periods with events at a carnival to emphasize critical characteristics of middle-school-age youth and to suggest unique program features counselors may use.

"The Unique Role of the Elementary School Counselor." *Elementary School Guidance and Counseling* 8, no. 3 (1974), pp. 219–223.

This position paper describing the role of the elementary school counselor has been officially accepted by the American School Counselor Association. It will be referred to in more detail in Chapter 6 and other sections of the book, but is important here as an outline of the work of the counselor in the elementary school.

"The Unique Role of the Middle/Junior High School Counselor." *Elementary School Guidance and Counseling* 8, no. 3 (1974), pp. 216–218.

This role statement will also be referred to in more detail in Chapter 6, but it is important here because it supplements the discussion of the middle and junior high school counselors' responsibilities and services.

CHAPTER FOUR

GUIDANCE:

HOW IT GREW

A survey of the history of guidance is helpful in understanding the field today as well as in projecting its future. This chapter describes the beginnings of guidance and reviews the major aspects of guidance over the past seventy years. Our study of the history of guidance highlights the impact of individual leaders and outlines the development of guidance into an organized profession.

GOALS

1. To understand the historical bases of current features of guidance.
2. To comprehend the effect of leaders who influenced the development of guidance.
3. To evaluate the direction guidance is taking and one's part in shaping the future.

GAINING INSIGHT
FROM A STUDY OF THE PAST

Counseling and guidance were not always as they are today.

Questions may be raised about the development of each aspect; answers to these questions take one back over the 60- or 70-year period of the development of guidance. Why, for example, is guidance considered to be a school function rather than a community-based service as in many European countries that served as models for so much in our educational system? How did the concept originate? Who conceptualized it and what generated its momentum? What are the origins of a developmental emphasis? How did testing become a function of guidance and counseling? What shaped the approaches to counseling that we see today, primarily emphasizing subjective aspects of a person? What gave rise to the present concern about subgroups, accountability, and strategies to spread the effects of guidance?

Questions may also be raised about the development of guidance at different educational levels. Why is elementary school guidance different from guidance at the secondary level, and why did it begin so much later? What shaped the approach to guidance in the transitional years between elementary and secondary school? While the college level is beyond the scope of this book, it would be informative to see how its development paralleled the public school trends.

Questions such as the above do not constitute an outline for a review of the history of guidance; they do focus attention on the threads in its development and alert the reader to the persons and events that lead us where we are today. They help point to relationships among seemingly disparate events that have interacted to produce a rationale and strategies for guidance and counseling.

An understanding of the history of guidance is particularly important for a profession that unlike teaching, law, or medicine, for example, has no official historical identity. Tracing the development of guidance illustrates the search for an identity that has been and still is a major problem confronting those who work in the field.

The chronological development of secondary school guidance, with the exception of the first 2,000 years, is portrayed in the pages that follow in phases identified by events, major movements, or professional developments. These phases are:

— Origins in social reform movement.
— The impact of testing.
— The impact of the depression.
— The new counseling.
— The National Defense Education Act (NDEA) and Guidance.
— Expanding the concept of guidance.

Guidance in the elementary and middle/junior high school and in higher education is taken up without division by periods, in sections that follow the secondary school account.

THE FIRST YEARS   Records show that Egyptian society was concerned with guidance as early as 2,500 B.C. (Borow 1964, p. 46). Plato recognized the value to society of differing work for differing abilities (Borow 1964, p. 46; Zytowski 1967). Roman parents helped boys and girls identify capacities through the use of role models and occupational exploration (Meyer 1965, pp. 35, 37). These early efforts reflect an interest in helping youth to plan, choose, and develop.

Events in the past 400 or 500 years show guidance beginning to emerge as an organized service. Publications became available in the 1400s soon after Gutenberg invented printing. Bishop Rodrigo Sanchez prepared a book on guidance for both secular and religious occupations entitled *The Mirror of Men's Lives*. It was in Latin, the language of scholars, and so probably did not serve the general public (Zytowski 1972). The number of books on guidance increased rapidly during the sixteenth, seventeenth, and eighteenth centuries (Brower 1942, Ch. 2). Zytowski (1972) identified some 400 that described occupations, but were as much for general information as for guidance. Titles are strikingly different from ours today. A book published in 1575 by a Spanish author, Juan Huarte, is called *The Examination of Man's Wits*, and one published in 1585 by an Italian, Tomaso Garzoni, is entitled *The Universal Plaza of All the Professions of the World*. This book qualifies as the sixteenth-century version of the *Occupational Outlook Handbook*, a U.S. Department of Labor biennial publication, the best known current reference on careers.

During the 1800s, publications began to appear in the United States. Whittock's *The Complete Book of Trades: or a Parent's Guide and Youth's Instruction* was, according to Zytowski (1972), the first with a title to indicate it was designed for guidance. Brewer (1942, pp. 21–41) describes a number of books by American as well as foreign authors that provided occupational and leisure guidance.

Much of what is known about early efforts at guidance is contained in publications such as those named above. How these documents were used and the attitudes and goals of the users may only be guessed, but certainly part of the purpose was to help people understand themselves better and gain a more realistic perception of opportunities.

AWARENESS OF NEED FOR CAREER PLANNING ASSISTANCE

Conditions around the turn of the century set the stage for the development of guidance. As Aubrey writes, "It arose in the dawning of the 20th Century as one of several movements answering the upheaval and turmoil created by the Industrial Revolution" (1977, p. 288). Leaders emerged to institute and upgrade help for young people faced with the new industrial movement and wanting to live productive lives and escape from poverty and wretched working-conditions.

Among these early leaders, George Merrill, Eli Weaver, Anna Reed, and Jesse B. Davis stand out. Each of these early leaders was associated with an educational institution, even though the roots of guidance were in

community agencies. Merrill's program in the California School of Mechanical Arts in 1895 included work-samples, program selection, placement, and follow-up, but strangely enough, he did not consider his work
to be guidance (Brewer 1942, p. 49). Weaver, a teacher and later principal
at Boy's High School in Brooklyn, originated a program for placing boys in
summer part-time work related to their school programs and provided
occupational information in courses. Critics condemned the placement
aspect, apparently oblivious of the guidance value of exploration. His
book, *Choosing a Career*, was published in 1906, and his approach was
widely followed in New York City schools at the time. In many ways his
work resembled that of the West Coast leader, Anna Y. Reed. She gave
more emphasis to in-school guidance and her programs reflected methods
utilized in business and industry. Both Reed and Weaver operated on the
principles of "social Darwinism" (Rockwell and Rothney 1961), believing
in evolution through competition and natural selection within the established world-of-work structure.

Jesse B. Davis, like many other early leaders in vocational guidance,
exemplified the tenets of the social reform movement. His work was well
known; he was a tireless lecturer and teacher, applying the "calling"
concept to vocational life in very much the same way as it is used in the
ministry and emphasizing work as serving humanity (Rockwell and
Rothney 1961). He instituted guidance classes on moral values and occupational study (Miller 1961, p. 150). Davis played a major role in the
beginnings of guidance. Shertzer and Stone (1974, p. 22) suggest that
counseling may have begun with his ten years as a class counselor helping
pupils with educational and vocational problems at Central High School
in Detroit. Later, as principal of Grand Rapids High School, he employed
counselors to work with pupils from the seventh grade on (Odell 1973;
Shertzer and Stone 1974, p. 22).

Other streams fed into guidance, notably measurement and clinical
treatment of learning difficulties. Binet, concerned about retardation in
French schools, collaborated with Simon to develop a mental ability scale
for classifying children (Miller 1961, p. 152). The 1905 scale was revised
several times and later introduced into the United States. Louis M. Terman
developed the best-known version in 1961, the Stanford-Binet Scale. At
Columbia University James McKeen Catell, probably influenced by
German psychologist William Wundt and English biologist Francis Gal-
ton (Williamson 1965, p. 64), began work on the measurement of students' abilities. Lightner Witmer established the first psychological clinic
for the study of student difficulties at the University of Pennsylvania
(Borow 1964, p. 48) and is credited with developing modern concepts of
counseling (Williamson 1965, p. 87).

Around the turn of the century, guidance was part of the broad movement of social reform; the movement's social and economic values were
combined in schools in a unitary concept of vocational guidance and

GUARANTEED TO DO THE WORK OF 5 FARMERS

SUPER FARMER

In the aftermath of the Industrial Revolution, early guidance leaders tried to help workers, like this farmer, find new jobs.

vocational education. The settlement house movement and the National Society for the Promotion of Industrial Education (NSPIE) were instrumental in shaping guidance and moving it into the schools (Stephens 1970, p. 5). But another influence was at work. While many of the early efforts were directed to introducing guidance as another subject into the curriculum, as Aubrey (1977) points out, it was the beginning of Progressivism in American education instituted by Horace Mann and John Dewey that ensured the visibility of guidance in the schools. More pronounced influences of the Progressive Education movement were to follow, but Aubrey (1977) characterizes Davis as an important example of American Progressivism in education. The ties with vocational education were close at this time; both were considered part of a larger helping strategy; separation eventually came, but at a later date.

ORIGINS IN SOCIAL REFORM MOVEMENT

Conditions in urban centers in the early 1900s generated national pressure for wide social reform and set the stage for Frank Parsons' remarkable achievement in formulating the concepts that were the beginnings of present-day guidance (Shertzer and Stone 1974, p. 24). While guidance was not his invention, the establishment of his Vocational Bureau in the Boston Civic Service House was the most significant event in its development in the past seven or eight decades and his work overshadowed that of his contemporaries.

Parsons was a social reformer whose philosophy of mutualism amounted to gradual socialism. Ahead of his time, he advocated many reforms, such as methods of selecting congressmen, women's right to vote, and a progressive income tax, which have since been realized (Rockwell and Rothney 1961). Parsons' concepts about guidance as revealed through his work and activities are remarkably up-to-date. Biggs (1963) points out that Parsons emphasized all-round development, continuity of guidance from childhood through adulthood, the need for professionally trained counselors, referral resources, follow-up, and evaluation (early signs of accountability!).

Parsons' personal experiences and the appalling living and working conditions of immigrants, particularly children, fed his zeal for social reform and led to an involvement in helping activities that continued until his death. He lost his job as an engineer in the panic of 1873. His liberal views brought him into conflict with big business, and railroad interests forced him out of his teaching position at Kansas State College in 1899. To effect reform in the industrial system and improve working conditions he became involved in activities of the Boston Civic Service House. He set up what was appropriately called the Breadwinner's Institute and then went on to establish the counseling service known as the Vocational Bureau. In a lecture on the "Ideal City," in which he described the help needed by young people in the choice of a vocation, Parsons developed the rationale for counseling. The talk aroused much interest, and many young people requested interviews with him. By 1907 a plan for a counseling office was prepared, and the bureau opened formally in January, 1908 (Brewer 1942, p. 59).

It is difficult today to visualize the social and economic conditions of Parsons' times. Children started looking for full-time work at age 14. Less than 10 percent of 17-year-olds graduated from high school, even though high school was regarded as the gateway to success. Parsons' efforts were directed at the lowest and most disadvantaged level in society—the 14-year-olds from underprivileged immigrant families, who made up the potential child labor force (Ginzberg 1971, p. 24).

Parsons' counseling principles are in many ways still sound. He advised choosing a vocation rather than merely looking for a job and urged young people to acquire a wide knowledge of occupations so as to avoid falling into the first convenient job opening. He gave considerable weight to expert advice but knew the value of basing predictions on research. Written self-analysis is still in use today, particularly in job search strategies. Parsons dominated the guidance work of his time with his innovative techniques. He died in 1908; his book, *Choosing a Vocation,* was published posthumously in May, 1909. The work of the center continued under David Stone Wheeler, and similar guidance services were established in Boston schools (Brewer 1942, pp. 65–66).

Some developments in other fields with which Parsons was not acquainted were overlooked, though they were later to have a profound impact on guidance. G. Stanley Hall brought Sigmund Freud to this country to lecture, and United States psychologists discovered psychoanalysis. The new personality theory and therapy had far-flung repercussions, affecting institutions as diverse as the theatre and child clinics, but it did not affect school counseling during the next ten or twenty years (Miller 1961, p. 167).

The mental-hygiene movement was getting underway, stimulated by Clifford Beer's book, *A Mind that Found Itself,* his account of a three-year confinement in mental hospitals. His activities led to the organization of the Connecticut Society for Mental Hygiene (Miller 1964, pp. 8–9), which was followed by the establishment of the group that is now known as the National Association for Mental Health. Over the years this organization has been increasingly active in promoting school and community counseling programs (Shertzer and Stone 1974, p. 26) and in drawing attention to affective aspects of guidance.

Aside from Parsons' use of assessment, psychological testing had little direct impact on the school guidance movement. Neither clinical nor group tests were used before World War I. Typically, guidance workers were cautious or negative about testing, and the pronounced effect it was later to have was not yet apparent.

This period of social reform was marked by great strides in guidance organizations and the spread of services into schools. The Boston Vocational Bureau and Chamber of Commerce organized the first national conference in Boston in 1910; its meetings attracted wide interest among employees, employers, social workers, and educators. It was a broadly supported, humanitarian crusade (Miller 1964, p. 5). A second national conference was called in New York in 1912.

The third national conference is of special significance. It was at this meeting, held in 1913 in Grand Rapids, Michigan, that the National Vocational Guidance Association, or NVGA, was founded. (Some thirty years later, it merged with other organizations to form the American Personnel and Guidance Association.) In 1927, the organization's professional publication was given the new name *The Vocational Journal,* which was later changed to *Personnel and Guidance Journal* (Siegel, 1972).

The Vocational Bureau was turned over to the Division of Education at Harvard University in 1917 and continued to prepare guidance workers under the title "Bureau of Vocational Guidance" (Brewer 1942, pp. 74–75). Later, and continuing until the 1940s, its work was taken over by the National Occupational Conference, the U.S. Office of Education, and NVGA (Brewer 1942, p. 75).

During the latter part of this period, guidance was making phenomenal inroads into schools, and a number of city school systems set up programs. Weaver's work in New York spread from coast to coast—from Philadelphia to Los Angeles (Miller 1961, p. 150). The Smith-Hughes Act in 1917, designed to promote vocational education, stimulated interest in placement and follow-up, but its funds could not be used for guidance until later (Miller 1964, p. 7–8). Education had accepted guidance wholeheartedly. In fact, the beginnings of school guidance reflected the concern of Progressive Education for building a more humane and productive life (Cremin 1965, p. 4). But conflicts were beginning to emerge. Barry and Wolf (1957, p. 29) observe that the 1918 Cardinal Principles of Secondary Education furthered the split between vocational guidance and general guidance, even though during and well past this period guidance was viewed as broadly, rather than narrowly, vocational (Miller 1961, p. 151).

THE IMPACT OF TESTING

The decade of the 20s witnessed a tremendous growth of measurements of all kinds, beginning with the unprecedented use of tests in World War I to classify and assign draftees. The confidence generated by the scientific allure of such instruments gave guidance status and respectability and infused its development with new life. But excessive dependence on testing is blamed for blinding guidance leaders to other potentially significant developments.

The time was ripe for a technique with the look of a precise technology, and widespread use had made the public familiar with its instruments. The army alpha- and beta-group intelligence-tests (the latter for illiterates) were developed through the combined efforts of the Psychological Committee of the National Research Council and the army's Committee on Classification of Personnel (Borow 1964, p. 51). By 1918 almost two million persons had been given one of these intelligence tests (Miller 1961, p. 154). Brewer credits these activities with having an effect on vocational guidance, although the emphasis of military testing was on selection (1942, p. 9). Input into the guidance movement at this time came from the armed forces, business, and education (Paterson 1938).

Clark Hull's work at the University of Wisconsin on predicting occupational success anticipated modern computer technology (Borow 1964, p. 53). Hull hoped that by the use of tests and job analysis, guidance could be made a science of matching men and jobs (Ginzberg 1971, p. 30). His landmark book, *Aptitude Testing,* was published in 1928, but results of his work led him to give up the idea of achieving a job-success prediction-system with tests (Williamson 1965, p. 103).

Interest measurement got started late in this period. E. K. Strong published the Strong Vocational Interest Blank in 1927 (Borow 1964, p. 52), following earlier work on interest measurement by James Burt, Bruce V. Moore, and Walter V. Bingham at the Carnegie Institute of Technology (Crites 1969, p. 5). Several approaches to interest measurement grew out of the institute's seminars, but Strong's has been the most extensively studied and used.

Many effects of developments in military personnel work were felt in the postwar years. Assessment instruments, including high school and college achievement tests and cumulative record cards were made available to schools (Paterson 1938, p. 39), and the Committee on Cooperative Experiments in Student Personnel (established in 1923) of the American Council on Education (founded in 1918) promoted use of the new materials and techniques.

Guidance with a vocational emphasis was spreading rapidly; during this period, it was probably at least taken under consideration by every system in the land. Seventeen large city systems set up programs in addition to those already established (Brewer 1942, pp. 100, 104). Legislation and leaders in the field reinforced the vocational thrust. The Smith-Hughes Act was not to have a clear-cut impact until later, but the Rehabilitation Act of 1918 was eventually placed under the jurisdiction of the Federal Board of Vocational Education (Borow 1964, p. 52). In his book, *The Psychology of Vocational Adjustment* (1925), Harry D. Kitson, a leading counselor-educator, emphasized that guidance is a specialized, professional occupation, and "not just for amateurs" (Brewer 1942, p. 88). He was influential in shaping the nature both of school guidance and the professional preparation of counselors.

Counselors and guidance workers were unaware of the emotional conflicts and tensions of the period, and failed for one reason or another to utilize insights from mental hygiene and psychotherapy (Miller 1964, pp. 8–9). Nor did they make use of the research of industrial psychologists pointing to the importance of workers' attitudes (Borow 1964, p. 367). For example, a significant study which added a new term to the vocabulary of counselors—the Hawthorne effect—was done in an industrial plant. Elton Mayo and a team of Harvard research workers analyzed the relationship of environmental conditions to production at the Hawthorne (Chicago) plant of the Western Electric Company and found to their surprise that the status and recognition of the workers they studied had a greater effect on output than physical surroundings and work scheduling (Miller and Form 1951, p. 50). The term "Hawthorne effect" has come to mean an effect that follows from being part of a study rather than from actual treatment.

Clinical methods for helping individuals were beginning to emerge; child study clinics, developing from the pioneering work of G. Stanley Hall, opened in a number of cities during the 20s. Their approach emphasized detailed study of individual development starting with the very early years (Shertzer and Stone 1974, p. 24). Vitales began applying clinical techniques to vocational guidance by integrating Witmer's clinical approach with psychological measurement (Williamson 1965, p. 87).

THE IMPACT OF THE DEPRESSION

Three characteristics of the time from 1929 to 1940 were of particular importance to the field of guidance. First, it was the period of the teacher-counselor. Second, it witnessed a substantial infusion of federal support for guidance and placement services. Third, the testing-information-giving model was beginning to give way to a more psychologically oriented approach.

Teacher-counselors divided their time between teaching and guidance work, devoting a half day to each. Preparation might be minimal; positions were filled with little regard for qualification. In fact, there was no consensus about personal qualifications, preparation, and duties. As a result, administrators tended to load counselors down with miscellaneous clerical tasks. Emphasis was on giving pupils information about occupations; little attention was paid to a clinical approach (Miller 1973, pp. 9–10). The professional counselor, with a background in interview methods, assessment, and mental health, had not yet arrived. There were some attempts to develop strategies for working with the total person, but typically the traditional guidance patterns remained in force; conflicts about new patterns v. traditional ones were still unresolved (Barry and Wolf 1957, p. 32), and ties with vocational education were still strong (Miller 1961, p. 167).

The economic depression caused initial setbacks in guidance, but the nationwide need for services soon stimulated substantial advances in the profession. Up to about the middle 30s, there was severe retrenchment, but the long range effect was marked expansion (Barry and Wolf 1957, pp. 29–30). In 1939, there were 2,286 school counselors employed at least half-time in 1,297 schools in 702 cities in 46 of the 48 states (Odell 1973,

p. 151). Brewer lists 24 large-scale programs organized during this period and identifies 22 different titles for guidance workers in 52 departments, with "guidance" being the modal one (Brewer 1942, pp. 104–105).

The depression years witnessed a sequence of federal programs and projects to reduce unemployment; their impact on school guidance varied. The CCC (Civilian Conservation Corps), established in 1933 to provide work for unemployed youth, amounted to a competing educational system, serving about 260,000 young people (Miller 1961, pp. 159–160). Two years later the NYA (National Youth Administration) was established and continued its activities into the 40s, providing income and career guidance to approximately 2,677,000 young persons (Miller 1961, p. 160). The effects of these programs on school guidance is difficult to assess, but both focused on occupational exploration, and the NYA gave guidance workers the opportunity to gain job experience (Miller 1961, p. 161).

The same year that the CCC was instituted, the Wagner-Peyser Act established the U.S. Employment Service for youth and handicapped adults (Ginzberg 1971, p. 28) with a wide-ranging program of testing, counseling, research, and publication (Miller 1961, p. 161). As additional guidance needs became apparent, services were expanded to include all persons who required career planning and placement help (Ginzberg 1971, p. 28). This legislation provided for out-of-school guidance; additional federal action expanded school guidance, but at the same time narrowed its focus. The George-Deen Act of 1936 amended the earlier George-Barden Act so that funds could be used for guidance (Miller 1961, p. 162).

A number of other projects and programs were to have a lasting impact on school guidance. In 1938 the Occupational Information and Guidance Service was established in the Division of Vocational Education of the U.S. Office of Education (Borow 1964, pp. 55–56). Under Harry Jager (Shertzer and Stone 1974, p. 27), it used funds provided by Vocational Education to promote school guidance and counseling. In 1939, the first edition of the DOT *(Dictionary of Occupational Titles)* was published by the U.S. Employment Service. The Occupational Outlook Service was established in the Bureau of Labor Statistics in 1940 and published the first *Occupational Outlook Handbook* in 1949 (Ginzberg 1971, p. 201). DOT and the *Handbook* have become basic references in school guidance.

Of various other programs initiated in response to the depression, two of the most potent in terms of their impact on school guidance were MESRI (Minnesota Employment Stabilization Research Institute), set up by the University of Minnesota, and the American Youth Commission, established by the American Council on Education. The former conducted research on employment and unemployment; the latter concentrated on problems of youth. MESRI's team of economists, engineers, social workers, medical personnel, and psychologists learned a great deal about the employment problems of adults and reported the findings as *Men, Women, and Jobs,* by Paterson, Darley, and Elliott (Miller 1961, p. 159) and other publications. The project developed tests which have been extensively used in school guidance and has had significant implications for adult vocational guidance as well.

The work of the American Youth Commission revealed much about the social and vocational problems of the young. Publications of the project such as *Youth Tell Their Story* and *Matching Youth and Jobs,* by Howard Bell, reported that in the late 30s nearly 4,000,000 youths between 15 and 24 were neither in school nor employed. These studies, like MESRI's, were based on the belief that better vocational guidance would result in better job adjustment.

In the 30s, the Progressive Education Association carried out a particularly innovative project supporting new guidance concepts. The Eight-Year Study broadened the concept of guidance and emphasized groups and curriculum changes, approaches that conflicted with the current adaptations of Parsons' work (Miller 1961, pp. 165–166). As Aubrey (1977) indicates, the school counselor stood for the Progressive Education Movement in schools, which was more a matter of theory than practice. Guidance professed the wish to concern itself with development of the total person; day-to-day work in the schools fell far short of this goal. But without the support of the Progressive Education Movement, there would probably not have been any counselors in schools at all.

During this period, the guidance model of matching traits with occupational requirements began to lose ground and more or less faded into oblivion in the 40s. Aubrey (1977) attributes its demise to its inability to adapt to the new demands of helping individuals with total developmental and adjustment needs. A new approach based on personality dynamics, developmental patterns, and affective communication was gathering strength.

THE NEW COUNSELING

Carl R. Rogers' book, *Counseling and Psychotherapy* (1942), triggered a revolution in all forms of counseling. His nondirective approach broadened the concept of counseling, emphasized the counseling relationship rather than diagnosis and information, and opened up therapeutic practice to those without medical or psychoanalytic training. In this period, counselors began to focus on pupils own perceptions of needs (Odell 1973, p. 152). The clinical emphasis, leaving out assessment, was now an integral feature of guidance (Miller 1961, pp. 167–168), and a closer relationship with psychology was established. The NDEA institutes in the late 50s and 60s greatly expanded the nondirective impact (see section on NDEA).

While Rogers' work influenced the face-to-face helping situation and changed the style of work with individuals and small groups, the research of Eli Ginzberg, Donald E. Super, and others offered new perspectives on the developmental process and the way individuals formulate and implement career goals. Ginzberg introduced his theory of vocational development at the NVGA Convention in the early 50s; Super began the Career Patterns Study in 1951. These developments led to new concepts for preparing school counselors and organizing school guidance programs. But researchers of the period were most fascinated with finding new ways to explore feelings and providing therapeutically oriented help rather than with discovering ways to facilitate vocational development. As Aubrey (1977) says, Rogers' impact tended to obscure other techniques and approaches, and to restrict the focus to counseling.

Another new approach, based in psychology, contributed to the eclipse of the Parsonian trait-factor method, and widened the gap between guidance and vocational education. In 1941 psychologists began working in the Employment Service, War Manpower Commission, and air force Personnel Research Units. Many counselors and counselor-educators served in these agencies and brought new techniques back to school counseling. Tests, notably the AGCT (Army General Classification Test), were developed and occupational aptitude norms were set up (Ginzberg 1971, p. 32).

In 1944 the Veterans Administration established centers to provide counseling for those receiving benefits under the GI Bill, which provided for training and education for all veterans. Many counselors were trained in VA supported counseling services on college campuses and, because of the financial support of the GI Bill, were able to go on for more advanced preparation. The Veterans Administration did much to broaden and professionalize the role of the vocational counselor. For example, the vocational adviser of earlier VA programs was not a full-fledged counselor, but in 1951 the VA established the position of counseling psychologist, in line with newer concepts from psychology and related disciplines (Borow 1964, p. 60; Miller 1964, p. 15).

Indirectly, the influx of veterans in colleges gave counseling another boost. Many schools added counselors to their staffs to help graduates gain admission to competitive institutions of higher education. The effects of this emphasis were felt for many years after the initial postwar period.

For some time there had been criticism of the teacher-counselor role with its splitting of responsibility between classroom instruction and guidance. Federal support gave leaders the opportunity to promote the employment of full-time school counselors. Hager used his powerful position to urge state guidance supervisors to improve certification programs for school counselors. His aim was to establish the school counselor as a full-time worker by advocating the role of the teacher-plus, i.e., a teacher with graduate training (Hoyt 1974, p. 503). In order to identify the special skills needed to implement this concept, reports on counseling competencies were prepared as bases for the institution of reimbursable programs and certification. These reports set the pattern for postwar school counseling and counselor preparation until the late 50s. New rehabilitation counselor and employment counselor programs were strongly influenced by this model, but there was little effect on counseling psychology programs in psychology departments (Hoyt 1974, p. 504).

School counseling also benefited from federal action to upgrade rehabilitation counselors. In 1955 the Office of Vocational Rehabilitation began providing training grants for these specialties (Borow 1964, p. 61). Support to departments and students in a no-strings program led indirectly to better preparation for school counselors. Indeed, some graduates of these new programs eventually did work as school counselors.

Publication of journals, books, and psychological measurements in the 40s and 50s added sophistication to counselors' theory and practice, and made available up-to-date information for occupational planning. *The Occupational Outlook Handbook,* Strong's *Vocational Interest of Men and Women,* and the U.S. Employment Service's *General Aptitude Test Battery* (building on some of the MESRI tests) are outstanding examples. A new periodical, the *Journal of Counseling Psychology,* published research and theoretical articles for counselors.

The professional status of the counselor was aided immensely by the expansion of already existing organizations and the initiation of new ones. Developments reflect a broader approach to helping and a further recognition of the need for a team approach. In 1951, the newly formed American Personnel and Guidance Association took over the journal of NVGA (National Vocational Guidance Association), *Occupations,* and gave it the new title *Personnel and Guidance Journal* (Siegel 1972, p. 518). The new organization brought together NVGA (the oldest association of its kind), the American College Personnel Association, the Association for Counselor Education and Supervision, and the Student Personnel Association for Teacher Education. The new group numbered about 6,000, more than half previously NVGA members (Barry and Wolf 1957, p. 104). In 1953, a year after it was formed, the American School Counselor Association became a division of APGA. In 1947 the American Psychological Association established division 17, Counseling and Guidance, which took an active interest in school counseling and although not a major school counselor organization had an influence on counselor preparation (Barry and Wolf 1957, p. 95).

A Supreme Court decision during the 50s set the stage for the challenges of this decade. The Plessy Doctrine of "separate but equal" was rejected and the process of integration, marked by conflict and resistance, began. From the start, guidance workers were in the middle of developments, but typically, counselors' background and training left them unprepared to deal with racial groups and the tensions. Major changes had to be instituted in counselor education programs to provide the understanding and skills for working effectively with minority groups. Awareness and concern about minority group differences probably got a real start during this time.

NATIONAL DEFENSE EDUCATION ACT (NDEA) AND GUIDANCE

During the late 50s, the American people were confident of the superiority of American education and guidance, but their complacency was rudely shattered by Russia's successful Sputnik launch in 1957. The National Defense Education Act of 1958 was designed to remedy shortcomings in our educational system and to produce more scientific talent through testing and counseling. The goal was to catch up in science; guidance was to play a strategic role in achieving it. Funds were provided first for high school counseling, but by 1964, amendments had extended support from elementary schools through junior colleges and technical institutions. During the first five years, about 13,000 counselors were trained in summer or year-long NDEA institute programs (Borow 1964, p. 62).

Several components of NDEA are of special importance. Title V-B, supporting counselor preparation through counseling and guidance institutes, was the greatest landmark in the history of counselor education. By 1967, over $58 million had been spent on training more than 14,000 counselors in short-term (usually summer) institutes and nearly 5,000 in year-long institutes (Hoyt 1974, pp. 504, 506). Title V-A strengthened and expanded state guidance services. Provisions for the reimbursement of counselors' salaries dramatically increased the number of counselors employed in schools. In the late 60s, funding was cut substantially and counselor preparation was incorporated in other education acts.

There is no question that school counseling profited at least quantitatively from NDEA, but it is not yet possible to assess the full effects. Some evaluations have been made and two major reports give positive conclusions (Tyler 1960; Pierson 1965). But some feel that it caused many of today's problems. One striking result was that the number of full-time counselors in secondary schools increased from 12,000 in 1958–59 to over 29,000 in 1963–64 (Odell 1973, p. 152). The reimbursement made possible counselor-pupil load ratios of 1 : 400 or 1 : 500 and facilitated the establishment of a developmental model of guidance from kindergarten through high school and beyond (Herr 1974, p. 41). Since assistance provided by the act went to states and counselor education programs through two separate sections (V-A and V-B), differences about the counselor preparation arose, and remained unresolved (Hoyt 1974, pp. 506–507). State counselor certification standards did not match the requirements of counselor preparation institutions.

The 1962 MDTA (Manpower Development Training Act) provided for training of unemployed and underemployed (Borow 1964, p. 62). Because of rapidly increasing unemployment in 1963, emphasis shifted from those displaced from work by economic and technological change to the disadvantaged (Ginzberg 1971, pp. 16–17). Project CAUSE (Counselor Adviser University Summer Education Program) of the U.S. Department of Labor provided for the preparation of guidance support personnel (Hoyt 1974, p. 507). The Vocational Education Act of 1963 and the 1968 amendments emphasized guidance for vocational planning; however, they had very little impact on school guidance (Hoyt 1974, p. 508).

Three major publications at this time dramatically moved forward the broad acceptance of guidance services. C. Gilbert Wrenn's book, *The Counselor in a Changing World,* the report of the Commission on Guidance in American Schools, defined the current status of school counseling and made far-reaching recommendations for economic, social and occupational change in the world of counseling (Borow 1964, p. 62). Two other books, *The American High School Today* (1959) and *Slums and Suburbs* (1961) by James B. Conant, strongly supported guidance services and highlighted the need of disadvantaged inner-city youth. These three publications reached audiences far beyond the profession and generated wide support for school guidance.

The period was marked by the development of new approaches used in the intensive NDEA institutes. The influences of psychology and client-centered counseling increased, and group counseling became popular for counselees in need of help as well as counselors in training. Odell (1973, p. 152) describes this stage as focusing on counselee-perceived needs and counselors' personal characteristics as opposed to theoretical orientations, and notes a drive toward professionalization.

Special attention was paid to preparation standards and role statements, and after the NDEA was passed concern about these aspects surfaced on a national scale (Hoyt 1974, p. 509; Hill 1968). The most significant document of the time, the *Statement of Policy for Secondary School Counselors* (Odell 1973, p. 152), was prepared by ASCA (American School Counselor Association) in 1964. The ACES (Association for Counselor Education and Supervision) published standards for counselor education in 1964, which were revised after tryout and distributed in 1967. These reports supported a two-year training program for counselors with practical work to develop skills. At about this time, ASCA became the largest division of APGA.

EXPANDING THE CONCEPT OF GUIDANCE

Perhaps the most appropriate label for the period from 1969 on might be "the age of accountability." Odell (1973, pp. 152–153) has characterized it as a time of innovation in which some groups recommend new roles, others question the need for counselors, and still others vehemently support them. Aubrey (1977) identifies the trend of searching for a system to unify helping persons with common purposes. It is unquestionably a time for building comprehensive approaches to solving problems and fulfilling needs. With the help of a continuous assessment of the desires of those served, guidance can be provided when and where it is needed. But it is a time when realistic priorities must be established, and energy is being expended with care.

The period might be characterized as a return to Parsons, Weaver, and the turn-of-the-century concepts in an updated, modernized, developmental, theoretically-based, technologically-sophisticated approach—career education. Some vestiges of Progressive Education are visible in the efforts to spread guidance throughout school and in the concern for the individual's total development. There are common themes, such as questions regarding counseling as therapy, work with minorities, licensing, specialist v. generalist, the counselor as change agent, the role of the consultant, and group work. Career education stands out from the others representing psychological education to facilitate personal development.

In the early 70s Sidney P. Marland developed the new concept of career education to stimulate vocational development in public schools and to help pupils learn to cope successfully in a technological society (Cramer 1974, p. 401). Marland, then Commissioner of Education, used discretionary and other funds to launch state efforts and establish research and demonstration projects (Herr 1974, p. 53). The National Institute of Education (NIE) has recently taken over responsibility for the program, which the Office of Education originally outlined in order to stimulate grassroots definitions and state developments (Career Education 1971), while at the same time supporting large-scale research and development programs in major cities. In a later policy statement, the Office defined the concept and outlined goals, suggesting responsibilities for school, home, and community (Hoyt 1975a) and spelling out the key role of the counselor.

The school-based career-education model, involving the total individual and geared to stages in vocational development, has gained wide support among lay persons and educators, but has also met with some resistance. Many blacks and other miniority group members see it as a way to build a supply of cheap labor, and reduce upward mobility. Opposition has come also from labor unions and advocates of a broad liberal education. This model appears to offer school counselors a unique chance to expand their role (Cramer 1974, pp. 410–411; Hoyt 1974, pp. 523–524; Odell 1973, p. 155), but it remains to be seen whether counselors will participate effectively in this new educational approach.

Career education is only one sign of a growing interest in career planning and decision making. The multifaceted concept has three variations besides the school-based model already mentioned: the experience-based, home-based, and special-residential models (Herr 1974, pp. 48–53; see also Chapter 13 for more complete descriptions). CETA (Comprehensive Education and Training Act) emphasizes guidance, training, and job placement for those out of work. Moreover, the education amendments of 1976 (Alford 1977) promote guidance assistance and career education through educational guidance centers for adults and programs to help counselors and teachers learn about occupations.

The decade has also seen an increasing concern for the rights of individuals. The widely publicized Buckley Amendment (see Chapter 14) safeguards the confidentiality of records, and Title IX of the educational amendment of 1972 prohibits discrimination on the basis of sex. New programs to provide jobs for the unemployed, particularly the young, are in planning.

We have been experiencing a leveling off of job opportunities in many fields, including counseling. Birth statistics, which are the basis for projecting the size of schools, allow predictions about the numbers of counselors who under present ratios will be needed in the future. (Another question is whether more counselors will be employed to obtain more reasonable counselor-pupil ratios.) A major concern is the discrepancy between the number needed under present employment rates and the number currently being prepared.

Predictions vary. It has been estimated that 54,000 school counselors were employed in 1970–71, with over four fifths in secondary schools (Odell 1973, p. 154). One estimate for 1975 (made ten years before) projected a need for over 150,000 (Odell 1973, p. 154). Others from the same time went as high as 200,000. Odell (1973) predicts that a total of 60,000 counselors will be employed in United States schools by 1980. The latest report available for 1973–74 shows a total of 55,743, with 31,277 in secondary schools and 17,537 serving both the elementary and secondary levels (National Center for Educational Statistics, U.S. Department of Health, Education and Welfare). Jones' (1976) study of supply and demand forecasts only moderate growth in employment opportunities until the 80s, when an upswing is anticipated.

A survey of critical problems and issues of our time makes a realistic conclusion to this review of the history of secondary guidance. (Chapter 16 picks up from here and looks forward to how the future will resolve these issues.) Odell (1973, pp. 154–155) identifies the major concerns as help for special target groups such as women, dropouts, and inner-city and rural individuals; improved career guidance and career information systems; upgrading competencies of preservice and in-service counselors; more effective work with parents; expanding drug-abuse programs; preparation of paraprofessionals including peers; better public relations; educating school administrators to counselor's roles; expanding the use of psychological education; and redefining the counselor's role in response to changing conditions and expectations. Other authorities add biofeedback (Kater and Spires 1975), consulting (Stiller 1974), social issues (Carroll 1975 a_2 p. 309), use of records (Burcky and Childers 1976), and licensing (Cottingham 1975). All of these concerns, developments, and issues add to the complexity of the question—how should the role of the counselor be defined?

Serious questions about role are not new, but have now reached a new intensity. Counselors should use a reasonable, inquiring, and focused attitude to understand the future, rather than engage in aimless searching (Giddan and Price 1975). Conversations on questions like "Where do we go from here?" (Cantell, Aubrey, and Graff 1974) examine issues and look for guideposts to the future. The quest for meaning is reflected in the "Pioneers in Guidance" series in the *Personnel and Guidance Journal* (Ewing 1975; Conyne and Cochran 1976). Counselors are looking back almost wistfully to times when problems and values were simpler and more sharply defined. But for all the complexities and confusion, these are exciting times, and progress, which is inevitable, is bound to be substantial.

GUIDANCE IN THE ELEMENTARY SCHOOL

Guidance had a much later start in elementary schools than in secondary schools. William Burnham was the first to see guidance in the elementary school as more than remediation, testing, and diagnosis, and his book, *Great Teachers and Mental Health* (1926), established him as the precursor of elementary school counseling (Faust 1968, pp. 11–12).

Burnham translated his developmental concepts into practices emphasizing the affective and cognitive components of the teacher's work. The 1930 White House Conference, influenced by Burnham, used the term "mental hygiene," which has since been replaced by "developmental guidance." But elementary school guidance got nowhere in the 30s, partly because the depression turned attention to vocational assistance (Faust 1968, pp. 15; 17; 21).

The 60s saw significant new developments. As late as 1965 there were no accurate counts of counselors, but five years later their number was established as almost 8,000 (Dinkmeyer 1973a, p. 172). The new elemen-

tary school counselor emerged, now that the NDEA institutes could include elementary programs, and institute proposals reflected new concepts of elementary school work (Faust 1968, pp. 25–26; 61).

A variation of the elementary school counselor role, identified as "child
behavior consultant," was developed by IRCOPPS (International Research Commission on Pupil Personnel Services) (Seidman 1970). The
five-year program, starting in 1963, included representatives from thirteen professional groups and was influential in shaping the role of the
modern elementary school counselor.

The 70s has been a period of continuing progress. There is a widely
accepted model, a professional journal (*Elementary School Guidance and
Counseling*, founded in 1965), and a substantial group of practitioners. In
1973–74 there were 6,929 counselors in elementary schools, and 17,537
serving both the elementary and secondary levels (National Center for
Educational Statistics, U.S. Department of Health, Education and Welfare
1973–74). Current estimates of the number of elementary school counselors are in the neighborhood of 10,000 (Dinkmeyer 1973a, p. 172). With
goals and model questions settled at least for the time being, much of the
literature is devoted to techniques, procedures, needs of special groups,
rights of children (Rotter and Crunk 1975), career education (Leonard and
Splete 1975), and building support through public relations (Bluhm and
Anderson 1976).

THE DEVELOPMENT OF GUIDANCE
FOR MIDDLE/JUNIOR HIGH SCHOOLS

Accounts of the development of guidance in the public school do not
often give much space to the middle grades even though school reorgani-
zation was discussed extensively around the turn of the century and the
first junior high schools were established in the early 1900s. In the 20s,
the central role of guidance was an important feature of this new school
plan (Johnson, Busacker, and Bowman 1961, p. 3; 14–15). But guidance at
this level followed the high school model, using teacher-counselors,
teacher participation, and with counseling, group work, and testing the
major functions. More recently, as the middle school has emerged, guidance for this level has gained a more clear-cut identity; statements have
stressed its transitional and exploratory role. Strategies are similar to
those used at other levels, particularly the elementary school.

The junior high school came into existence to a large extent as a reaction against the 8:4 system (Barnes 1974, p. 150). The new concept
seemed to imply a strong guidance function. In fact, early origins can be
traced to the reform movements promoting social and economic effi-

ciency (Stephens 1974, p. 14). The first designated junior high school was Indianola Junior High School in Columbus, Ohio, opened in 1909 (Lounsbury 1974, p. 5), but by the 1930s the junior high school had become an accepted part of the American school system (Lounsbury 1974, p. 5).

In its early years the junior high school adopted guidance patterns from those developing in the high school, using class advisers and vocational counselors. Unfortunately, this system was more suitable for the secondary level, and did not meet the special needs of junior high pupils. Later, through the influence of psychologist G. Stanley Hall and the Cardinal Principles of Education, the narrow educational and vocational scope broadened to include the whole range of needs of the individual (Howard and Stoumbis 1970, pp. 57–58).

Growth in the number both of institutions and guidance services has been substantial. For example, over a ten-year period from the middle 50s to the middle 60s, the number of junior high schools more than doubled, and the percentage of those having an organized guidance program increased from 61 to 91 percent (Lounsbury and Douglass 1974, pp. 168; 176).

In some ways the growth of the middle school has been a response to a failure of the junior high school to carry out the guidance function. If the junior high school had continued to serve as a bridge between the self-contained classrooms of the elementary school and the subject-field organization of high school, provided exploratory experiences for high school planning, and offered comprehensive guidance, there would have been no need for a change to the middle school (Compton 1974, p. 198). While there are still a large number of junior high schools in operation today, the 60s could be called the decade of the middle school (Brough and Hamm 1974, p. 179).

Over the years guidance services have been regarded as essential parts of both middle and junior high school programs, and some authorities feel that some of the best guidance anywhere is to be found at this level (Barnes 1974, p. 154). But guidance will have to move out of the office and help teachers in the classroom; the program must be spread throughout the school, using consulting, teacher participation, training, and community outreach. The timely model proposed by Hansen and Hearn (1971, p. 305) illustrates current thinking. They set up four levels of guidance roles and responsibilities within the middle school. The first two, meeting immediate and long-range needs, are primarily the teacher's responsibility. Counselors share in helping with long-range needs and have major responsibility for the third, consulting with other staff members. The fourth level, long-term treatment, is the responsibility of the school psychologist. Major emphasis is on the counselor as a consultant, but there are other responsibilities, among them counseling with individuals and groups, coordinating activities like staff conferences, and providing in-service education for teachers.

GUIDANCE AT THE COLLEGE LEVEL

A brief review of the developments at the post-high-school level illustrates similarities and differences in public and higher education. While the settings are unlike in many ways, rather striking parallels are apparent in trends like the team approach, outreach, prevention, and training to enable others to carry out guidance functions.

In the early 1900s guidance at the college level was not affected by factors that stimulated developments in public secondary school. Only a few could attend college. The German influence contributed to a wide gap between students and faculty; adaptations of the English tutorial system placed the focus on academic development (Brewer 1942, p. 237). College personnel work (comparable to pupil personnel work in schools) originated with the work of deans of women. By 1910, they had a variety of helping responsibilities, including vocational counseling. Deans of men arrived on campus somewhat later, and served mainly as disciplinarians (Barry and Wolf 1957, pp. 19–20). Educational guidance at the University of Chicago in 1905 focused on students' personal qualities and the selection of programs (Brewer 1942, p. 237). A 1912 survey identified many examples of educational guidance, but there were also few programs of vocational guidance. Some colleges held vocational conferences once a year; women's colleges were more active in this service than men's (Brewer 1942, pp. 242–243, 245–246).

During the 1920s college personnel work was feeling the effects of studies and developments stimulated by World War I (Barry and Wolf 1957, p. 21; Williamson 1965, p. 100). New types of tests were made available for guidance, admission, and placement; more attention was focused on mental hygiene. Specialists began to develop, and by the 20s beginnings had been made in formulating purposes and specifying activities (Paterson 1937, p. 39; Barry and Wolf 1957, p. 22). In 1924 the National Association of Appointment Secretaries, later renamed American College Personnel Association, was organized (Borow 1964, p. 52). A few institutions offered occupations courses and vocational counseling; a greater number provided placement services (Brewer 1942, pp. 244–249). The college population was not heterogeneous as it is today; the proportion of 18- to 21-year-olds in college in 1900–1910 was approximately 5 percent; by 1924 it had climbed only to 10 percent (Ginzberg 1971, p. 27).

During the 30s guidance at the college level continued to expand and search for directions. During the depression, both its status and acceptance rose, partly because enrollments increased and student groups were becoming more heterogeneous (Barry and Wolf 1957, p. 23). By the end of the decade college enrollments reached about 16 percent of 18- to 21-year-olds (Ginzberg 1971, p. 27). Concern was growing about the nature and function of college personnel work. Debates resulted in the Clothier Report on principles and functions (1932) and the ACE publication, *Student Personnel Point of View*, which recommended an array of separate services for students (Barry and Wolf 1957, pp. 23–25). Both the American Council on Education and the American College Personnel Association were active in policy development (Borow 1964, p. 52).[1]

During the 40s, 50s, and early 60s, student personnel workers continued to study and evaluate the traditional services: counseling, collecting and providing information, and exploratory activities for students (Barry and Wolf 1957, p. 138). Williamson (1961, pp. 29–32), regarding student personnel work from this point of view, advanced the concept of personnel work as a way of individualizing education. Major doubts and conflicts about the purpose and value of the service did not arise until later.

The present modifications of college personnel work began in the late 60s. Critical voices were heard (Warnath 1973a, pp. 2–3). Personnel workers were caught up in campus demonstrations; wave after wave of new problems developed, many due to the Vietnam War (Kincaid and Kincaid 1971, pp. 727–735). But even with the greater needs of students, college personnel work was described as a collection of separate services, lacking in professional identity and consistent point of view (Penney 1969, p. 961). The rapid growth of community colleges was well underway, and the budget crunch that would soon confront all levels of education was just around the corner.

The pressures, conflicts, and economic problems of the 70s have affected all levels of counseling and guidance, but have had their greatest impact on services in higher education. Budgets for counseling and personnel services have been cut. Traditional counseling models have been sharply criticized (Warnath 1973a, pp. 18–20; Williamson and Biggs 1975, pp. 7–10). New approaches to student development are being tried out; collaborative work with students, peer counseling, and outreach are popular current strategies. But there is no evidence that these will gain the firm support that earlier programs once enjoyed. The anticipated decline in college enrollment may affect both programs and employment opportunities for counselors in training. New models for higher education, although still mostly small-scale, suggest alternative types of guidance and counseling services.

1 The latter organization emerged during the 30s from the National Association of Appointment Secretaries.

USING HISTORY TO LOOK
INTO THE FUTURE

It is difficult to show cause-effect relationships in the history of guidance, but by identifying related events one can understand the present and predict the future. The conditions that gave rise to Parsons' work are an example. Parsons was not alone in his recognition of problems and concern, but his experience and philosophy had prepared him for constructive action. The proposals he developed were designed to meet the needs he recognized. This pattern has been repeated over and over through the years as in the Depression, World War II, and after Sputnik. Regardless of names or labels, there will be a demand for services to help people make the most of their lives; demand will increase as human needs increase.

Those who conceptualize the future role of guidance should keep in close touch with opinions of many different factions. It is tempting to think that in the future counseling will take the ideal shape guidance workers would prefer, but predictions can be misleading. A few years ago predictions were made calling for a great increase in the number of counselors; relatively little attention was given to evaluation. At the time no one questioned effectiveness. Now the picture has changed; economic conditions have cut budgets. Questions about results, previously ignored, are being asked, but data for answering them are lacking. Accountability is not a new problem—Brewer raised it over three decades ago (1942, pp. 294–295)—but completely unexpected social and economic conditions have thrust it to the foreground.

History tells us that there is continuity in the development of guidance work, but that progress is not linear. Today some elements of the earliest models still remain or have been revived: people still need information about the environment; a concerned and interested listener still can help. With the present being so different from the past and the future sure to be more novel still, some may feel that the past is no guide. Guidance workers in any period may have felt this to be so, but history shows that there are periods of rapid advances, of stagnation, and of retrenchment. Smug satisfaction has given way to anxiety and bewilderment. History suggests that we shall see more of these conditions, but it gives some guidelines for coping with them.

EXPERIENCE

TRAVEL BACK THROUGH TIME

Imagine that you are a counselor in Parsons' Vocational Bureau. Go through the day. What sorts of people do you meet? What kinds of problems do they face? How do you feel about working with them?

Imagine that you and your fellow counselors are having a staff conference with Parsons at the end of a week's work. Present your feelings and ask questions about his approach, e.g., is it too limited? (Role play in small groups.) Have one member assume the role of Parsons and respond to comments.

EXPERIENCE

CONVERSATIONS WITH LEADERS

Assume the role of a counselor in one of the earlier periods covered in this chapter. Think about duties, responsibilities, types of counseling problems. What is the most striking experience you will report when you return to your own time? What sorts of colleagues and counselees have you encountered? What was a day like? (If groups are used, take turns reporting.)

EXPERIENCE

THE YEAR 2000

Imagine that you can move this class ahead to the year 2000. Spend a few moments imagining what the setting might be. What would be the major topic to take up today? How would the class be conducted? What type of work would you expect to do after completing your training?

EXPERIENCE

CHARADES

In small groups, select one of the periods in this chapter and discuss major features that would identify it. (Do not reveal your group's choice.) Then portray nonverbally its identifying features. See if other groups can guess the period you have chosen.

EXPERIENCE

THE MOTIVATIONS OF LEADERS

Try to put yourself in the place of one of the leaders of the guidance and counseling movement named in this chapter. Infer this person's attitudes, values, and goals. Express these to others in sentences beginning with "I am," or "I feel."

At the conclusion share feelings about the leaders you selected.

OBJECTIVES

1. To develop an interest in the history of guidance. Read at least two additional references on history.

Read any of the references in the annotated list at the end of the chapter or referred to in the text.

2. To be able to list a chronology of major persons and social, economic, and political events in the development of guidance. List the three most significant ones and explain why you selected them.

This objective is designed to emphasize that facts are needed for understanding and drawing conclusions. A listing would be too extensive to include here, since you are asked to consider the whole span of history. Note that effects of persons or events can cut across a whole period, as when, for example, international events resulted in Congress setting up the NDEA, thus in turn stimulating new preparation methods.

3. To be able to explain the impact of leaders in the field. Give brief statements of the impact of three leaders.

This objective goes beyond Objective 2 and asks you to assess the impact of leaders. The major point is to identify how a person's influence goes beyond the broad historical forces of a period.

4. To be aware of the value of historical knowledge to a professional guidance worker. Give three sentences designed to convince someone of the importance of history to the professional worker.

Sample topics are:

— Knowledge of heritage.
— Awareness of trends.
— Understanding roots of issues.
— Anticipating the future.

5. To understand the influence of other areas to the development of guidance and counseling. Name three aspects of guidance that represent contributions of other professions or disciplines.

Guidance draws on psychology, psychoanalysis, sociology, and economics, and on professions such as psychiatry and social work. Typical contributions are psychological tests, personality theory, and interview techniques.

6. To understand the positive and negative aspects of tradition on the adaptability of a profession. Identify the oldest and youngest levels of school guidance. Rate each on adaptability.

Secondary is the oldest and most difficult to modify. Elementary is the youngest and the most flexible.

7. To be able to judge the similarity between conditions that generated guidance services and conditions today. Identify three conditions or needs that give rise to guidance and state to what extent these conditions exist today.

Typical conditions discussed in the text:

— Slums and ghettoes.
— Low levels of work competencies.
— Special groups need help in catching up.

8. To be able to predict trends and directions of guidance. Give three statements indicating the major characteristics of guidance in the year 2000.

Only time will reveal if your predictions are accurate. Help for special groups, outreach, expanded use of paraprofessionals, and increased use of technology appear to be likely trends.

ADDITIONAL READINGS

Aubrey, Roger F. "Historical Development of Guidance and Counseling and Implications for the Future." *Personnel and Guidance Journal* 55, no. 6 (1977), pp. 288–295.

A well-organized and very readable account of the development of guidance and counseling providing insight into the status of the profession today and into directions it may take in the future.

Brewer, John M. *History of Vocational Guidance*. New York: Harper and Bros., 1942.

The standard reference on history up to 1942. Chapters 5 and 6 on Parsons and the reprint of his first and only report (Appendix, pp. 303–307) are recommended reading.

Kaplan, Bernard A. "Federal Legislation Influencing Guidance Programs." In *School Counseling*, edited by Alfred Stiller, pp. 55–70. Washington, D.C.: American School Counselor Association, 1967.

Covers federal aid during a significant period in the growth of school guidance and includes the historical background of funding.

Miller, Carroll H. *Foundations of Guidance*. **New York: Harper and Bros., 1961.**

This book, together with chapters in Borow's (ed.) *Man in a World at Work*, "Vocational Guidance in the Perspective of Cultural Change," pp. 3–23; and Borow's (ed.) *Career Guidance for a New Age*, "Historical and Recent Perspectives on Work and Vocational Guidance," pp. 3–40, establish Miller as the major historian on the guidance movement. The scope of his writing is broader than the term "vocational" implies.

Reed, Anna Y. *Guidance and Personnel Services in Education*. **Ithaca, New York: Cornell University Press, 1944.**

A comprehensive account of the development of guidance and student personnel work. Part I covers events up to 1916; "Retrospect" (pp. 457–472) gives an authoritative and concise review of the period up to and including World War II. The author's "Prospect" section makes interesting reading as the passage of time allows the reader to check the accuracy of predictions.

Stephens, W. Richard. *Special Social Reform and the Origins of Vocational Guidance*. **Washington, D.C.: National Vocational Guidance Association, 1970.**

While the title suggests a narrow focus, the book covers general school guidance. The thoughtful analysis of factors leading to the present school model shows how the past can illuminate the present.

Zytowski, Donald G. "Four Hundred Years Before Parsons." *Personnel and Guidance Journal* 50, no. 6 (1972), pp. 443–450.

An interesting account with illustrations of early guidance publications that provide a readable record of past efforts.

CHAPTER FIVE
BASIC VALUES

Guidance is built up on principles from philosophy and the social sciences, and also contains an element of art. A practitioner develops working methods that are personal and unique, but must have, in addition, a set of values that express underlying attitudes toward people and helping services and a command of theory and research into human behavior. Values answer the question <u>why?</u>; they justify, for example, achieving happiness through helping others. Theory tells how; it predicts, for instance, the procedure that will enable a person to relate to others more effectively.

Guidance also reflects the character of society as a whole. The political system, for example, determines the climate and limits on the life of the individual; the economic system affects opportunities and life-style.

This chapter raises a series of crucial questions for anyone considering a career in counseling and then reviews useful data from various disciplines provided to help answer them. Prior study is not a prerequisite; the bases upon which counseling and guidance rest are introduced here.

GOALS

1. To be aware and appreciate the importance of values in the helping profession.
2. To appreciate how theory and research support effective practice.
3. To examine your own values and ways of interacting with people as a first step toward a personal rationale for helping others.

VALUES UNDERLYING GUIDANCE WORK

Values are philosophical positions not directly testable by research. If, for example, you say: "I believe that persons are inherently good," you are stating a value. I may recount numerous incidents of harmful acts, and attempt to show you that you are wrong—and that persons are usually bad—but very likely you will not change your opinion. It is deep-seated, resistant to change, and very important to you, that is, if it is really a value rather than a superficially held opinion.

The subject of values has always been a deep concern of guidance workers, but attention has varied over the years. Beck's analysis (1963) is a landmark in the search for the philosophical position of guidance. Interest in the ethical standards of the profession is increasing (see Chapter 14). These standards, as Smith and Peterson (1977) point out, represent the underlying belief of members of the profession in the value and dignity of the individual.

Values today play an increasingly vital role; guidance workers are facing more pressing conflicts and ambiguities than ever before. Smith and Peterson (1977) provide an extremely helpful discussion of the levels of values in society and identify the kinds of conflicts the counselor must deal with. The most general level, the "universals," is made up of values of profound importance to all, for example, right and wrong. The next level consists of "specialties," which are relevant only to a part of society, for instance, the values of a social class or subcultural group. At the third level are "alternatives," variations from the usual societal modes requiring choices. This last category is usually where changes occur; if universals are subjected to controversy, society tends to lose cohesiveness and established patterns deteriorate.

Smith and Peterson go on to identify a number of areas of conflict that cut across all three levels. Prominent among these are: the place of the counselor's values in the helping relationship; regulation of practitioners; adequacy of preparation; changes in sexual mores and differing views of marriage; and the meaning and purpose of life. There are others but the point is clear from those given—conflicting trends reach to the most basic levels of our society's values.

The counselor must have a value base for dealing with issues and pressures and as a guide for the daily responsibilities of counseling and other guidance tasks. These are major points (see also Tolbert 1972, pp. 95–96):

— For a full understanding, the counselor must view the counselee as a total person.

— You can only know the counselee's personal world to the extent that the counselee is willing to share it.
— Each counselee is motivated by a positive growth force.
— To develop fully, everyone needs others and needs to feel needed.
— All people have the freedom to choose what they are and will be.
— To develop fully, each person must accept responsibility for his or her choices.

The counselor thus views each counselee as a unique, valued, and independent person. Beck's comprehensive statement (1963, pp. 145–147) emphasizes further the need to maintain and enhance the self, and the potential for positive development if barriers and limitations are removed. These statements give the counselor's work a comprehensive and profound philosophical foundation.

A more down-to-earth statement of values may be drawn from ethical codes. Smith and Peterson (1977) suggest the following central concepts:

— The counselor values the uniqueness, worth, dignity, and potential of each individual.
— The counselor respects the rights of the individual to make choices. (An exception would be choices that are potentially destructive to the counselee and others.)
— The counselor provides an effective service to society based upon the first two value statements.

The values supporting counseling and guidance appear to be clear-cut, reasonable, and appropriate. But actually dealing with individuals is another matter. Personal situations usually involve complexities that make a quick solution impossible; needs of the individual frequently are in conflict with those of others or of society, and judgment is difficult. A counselee who is using drugs, for example, may be anxious to kick the habit through counseling, but school regulations require that drug use be reported for disciplinary action. The counselor may feel that there is a good chance to help the counselee if parents, school administrators, and police can be kept out of the case for a short time. How do counselors reconcile respect for the individual with responsibility to society? If they appear to "protect" drug users, will others be encouraged to regard drug use as acceptable? Is the counselor who turns a pupil in neglecting responsibility to the individual?

The counselor must answer philosophical questions every day and make decisions about the most effective types of help. Suppose the counselor is faced with Mark, a resistant pupil who is performing below expectations, is in a very difficult home situation, and is suspected of bringing drugs to school. What philosophical questions need to be answered? How do answers determine the methods of intervention? Here are some examples:

— Should Mark's behavior be changed? Do you have some standard of "good" and "bad," and if so, on what is it based? If you decide that behavior should be altered, will you use a process that, for example, permits him to decide what he wants to do or one that more or less dictates what the changes will be?
— Should he be required to participate in counseling? Suppose he did not want your help? Will you leave participation up to him? What if the school administration requires him to enter counseling even though he doesn't want to? Would you work with him?
— What is the source of his needs? Can you decide what is best for him? Are there "absolutes" good for all? If so, where do they come from?
— What is the place of school and community standards in working with the pupil? Should he be required to live by them? Does he, for example, *have* to get better marks? Which is more important, the individual or the organization?
— Suppose he does participate in counseling, how will you select an approach? Each personality theory and counseling approach (discussed in Chapter 7) makes certain assumptions about human nature. Some give weight to a positive growth force in the individual; others attribute much individual behavior to the effects of society.
— Who is responsible for his behavior? The family? The community? The pupil himself? Is he able to make decisions and change, or is his behavior determined?

When the philosophical questions are answered, the counselor looks to theory— psychological, sociological — to answer questions *how?* Theories discussed later in this chapter deal with how individuals learn, develop, and find rewarding life-styles. Chapter 7 identifies methods of counseling, which are largely based on these theoretical positions. Counseling techniques, also discussed in Chapter 7, enable the counselor to put the theory of helping into practice.

EXPERIENCE

MAKING VALUE DECISIONS

A capable pupil, Mary, has been skipping afternoon classes and is threatened with suspension. You have talked with her and found her truancy allows her to work part-time in a lunchroom. She has lied about her age to get the job. She says that she is helping out at home; her father is unemployed, her mother needs medical care, and unemployment payments have run out. If her parents know that she is working, they will force her to stop. In that case, she says she will drop out of school and work full-time, even though her ambition is to continue at least through two years of community college. (Cooperative education is not a possibility.) She has given you this information with the assurance that you will keep it confidential.

What would you do?

What values underlie your decision?

What is the basis for your decision? Check the following list of moral criteria (based on Kohlberg in Geiwitz 1976, pp. 320–324). Note that the list does not refer to the decision itself, but your reasons for it.

— What you consider to be right or wrong particularly to avoid difficulty or punishment.

— How much it suits you, i.e., fits in with your personal desires.

— What you think a "good" person should do according to school policy.

— Your recognition that there need to be rules and regulations.

— Your belief that rules and laws represent the consensus of the majority while recognizing that laws can be changed.

— Your belief about a higher principle of what is ethically correct.

PERSONALITY DEVELOPMENT

One of the most useful foundations of guidance and counseling derives from theory and research on personality. The interplay of physiological, psychological, and environmental factors leads to the development of unique individuals. The guidance worker who understands these factors and their probable effects has a firm basis for understanding pupils and planning strategies for change.

Physiological factors play an important role, but do not exert the strongest influence. Physical size, build, and other such characteristics have some slight relationship to personality, and can produce major patterns in interaction with other conditions. The obese boy may avoid sports, where he is always outclassed, and turn to less physically demanding social activities or hobbies. But he could also choose to continue in sports. The way the person views the characteristic makes the major difference. In the school years, size, appearance, and physical ability are extremely important and exert a great influence on a person's self-concept.

Individual differences in abilities and temperament also play an important role in personality development. Learning ability, commonly referred to as intelligence, is the most significant. There are no clear-cut data that convincingly demonstrate how much intelligence is genetically determined and how much it is modified by the environment, but limits do seem to be broad; the home, family, and community are all major factors. Mechanical, artistic, or musical ability appears to be largely determined by personal experiences, interests, and the level of general ability. Special abilities play a significant part in personality development; for example, a boy with some talent in science may see himself as a great scientist.

Intellectual ability develops by stages, which is very significant for personality formation. At age six or seven, the child can think about things in logical or organized ways and classify objects; the ability to classify increases gradually in the later teens. Around 11 or 12, adult-type thought processes begin to develop; new abstract abilities are used extensively in arguing, debating, and discussing complex subjects. Children begin to develop personal theories of how their actions affect others and what will happen as a consequence of their behavior (Geiwitz 1976, pp. 296–299). Differing intellectual capacities determine how people deal with everyday problems and issues, and a young child does not have the same thought processes as an older one.

Social life also develops through identifiable stages. One way to look at social maturity is in terms of psychological crises as formulated by Erik Erikson.

Age	Psychological Crisis	Virtue
1	Trust v. mistrust	Hope
2	Autonomy v. shame, doubt	Willpower
3 to 5	Initiative v. guilt	Purpose
6 to onset of puberty	Industry v. inferiority	Competence
Adolescence	Identity v. role confusion	Fidelity
Early adulthood	Generativity v. stagnation	Care
Old age	Integration v. despair	Wisdom

Each of these crises must be brought to a positive solution in order to attain the corresponding virtue. From this point of view, identity formation in adolescence is essential to personality development, yet many social factors tend to interfere (Goethals and Klos 1976, pp. 12–13). It is also apparent that interpersonal relations are critical factors in the resolution of the psychological crises.

Personality development may also be viewed according to Freudian theory as a series of stages through which the individual passes in biological maturation. In the first, the oral stage, focus is on oral satisfaction. The ease with which the child gets what he or she wants is important in later personality. In the second and third years, called the anal stage, toilet training is the major task to be mastered; it is the first major source of conflict with parents, and the solution affects the development of autonomy, independence, and tendencies to control others. Still later there is the phallic stage, which is the early beginnings of normal sexual development. At this stage, the child experiences erotic and possessive feelings toward the parent of the opposite sex. The solution of this triangle has a lasting effect on personality and later interpersonal relations. If, for example, the father is extremely threatening and the mother very loving, the child may not be able to form normal social and marital relations later (Geiwitz 1976, pp. 304–313). Rivalry between children is based on the same dynamics; the child is jealous of the affection shown for his or her siblings by the parent of the opposite sex (Brown and Herrnstein 1975, p. 548). The Freudian approach puts particularly strong emphasis on the early years for the formation of adolescent and adult personality. The young person of high school age needs to reject a former dependent role and turn toward peers of the opposite sex, a process that can be helped or hindered by early parental attitudes.

Following along the same Freudian psychoanalytic approach, the structure of personality is composed of a source of energy, basically sexual and aggressive *(id)*, an aspect that deals with the real world *(ego)*, and the conscience *(superego)*. Primitive basic drives are converted to socially acceptable behavior by the ego, while the superego judges whether the actions are good or bad. The individual who has a need to dominate others may work hard to make the best marks on a test, and thus meet the need in a socially acceptable way.

Personality may also be viewed as the result of social learning, according to Bandura, Walters, and others (Ringness 1975, pp. 80–90). In interactions, first with parents and then in a wider circle, the individual builds a pattern of responses to obtain rewards like affection, acceptance, material goods, and learns to provide self-rewards in the absence of others, thus giving behavior a continuity. This view of personality also stresses the importance of models to identify with and copy. The environment is crucial as the source of rewards, behavior patterns, and models. Through behavior the individual builds up expectations; unanticipated results are likely to cause difficulty unless new or productive responses are found. For example, the child previously rewarded for an open, friendly manner may be baffled by suspicious and hostile classmates in a new school.

Another view of personality development focuses on the striving towards growth and self-actualization, towards becoming the best person one can. Key concepts are the basic drives and goals that account for behavior. In Maslow's version of this theory there is a hierarchy of needs. At the lower levels are those that must be met for survival, such as food and shelter. Next are safety and security, followed by love, affection, and the sense of belonging. Higher yet on the hierarchy are the needs involving self-esteem: respect for self and pride in accomplishments. Finally, there is the stage of self-actualization, which consists of being the best one can be and promoting the best for the society. Lower order needs must be met before moving to higher levels and the individual may regress to lower levels from time to time. Protection and enhancement of the *self* (self-identity, self-image) is central to this concept of personality. Conflicts can arise between what one wishes to do to make the most of potential (to become self-actualized) and the need to enhance the self through positive reactions from others. One may feel pressured into a role incongruent with the self with a resulting gap between what one would like to be and what one is.

The main purpose of this review of theories of personality development is not intended as a complete summary or detailed description of how each position relates to guidance, but aims rather to show that personality theory provides one of the essential bases of counseling. From the brief discussions, you can extract useful concepts for understanding and facilitating the growth of counselees and structuring guidance services. An example of this usage is given in the following case study.

EXPERIENCE

UNDERSTANDING PERSONALITY

Joe is a high school student who seems to have no goals or interests. When you talk to him he seems fairly alert and responsive, but when it comes to what he wants to do, how he sees himself, and how he thinks others view him, he shrugs his shoulders and says: "I don't know." His grades are low; he has few activities and friends.

Joe has two brothers who did not finish school. One is unemployed and living at home, and the other left home without saying where he was going. It is reported that he lives with a drug-using group some distance away. Joe has always been his mother's favorite. She has taken up for him, tried to protect him from responsibility for his actions, and made his decisions for him. His father is harsh and demanding, and expresses disgust that none of the boys is "worth a darn." He has never shown any affection for them. He gives Joe no money, saying this will make a man of him. The boy has no spending money for school activities. His father frequently threatens him with physical abuse. Joe's mother's efforts to protect him result in bitter arguments with his father that can be heard around the neighborhood.

Do any of the brief outlines of theory give any clues to bases for Joe's personality?

What is he gaining by his present behavior?

If you could change only one condition that he faces, which one would you choose? Why?

EXPERIENCE

THE LEADER

Bill is a fourth grader who seems to have considerable influence on other pupils. When he wants to, he can cause turmoil or hilarity in the classroom. But other times he helps organize activities, quiets troublemakers, and serves as an efficient helper for the teacher.

The first thing you notice about Bill is that he is open and friendly and evokes the same qualities in others. He appears to be quite secure in believing that he is important, likable, and capable. His grades are above average and measured ability is high. He is active in sports but not a star. In fact, he seems to have no spectacular accomplishments that would make him a hero in the eyes of classmates. Even so, he is the one who ranks highest on sociometric tests, he can build support for an activity or insure its rejection, and he knows just how far he can push the teacher.

What would you say about conditions that have contributed to the development of Bill's personality?

How would you suggest that the teacher deal with bill to evoke positive, productive reactions?

HELPING A PUPIL CHANGE

The central task of the counselor is to provide conditions—individual, group, or school-wide—that allow others to develop, grow, and be more effective persons. Personality theory gives some indications of tasks that should be accomplished at specific ages, but hint only indirectly at strategies to promote development.

Assuming behaviors, attitudes, values to be learned, it is important to consider how learning takes place. How, for example, does one person learn to expect that others are friendly and supportive? Why does another view others as threatening, unresponsive, and cold? Why does a pupil work for hours at shooting goals on the basketball court or in football practice? How did the sport become so much more important than school subjects? Why does one person dread mathematics while another who is no more intelligent learn it with ease? Why does one child seem to be ready for the next steps in school, work, or social life while another is unprepared? How does a person learn to get in touch with feelings after years of denying their existence?

There is no one answer to any of these questions. Learning new behaviors and attitudes, developing new styles of living, and formulating new goals takes place in numerous ways. Counseling and guidance, therefore, have a wide range of strategies for helping people to grow and develop. The counselor may look to the following explanations to understand how a counselee has learned in the past.

Critical to any learning is the developmental stage of the individual or group. Stages in cognitive development indicate what type of thinking may be expected at certain ages, and which tasks need to be accomplished at special periods. Physical development tends to follow general age-based patterns, and there is evidence that moral development too is related to age. Career development involves a series of tasks to be mastered at specific periods in the individual's life. Developmental phases imply developmental tasks and constitute general stages for learning.

The stages of moral development were implied in the exercise on values adapted from the studies of Kohlberg (page 85). The theory includes three levels of two stages each. In level 1, the *preconventional* level, the individual forms a judgment of what is right or wrong without any basic reason for the choice. The first stage in this level involves obedience and the avoidance of punishment. The second, more advanced stage involves satisfaction of one's own desire or action expected to elicit reward from others. Seven-year-olds tend to respond at this level, and particularly at its second stage.

Level 2 is identified as *conventional*. In stage 3, the first stage of level 2, the urge is to portray oneself as good or pleasing to others. In stage 4, which is characterized by an orientation towards law-and-order, the individual supports the established way of doing things. Sixteen-year-olds in the research typically respond at this level, and particularly at stage 4, which is the most typical developmental stage of all persons studied.

Level 3, the highest level, is called the *postconventional*. It involves judgments that imply autonomy and principle. Stage 5, the first stage on this level, involves awareness of the need of society for order and regulation—these are essential. But there is an awareness too that rules may be changed by an orderly process. Research shows that individuals at stage 4 in high school tend to move up to the next stage if they did not go to college, while college entrants regress to stage 2. The challenges of the academic setting seem to overwhelm stage-4 judgments, but students are often not yet ready for the next higher level. Such regression is temporary.

Only a few individuals in the research reached stage 6, and it is assumed to be rare in the general population. It involves the application of self-chosen universal ethical principles that promote the greatest good for the greatest number.

Stages represent a step-by-step progression, with regression only as mentioned earlier. They correspond roughly to ages, but the relationship varies with groups and cultures (Brown and Herrnstein 1975, pp. 310–324; Geiwitz 1976, pp. 320–329).

Another view of moral development uses only two stages: *heteronomous*, based primarily on authority, and *autonomous*, based on one's own capacity to judge according to one's level of cognitive development. Autonomous moral judgments are possible by about age 12 or 13 (Brown and Herrnstein 1975, p. 309).

Career development is another facet of the developmental process having a bearing on the problems that need to be resolved. One well-known concept of the process proposes five stages covering the entire life span (Super and Bohn 1970, pp. 136–137). From birth to about age 14, the child goes through the *growth stage*, which includes successive substages dominated by fantasy choices, next by interests, and a final one where abilities are the major focus. Next comes the *exploration stage*, covering the decade of life from middle teens to about the middle twenties, and involving first tentative choices, then efforts to move into desired work, and finally by a tryout of the chosen occupation.

Following the entry into what appears to be a suitable type of work, the phase of *establishment* continues for the next 20 or 30 years, until about the middle forties. The early part of this stage is usually devoted to verifying the suitability of the choice and making any needed changes. Following a generally satisfying placement, efforts are devoted to becoming established in the occupation.

Developmental tasks for the exploratory and establishment phases are (Super 1969, p. 4):

— Settling on an occupation as desirable and appropriate.
— Formulating a clear idea of what the occupation involves and how it meets one's needs.
— Putting plans into effect (getting the job).
— Becoming settled in the work.
— Achieving status and security.
— Moving ahead in the occupation.

Phases in both career development and developmental tasks show that certain decisions, plans, and new learning are related to life stages. For example, a pupil who should be exploring possible occupations would not profit from assistance in narrowing preferences with the purpose of making a specific choice.

Looking at general development, a well-known framework (Havighurst 1972, pp. 1–98) identifies tasks at a series of age levels, and involving physical, psychological, and cultural factors. The six stages are: infancy and early childhood, middle childhood from about 6 to 12, adolescence from around 12 to 18 years, early adulthood, middle age, and later maturity. At each stage tasks must be mastered in order to move to the next stage. The six to ten tasks at each stage cannot be summarized here, but a brief description of each period illustrates the significance of the concept for guidance and counseling strategies.

The emphasis of the period of *infancy* and *early childhood* is upon instrumental behavior—learning to walk, talk, and relate to parents; there is also an incipient ability to judge right and wrong. *Middle childhood* is characterized by moving out from home-centered life to peer-group activities, increasing ability to communicate, awareness of role, and development of values. The *adolescent period* is marked by getting ready for adulthood, developing sex roles, building relationships with peers of both sexes, gaining emotional independence from parents, and increasing readiness for occupational selection and preparation. The period of *early adulthood* usually involves major events—marriage, starting a family, choosing an occupation. It is a unique period in that the individual moves from a relatively structured life to one that is often ambiguous and confusing. There are variations in tasks at different socioeconomic levels.

This review illustrates how guidance and counseling strategies based on individual developmental stages suggest what should have been accomplished previously, what is currently important, and what lies in the immediate future. The developmental stage must be taken into account to determine the appropriate content and process for learning and problem solving. Adolescents should learn how to identify who they are, for example, but their developmental stage also implies that their learning can be facilitated by activities involving verbal interaction between both sexes.

Actual learning takes place by a number of processes that can be set up in guidance and counseling situations. One of the best known is pairing of stimuli to give previously unrewarded behavior motivational value. Behavior is built in this way every day. Suppose, for example, that an elementary pupil who is frightened by hostile, loud, threatening persons has a teacher who is loud and abrasive, and rules the class by sheer voice power. After a few days, the pupil begins to be afraid of previously non-threatening persons, objects, and events—teachers in general, schoolwork, going to school—having established an association between them and the feared person.

The same child may demonstrate another type of learning. Suppose, for example, that in trying various types of coping responses, the child gets up and walks around the room and discovers that the teacher becomes baffled and changes her style of discipline. A type of rewarded behavior has emerged, more or less by chance, and gains strength.

Another process of learning involves insight, a more or less sudden understanding of the solution to a problem, a new way of behaving, or comprehension of a situation. This type of learning is based on previous experiences, such as previous discussions of a subject (Geiwitz 1976, p. 149).

Social learning makes use of these types and also involves thinking processes for selecting a stimulus and a response to it. The environment has a pronounced effect, but people can reinforce their own behavior individually. A person can choose a model and maintain a consistent behavior of thinking, "I am acting the same as the person I admire." Guidance programs have used this process to promote new behaviors like openness in group discussions or searching for occupational information. The powerful effect of modeling can be seen every day in schools. It is one cause of concern about phenomena like TV violence.

Another useful explanation of learning focuses on cognitive restructuring (Ringness 1975, pp. 96–97). It involves thinking and individual processing of information, which the learner accepts, rejects, or modifies. The process and its results rely on previous cognitive and affective learning. For example, you may see a TV commercial that tells you a certain type of car will make you more attractive to the opposite sex. The terms and concepts have a powerful affective impact from previous learning. You process the persuasive message and are convinced that this is the car for you even though you had planned to keep your old one for another year. You have carried out the process of cognitive restructuring. Obviously guidance processes that involve cognitive restructuring can be useful in dealing with attitudes and prejudices.

A quite different approach to learning and change assumes a person's major concern is with maintaining and enhancing the self, and the most significant aspect of individuals' worlds is how they perceive them. Each person has a drive for positive development as described in the hierarchy of needs given on page 89. Change is possible when individuals feel safe enough to share their world with someone else and feel that threat to the self is low enough actually to consider alternative attitudes or behaviors and to face the feelings of adequacy or inadequacy that may arise. A person may be representing a personable, competent, successful ideal, while the real self is weak, irritable, narrow, anxious. The undesirable characteristics may be so threatening that the person cannot admit they exist. Change can take place when people face the way they really are, compare what is and what is desired, and bring the two closer together.

The young are quick to imitate their chosen heroes. Counselors should realize that they, too, may be behavior models.

The process helps the individual be more natural, spontaneous, and effective in all aspects of life. Situations in which the person can learn more about reactions of others, bring out feelings, and gain more realistic self-perception can facilitate the development of new and productive ways of dealing with oneself and the world. Many types of counseling and guidance activities, including growth groups and human potential programs, use this general approach to help people become happier, more productive, and more responsive to their own needs.

Counseling and guidance approaches, as shown in Chapter 7, make use of these types of learning singly or in combination; technique and the content are related to the developmental level of the individual being counseled. The exercise that follows illustrates some applications.

EXPERIENCE

WHAT CAUSED THE CHANGE

You are starting to work with a group of six middle school pupils who have said they want to learn to improve communication with others and get along better with peers. They are not disciplinary "problems," but teachers feel they could profit from some help of this type.

At the first meeting you ask members to talk to each other in groups of two for a few minutes and then to introduce each other, pointing out some interesting features. The activity goes well until one boy makes fun of another and talks much longer than his turn. As the meeting proceeds, he interrupts others, falls backwards in his chair, and does other things that distract the group's attention.

Finally, about when you conclude that the group will not be able to accomplish anything as long as the troublemaker is present, two influential members say they think he should be sent back to the classroom. Other members quickly agree. You have said that decisions about the group will be made democratically, and realize that you should act upon this judgment. In order to help the boy, however, you suggest that first he be excluded from the group five minutes and then be allowed to return. Your suggestion is accepted, and you talk to him briefly alone, assuring him that you want him to participate and that you feel sure he has much to contribute, but think he is not being fair with the other members. You add that he will not be able to stay in the group unless he respects and helps others.

After five minutes are up, the boy is invited back. For the rest of the meeting he takes part more constructively, interrupting only occasionally and displaying only a few mildly distracting behaviors.

You wonder if the change is transitory and expect problems to arise in the future. Even so, you feel progress has been made.

Is there anything about the typical levels of development of middle school to help explain the boy's behavior?

On the basis of what you know about the situation, what factors do you think have contributed to the change in his actions?

What more would you like to know about him if you were responsible for the group?

What philosophical assumptions underlie your answers?

EFFECTS OF CULTURE
ON GUIDANCE AND COUNSELING

The larger setting of guidance determines its philosophy, the nature of its services, and the objectives it establishes, and the democratic principles underlying our form of government determine the nature of guidance in our country. The Declaration of Independence supports values of life, liberty, and the pursuit of happiness. The Constitution, too, emphasizes the importance of the individual, particularly through the Bill of Rights. The philosophical position set forth in these documents demands a service devoted to the full development of the individual. All command their own destiny. Rights imply obligations; people must be able to act constructively. Freedom of choice involves an awareness of options.

In practice there have been shortcomings in ensuring all the opportunities to choose, develop, and grow; deficiencies were discussed in Chapters 1 and 4. But history reveals a continuing effort by government through legislative, judicial, and executive action to implement democratic principles. Concerned groups and political leaders have brought public pressure to bear on deviations from democratic principles; voters have typically responded to improve conditions.

Governmental economic policy has a profound effect on freedom and choice. Regulations directed at business and industry, labor legislation, monetary policy are examples. Positive actions like unemployment insurance, employment services, aid to the handicapped, and special training and work programs for minorities illustrate social concern.

Direct support to educational and guidance programs is another sign of underlying values. Program support usually arises in response to national emergencies or problems such as discrimination, need for scientific talent, education of veterans, or work for the unemployed. Direct legal action has been used to expand opportunities, for example through desegregation.

Balancing the individual's rights with the requirements of the society poses difficulties for any democracy. Society is not static; needs change. What is necessary for the survival of the nation may not, at the moment, be in the best interests of the individual. This dilemma comes up again and again; solutions often generate hostility or resistance. There are no simple, quick solutions. Guidance workers must go back to the values discussed at the beginning of this chapter to get their bearings and formulate a personal rationale for their activity.

The study of the family, the community, institutions, and other facets of group life provide bases for working with pupils and parents, providing outreach services, and making changes in the school and community environment. The family is a major concern of guidance workers. Counselors need to be aware of its changing role to understand young people, work with parents, and plan parent-oriented guidance activities. The middle-class espouses, among other things, education, delay of rewards, and a small number of children; but values differ for families in other subcultures. The trend toward a nuclear family under one roof and away from an extended family has profound implications for guidance. As more wives have taken work outside the home, the family situation has changed; day-care centers are often used for child care. Mobility of families, the increase of commercial entertainment (TV, record players), and the automobile have reduced the importance of the home as the family's social and recreational center. Many responsibilities formerly taken care of by the home have shifted to the school. The predicted energy shortages are certain to reverse or alter some trends in family life. What will happen, for example, when it is no longer practical to drive to school or to have two or three cars in a family?

Community life has direct implications for guidance. The traditional community has declined as society has become urbanized (McKee 1969, p. 201). The movement of families to the suburbs has speeded the deterioration of the inner city. The difficulties faced by those who remain there—crime, drugs, unemployment—pose formidable challenges for guidance workers. Obviously one task will be to build closer relations with community life and to adopt strategies that involve outreach, paraprofessionals, and expanded use of school resources and facilities.

Much of the school guidance program involves groups—small counseling groups, large guidance groups, training activities with classroom sized groups. Principles of group behavior are important bases for guidance. Age plays a part in group participation; six-year-olds, for example, can do very little cooperative work in groups, but older children can go by regulations and interact as teams (Jersild, Telford, and Sawrey 1975, p. 267). Groups based on social stratification establish life-styles and attitudes (McKee 1969, p. 248), but not all group members are the same nor do they fit a stereotype. Principles of group behavior are essential as background knowledge for the counselor or guidance worker, particularly when dealing with prejudice and discrimination.

Social organizations, religious, fraternal, educational and political institutions, the family, and the community all exert powerful influences on members' attitudes, opportunities, and life-styles. (The attitudes of teachers, for example, tend to differ from those of semiskilled plant operators.) A single individual may be a member of a number of groups through work, recreation, social, religious, and labor organizations, and political party. Each calls for a different role. But institutions can be changed. The campus unrest during the 60s is an example of collective action to alter an institution. One outcome for educators, particularly those in student personnel work, was a recognition of the critical role rumors play in touching off disorder, and the need for a rumor control center.

The cultural context of guidance affects all aspects of the work of the counselor—goals, processes, rationale, target groups. In an environment that is rigid, authoritarian, and hostile to individual development and freedom, there would be no need or place for guidance as we know it.

The following exercise illustrates cultural effects.

EXPERIENCE

WHY DO THEY ACT THAT WAY?

Your conservative school has been experiencing abrupt changes recently, and the principal and teachers are becoming confused and frustrated. The chief difficulty stems from an influx of new families from a different part of the country attracted by several new industrial developments. Until recently, most of the pupils were from middle-class families that had lived in the community for several generations. Teachers are mostly from the same group, have the same traditional values, and know the families of pupils. Most of the pupils planned to attend college, and those who did not either dropped out, or took one of the vocational education programs.

The new pupils are different. The first thing teachers noticed was the way most of them dressed. They spent more money on clothes and bought all the latest styles. The envy of locals is obvious, but they are less affluent and follow a rather conservative trend required by parents. But the most disturbing features are the language, attitudes toward drug use, and lack of interest in schoolwork. Conversation in the halls and cafeteria is in an almost unintelligible slang, sometimes punctuated by four-letter words. Even in class, the new pupils are disrespectful and offensive. Some of the newcomers admit they have used drugs. They scoff at local pupils' interest in school activities, and express little concern about schoolwork. To the dismay of teachers, parents of some of the new pupils seem uninterested in discussing their sons and daughters; they are totally involved in a continuous round of parties, golf, and travel and often turn their houses over to young people for their own parties.

At first teachers tried to pressure the newcomers to fit the pattern of the local school, but this aroused strong resistance. Typical pupil reactions are: "There's nothing wrong with what we do. You are living in the past, and don't know what the world is like." "Who says you have to respect teachers and parents. You do your thing and I'll do mine."

From what you know of the homes, there is a great deal of permissiveness, no regulations about study, and no set time to be in in the evening. The parent-child relationships generally seem to be casual and marked by a lack of concern. Some families expect to be transferred again and show no interest in participating in community affairs.

As counselor in the school, teachers have asked you to help them understand the new pupils. They ask: "Why do they act the way they do?" "Why do they reject everything about the school?" "Why do they laugh at our life here?"

As one senior teacher put it, "If we could understand them a little better, maybe we could meet them half way. As it is, these newcomers are influencing the others so much that the approaches we have been using don't seem to work anymore."

What would you say to the teachers?

USE OF THEORY
TO IMPROVE PRACTICE

Guidelines for selecting practices to implement values are found in the social sciences. The major reason for examining the theoretical bases is to provide a foundation for an effective guidance program. How it is done depends upon the individual guidance worker. One strategy is first to identify your philosophical beliefs and then draw on the social sciences to establish what to do and what to expect to achieve.

A helpful way to look at the process is described by Strickland (1969). He uses the term *philosophy* to denote the counselor's values and attitudes (What is important? What is desirable? What is the nature and purpose of a human being?). *Theory* refers to the general plan for helping ("If I do this, the counselee will do that"). Theory emerges from and is consistent with philosophy. If I believe that the individual is by nature seeking self-enhancement, then I will use a relationship that helps free positive forces for effective use. *Practice,* in turn, is derived from theory and consists of the techniques used to implement it; the helping relationship to free positive forces may be, for example, implemented by demonstrating interest, concern, and understanding.

The starting place is to formulate your own values, attitudes, and beliefs. What do you believe about yourself? About others? What are they like? What do they want to do? What is the good life? The answers do not have to reflect one particular philosophical orientation (Tolbert 1972, p. 95), but they should be consistent. It would not make sense, for example, to say that individuals are of equal importance and operate on the assumption that some deserve more help than others.

The next step is to draw theoretical elements from the social sciences discussed earlier—psychology, sociology, and economics. These major sources of theory are used in subsequent chapters on counseling, group work, assessment, and other services. Research and theory do not prove unequivocally that any one method is better than others—no science provides final, fixed laws. Research and theory make a better base than intuition or trial and error; still, it is true that the counselor builds a store of experience that can often serve as a useful guide. Sue (1975b) clarifies the issue by pointing out the essential nature of a research base for the profession while acknowledging the value of experience and intuition. Research is not the complete answer, but it is one essential element.

Returning to the problem of improving practice, suppose you want to improve the general climate in your school. Through interviews, surveys, and personal observation you have verified the existence of tension, hostility, and a lack of communication in the school. The obvious signs are absenteeism, vandalism, disciplinary problems, and low achievement. Drawing on psychology and sociology, you set up a plan, try it out, and evaluate results. The plan is itself a tentative theory. You have used theory to improve practice in two ways. First, you have used material from the social services for guidelines and second, you have organized your own plan into a theory-practice model.

ADDITIONAL READINGS

Broom, Leonard, and Selznick, Philip. *Sociology*. 4th ed. New York: Harper and Row, 1968.

An excellent source of theory and research illustrating psychological stratification is particularly helpful.

Brown, Roger, and Herrnstein, Richard J. *Psychology*. Boston: Little, Brown, 1975.

An excellent source of theory and research illustrating psychological bases of guidance. Chapter 11 on personality is especially recommended.

Goethals, George W., and Klos, Dennis S. *Experiencing Youth*. 2d ed. Boston: Little, Brown, 1976.

Twenty-seven vivid first person accounts of the lives of college students, analyzed from various theoretical approaches, e.g., those of Freud and Erikson. While the subjects are beyond high school, the accounts cover the developmental process during childhood and early adolescence.

Lloyd-Jones, Esther M., and Rosenau, Norah eds. *Social and Cultural Foundations of Guidance*. New York: Holt, Rinehart and Winston, 1968.

An outstanding reference relating foundations to programs and practices. Any section will be valuable reading.

McKee, James B. *Introduction to Sociology*. New York: Holt, Rinehart and Winston, 1969.

A lucid and interesting survey that shows sociology's contributions to guidance.

Miller, Carroll H. *Foundations of Guidance*. New York: Harper and Bros., 1961.

The classic on foundations of guidance, covering major cultural, economic and psychological factors. The author surveys and synthesizes research in psychology, sociology, and other areas. Any chapter will add depth to the reader's understanding of guidance.

Ratigan, William. "School Counseling: Relation of Theory to Practice." In *School Counseling 1967* edited by Alfred Stiller, pp. 93–130. Washington, D.C.: American School Counselor Association, 1967.

The author describes the difficulties school counselors face in utilizing theory and gives some practical guidelines for day-to-day work. Although the article was written some years ago, it is still fresh and to the point.

Ringness, Thomas A. *The Affective Domain in Education*. Boston: Little, Brown, 1975.

A clear exposition of how theories may be translated into day-to-day practices. The applications of classical and operant conditioning are examples of treatment that covers the whole range of learning.

Smith, Darrell, and Peterson, James A. "Counseling for Values in a Time Perspective." *Personnel and Guidance Journal* 55, no. 6 (1977), pp. 309–318.

A vivid presentation of the value issues the counselor must deal with. The article is particularly helpful for readers beginning to identify where they stand on counseling values.

Soule, George. *The New Science of Economics*. New York: Viking, 1964.

An understandable introduction to economics, particularly for the beginner. The first chapter provides a useful orientation.

Tolbert, E. L. *Introduction to Counseling*. 2d ed. New York: McGraw-Hill, 1972.

The author's own point of view of the philosophy, theory, and practice of counseling (pp. 95–107). Not the total guidance program is covered directly, but the discussion illustrates how the three aspects may be related.

Tyler, Leona E. "Theoretical Principles Underlying the Counseling Process." *Journal of Counseling Psychology* 5, no. 1 (1958), pp. 3–8.

The author describes how she collects techniques, principles, and values from a variety of fields and uses them to build an approach to counseling. An excellent illustration of the point of view of this chapter. Pepinsky's comment (pp. 8–10) underlines the difficulties of building a rigorous theory as opposed to a general rationale.

Wrenn, C. Gilbert. *The World of the Contemporary Counselor*. Boston: Houghton Mifflin, 1973.

A perspective on bases from the standpoint of changes, conflicts, and needs in society. Chapter 2 on changing values, and Chapter 7 on attitudes of youth about work are particularly useful.

CHAPTER SIX
THE FRAMEWORK
FOR GUIDANCE: PROGRAMS,
ROLES, AND SERVICES

This chapter is about the guidance program—how it is organized, who is involved, and what is done. It goes beyond the illustrations in Chapters 2 and 3 and describes rationale; goals and objectives; and roles of guidance and pupil personnel workers, parents and pupils. With this framework the place of specific services such as counseling and testing are clearer. There is not one single model for all guidance programs; variations occur to meet needs of specific schools. Even so, similarities cut across all settings; programs are more alike than different.

School guidance is more than the services of counselors; the contributions of teachers and administrators are essential for positive results.

GOALS

1. To develop an awareness of the different approaches to building school guidance programs.
2. To understand the roles of those participating in the guidance program.
3. To achieve insight into your own feelings about working as a member of the guidance team.
4. To become aware of the importance of providing guidance through a comprehensive, organized program.

MODELS OF GUIDANCE
IN THE SCHOOL

Two major approaches to guidance are used in schools, one emphasizing the providing of services and the other a particular program. The services organization tends to offer an array of helping activities (e.g., counseling, information-giving), and to have them ready for pupil and teacher use (National Study of Secondary School Evaluation 1969). The program concept coordinates services in a plan or system with specified objectives (Shaw 1977). The services approach is more frequently used and determines the framework of much of the rest of this book; each chapter describes a service. But the program mode is gaining ground rapidly and is certain to gain wide acceptance.

A school that emphasizes services usually provides counseling (individual and group), an information system, an assessment service, a counseling service, and research and evaluation, sometimes setting up goals and objectives. The difference between a services and a systems approach—a program as used here is actually a system—is that the systems approach is more specific and precise about what should be accomplished, provides methods for assessing outcome, and relates objectives to functions. But the services approach can be productive and efficient and can lead to a needs-based, developmental, comprehensive guidance program. It emphasizes functions, however, and evaluation tends to be in terms of adequate provision of these functions rather than of their effects on pupils.

Under the systems approach there are essential program elements consisting of (1) rationale, (2) needs assessment, (3) objectives, (4) staff, (5) methods of administration, and (6) procedures for evaluation. This model is more than a listing of services; it involves an organization of the parts according to a particular pattern. Different models can have similar goals; the model describes the way of reaching them.

The systems approach is a method of organizing parts of a program so that each contributes to the general mission, and specifies relations among elements. There are provisions for continuous evaluation to determine the effectiveness of the total system as well as of each subsystem. The following three figures, arranged according to conceptual comprehensiveness, illustrate three important models: direct application of the systems approach in program building (Hosford and Ryan 1970), the generalist-specialist model (Shaw 1968b), and the Cube paradigm (Morrill, Oetting, and Hurst 1974). The models do not determine program priorities, functions, and target populations, but give systematic procedures for identifying and reaching them.

Figure 6–1. Counseling and guidance program development system model.

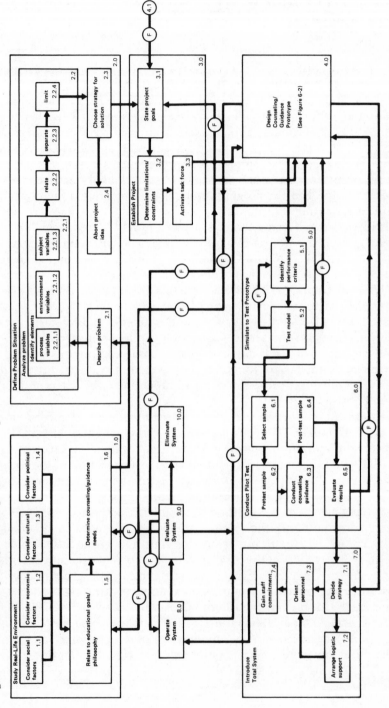

Source: From R. E. Hosford and T. A. Ryan, "Systems Design in the Development of Counseling and Guidance Programs," *Personnel and Guidance Journal* 49, no. 3 (1970), p. 226. Copyright 1970 American Personnel and Guidance Association. Reprinted with permission.

The flowchart in Figure 6-1 shows the Hosford and Ryan model. The ten major functions in this figure are:

1. Study real-life environment (1.0)
2. Define problem situation (2.0)
3. Establish project (3.0)
4. Design counseling/guidance program prototype (4.0)
5. Simulate to test program prototype (5.0)
6. Pilot-test model (6.0)
7. Introduce system (7.0)
8. Operate system (8.0)
9. Evaluate system (9.0)
10. Eliminate system (10.0)

"F" represents feedback for evaluating and modifying subsystems.

Stage 4, designing the counseling system, is shown in detail in Figure 6-2. This system involves a process that can be described as follows: First, there is an analysis of the environment and the target groups. This is essentially a needs survey. Second, from needs, problems are specified. For example, pupils may require help in developing positive social relations with each other, or fitting courses to career plans. Third, program goals and objectives are set up. Goals are general statements of what is to be accomplished; objectives are specific behaviors that can be observed and assessed. Objectives are particularly important; there is no way to estimate the effectiveness of the system if results cannot be measured. Fourth, all information, resources, and staff are organized into a guidance plan or program (usually referred to as a model). Fifth, the model is tested. This may be done by such methods as computer simulation or the use of a small selection of pupils. Needed modifications are made. Sixth, the model is instituted. Systematic evaluation is carried out. Seventh, outdated or ineffective parts (or the total program) are replaced.

The systems approach provides a unique program characterized by measurable objectives, clear-cut ways of achieving them, and evaluation in terms of effects on pupils. The model meets the accountability requirement and provides information on relative costs of strategies (Krumboltz 1974). The Los Angeles, California, plan for pupil personnel services is an example of this approach (Mitchell and Saum 1972, pp. 75–91; Sullivan and O'Hare 1971, pp. 1–6).

Shaw's generalist-specialist model, shown in Figure 6-3 is another way of looking at the program. The horizontal line across the top of the figure is divided into three sections by major emphasis of the program; this emphasis is determined by the growth stage when guidance intervention takes place. Part A, identified as *Indirect Focus*, illustrates the effort to

Figure 6–2. Counseling/guidance programs prototype.

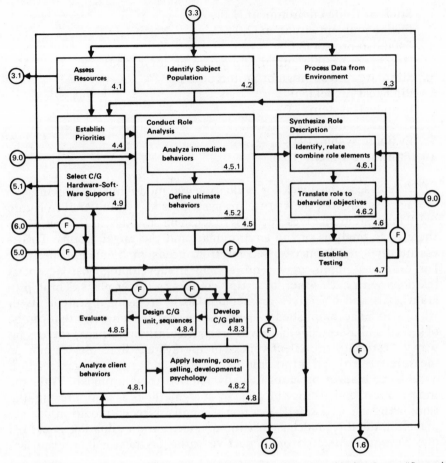

Source: From R. E. Hosford and T. A. Ryan, "Systems Design in the Development of Counseling and Guidance Programs," *Personnel and Guidance Journal* 49, no. 3 (1970), p. 227. Copyright 1970 American Personnel and Guidance Association. Reprinted with permission.

improve environmental conditions and to work with others to help the counselee. Part B, *Direct Focus*, involves face-to-face helping like counseling.

This approach uses the same elements as the first, but in different ways (Shaw 1968*b*). Starting with values, program-building moves through general objectives, specific objectives, assumptions, functions, implementation, and evaluation (Shaw 1973, pp. 71, 272), but the organization of functions depends on the selection of the general goal or goals; general prevention, early identification and treatment, and diagnosis and therapy.

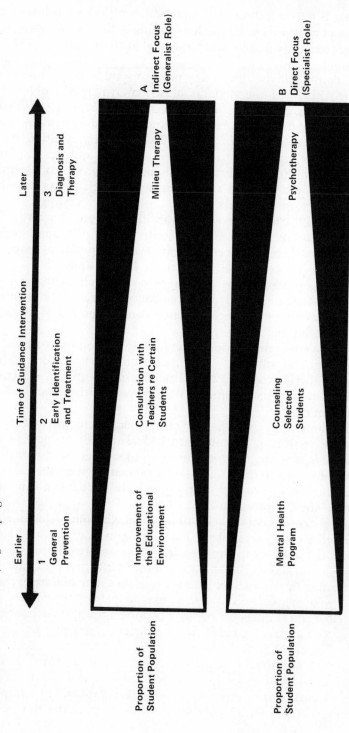

Figure 6–3. General model for guidance services. The horizontal dimension represents the time at which guidance intervention takes place. The two different rectangles represent two basic techniques for achieving objectives — directly through working with students or indirectly through working with significant adults in the learning environment. The proportion of the population which can be reached through a given technique initiated at a given time is indicated by the white areas. Black areas represent the proportion of the population *not* reached by a given program.

Earlier

Time of Guidance Intervention

Later

1
General
Prevention

2
Early Identification
and Treatment

3
Diagnosis and
Therapy

A
Indirect Focus
(Generalist Role)

Improvement of
the Educational
Environment

Consultation with
Teachers re Certain
Students

Milieu Therapy

Proportion of
Student Population

B
Direct Focus
(Specialist Role)

Mental Health
Program

Counseling
Selected
Students

Psychotherapy

Proportion of
Student Population

Source: From M. C. Shaw, *The Functions of Theory in Guidance Programs* (Boston: Houghton Mifflin, 1968), p. 15. Copyright 1968 Houghton Mifflin Co. Reprinted with permission.

Each goal is pursued through direct treatment by counselors or through the indirect efforts of the counselor working with other persons. Six variations are possible (e.g., generalist—general prevention, specialist—general prevention).

Shaw points out that few if any programs are based on just one of the six approaches. Still, the model is an extremely helpful tool for clarifying the nature of a guidance program, making it specific and realistic, and illustrating the differences between functions and objectives. It also implies appropriate counselor action. The general-prevention model, for example, must begin early in the school sequence and aim at all pupils. If the focus is on direct treatment, individual and group counseling play a major part. If it is indirect, counselors devote their efforts to influencing significant persons in pupils' lives.

Early identification and treatment are aimed at pupils who are developing problems, and therefore reach only part of the pupil population. Diagnosis and therapy concentrate on developed problems, come later in the school sequence, and serve relatively fewer pupils.

Many ongoing programs appear to contain elements of several of Shaw's six strategies. Analyzing a guidance program by this model, it is relatively easy to detect inconsistencies and vague assumptions in cases of careless planning.

The innovative cube model, Figure 6-4, cuts through the confusion, overlapping, and ambiguity that sometimes pervade secondary school guidance. It illustrates graphically the three major dimensions of programs—target group or institution, purpose of the action, and method of intervention.

The A dimension contains four target groups ranging from the individual to the institution or community. The specific purpose of guidance assistance falls in the B dimension; purposes range from remediation for existing problems to training and development. (Psychological education, for instance, is an example of training.) The method of intervention is shown on the C dimension.

This efficient model makes a unique contribution by helping guidance practitioners clarify their work. The target group dimension, for example, includes the individual; the primary group, such as family; the association group, such as a class or club; and the institution or community. The classification of purposes of intervention into remedial help, prevention, and development facilitates the choice of an appropriate method. ("Developmental intervention" is a technical term; it describes methods aiming to encourage growth, build strengths, and prepare for meeting needs.) The third dimension of the cube, showing methods of intervention, relates to the way help is provided. There are three approaches— direct face-to-face help, indirect assistance by consultation and preparing others to work with counselees, and the use of medialike computers and programmed materials. All of the activities of a guidance service are based

Figure 6–4. Dimensions of counselor functioning.

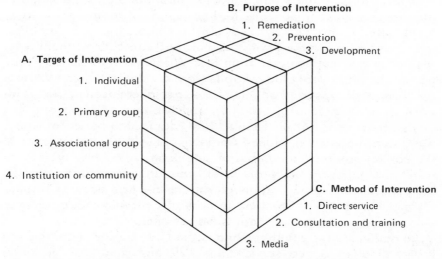

Source: From W. H. Morrill, E. R. Oetting, and J. C. Hurst, "Dimensions of Counselor Functioning," *Personnel and Guidance Journal* 52, no. 6 (1974), p. 370. Copyright 1974 W. H. Morrill, E. R. Oetting, and J. C. Hurst. Reprinted with permission.

on choices from elements in the three dimensions. A complete plan includes objectives, assessment methods, and coordinating procedures. Sprinthall and Erickson (1974) and Tuma (1974) describe applications in schools.

EXPERIENCE

CHOOSING A MODEL

Set up four sections of the room, one for each of the guidance models. Students choose the one they prefer, assemble in that area, and discuss their choice. Each group then gives the three major reasons for their choice.

RESEARCH

EFFECTIVENESS OF PROGRAMS

Very little research has been done on the evaluation of programs; studies have usually centered on a specific service (e.g., counseling). Thus, there is a scarcity of evidence to support one model over another.

Several large-scale studies provide information on the value of guidance services in schools. Rothney's (1958) longitudinal study emphasized counseling by study staff members but included other activities such as working with teachers and curriculum committees. A total of 890 sophomores from four Wisconsin high schools took part in the eight-year study. Pupils were divided into experimental and control groups, and effects of the special counseling and guidance were checked at graduation and two and one-half and five years afterwards. Results showed that, during the period of study, the group provided guidance (mainly counseling) was superior to the control group on a number of significant variables. Even in an additional followup ten years after graduation the results favored the experimental group, although differences had become smaller (Tyler 1969, p. 232). The long-term results showed that guidance, using the services model, does have beneficial effects.

An earlier study by Rothney and Roens (1952) used regular junior high school guidance services for 129 eighth graders in three schools. Both experimental and control groups were composed of pupils identified as either superior or needing help. Evaluation was based on followups at the end of five years of school and after one year of post-high-school experiences. Results showed that the staff of professional counselors working intensively with pupils and teachers had positive effects; pupils learned to plan effectively for realistic goals, and acquired productive, more effective styles of interpersonal behavior. This study, too, illustrates the services model, and emphasizes the need for teachers to participate in the program.

A study with college students also supports guidance services. Campbell (1965) followed up students who had participated in a research project at the University of Minnesota twenty-five years earlier. The long-term results revealed that counseled students had achieved at a higher level and had demonstrated more effective ways of coping with problems. The helping approach used was somewhat like the services model.

Gamsky (1970) reports on an evaluation of the services model. Data consisted of teachers' judgments of help to referred pupils. Results were quite positive; teachers noted substantial improvement and learned, moreover, how to understand and deal with pupil behavior.

The Mesa (not dated) and the Grossmont Union High School district (Jacobson and Mitchell 1975) utilized various aspects of a systems approach in their programs. Early preliminary evaluations of the Mesa accountability program showed substantial benefits from use of this model, and provided data for revising procedures and materials.

A number of research studies cover elements of these models, but comparisons of effectiveness are not possible.

OBJECTIVES

1. To be able to identify the major models of contemporary guidance programs. Name four models and give an important characteristic of each.

The models discussed in this chapter are: services, systems, generalist-specialist, and cube.

The following are illustrative characteristics:

— Services model: provides functions designated in official role-statements.
— Systems model: utilizes an orderly sequence of steps to build a program that meets needs.
— Generalist-specialist model: requires that the major emphasis of the program be identified.
— Cube model: uses the major dimensions of target group, type of intervention, and purpose of intervention.

2. To understand your own attitudes and preferences about each type of program. Rank the four models in order of preference and state the feelings that determine your choice of order.

There is no right or wrong answer; the objective is met if you rank them and can express feelings about choices. For example, do some models appear to be more likely to give you freedom to work in your own style?

APPLICATIONS TO SCHOOL LEVELS

The guidance models described in the previous section can be applied at all school levels—secondary, middle/junior high, and elementary. Utilization varies with the needs of pupils and the organization of schools at different levels. Secondary schools make considerable use of the services approach, although this model may actually amount to a type of "system" (Hollis and Hollis 1965, Ch. 7). Approaches using more recent systems concepts, however, are gaining acceptance, particularly in career-education-oriented programs (see programs described in Chapter 13).

PROGRAMS IN ELEMENTARY SCHOOLS Guidance programs in elementary
schools are more clear-cut and consistent than at the secondary level,
partly because of their more recent arrival on the school scene and the
simpler organization of schools at this level, partly because of a clearer
focus (counselors do not, for example, have to concern themselves with
electives, choice of programs, job preparation, or college admission). But
these conditions would not have led to an efficient and systematic pattern
without the conceptualization of early leaders whose work set the stage
for school programs today (Faust 1968).

The elementary school guidance program usually involves a school-
based counselor providing the services of counseling, consultation, and
coordination (priorities vary). Further guidance responsibilities within
these areas are diagnosis and referral. The counselor is in a key position to
help identify pupils with special needs, disabilities, or handicaps, and to
refer those in need of special assistance (Cottingham 1969; Faust 1968;
Patterson 1969a). By general agreement, the program has developmental
emphasis (American School Counselor Association 1975, p. 3; Holt 1975,
p. 12).

Programs differ according to priorities established among the three
basic services. Faust ranks consulting with teachers along with counseling as the first priority for help to teachers and pupils. Consulting with
school administrators, parents, and others is placed at a lower level (Faust
1968, pp. 13–14, 41). The recent statement of the role of the elementary
school counselor does not make this distinction. Primary functions are:
counseling with individual pupils; counseling with groups of pupils; consulting with teachers, other staff members, and parents; and evaluation
(American School Counselor Association 1974c, pp. 221–222). Though
the teacher is the person who works most closely with children, services
to teachers are not given top priority. In a statement that relates psychological bases to practices, Dinkmeyer (1971b) recognized that the counselor
must set up priorities, and recommends this order: first, working with
administration; second, working with groups of teachers; third, counseling with children in groups; fourth, consultation with parents in groups;
and fifth, individual counseling with children. The setting of priorities,
once objectives are established, is a critical task; it indicates where to
begin and the sequence of activities to be followed in implementing the
program (Heddesheimer 1975, p. 29).

Tuma's report (1974) illustrates her use of the cube design in an elementary school developmental guidance program. The chief problem during
her first year was gaining access to classrooms in order to initiate activities necessary for the program's success. To overcome this difficulty,
she utilized the cube strategy to select the target population, the method
of intervention, and purpose of intervention. She also employed the model
proposed by Blocher and Rapoza to effect change in the human system

(1972), in this case to gain teachers' cooperation. Thus, she defined services, identified potential clients, introduced new concepts to clients, and set up mutually agreed-upon goals. With teachers' acceptance, and with the help of the principal, the counselor succeeded in introducing a number of techniques and guidance strategies. By the end of her second year, she had established working relationships with nearly all staff members. Direct contact with small groups and individuals was part of the program, but the major emphasis was on classroom demonstrations and consultation with teachers.

How the major elements of Shaw's model and the approach of Morrill, Oetting, and Hurst can be synthesized in program-building is illustrated by Heddesheimer (1975, pp. 6, 81–87). The cube elements (e.g., target of intervention) are related to methods of intervention (e.g., remediation) to identify program activities. Relating these two models, their similarities are much more striking than their differences.

These models also provide a framework for incorporating the trends of the late 70s, which Muro (1977) characterizes as a decade of delivering new services in new ways. The major feature of this trend includes the view of the counselor as a fully involved member of the school, a mobilizer of resources, a stimulus and energizer, a curriculum expert, and an implementer of productive placement to promote the students' success and growth.

PROGRAMS IN MIDDLE AND JUNIOR HIGH SCHOOLS   Programs for this level resemble those in either the secondary or elementary school; they involve all school personnel and are attuned to developmental needs of pupils. There is a heavy emphasis on exploration, gaining self-identity, developing good peer relations, and achieving sex-role identification (Gatewood and Dilg 1975, pp. 11, 16–17). The school years between elementary and high school help bridge the transitional period in adolescence, and aim not only to help pupils get ready for the next level, but more importantly to make the most productive use of this period of development. The involvement of parents is particularly important; suggested participation includes conferences and career guidance (Fletcher 1976).

The counselor provides specialized assistance such as individual and group counseling. Consulting with the administration and teaching staff is also an important area (Hansen and Hearn 1971, p. 308). Consultation includes assistance to teachers on questions involving pupil learning, personality development, and career exploration. There is also a need for crisis counseling. Problems cover a wide range, including drug use, venereal disease, and potential runaways, and not only demand immediate attention, but pose problems of confidentiality (Kirk and Martin 1977, pp. 145–148).

Planning and coordinating the total program is a major responsibility (American School Counselor Association 1974c). Special attention is on teacher participation and developmental activities, but the focus is on pupil needs. The Aurora Hills Middle School guidance program, Aurora, Colorado, illustrates this point (Reid 1977; Johnson 1977; Arnow 1977). It has a preventive emphasis, and teachers do much of the intervention in the classroom using skills developed in counselor-led in-service education.

GOALS AND OBJECTIVES

No one element of the school guidance program is expendable, but goals and objectives are without doubt the most critical for success. Guidance workers are realizing without them programs are often terminated when expenditures are reviewed for budget cuts. The public is insisting on an accounting for the use of funds and evidence that an agency justifies its existence; services that cannot document results are dropped.

Goals and objectives communicate what the service is attempting to accomplish and enable progress in meeting objectives to be judged. Functions like counseling and consulting are important, of course; without them nothing would be accomplished. But goals and objectives provide the ultimate justification for the total guidance program. Still, despite its importance, this aspect of the program typically gets little attention.

DEFINITIONS   One major problem in defining goals and objectives of a guidance program is confusion about terms. Widely used definitions are as follows:

Goals.   General statements of what is to be accomplished. They do not provide a basis for assessment of progress. This is an example of a goal statement from a school guidance plan: "To help pupils develop positive feelings about themselves." How can positive feelings be measured? What do we mean by positive feelings? How can we tell if pupils have developed them? How much do they have to develop for us to judge our efforts successful? Obviously, something more is needed to serve as a guide for planning and evaluation.

Objectives.   Sometimes called "specific goals," these state explicitly what we hope to accomplish. A good statement of an objective indicates what skill, attitude, or value is to be learned, who will learn it, how it will be demonstrated, and how much is needed to represent success on the part of the pupil. The two following statements are examples:

1. Secondary school pupils make the most of educational opportunities at the school.
2. Help ninth graders choose a program consistent with stated goals and demonstrated ability in which they perform satisfactorily for the year.

Which one gives guidelines for action and provides for evaluation? Obviously the second. The example is oversimplified; better-developed ones are given later, but this one does show the basic difference between a vague, general objective and a specific one. Objectives provide the means to estimate attainment of goals; usually several objectives are needed for each goal.

Process Objectives.   These are objectives in terms of process (for example: counselors will see all tenth graders; counselors will confer with all teachers every two weeks). Such objectives are valuable if they are logical consequences of appropriate vehicles for change and have a basis in theory, but they tell little about pupil outcome.

Outcome Objectives.   This type is illustrated in the examples; it describes what is supposed to happen as a result of guidance. Process objectives can be translated into outcome objectives. If, as a result of counselor conferences, teachers initiate one new group-technique each week, the result is an outcome objective for the counselor—it indicates what happens as a result of services. For the teacher, however, it is a process objective.

Performance Objectives.   The most useful type, though there is argument over how suitable such objectives are for counselors (Gubser 1974). Guidance should make a difference in people's lives, but counselors do not agree on the type of evidence and the methods needed to measure its effect. Can significant pupil growth such as developing a sense of identity be put in objectively measurable terms? Is it possible to assess how many pupils have stopped using drugs because of the guidance program? (Accountability is discussed in detail in Chapter 15.)

SETTING UP GOALS AND OBJECTIVES   Setting up goals and objectives is a clear-cut process and relatively simple to carry out. There are a number of useful guides that can help (Sullivan and O'Hare 1971; Mease and Benson 1973; Michigan School Counselors Association Executive Board 1974; Mitchell and Saum 1972; see also Chapter 15 for Wellman's system for establishing objectives).

Goals and objectives are based on needs; needs assessment is therefore the first step. This includes all persons concerned: What problems do they face? What do they hope to achieve? What do they think the school should do?

The greatest difficulty often seems to come at the end point of translating needs data into goals and objectives. There is a tendency to make objectives so broad that they are impossible to carry out and evaluate (e.g., "Help all pupils to make optimum use of potential"). There is also a tendency to substitute functions for objectives (e.g., "Provide group experiences for pupils"). There is also a tendency to establish objectives to cover everything. Usually priorities have to be set up and some important needs must be left out. Philosophy, goals, and objectives have an important relationship. Philosophy tells what is true, good and real; needs tell what people feel they lack for a good life. Needs can conflict with values, e.g., some pupils want preferential treatment. It is necessary, therefore, to check goals and objectives against the philosophy of the program.

A prize-winning effort in counseling goes beyond the formulation of good, specific objectives to the achievement of them.

A philosophy should contain statements such as the following excerpts from *Perspectives on Secondary Guidance* (Lombana 1977, p. 1).

Secondary school guidance services exist to provide assistance to students as they attempt to cope with the difficult, often puzzling, and complex problems associated with educational, personal, and vocational development. Facilitative in character, guidance services are planned, developed, and implemented on the basis of student-referenced assumptions:
   that each student is a unique individual capable of achieving self-direction in problem-solving and decision-making;
   that each student has a right to full acceptance and opportunity for personal development within the school milieu;
   that each student has a responsibility to seek fulfillment through maximum participation in the educational and career guidance programs in the school.

EXAMPLES OF GOALS AND OBJECTIVES   The SPOP (Situation, Population, Outcome, Process) approach developed by a task force of the Bureau of Pupil Personnel Services of the California State Department of Education illustrates a systematic and effective way to spell out the specific accomplishments pupils are expected to attain. Each objective statement indicates the following (Sullivan and O'Hare 1971, pp. 16–21):

— Situation: describes the target group.
— Outcome: the desired behavior and expected level.
— Process: how the desired behavior will be learned.

The model further classifies objectives on three dimensions: school level; educational, social, vocational needs; and action, awareness, or accommodation.

The SOOM (Self-Other Outcome Management) plan using "success indicators" for objectives is described by Mease and Benson (1973). The plan calls for needs assessment, identifying needs for specific groups, goal statements, identifying facilitating and inhibiting factors, and success indicators, which are similar to objectives. *Self* refers to the guidance worker's own perceptions, feelings, and competencies. *Others* indicates people the counselor works with—pupils, teachers, parents, and school administrators. Implementing activities are established to achieve success indicators, and feedback is used to improve the system. While the plan emphasizes behavioral objectives, the authors show that it is people-oriented, and not restrictive and without concern for affective elements (pp. 15–17). The monograph, distributed by the Minnesota Department of Education, gives detailed instruction for instituting the system.

An interesting and simplified explanation with cartoon illustrations for establishing goals and objectives has been prepared by the Michigan

School Counselors Association (1974). The approach centers around the issue of accountability, but the section on needs analysis, development of goals, and specifying objectives is lucid and helpful. It contrasts "action" and "reaction" programs, and describes good use of task groups to involve faculty, pupils, and parents.

Krumboltz' plan for accountability (1974) compares program costs with effectiveness, and requires mutually agreed-upon goals and objectives. Krumboltz recommends specific objectives for each counselee; this aim is more feasible in individual and small-group work than in school-wide guidance activities. While his plan is more a strategy than a way to establish objectives, he makes the point that large numbers of behavioral objectives (e.g., "90 percent of seniors will have chosen a career") result in efforts to force conformity regardless of individual needs. For example, Bill Brown may need to consider several alternatives rather than concentrate on one choice, while specific objectives set up in a program indicate it is time for him to make one specific choice.

EXPERIENCE

LOOKING AT GOALS AND OBJECTIVES

Obtain a statement about guidance and counseling from a local school. Identify the section containing goals and objectives. (It may have a different heading, e.g., "Purposes.") Select one or two statements that most nearly resemble specific objectives. See if you can explain how progress toward each might be assessed. Then ask a counselor in the school how it is assessed.

OBJECTIVES

1. To understand the differences between program goals and objectives. Explain why objectives but not goals can be assessed directly.

Objectives are expressed in terms of observable behaviors that can be measured. Goals are general statements of what is desired, but lack specific assessable criteria.

2. To understand the different types of objectives that are used in guidance. Can a process objective be converted into an outcome objective?

Yes. Building a process into the guidance program may be an outcome objective for the person who has the task to accomplish. For example, the counselor may be interested in helping teachers give positive responses to pupils. The result of the counselor's efforts may be a process used by teachers. For the counselor, therefore, success in getting the procedure used is an outcome objective.

3. To understand the importance of program objectives. What contributions do objectives make to school guidance?

Objectives provide guidelines for establishing services; allow effectiveness to be assessed; serve as a basis for communicating what the program aims to accomplish; and provides data to report results of effectiveness.

ROLES

For a guidance program to be successful, teachers, administrators, parents, and pupils need to understand the role of guidance staff members. Counselors should be aware of the special contributions of others, particularly teachers and other pupil personnel workers. Unfortunately, there is considerable confusion about roles, and even wide differences of opinion among counselors. The same difficulty surrounds the guidance of other pupil personnel workers, teachers, administrators, pupils, parents, and community members. Specific functions may vary with local needs, but all have a part to play if the program is to be successful. Roles need to be explicitly stated and agreed upon.

Role statements provide a general explanation of what counselors and other pupil personnel workers do, summarizing the general types of service they provide. Goals and objectives are aims based on needs of the target population. The guidance program provides strategies for determining these goals and objectives and for the delivery of services. Roles, therefore, serve as guidelines in determining both what will be done and how it will be carried out. Since, for example, counselors are competent to help pupils improve communication skills, an objective could be communications training; implementation could involve a strategy of group interaction.

GUIDANCE WORKERS   This category includes secondary, elementary, and middle school counselors, guidance paraprofessionals, and clerical personnel. They make up the guidance staff.

School counselors are basically helpers who work with pupils, staff, and others on personal problems and needs. While a large portion of their time is given to face-to-face work with pupils individually or in small groups, responsibilities include consulting, coordinating, providing information, follow-up, placement, and evaluation. Assistance is aimed at enabling others to decide, grow, and develop; the counselor does not provide answers, administer rules, or carry out teaching or administrative functions.

At the secondary-school level, the counselor may be one of several full-time professionals, depending upon the size of the institution and the counselor-pupil ratio. Ideally this ratio would be about 1 : 250 (American School Counselor Association 1965), so that, for example, in a school of 2,000 pupils there would be eight counselors. Usually the load is greater. Through individual and small-group contacts, much time is devoted to face-to-face help for a variety of problems and needs, e.g., social relations, personal identity, career planning, and educational progress. Regardless of the approach (taken up in Chapter 7), the emphasis is on clarifying goals, self-understanding, and decision-making rather than directing, advising, or controlling. This helping relationship uses the counselor's major area of expertise.

The role entails other responsibilities, some involving relationships and some more heavily technological, organizational, or administrative. The first type includes consulting with teachers, administrators, parents, and community persons. Each of these activities, particularly the first two, involve relationship skills in building trust, effective communication, and demonstrating sensitivity to the views and needs of others. The third type—administrative—involves such activities as planning and supervising the information service, the testing program, and evaluation service. A specialized and necessary public relations function is implicit in all activities and in working with the community, e.g., through the media, organizations, and agencies. The use of school and community resources is a major responsibility, and involves organizational skills.

The role of the elementary school counselor is that of helper to pupils, teachers, and parents. To carry out this role the counselor works face-to-face with pupils individually and in small groups on remedial and developmental needs, provides classroom guidance activities focusing on affective aspects of personality, and assists teachers to develop skill in use of these techniques. Consultation with teachers is designed to help them work effectively and positively with individuals and groups. Both individual conferences and group meetings with parents are used to help with problems and give information about guidance services. The counselor also coordinates services such as team help for learning deficiencies and referrals to out-of-school agencies.

The elementary school counselor's role fully recognizes the importance of success experiences for *all* pupils. (American School Counselor Association 1974c, pp. 219–220). Every pupil must be made to feel competent, worthy, and valued.

The role of the middle school counselor encompasses responsibilities already described, adapted for the developmental level of the middle/junior high school (American School Counselor Association 1974c, p. 216). Counseling, staff consulting, parent consulting, community contacts, and educational placement, are major responsibilities.

At all levels, there will be increased work with the handicapped result-ing from the requirements of PL 94-142 which makes the school respon-sible for providing appropriate education for all children, whatever their needs. This legislation will very likely bring the roles of the counselor and school psychologist closer together.

Differentiated staffing can be implemented at all grade levels. The use of support personnel, including peer counselors, is one example. Within the counseling profession itself, however, differentiation is not yet wide-spread. With the increased importance of the consulting function, it seems likely that applications will develop among counselors as well as between counselors and teachers or parents. An experienced and highly qualified counselor could, for example, serve as a consultant to those new on the job (Tolbert 1974, p. 205).

The role of the paraprofessional is gaining increased importance for school guidance and counseling. Nomenclature varies. Typical titles are "peer counselors" or "guidance assistants" (Delworth 1974, p. 250). Paraprofessionals may be paid guidance workers, unpaid volunteers, or pupils. Roles are narrowly defined; under supervision, paraprofessionals perform specific responsibilities, e.g., interviewing, testing, providing in-formation, keeping records, and job placement. There has been a tendency to think paraprofessionals carry out only relatively simple cognitive ac-tivities, but roles are expanding and paraprofessionals now have such advanced duties as leading facilitative conferences (Danish and Brock 1974; Lechowicz 1975).

Clerical personnel contribute to the guidance program through record keeping, arranging appointments, and meeting pupils, parents, and others. These functions can do much to facilitate goals of the program. The short-age of clerical personnel is one of the major problems in guidance today; counselors often have to devote considerable time to routine record-keeping tasks.

PUPIL PERSONNEL SPECIALISTS Pupil personnel specialists staff the school program aimed at the affective, personal side of education. Teachers may devote time to helping pupils develop self-understanding, perceive the personal meaning of course material, remove learning blocks, and clarify values and goals, but the major responsibility for these parts of education falls on the team of pupil personnel specialists. The counselor is one team member; others are the school psychologist, school social worker, and the health and medical service worker. The counselor needs to understand the roles of these professionals to develop effective working relationships.

The School Psychologist This specialist works with elementary, middle/junior high, and secondary pupils and traditionally has spent considerable time giving individual tests to pupils being considered for special education or suspected of having learning problems (Bardon 1968). Additional functions have been consultation to teachers and parents. Though they have not in the past been major functions (Liddle and Ferguson 1968, p. 44), therapy and services to handicapped children are likely to increase (Kaplan, Charin, and Clancy 1977). The new emphasis on working with the handicapped resulting from PL 94-142 will add responsibilities for diagnosis, referral, participation in planning programs for special education pupils, and helping make the classroom situation productive for all who can participate in it. Major differences between the counselor and school psychologist are that the psychologist is based in the district office and is qualified to administer and interpret specialized tests but the role is difficult to define because it depends upon interests and job demands (Ringness 1976).

The School Social Worker   The counselor calls on this specialist when a problem requires casework involving data about home life or when help is needed for the family. An earlier title for this function was "visiting teacher," which emphasized school-home-community relations. The current title highlights casework, i.e., synthesizing data about the pupil, planning treatment, consulting with school staff, and working with home and family to make the school experience productive for the pupil.

Health and Medical Personnel   The school nurse assists in screening health records, provides first aid and emergency medical treatment, and works with pupils on health problems. The school nurse also coordinates health and physical examinations and the school health program, and participates in planning and policy making to improve services (Hatch and Stefflre 1965, pp. 132–136).

Other medical services are usually provided on a consulting basis in areas such as health appraisal, health counseling, emergency care, and prevention and control of communicable diseases (Gibson, Mitchell, and Higgins 1973, pp. 32–33). A psychiatrist can be particularly helpful in dealing with severe emotional problems.

Teachers   Teachers have a key role in the guidance program. They implement remedial, therapeutic, and developmental strategies planned cooperatively with the counselor. Hill (1974, p. 175) suggests that this is especially true at the elementary level, but it also holds for middle and secondary schools. Most important are understanding, accepting, and working with the program. The burden of building positive attitudes and cooperation rests with counselors, the newcomers to the educational scene.

Teachers use group approaches to promote a positive learning climate in the classroom. Individual conferences and referrals to counselors are further important functions. Teachers are in the best position to identify those who need help and to enlist the counselor's assistance before problems have grown acute.

The role also includes providing data for records, taking part in staff conferences, imparting study techniques, and supplying career information relevant to the area of study.

Administrators   Educational administrators, primarily school principals and district superintendents, have an essential role to play in guidance programs. Shertzer and Stone (1976, p. 379) rightly point out that if principals do not support a program no one else will feel the need to. One important administrative function is employing qualified counselors, which requires knowledge and respect for professional and personal standards. Visible enthusiasm for the program on the part of administrators is most important. They can demonstrate support by indicating a positive attitude to teachers and community; providing time, facilities, and staff; recognizing achievements; and encouraging counselors to structure their programs in keeping with high professional goals.

The administrator is in the best position to present the guidance workers' point of view to those who control funds on the board of education. In times of budget cuts, such involvement is critical.

PUPILS   Pupils have served in many responsible positions in the past, for example, as orientation guides, big brothers and sisters, or aides in the guidance office. But with the advent of peer counseling and psychological education involvement has increased on levels from elementary through college.

Pupils have other important roles to play. They can participate in committees for planning and policy-making or in clubs that promote guidance work through public relations; many also serve in clerical capacities for record-keeping, building informational files and helping with community and follow-up surveys.

The pupils' major role, however, is to use the guidance service, tell others about it, make referrals, and let others know that guidance is an essential part of the educational program. Pupils are increasingly appearing on programs, even at the national level, to describe new strategies and the personal benefits of participation (Elkins 1975, p. 239).

PARENTS   New avenues for participation are opening up for parents as counselees, consultees, and active helpers. More and more groups to teach parents effective child-raising procedures and ways to handle parent-child conflicts are being formed. Parents also serve as helpers, paraprofessionals, and resource persons in guidance programs.

A major function involves cooperative work carrying out helping plans developed together with school counselors. This is an essential role, as many plans, decisions, and new behavior patterns depend on support at home.

RESEARCH

PERCEPTIONS OF THE COUNSELOR'S ROLE

Role statements help clarify what counselors do, but the evidence is that teachers, administrators, and counselors themselves do not fully understand or accept the counselor's role. Graff and Warner (1968), using a scale on attitudes towards guidance, questioned 83 teachers, 9 administrators, and 10 counselors in a large suburban high school and found differences as follows (lower scores more positive):

— Administrators' average, 291.66
— Teachers' average, 306.90
— Counselors' average, 236.50

Counselors differed from both teachers and administrators at the .05 level, but administrators and teachers did not differ significantly.

The results of this limited study tend to agree with other research; Hart and Prince (1970) found, for example, that job demands were in conflict with roles counselors were taught in preparation programs.

Buckner (1975), using items similar to those in the ASCA-ACES policy for secondary school counselors, found that a substantial number of counselors in four Utah school districts did not know the functions set forth in the statement. For example, responsibility for conducting class discussions about school rules was not considered to be an ASCA-ACES role responsibility, yet 63 percent of the counselors stated that it was.

Carmical and Calvin (1970), using a sample of 153 counselors in the Houston area, found that the top three items selected as desirable functions were: to give pupils the opportunity to discuss problems, counseling potential dropouts, and counseling those failing. Scheduling pupils ranked forty-seventh. Comparisons with Buckner's study are not possible, but it appears that in the main counselors' conceptions of their role were consistent with the official role statement. However, counseling pupils about personal decisions ranked twenty-second, below organizing a school testing program.

Support for the guidance program is a major role. It is demonstrated through making referrals, requesting conferences, lobbying, and electing local and state officials in favor of guidance services. Legislative power rests with the local community; elected leaders have learned to listen carefully to wishes of constituents.

The community has a guidance role, although the relationship is usually stated the other way around as the role of guidance in the community. The resources of the community facilitate the school's efforts to make the program contemporary and meaningful. In fact, the new concept of community education (discussed in Chapter 11) involves community-wide problems and needs.

Local referral resources are one significant aspect of the role. They range from agencies providing therapy, welfare, medical rehabilitation, and employment services to individuals—specialists in various occupations, retired persons, and others—who are willing to donate their time and talents to help pupils. Many appreciate the chance to provide a meaningful service. Retired persons, for example, are found staffing special remedial programs and career information centers.

The community participates in the guidance program by providing social, recreational, and career-exploratory opportunities; the school cannot cover all needs in these areas. The opportunities for career exploration through part-time jobs and co-op programs depends on the community's willingness to participate in providing educational experiences. The new concept of career education makes greater use of community resources than ever before.

RESEARCH

ELEMENTARY SCHOOL TEACHERS' PERCEPTIONS OF GUIDANCE ROLES

Witmer and Cottingham (1970) used a stratified random sample of 556 Florida K–6 teachers to investigate their use of, the value they ascribed to, and preferred method of improving their guidance functions. They concluded that teachers have accepted the function as a major responsibility, implement it in the classroom, and see themselves as the ones to improve practices, but feel additional time and the assistance of specialists are needed to improve services.

The value accorded guidance practices was significantly greater than their actual use (at the .01 level), and a majority of teachers expressed the desire to develop greater competency in practically all of the functions.

EXPERIENCE

AWARENESS OF ROLES

Interview a teacher, a parent, and a pupil to determine perceptions of their roles in the guidance program. Compare with the factors given in this chapter. How well do these individuals appear to understand guidance?

Ask several fellow students to think back to high school days and give their most vivid impression of the guidance service. Do these recollections imply an awareness of participatory roles?

EXPERIENCE

CLARIFYING THE COUNSELOR'S ROLE

Using several small groups, ask each to agree on a three-minute role statement to present to teachers, parents, and school administrators. Have each group present in turn, with others assuming roles of members of the target audience.

At the conclusion discuss:

— Difficulties experienced (if any) in agreeing on a role statement.
— How willing the target groups would be to support the role presented and how essential they considered it to be in the educational process.

OBJECTIVES

1. **To understand the guidance roles of all who have a personal interest in school guidance services. Identify the persons who are concerned with the guidance program and give one key role element for each.**

The list of concerned persons includes teachers, administrators, other pupil personnel workers, parents, and pupils. (The community itself also has an important role to play.)

Illustrative role activities are as follows:

— Teachers—refer pupils to counselors.
— Administrators—display an attitude of support for the program.
— Pupil personnel workers (school psychologists, school social workers, and medical personnel)—accept referrals in need of their services.

— Parents—participate in learning experiences provided by counselors.
— Pupils—serve as peer counselors.

2. To gain an appreciation of how well the counseling role would suit your preferred life-style. Write out five statements beginning, "I am . . ."; then write another five beginning, "A counselor is . . ."
The purpose of this objective is to elicit insights about yourself, the counseling role as you perceive it, and to see how well the two match.

ADDITIONAL READINGS

Bonnell, Jane A., "Role of the Instructional Staff." In *The Organization of Pupil Personnel Programs*, edited by Raymond N. Hatch, pp. 202–222. East Lansing, Mich.: Michigan State University Press, 1974.
    One of the most complete references specifically on the teacher's role in guidance.
Ferris, Robert W. *Pupil Personnel Strategies and Systems.* Springfield, Ill.: Charles C. Thomas, 1975.
    Pages 37–67 provide a helpful discussion of pupil personnel roles emphasizing the team approach.
Hatch, Raymond M., ed. *The Organization of Pupil Personnel Programs.* East Lansing, Michigan: Michigan State University Press, 1974.
    The four pupil personnel programs described on pages 223–394 give added understanding of roles and organizational patterns, and the role descriptions in pages 3–40 are unique in pointing out consulting and coordinating functions.
Hill, George E. *Management and Improvement of Guidance.* 2d ed. Englewood Cliffs, N.J.: Prentice-Hall, 1974.
    Chapter 7, "Definition of Guidance Functions of Teachers and Others," describes the teacher's role in detail, covers other staff members, and gives a helpful point of view about the part that parents and pupils can play.
Hosford, Ray E., and Ryan, T. Antoinette. "Systems Design in the Development of Counseling and Guidance Programs." *Personnel and Guidance Journal* 49, no. 3 (1970), pp. 221–230.
    An excellent presentation of the systems approach in building guidance programs. The discussion in this chapter utilizes concepts from this article.
Krumboltz, John D. "An Accountability Model for Counselors." *Personnel and Guidance Journal* 52, no. 10 (1974), pp. 639–646.
    An excellent discussion of the types of objectives needed in guidance and procedures for computing cost-effectiveness of services.

Morrill, Weston H.; Oetting, Eugene R.; and Hurst, James C. "Dimensions of Counselor Functioning." *Personnel and Guidance Journal* 52, no. 6 (1974), pp. 354–359.

The article that introduced the cube concept as a basis for guidance programs. Examples of application are given in other sections of the same Journal.

Peters, Herman J., and Shertzer, Bruce. *Guidance Program Development and Management*. 3rd ed. Columbus, Ohio: Charles E. Merrill, 1974.

An elementary school guidance program is described on pages 551–563 and a metropolitan school district on pages 564–575. Physical facilities and their effects are described on pages 477–487.

Rollins, Kenneth W. "Staff Roles and Relationships." *The Organization of Pupil Personnel Programs*, edited by Raymond N. Hatch, pp. 162–201. East Lansing, Mich.: Michigan State University Press, 1974.

A useful source on roles with a particularly good discussion on the part teachers can play in guidance.

Shaw, Merville C. *School Guidance Systems*. Boston: Houghton Mifflin, 1973. Chapter 3, "A General Model for Guidance Services."

Describes the generalist-specialist approach. The reading shows the potential of this well-designed model.

Shertzer, Bruce, and Stone, Shelley C. *Fundamentals of Guidance*. 3rd ed. Boston: Houghton Mifflin, 1976.

Another classification of guidance models is given in pages 67–84. The authors base their classification on general aims, e.g., "social reconstruction."

Tamminen, Armas; Gum, Moy; Smaby, Marlowe; and Peterson, Terrence. "Teacher-Advisors: Where There's a Skill There's a Way," *Personnel and Guidance Journal* 55, no. 1 (1976), pp. 39–42.

The article describes how counselors help teachers to develop skills leading to a more effective participation in the guidance program. It is an example of "giving guidance away."

CHAPTER SEVEN
FACE-TO-FACE COUNSELING
FOR INDIVIDUALS

This chapter is about the single most important function of the counselor—face-to-face work with individuals. Counseling is the service that puts the counselor's unique skills to best use and makes the greatest personal or professional demands.

The first section summarizes issues, problems, and trends in counseling. Next, comes a discussion of counseling strategies, followed by a review of the techniques whereby theories (which are in the main independent of techniques) are implemented. Regardless of your style of expressing yourself in a creative composition, you observe the rules of grammar. Similarly, with few exceptions, in counseling certain basic techniques apply.

GOALS

1. To understand the major new developments in the counselor's role.
2. To become aware of the variety and nature of approaches to helping.
3. To know how techniques contribute to the counseling process.

DEFINITIONS, EXAMPLES, AND TRENDS

Counseling is by no means a static concept; the way it is defined and implemented is undergoing significant change. Debates over its limits continue. One frequently expressed concern is its degree of similarity to psychotherapy; another is the question how counseling and guidance differ. These issues and others reviewed in this section will help acquaint you with professional concerns that have significant implications for career planning. If career and life-style are to harmonize, it is important to learn about and seriously consider these aspects in the early planning stage.

COUNSELING AND PSYCHOTHERAPY Similarities and differences between counseling and psychotherapy cause persistent concern. Some equate the two terms, but there are significant differences. The two most important involve the type of problem and level of adjustment of the counselee. Counseling is the process of helping relatively normal individuals develop, make decisions, and solve mild situational problems. Psychotherapy is assistance for individuals with deep-seated, long-term emotional problems that rate as severe and often debilitating. Psychotherapy is the typical work of the psychiatrist, the psychoanalyst, and the clinical psychologist. Still, the distinction is difficult to maintain; many writers use the terms synonomously, and it is true that quite often the psychiatrist is offering short-term help to relatively normal individuals and the counselor is providing a therapeutic experience for the counselee. Moreover, counselors draw on approaches and techniques from psychotherapy in working with counselees. But the difference is important both for day-to-day helping activities as well as for public relations. Many pupils find it easier to approach the counselor than a psychotherapist. Schools are more likely to support counseling services than psychotherapy.

PUPILS' PERCEPTIONS OF THE COUNSELOR'S ROLE Various people perceive the role of the counselor in different ways; these perceptions have a certain impact on the counseling-psychotherapy question. Regardless of their adjustment status, pupils seem to consider personal characteristics of helpers when requesting counseling (Larson and Rice 1967). The designated counselor is likely to be turned to in program planning; other types of problems are taken to different persons. These findings are in keeping with those of an earlier study in which pupils were found to select helpers in the school they perceived as beneficial regardless of their titles, and were also found to know very little about the persons designated as school guidance specialists (Tolbert 1947, pp. 119–120). Brough (1968) found no differences between ninth graders who requested counseling and those who did not. The evidence suggests that pupils prefer and use voluntary services. There is some indication that those who request counseling come from more affluent families and are more ambitious and success-oriented (Tseng and Thompson 1968). Socioeconomic status of pupils also affects their perceptions of counselors (Haettenschwiller 1969). Those of higher socioeconomic status, for example, have more expectation of respect from parents, teachers, and counselors. Pupils in general expect more empathy, respect, and concreteness from counselors than from parents, and girls anticipate more respect from parents, teachers, and counselors than did boys.

Obviously, the counselor can expect pupils to bring many personal preconceptions and preferences to the counseling session (those from higher socioeconomic levels, for example, are likely to be more positive), and they have little understanding of the counseling process and their part in it.

Certain preferences form definite patterns. Counselees tend to choose counselors of the same race (Riccio and Barnes 1973); race, subculture, and sex of the counselor are all important to black students. High school seniors have a much clearer perception of who could be of help with problems of social adjustment and religious and racial prejudice than do freshmen (Tolbert 1947). A common racial background does seem to facilitate the counselor's rapport in the first contact, but there is insufficient evidence to say that there is a compelling need for the counselor to belong to the same race as the counselee.

Counselees also have definite ideas about who they will turn to for what types of help. Rosen (1967) found that high school pupils consider school counselors fairly helpful with educational and vocational problems, but prefer not to take emotional problems to them. They prefer a directive type of counseling, but differences in personality and sex affect the choice of counselor. Pupils value appropriate and adequate information, understanding the purposes of counseling, interest, empathy, availability, and sensitivity to feelings and attitudes (Staudenmeier 1967). Males rate high the encouragement to speak, while females consider listening very effective counseling behavior.

The counselor-psychotherapy issue appears to be a factor in pupils' minds when they are asked to refer individuals with various sorts of problems. Heilfron's study (1960) demonstrates pupils' tendency to refer the obviously maladjusted to the counselor but to take no action for those needing developmental help.

SCHOOL STAFF MEMBERS' PERCEPTIONS OF THE COUNSELOR'S ROLE School administrators and teachers see the counselor's role quite differently than the counselor sees it. (Riese and Stoner 1969; Hart and Prince 1970). One of the major differences involves providing personal emotional counseling. Principals feel that counselors should share many of the clerical and noncounseling duties in the school. Even so, principals and counselors agree on the importance of the same functions, but disagree on their relative standing (Sweeny 1966). Both give services to individual students first priority, and place establishing and maintaining staff relationships second; counselors, however, rank community relationships third, while principals give that rank to promoting the school program. It does not appear that principals understand the work of the counselor (Boller 1973), and there appears to be a need for counselors to become more central to the school program (Haettenschwiller and Jabs 1969). Teachers and administrators apparently expect the counselor to be more active in classroom sessions and in summarizing and interpreting information for school use. Elementary teachers generally are positive about work with counselors, but see the function as mainly remedial (Masih 1969).

PARENTS' PERCEPTIONS OF COUNSELOR'S ROLE The school counselor typically ranks high in the eyes of parents; major suggestions tend to reflect a desire for more assistance for their children (Perrone, Weiking, and Nagel 1965). Junior high school parents are satisfied with work being done by counselors, ranking vocational help first, educational help second, and personal help third (Jacobs, Krogger, Lesar, and Redding 1971). They express the wish for more contacts with the counselor, both individually and in groups. In general, counselors have a base of support in parents and could further enhance status by more interactions with them.

COUNSELORS' PREFERENCES AND CONFLICTS It is not surprising that counselors' attitudes and preferences have an effect on how their role is implemented. Counselors must, of course, be sensitive to the effects of their attitudes on the perceptions of counselees. For example, counselors have ideal counselees from whom they expect greater progress; typically, these pupils are more like the counselor in personality, agree about the cause of the presenting problem, value counseling, and have better grades. Counselor biases about sex, age, race, and social class can prevent effective help. The better the counselor's understanding of the values and mores of minority and other special groups (e.g., the opposite sex, older persons) the more effective counseling is likely to be.

Counselors tend to value a personal-problem type of assistance, regardless of the needs of pupils. Warman's studies (1960) show that college counselors rate adjustment problems first, career problems second, and school-routine problems third. School counselors, however, rated career problems first in importance, school routine second, and adjustment third. These studies were done some time ago; it might be expected that upgrading the preparation for school counseling would result in preferences more like those of college counselors, and the literature on major intervention strategies seems to bear this supposition out. But as Leviton

(1977) points out, pupils have other expectations; they want help with career and educational problems. This is one of the areas of concern to prospective counselors—what type of help would they feel comfortable in providing? Is this preference in line with needs of pupils?

Another critical question for the counselor is the congruence of personal values and those espoused by the school. To what extent should the counselor adopt the values of the work setting? Rothney (1970) argues that counselors have a responsibility to conform to the standards of the employing institution, and takes issue with the attitude that they can follow their own philosophical orientation and social views, regardless of impact on others. But the secondary school is a conservative institution that changes slowly, and the needs of contemporary youth may not be met (Stubbins 1970). Moreover, the counselor experiences the conflict between the needs of the individual and the demands of the marketplace for salable skills (Brigante 1958). Wrenn (1970) brings up other ways that questions concerning values impinge on the counselor's work. Can counselors hold to their own values and yet enter into the world of the young people? Can they show they care for counselees as individuals and yet get involved in controlling their lives? Can a counselor continue to be a warm, accepting, helping person, and yet carry out the numerous demanding tasks required of the professional practitioner?

NEW COUNSELING ROLES

There is a wide range of opinions about the most appropriate role for the school counselor. Attempts to be all things to all people are futile; the counselor must establish a clear-cut, specific role (Kushel 1970). Suggestions involve new concepts as well as urging counselors to adopt a specific approach. The model of the human-development consultant or applied-behavioral-scientist is one option (Berdie 1972; Seidman and others 1970). This new worker would replace counselors and would use behavioral-science theory and research to improve individual and institutional efficiency. The role resembles that of the child development consultant, a new role in the elementary school.

Another way of clarifying the role is to emphasize the counseling function. Brammer (1968) suggests that the counselor drop guidance activities and concentrate on psychological counseling. Felix (1968), however, characterizes the school worker's duties as primarily educational and argues for noncounseling guidance activities. Their controversy triggered many responses, pro and con (Easton and Resnikoff 1969; Hopkins 1969; Wyatt 1969; Dash 1969). A related question is the therapeutic v. the school-counseling model. Aubrey (1969) takes issue with the school use of therapy and recommends attention to the sociological factors in the school and strategies to change the educational setting over intensive treatment of individual pupils. This position, too, evoked many responses, which attests to its significance (Call 1970; Jones 1970; Keefe 1970).

Roles are intimately related to the program models described in Chapter 6, and the merits of counseling v. other interventions should be considered from the standpoint of utility. Individual counseling is one type of intervention. If others are needed, as the cube and generalist-specialist models suggest, then obviously the counselor's role must embrace a wide range of interventions. This expansion appears to be taking place as new treatment methods are developed.

A new model is emerging that combines elements of formerly disparate roles; the major feature is the use of psychological principles as the base for a variety of approaches including counseling, consulting, and teaching. Pine (1975) argues that this is the model needed to maintain counseling as a viable service in schools. Major emphasis is on giving school counseling away to teachers and others who work face-to-face with students, and helping them respond to pupils' feelings. The counselor is thus a consultant, a trainer, and a psychological educator whose function is to help pupils, parents, teachers, families, and members of the community make use of helping techniques. The counselor also functions as ombudsman and agent for change, with problems of racism, sexism, and social injustice, using a wide variety of strategies such as values clarification, human development training, peer counseling, family counseling and education, organizational development, and community development (Becvar and Dustin 1974).

These new functions enjoy wide support in the profession. Ciavarella and Doolittle (1970) advocate the role of ombudsman—someone who will listen to the pupil's complaint and take action by helping or making efforts to change the institution. This activist role would make the counselor an advocate for civil liberties (Lewis and Lewis 1970) and lead to the proactive role (Becvar and Dustin 1974). Such developments represent a shift to a more active and assertive role (Carkhuff and Berenson 1969).

Action orientation and outreach are major strategies by which the counselor may have an impact on the environment. Starting with a study of the effects of the school and community, more productive and positive environments are designed (Conyne 1975). Blocher (1974) describes this as the "ecological" approach, because it deals not only with the student potential, but enhances it by improving their various environments—the school, community, and home. Building constructive learning environments is a high priority task.

The term "change agent" is an older role-concept recommended for counselors (Warnath 1973). As Cook (1972) points out, counselors have avoided the role, as it involves risk. But the role can be implemented both through serving as a student advocate and through helping to modify the organization to meet students' goals. Student advocacy is more in line with the counseling and ombudsman functions than the civil liberties role.

Outreach is another major trend (Lipsman 1969). New techniques and strategies — e.g., peer counseling (Drum and Figger 1973), behavior modification (Toews 1969), building coping skills, and changing the social system (Lipsman 1969)—provide the tools the counselor needs. But opinions differ about suitability of such new ways of changing behavior as behavior modification (Lane 1970; Lifton 1969).

Career counseling and guidance have regained status in recent years because of career education and a new recognition that career counseling involves the total person rather than a superficial consideration of test scores and occupational information (Dolliver and Nelson 1975). Moreover, the report by Christopher Jencks (*Inequality: A Reassessment of the Effect of Family and Schooling in America*, 1972) leads Menacker (1975) to suggest new developments in career counseling to expand and make more active the role of the counselor, and to give added importance to the counselee's family and peers. Out-of-school variables are becoming more important (Giddan and Price 1975). This expanded concept of career guidance and counseling incorporates aspects of the role of change agent and elements of outreach, consulting, and action strategy.

The trend in evaluation, quite appropriately, is on counselee accomplishments, rather than counselor duties. All types of services are used to help the counselee reach goals mutually agreed-on. The approach reflects the trend toward a clearer specification of what counseling is supposed to do and how well it accomplishes its objectives.

Many of the new emphases already described are similar to those of the 1973 Vail Conference on professional psychology (Ivey and Leppaluoto 1975). The recommendations of the conference, which supports developments already under way and introduces new ones, are likely to have a significant impact on school counseling. For example, the report emphasizes the need to espouse values and attitudes that enhance society; counselors need to work for a society responsive to people's needs, and greater attention is going to the practitioner (as opposed to the practitioner-scientist). A major emphasis is on an active role in which the counselor participates in institutional changes, provides services to large groups, and has an impact on local institutions and the community. These recommendations sharply contrast with the older focus on one-to-one, self-initiated help, and it has been suggested that the new concepts outlined at the conference would justify creating an Association for Human Development within the American Personnel and Guidance Association.

RESEARCH

COUNSELORS AS CHANGE AGENTS

While counselors are urged to incorporate the change-agent function into their role, research shows mixed reactions to the advice. Baker and Hansen (1972) used an attitude inventory to measure counselors' preferences for roles ranging from maintaining the status quo to acting as a change agent. The 473 subjects included 251 employed school counselors and 222 students in counselor preparation programs. (Although subjects came from all parts of the country, sampling was not random; generalizations should therefore be made with caution.)

The inventory provided for six responses for each of the twenty items. Response 1 strongly favored the status quo while Response 6 strongly supported the position of change agent. Intermediate positions fell in between. Partial results are as follows:

Responses	Practicing Counselors (in percentages)	Counselor Trainees (in percentages)
1. Strong status quo	0	1
2. Interested in helping counselee but not in changing status quo	2	2
3. Preference for helping counselee adjust to the situation	12	11
4. Preference for helping counselee change conditions	59	62
5. Interested in change, and will help counselee find sources of help	16	15
6. Interested in change and wants actually to participate in bringing it about	11	9

Counselors and students showed a strong preference for assisting the counselee to make changes rather than taking on this role responsibility themselves. Though the students were younger, their responses are very similar to practicing counselors, suggesting that the reluctance for serving as a change agent is not a function of age.

Consulting involves changing attitudes, and is an established function at the elementary school level. Splete's study (1971) involved elementary school teachers' opinions of effective and ineffective counselor behaviors in helping teachers to better understand themselves and pupils. Two results are particularly relevant here.

1. Both teachers and counselors reported more examples of effective consultation in helping teachers understand pupils than in understanding themselves. Results were significant at the .01 level.
2. Both teachers and counselors perceived the elementary school counselor as more effective than ineffective in a consulting relationship with teachers.

Other research reported in Carlson, Splete, and Kern (1975) and in Chapter 9 give additional evidence that the counselor can help to improve the social environment through consultation.

EXPERIENCE

ROLES

Write out the roles that appear below and have members of a small group select one each without revealing the choice. Then go around the group with each member explaining in a minute or less how to help the pupil described below. At the conclusion ask members to describe their feelings about the helping procedure.

Roles:

1. Counselor X—A record keeper and program adviser. Stays in office and can quickly provide up-to-date data on students. Knows a great deal about the school and is in good standing with the faculty.
2. Counselor Y—An individual therapist. Believes in one-to-one work emphasizing feelings. Has been very effective with difficult cases. Prefers to handle problems without conferring with others.
3. Counselor Z—Gives counseling away. Works with teachers, administration and parents. Provides direct individual and small group help only if needed. Prefers to get others involved in the helping process. Sometimes difficult to find.

The pupil:

A high school freshman who is having a great deal of difficulty with school subjects. Parents are separated, and he lives with each for a period of time. Recently he has been skipping school, and there are rumors that he is using drugs. Both parents express concern, but say they don't have time to come to the school for a conference.

EXPERIENCE

ROLES AND REWARDS

You have worked in the school for about a year along with three other counselors who have been employed for a much longer time. By now you know that Counselor X (from the previous exercise) has received the greatest salary increases, Counselor Y, smaller ones, and Counselor Z the lowest. You are trying to decide whose pattern you will follow.

What is your decision? Why?

If small groups are used, ask each group to come up with a ranking. Then discuss reasons and factors considered in the task.

OBJECTIVES

1. To be able to identify ways in which the counselor's role has expanded in recent years. Name three aspects that take the counselor out of the office.

The major ones covered in this chapter are outreach, work as a change agent, and psychological education.

2. To realize the significance of the concept of "giving counseling away." Identify one item that could be given away and name two potential recipients.

Practically any guidance and counseling technique could be given to others who could put it to good use. A particularly effective one would be listening for and responding to the feelings expressed by another person.

POINTS OF VIEW ABOUT COUNSELING

A counseling point of view is a set of principles that guide the counselor's work and is the basis for choosing techniques. Other terms can be used, e.g., theory, orientation, system, school, or approach. All mean the same thing, although "theory" implies to some experts something more comprehensive and rigorous than a counseling point of view.

Theories (points of view) are sometimes thought to be impractical ("Once I began work, I had to forget all that theory!"). The attitude is wrong; a good theory is the most practical part of the counselor's preparation. It provides the road map that shows where one is going and how to get there. It justifies the counselor's activities and provides a basis for predicting effects. To operate as a professional without a theory is dangerous and unethical.

Negative feelings about points of view may arise from resistance to the need to adopt a particular theory. But a counselor's rationale is highly individual and involves personal characteristics, elements of formal positions, and preferences (Ratigan 1967, p. 139; Shoben 1962). Very likely no single specific point of view given here will suit you "as is," and you

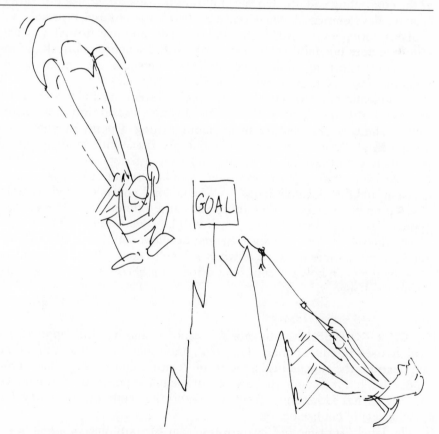

No one counseling method is indisputably the best. It is the counselor's prerogative to choose one approach or combine several.

may wish to combine parts of various approaches, using, for example, an approach like Ponzo's (1976). He divides the counseling process into stages (e.g., awareness of the problem), and adapts aspects of five of the approaches discussed here to facilitate counselee progress. But learning about approaches is a necessary first step in developing a personal style.

Regardless of points of view, effective counselors tend to be very much alike in the ways they help and relate to others (Combs and Soper 1963; Fiedler 1950b; La Crosse and Barak 1976). While research has dealt more with therapeutic practice, it is reasonable to assume and there is evidence to support the position that the same is true for school counselors.

Depending on who is writing or talking, the number of counseling points of view ranges from three or four to twenty or thirty. Twelve which are of importance, directly or indirectly, to the school counselor are arranged here on a continuum from counseling to psychotherapy. Starting at the counseling end, the list is as follows: trait-factor, decision-making, eclectic, developmental, behavioral, reality, client-centered, transactional analysis, rational-emotive, existential, Gestalt, and psychoanalysis. The sequence does not indicate degree of use in the school; practically all of these approaches, in complete or modified versions, are employed by school counselors at one time or another.

The eclectic point of view constitutes a systematic and widely used approach, although agreement on this position is certainly not unanimous. There is also disagreement about calling a point of view "developmental"—the term is more frequently used with guidance. It is possible to group several approaches under more general headings; cognitive decision making, for example, would include the trait-factor, decision making, developmental, and behavioral points of view. To help develop an awareness of the similarities and differences of the various approaches to helping, however, each will be considered separately.

The theories of learning and personal development discussed in Chapter 5 are the sources of much of what is done in counseling. The focus in this chapter is on how the counselor utilizes the theories in helping counselees to change.

TRAIT-FACTOR COUNSELING   In one variation or another this approach is widely used in educational, placement, and rehabilitation settings. One application, the mechanical process of "testing and telling," has come under fire, but it is, none the less, one of the major points of view covered in reviews, has a long and respectable history, and contains much of value for the school counselor.

The label "trait-factor" has always been to some degree a pejorative misnomer. A more suitable term would convey that the approach is scientific, systematic, instructional, largely cognitive, and leads to choice, also indicating the important role given to affect and values. It has been described as mechanical and factual, but Williamson (1965, p. 203) makes clear that the approach does include the personal and emotional aspects of helping. Major emphasis is put upon attaining the "good life," involving happiness through the productive use of potential for personal and social improvement.

The approach rests on the assumptions that individuals with adequate information can make logical, rational decisions; that the traits of individuals differ measurably; and that educational and occupational settings require differential levels of such traits as verbal intelligence or mechanical understanding.

Trait-factor counselors employ a sequence of five steps, starting with identifying the reason for counseling and ending with a check on the suitability of plans. The first step, analysis, involves collecting all sorts of data about the individual and may be done in part before the first interview. The interview itself, however, provides essential data about attitudes, motivations, conflicts, and goals.

The second step, synthesis, is a process of organizing data and inferring meaning, detecting patterns, and identifying strengths, potential, weaknesses, and problems. Success in this step depends upon the adequacy of the analysis phase.

Diagnosis follows; the problem is identified, causes are ferreted out, and a prognosis is made about the likelihood of success of problem-solving strategies. Diagnosis is a cooperative process in which the counselee takes an active part.

Counseling, the fourth step, follows next. It may emphasize teaching new ways of behaving, helping to utilize information in decision making, formulating steps to solve problems—it is the cooperative activity that leads to planning and learning an approach to problem solving.

Finally, there is the fifth step, the follow-up. As the name implies, it is a check on how well plans have worked out and whether or not additional assistance is needed.

While newer models of school counseling emphasize affective elements and play down the use of diagnostic data (e.g., cumulative records), this point of view is useful to many counselees in the school, particularly in educational and career planning. It clearly makes the counselor an "expert" (with respect to assessment, diagnostic interviewing, career and other information, and in techniques of cooperative planning).

DECISION-MAKING COUNSELING   While practically all theories include this element, decision making derived from economic decision theory and psychological studies of the decision process amounts to a unique counseling approach not only for educational and career assistance, but for the whole gamut of problems faced by the high school counselor. It is some-what similar to the trait-factor approach because it incorporates a sys-tematic decision-making process that provides a framework for the coun-selor's work.

Both group and individual counseling may be based on this approach; this point of view is adaptable to a great variety of situations (e.g., classroom-size groups, orientation, packaged programs, and computer guidance systems). It uses the framework of a decision process such as Gelatt's model (1962) in which a strategy is used to help counselees solve problems, prepare to meet needs, and learn a process that will serve them in future situations. The actual techniques are the same as those used in other approaches—providing information, assembling data about abili-ties, reflection of feeling, inventorying of values, and use of the core facilitative conditions (see next section).

This approach, developed by Gelatt, Varenhorst, and Carey is used in *Deciding* (1972). The group process begins by helping pupils identify values and then goes into locating and using information and identifying alternatives. Next, pupils are helped to examine how much risk they will accept. Finally, pupils review strategies for achieving goals. *Deciding* exemplifies a group application of a decision model.

Two new programs have been developed. One, for teenagers, older stu-dents and adults, is *Decision and Outcomes* (Gelatt, Varenhorst, Carey, and Miller 1973); the other, for women, is *How to Decide* (Scholz, Prince, and Miller 1975). All three programs are somewhat along the lines of the decision model described by Gelatt (1962; 1967, pp. 101–114) and sum-marized above.

Other decision-making theories emphasizing different processes have been developed; each provides a framework for counseling (Tolbert 1974, pp. 68–69). Several provide rationales for computer programs that enable the counselee to move through the decision process step by step.

ECLECTIC COUNSELING   This often maligned approach to counseling mixes elements from many other points of view. Patterson's definition clarifies the confusion that has typically been associated with the term:

Eclecticism differs from theoretical positions of schools or cults, in that, on the one hand, it is more comprehensive, attempting to integrate or synthesize the valid or demonstrated elements of these narrower or more restricted theories, and, on the other hand, it is a more open-ended, loose, or tentative theoretical position (1973, p. 461).

Thorne (1973) takes basically the same position, particularly emphasizing the openness to revision and the importance of the unique features of the particular case in adapting counseling strategies. All writers agree that the critical aspects are to determine the causes of problems and to select the most appropriate helping strategies.

The eclectic approach is more widely subscribed to than is apparent, and has much to offer school counselors because of its adaptability, utilization of new research and theory, and suitability for the new functions of the school counselor.

It is difficult to define eclecticism in a universally acceptable way and equally hard to define an eclectic counselor. Still, Tyler (1958; 1960; 1969) and Ratigan (1967; 1972) are certainly two counselors who can be identified as eclectic. Tyler's method of building a personal theory from social sciences, religion, and personal experience, in order to help a wide variety of clients implies that she agrees. Ponzo (1976) takes an eclectic position in a carefully developed statement of how he forges his helping theory. There are others; Patterson (1973; p. 462) reports that in the 25-year period from 1945 to 1970, the percentage of members of the APA's Division of Clinical Psychology who identified themselves as eclectic rose from zero to about 50 percent. A similar trend in school counselors' preferences can be inferred.

There is considerable value in the eclectic position, provided it is more than indiscriminate picking and choosing. Eclecticism promotes an openness to new research findings and new theorizing, in addition to being well-suited for incorporating the insights arising from daily experience. An eclectic approach can make use of learning theory, career development theory, sociology, economics, and decision making; developmental tasks can be used for goal setting. A useful major emphasis can be placed on generalizing accomplishments in counseling to daily life (e.g., homework involving exploratory and tryout experiences), on the assumption that real growth must take place in the counselee's own daily environment (Tolbert 1959, pp. 156–178; 1972, pp. 95–107; 1974, 75–76, 165–174; 192–199).

There are important counselor characteristics that cut across various approaches. Understanding these basic characteristics (e.g., caring, experiencing), the eclectic counselor varies them to fit the needs of different counselees (Brammer 1969). While providing a relationship that involves acceptance, understanding, and sincerity, the counselor intervenes with strategies that directly respond to counselee needs. Thus, information may be provided, assessment may be used, and tryout activities may be utilized. Typically, the initial counseling contacts are used to explore feelings and to identify problems and needs. Later, there is usually more emphasis on setting up objectives, deciding on alternatives, and planning reality-testing experiences.

Eclecticism is a different matter for the psychotherapist with an affluent clientele and the school counselor with a heterogeneous group to serve. The cases a psychotherapist takes on may run for months, but the school counselor may have five minutes in the hall between classes with the pupil who expresses irritation at a teacher, or be involved in long sessions with a troubled and angry potential dropout (Shoben 1969). Would concepts developed in long-term therapeutic relationships be useful to the counselor? The answer is yes, although obviously extensive adaptations must be made. In a sense, every counselor is an eclectic. "Freud was a Freudian and Rogers a Rogerian . . ." (Brammer 1969, p. 193) because of personal experiences and preferences. No one can exactly duplicate someone else's approach.

DEVELOPMENTAL COUNSELING   This approach is among those that come closest to the day-to-day work of the school counselor. It is in line with school counseling policy statements about a developmental emphasis in grades K through 12; it is appropriate for the career, educational, social, and personal needs that arise; and is well suited for brief on-the-scene contacts as well as more formal ones in the counselor's office. It also serves as a rationale for group as well as individual counseling.

Developmental counseling is difficult to define as a specific, unique approach, and some writers do not even include it in lists of counseling theories (Arbuckle 1974; Stefflre and Grant 1972; Stefflre 1965). However, a significant number do (Dinkmeyer 1971; Peters 1970, pp. 43–58; Tolbert 1972, pp. 75–76). The main features of this point of view show convincingly that it has a great deal of relevance for school counseling. Central concepts are its basis in developmental tasks, its use of counselees' own strengths and effective ways of coping, and its continuance until new behaviors are mastered or decisions are tried out. A typical developmental task, getting along with peers (Dinkmeyer 1971, p. 248), shows the importance of anticipating problems rather than waiting for them to emerge. Its theme is to develop effective ways of coping and building commitment to new and productive ways of thinking, feeling, and acting. The actual process of working with a counselee or leading a group utilizes techniques that show acceptance, understanding, and interest. Counselor and counselee(s) work together as active collaborators, with the latter experiencing enough dissonance to stimulate new learning without being overwhelmed by outside pressures and anxiety.

Peters (1970, pp. 43–52) gives a lucid explanation of the process, using five conditions that must be satisfied. These are *dimensionality* (level of concern, based on the seriousness or complexity of the problem); *mutuality of participation, movement, searching,* and *follow-through*. Peters' subject is individual counseling, but the model can be applied to group counseling; mutuality can be a condition among a counselor and a small group of counselees who are sharing feelings and dealing face-to-face, openly, and honestly with each other. The individual or group could be more concerned about some specific information (e.g., college entrance requirements or facts about effects of drugs). The dimensionality might then be at what Peters calls the "directional level"; the counselee needs information for decision making. Movement relates to progress (e.g., in learning a new behavior), but primarily it refers to achieving feelings of fulfillment. Searching involves finding ways to meet needs, regardless of their nature (e.g., developing self-understanding, learning to communicate more effectively).

Help for career development fits quite naturally within this approach. Recent research and theory provide support for strategies that recognize stages in development and help pupils get ready for tasks they will soon encounter (see Chapter 5).

A career involves the lifelong series of experiences in education and work. It is more than the jobs held, and includes the life-style of which the occupation tends to be the central focus. Thus, counseling involves the total person and deals with both cognitive and affective material.

The major career-development concepts for a counseling point of view are choice as a developmental process; developmental stages in which specific career behaviors should appear; vocational maturity; translating the self concept into a work-self concept; and career patterns. The individual goes through a series of developmental stages, each of which involves characteristic behaviors and tasks. Career maturity, like social or other types, gives an indication of how far individuals have progressed and how they stand in relation to peers in such areas as learning about occupations, realizing the need to make decisions about work, and personal attributes that can be utilized in planning.

Career patterns reveal the sequences of occupations; preparation; exit from and entry into the world of work; and advancements or regressions for individuals or groups of individuals. These data provide useful guidelines for career planning. The counselor takes all these aspects into account in designing helping strategies. The individual needs realistic information about work settings and life-styles of occupational groups. Self-understanding, particularly with respect to values and goals, is essential. The counselor thus may help individual or groups understand and master developmental tasks, give appropriate weight to factors in decision making, test reality in work settings, and carry out plans.

Career-development counseling makes use of facilitative techniques very much as other approaches do, but it employs them in the framework of career-development theory (e.g., to help the counselee discover ways to implement the self concept in work).

BEHAVIORAL COUNSELING This point of view of counseling, clearly illustrating the application of learning principles to the helping relationship, has experienced tremendous growth in the past few years. It is covered in one form or another in most publications on the theories of counseling and psychotherapy; it has applications in settings ranging from the elementary school to community clinics. It is also the basis for a book and a series of eight films recently put out by the American Personnel and Guidance Association (Hosford and de Visser 1974). It is not the only approach portrayed on film, but the process is alone in being the subject of a book keyed to a series of explanatory films. The presentation has been described as a "revolution" in the counseling profession (Hosford 1969, p. 1).

"Behavioral" is a term that can be applied to both counseling and psychotherapy and actually involves a wide variety of different but closely related approaches (Patterson 1973, pp. 83–84). Psychotherapeutic methods have been developed to work with all sorts of neuroses and psychoses (O'Leary and Wilson 1975). Counseling applications cover a wide range of activities such as conditioning (both classical and operant), modeling, and behavior modification. The behavioral approach has wide application in school situations and appears to be gaining acceptance in individual counseling, group work, and in the classroom. Interestingly enough, college students expressed a preference for this type of counseling over others when given the choice after listening to tapes of various counseling approaches.

The basic assumption is that behavior is learned; thus old behaviors can be unlearned and new behaviors can be mastered. Counselors employ various learning strategies to assist the counselee in mastering new and desired behavior. The goal of counseling is usually stated in specific terms so that progress may be assessed and methods for reaching it may be planned. The counselor then decides which strategy is likely to be the most effective. Hosford and de Visser (1974, p. 23) divide the process into six steps. First, the problem is identified. A counselor may use various types of learning techniques (e.g., reinforcement) to motivate the counselee to bring out needed information. The problem must be specified in behavioral terms and important reinforcers identified (p. 49).

Next, counseling goals are formulated; the counselee decides on a desired course of action. Goals must be in specific terms so that it will be possible to specify what is to be learned, under what conditions it will be demonstrated, and what it will achieve (p. 65).

The third step (pp. 80–81) is to identify the counselee's status with respect to the desired goal. This information helps in setting up a strategy and gives a base for estimating progress. For example, if the counselee wants to develop positive feelings toward peers and classmates it would make quite a difference in the strategy if at the beginning of counseling the person were very hostile and withdrawn rather than moderately outgoing.

The next step is to select and carry out a counseling strategy for reaching the goal (pp. 96–97). Typical ones involve operant and classical conditioning, social modeling, or assertiveness training. There are others, but these are the major types.

Next, there is an evaluation of success in reaching the goal. Since it has been stated in specific terms including levels of performance, evaluation is relatively easy. The last and final step involves termination of counseling; if the goal has not been reached, however, the whole process may be repeated. There may even be a need to further identify the problem.

The behavioral point of view has strong supporters and equally strong critics. Detractors often assert that the behavioral therapist or counselor is a manipulator, not concerned with the quality of the therapeutic relationship, who takes responsibility away from the counselee. Supporters reply that the relationship is extremely important and that rapport is considered essential. They insist further that the counselee has a choice in setting goals; after all, it is the counselee who comes and requests help in achieving a desired objective and there is no compulsion to undergo behavior modification.

There are numerous examples of effective use of the approach. Career counseling is one (Woody 1968; Krumboltz and Baker 1973, pp. 235, 283). Successful results have been obtained with juvenile delinquents (Sarason 1968). Behavior modification is widely used in schools, for example, by reinforcing pupils for improved behavior (Vannote 1974). Groups using reinforcement techniques to improve study habits have been shown to be more successful than discussion groups (Harris and Trujillo 1975). Learning theory utilizing reinforcement and modeling can be used to teach disruptive children new productive skills to gain rewards from teachers and classmates (De Voe and Sherman 1975). Other programs have used behavior modification to effect positive change in pupils through positive reinforcement, a token economy, modeling, and systematic desensitization (Stolz, Wienckowski, and Brown 1975). Many applications have been made in elementary school. In one example the counselor and teacher used a reinforcement schedule to strengthen positive behavior and reduce negative responses. After setting up a baseline, the procedure was tried and disruptive behavior was sharply reduced; positive behavior increased (Englehardt, Sulzer, and Alterkruse 1971).

REALITY THERAPY   The term "therapy" is typically used in this point of view although it is not necessarily limited to individuals with emotional problems. It might, for example, be used with high school pupils both in groups and individual settings for a wide variety of behavior problems, personal difficulties, and decision-making tasks. Most use, however, has been with young (incarcerated) delinquents whose need to face reality is very apparent.

Reality therapy is very much like behavioral counseling with one major difference—the individuals in therapy are held responsible for their behavior (Arbuckle 1974). Learning theory is used, and the counselee is taught new and more productive and appropriate behavior (as determined by the therapist). For example, the young, incarcerated delinquent who gets in fights with fellow inmates and rebels against regulations will be told that such behaviors are irresponsible; consequences will be pointed out, and the therapist's ideas of appropriate behavior will be described. If the new behaviors are not learned, the consequences must be accepted. If they are mastered, however, rewards will be forthcoming.

This therapy is based on the idea that the most important human need is to attain a success identity. To achieve this identity, an individual must feel loved and of personal value. Each person can choose; responsible choices lead to the success identity. On the other hand the individual can choose a failure identity by engaging in activities that do not lead to love and a sense of self-worth. The results are pain, disappointment, and feelings of rejection.

The fact is made clear that the individual has a choice, and can choose to flaunt the reality of the situation. But the approach also underscores personal responsibility for one's actions. The therapist decides which new behaviors will provide reward and thus be reinforcing. Usually the established goals are in keeping with the realities of society. The therapeutic process requires a close counselor-counselee working relationship that focuses on present behavior rather than an examination of the past. Assigning a value to the present behavior, counselees must decide whether they want to change. If so, a plan is developed for positive actions to attain the goal of a success identity. Commitment is necessary and counselees must take responsibility for actions. The counselor neither accepts excuses nor punishes for failure to carry out commitments (Wubbolding 1975). But the climate is far from unfeeling; the counselor communicates caring, understanding, and warmth (Glasser and Zunin 1973, p. 298).

The approach has considerable merit for applications in a variety of situations with high school pupils and those in other grade levels. Successful programs to teach the method to counselors and teachers have been reported (Wubbolding 1975). Anxiety problems, marital conflicts, and perversions have been treated by this approach. In fact, Glasser and Zunin (1973, p. 308) recommend reality therapy for any problems faced by individuals or groups, even those national in scope.

CLIENT-CENTERED COUNSELING Only a few years ago the guidance profession was preoccupied with the great debate about the relative merits of directive v. nondirective counseling. The debate still surfaces in various disguised ways, but the terms have disappeared. Now we hear about other conflicts, e.g., humanism v. reinforcement. The nondirective approach of Rogers that appeared in the 40s (Rogers 1942; Rogers and Wallen 1946), called "client-centered," probably has had a greater impact on school counseling than any single other factor (including accountability, NDEA institutes, or any others.) It is given a place of prominence in publications on counseling and therapy (Patterson 1969, 1973; Grummon 1965, 1972; Meador and Rogers 1973). It is one of the major approaches you will encounter in preparation and work.

This counseling approach is based on a theory of personality that views the individual as in a process of becoming, growing, achieving worth and dignity, and seeking to actualize potential (Patterson 1969, 1973; Meador and Rogers 1973). Maintenance and enhancement of the self are the overriding concerns in a person's life. The individual's own perceptions of his or her world, not someone else's are reality.

The personality theory grew out of the therapy experience (Rogers 1951, pp. 481–483). Recordings of counselor-counselee interactions were analyzed and patterns and themes were detected that gave support to the theory's explanation of behavior and the processes individuals use to solve problems.

As enhancement of the self is a basic process of growth and development, threats to it, such as lack of love or lack of positive regard, arouse defenses that tend to distort reality and arouse anxiety. Excessive threat causes a breakdown in defenses and results in emotional disturbances.

Therapy is aimed at helping the individual utilize growth potential in the drive toward self-actualization. The therapist supplies the necessary and sufficient conditions for positive change, positive regard, empathy, and genuineness (Patterson 1973, pp. 388–389). Reflection of feeling is the primary technique used, but the emphasis is on building a relationship that is accepting, safe, and understanding. Empathy is considered to be the most potent of all counselor qualities (Rogers 1975, p. 3). Because of the relationship, the counselee can identify and look at threat, adjust perceptions, and carry out self-exploration to understand values, needs, and beliefs. Self-exploration, usually negative at first, leads individuals to trust their own perceptions more fully, to become more actualized, and to make fuller use of potential.

Other types of assistance, such as providing information, are not part of the therapeutic process (Patterson 1969, pp. 9–10, 21). Therapy, by definition, applies only to the process of interaction for self-exploration; by freeing potential, therapy enables the client to take positive action to find the information.

The counselor does not direct, manipulate, or control. Responsibility for what to discuss, goals to be reached, and decisions about the length of therapy rests with the counselee (Arbuckle 1974). A facilitative human relation is provided; positive growth results.

Rogers has recently been more involved in encounter group work than individual counseling. The approach serves quite well as a basis for group work, and his concepts of facilitative conditions have been utilized by Carkhuff, Truax, and others in building training and research models (Calia 1974).

How applicable is this approach to school counseling? Opinions differ, but there has been an extensive adaptation of the basic attitudes, techniques, and particularly the facilitative conditions for counselor preparation and work. While the fairly lengthy process implied by this point of view may often not be possible with the day-to-day demands in the school setting, adaptations are useful for counselors as they develop their own unique styles.

TRANSACTIONAL ANALYSIS (TA) This method of therapy has achieved phenomenal visibility in recent years. Next to encounter and sensitivity groups, it is probably one of the best known psychological innovations. The expressions "games people play," and "I'm O.K.—You're O.K.," for example, have their origin in this theory.

TA is a group approach (Harris 1969) with its own vocabulary. The interaction of group members is an essential part of the process, but TA is therapy in a group rather than group therapy. It is based on interactions between persons, the roles they take in these interactions, and the needs they display. The transaction is an exchange between two people (an action and a reaction, or a statement and a reply). Each transaction is based on one of three roles: parent, adult, or child (Harris 1969, pp. 16, 36). The parent role embodies the "shoulds" and "oughts" and rules derived from early interaction with parents. The child reflects smallness, dependence, clumsiness, and helplessness. The adult is a computer (Harris 1969, p. 30) using data from the child, parent, and adult to determine the best response in the present situation. The concept of "strokes" is involved in either positive or negative responses from other people; everyone needs them. In fact, people "play games" to obtain strokes.

There are four positions in which a person may visualize himself (Harris 1969, p. 43). Each consists of classifying oneself and the other person as "O.K." or "not O.K." Each person has a life script that he or she plays out to demonstrate one of these roles. "I'm O.K.—You're O.K.," is the most desirable of the four positions. The therapeutic process analyzes transactions. The objective is to base more and more transactions on the adult role.

The approach was developed by Eric Berne (Holland 1973, pp. 356–357) as a theory of personality development and group treatment. "Script analysis," an investigation of life dramas that persons play, is the means used to free them from irrational decisions based on fixed scripts. For example, some people may have to be liked by everyone in order to feel "O.K."

The treatment was originally developed for psychiatric populations but has wide applicability. It has been employed to help college students in career planning by analyzing scripts and determining roles for realistic planning (Kurtz 1974). Teachers have been helped to understand the roles they are playing in order to develop more positive opinions of themselves (Hannaford 1974). It has been used with adolescents who are having difficulties with teachers, peers, and parents (Hipple, Muto 1974). Some critics accuse TA of promoting sex stereotypes; for example, qualities considered "feminine" in the TA context seem to resemble those of a child, and include little of the decision-making qualities of the adult (Roney 1975). Holland (1973, p. 398), however, see effects as positive and the approach as useful in practically any situation where psychological principles may be applied.

RATIONAL-EMOTIVE THERAPY (RET)   This is another therapy-type of treatment widely used in schools and colleges. Often a counselor will say, "I used some RET to help the client look at what he's telling himself." Applications to school counseling are based on the assumption that the approach is essentially educational rather than medical, suitable for treating relatively normal persons, and useful for individuals experiencing problems, conflicts, and needs that are part of growing to maturity (Protinsky 1976; Ellis 1975b).

This point of view is recommended for individuals and groups, from elementary school age to older persons. The originator of RET sees it as valuable for working with teachers and parents, as well as pupils (Ellis 1975).

Although some counselors consider the approach to be uncaring and to ignore the individual's feelings, proponents argue that RET incorporates techniques from other approaches to provide the facilitative core conditions. Clients are accepted and supported regardless of their negative feelings or resistance to the therapist (Ellis 1975). But the therapist does at times push the individual to bring out and look at ideas that cause problems.

"Problems" are defined quite simply as an individual's irrational ideas. It was thought earlier that since they are so universal, they are innate; the current position is that they arise from home, family, and social development (Ellis 1975b). The aim of the therapy is to rid the client of these irrational ideas.

The approach is based on the assumptions that emotions result from thinking. Rational thinking results in good feelings; irrational thinking causes pain and unhappiness (Patterson 1966, p. 109; 1973, pp. 51–52). An *ABCDE* model may be used. *A* is the activating event; irrational thinking results in internal verbalization. For example, the pupil may say to himself, "I must have perfect grades to be good." This is an irrational idea, and therapy helps to bring it out.

B, the belief system, may contain both rational and irrational thoughts, but the one used by the individual is irrational. (It would be rational enough, of course, to be disappointed by failure, but not to consider oneself worthless!) *C* represents the painful emotions resulting from the irrational belief system. The *D* stage is the therapist's efforts (e.g., confronting, teaching, explaining) to get the individual to face the irrational self-talk and replace it with rational thinking (Protinsky 1976). For example, the therapist might urge the client to look at the sentence, "To be less than perfect means I'm worthless." The therapist might dispute the sentence, question why it is so, and ask from whom it was derived.

E, the final step, is the formulation of more effective and rational goals for the future. The client now has replaced the irrational thoughts in the belief system, e.g., can now say, "I failed that program and I'm disappointed, but I can do other things well."

EXISTENTIAL COUNSELING   As a philosophy or attitude about school counseling this point of view has had considerable impact, but its theory and techniques are not greatly in evidence (Patterson 1973, p. 424). The relationship of intimacy—what Arbuckle calls "human to human sharing" (1974, p. 216)—is the essence. Beyond this the counselor may employ all sorts of techniques (e.g., reflecting, confronting, giving information).

A major facet of the approach with considerable appeal relates to freedom and responsibility (Brown and Herrnstein 1975). Individuals have some degree of free will. They choose to be what they are and are responsible for what they become (Patterson 1973, p. 431). Thus counselors care about their counselees, but do not attempt to interfere with their freedom and responsibility.

Another major emphasis is on the concept of "being-in-world" (Brown and Herrnstein 1975, p. 564; Kemp 1971, p. 10). A person's being extends beyond bodily boundaries and involves all personal concerns. Thus, the counselee is in the counselor's world, and the counselor exists in the counselee's world. The counselor is "with" the counselee; the process of becoming and evolving includes both persons.

Major goals are to help individuals achieve self-realization and to be authentic (reducing guilt over neglecting their potential); and to help them gain meaning for life and come to feel they are of value (subduing feelings of emptiness and nonbeing).

The relationship of oneness with the other person provides the setting in which these tasks can be accomplished. Beyond that, the counselor attempts to understand the counselee's world as the counselee experiences it, acts in an authentic manner, and communicates his understanding to the counselee (Tolbert 1972, p. 86). He may provide information, help in identifying alternatives, reflect, ask questions, and set up turning points for major changes in direction (Ratigan 1967, p. 122).

Existential therapy is actually a conglomeration of several points of view. All share the central concern of understanding individuals in their own world as they themselves see it. But there are different applications.

GESTALT THERAPY This approach is mainly used with groups rather than individuals, but can be applied in one-to-one settings. Even though the name implies help for emotional problems, the approach is experiencing wide use in schools and college settings (Raming and Frey 1974).

Because of the name, it may be assumed that it is based on Gestalt psychology, and to some extent it is (Emerson and Smith 1974, pp. 8–12). Both deal with the relative importance of figure and ground in perception, the impact of total configuration as opposed to separate parts, and effects of unfinished business. While Perls, the originator of the theory, acknowledges his debt to the academic school of Gestalt psychology, he has not been claimed by the school (Emerson and Smith 1974, p. 12).

Gestalt therapy aims at promoting growth defined as openness to experience and willingness to interact with others (Harman 1975, p. 363). A problem results when there is a split between what individuals are and what they should be or feel they should be (Ward and Rouzer 1974, p. 20). Attempts to actualize the ideal picture of self by excessive control fail because of an unrealistic self-image (Ward and Rouzer 1974, p. 20). Therapy is designed to remove obstacles to growth by emphasizing the here and now in therapy and making it a period of actual emotional challenge rather than a safe comfortable place.

The therapist uses several modes of helping the client to deal with the present. One is to make the client aware of the present, e.g., by pointing out nonverbal behavior. Fantasy may be used to explore situations from the perspective of "What would happen if . . . ?" (Harman 1975, p. 365). The empty chair is one of the best-known and most powerful techniques (Fagan, Lauver, Smith, Deloch, Katz and Wood 1974, p. 33). Clients interact with the "occupant," who may represent part of their own personality or some significant person in their lives. The therapist helps clients understand the conflicts that emerge, with attention to nonverbal as well as verbal data.

To carry out the role of helper in this context, the therapist acts honestly and spontaneously, sometimes frustrating and challenging clients, and placing responsibility for change on them, for instance by forcing them to find their own direction, to "own" responses, and to face denied or unpleasant experiences (Raming and Frey 1974, p. 182).

The approach is used with either individuals or groups, but the group approach may be considered as individual work done with others present (Harman and Franklin 1975, p. 49). For example, a major technique is concentrating on members in turn. The group setting offers a number of advantages; there are opportunities to try out roles for observation and interaction (Harman and Franklin 1975). In marathon groups, one-to-one techniques have been used (Foulds and Hannigan 1976). The number of persons involved depends on the needs of those seeking help (Kempler 1973, pp. 275–276).

In the classroom, a counselor or teacher could, for example, help a pupil to deal with unfinished business with another pupil by having the first pupil talk to the second or to an empty chair representing the second, and then have the first pupil reverse roles and take a role completely opposed to typical behavior (Poppen and Thompson 1974, p. 49).

PSYCHOANALYTIC THERAPY   More than any of the other theories discussed, this is therapy for those with deep-seated, long-term emotional problems. A school counselor is not a psychoanalyst; psychoanalysis is included here because it is well-developed and offers a comprehensive personality and therapy theory, and because many techniques of Freud and his followers are used in some current counseling systems. Besides, many psychoanalytic concepts appear in literature, everyday conversations, and practically every facet of daily life.

As pointed out in Chapter 5, the personality and psychotherapy theory includes three structures, the ego, the id, and the superego. Psychic energy (libido) comes from the *id*, which is the source of instinctual energy and strives for immediate gratification. The *ego* is reality-oriented and decides how gratification demanded by the id can be obtained in the real world. It also has a certain reserve of energy which it uses, for example, to hold back primitive, pleasure-seeking id forces. The *superego*, which can be thought of as the conscience, is made up of values, attitudes, and moral precepts; its energy may side with the ego or with the id, though usually it sides with the former. These three terms are frequently used in everyday conversation with somewhat the same meaning.

Each stage of biological development has its own significance for personality development and therapy. In the first, the oral stage, the mouth is the primary source of gratification. Such adult personality characteristics as dependency stem from parental treatment at this stage. Later stages include the anal, phallic, latency, and finally the genital stage of adulthood. Fixation may cause the individual to remain at a particular stage, and may be due to parental overindulgence or denial. (But the characteristics associated with each level never completely disappear.)

The individual copes with the world by mechanisms such as repression and sublimation. The unconscious, encompassing repressed material and id demands of which the individual has never been fully aware, exert a powerful effect on personality and are the source of much behavior, particularly that which to the observer appears irrational.

Therapy is designed to bring out hidden motives, conflicts, and distortions of perceptions to allow individuals to gain control over their emotional lives. The process taps the unconscious by free association, dream analysis, and other techniques; clients can bring out material threatening and unacceptable to themselves. A transference relationship is developed in which clients react to the therapist in modes used in past relationships. Through interpretation of dreams, resistance, free association material, and other data, clients are able to understand their defenses, conflicts, and anxieties, and integrate new insights in their emotional lives.

RESEARCH

SOME TYPICAL STUDIES OF COUNSELING

Research on counseling and psychotherapy has covered a large number of designs, populations, and counseling styles. Summaries by Tyler (1969, pp. 217–237) and Meltzoff and Kornreich (1970) give an overview of the variety and indicate the difficulty of this type of work. (Fewer studies deal specifically with school counseling; more cover therapeutic types of help.) Results of these reviews are too extensive to summarize here as they cover all facets of counseling, but several representative ones are described below to illustrate the nature of this type of research.

Several representative studies are those by Fiedler (1950), Combs and Soper (1963), Rogers and Dymond (1954), and Carkhuff and Alexik (1967). They illustrate how efforts have been made to understand and improve the counseling process. In the Carkhuff and Alexik study, people playing the role of counselees used different levels of self-exploration with experienced counselors. Those counselors who had been functioning at high levels of the core conditions (empathy, respect, genuineness, and concreteness) tended to maintain their levels of effectiveness, but those who had been functioning at lower levels were negatively affected by counselees' lowering level of self-exploration and failed to regain their initial level of facilitation.

Fiedler's study (1950b), starting from the proposition that in all types of therapy (and counseling) the counselor-counselee relationship is considered to be of paramount importance, investigated the opinions of professionals representing several different points of view about the ideal therapeutic relationship. He asked nondirective, psychoanalytical, and eclectic therapists to sort statements describing the ideal therapeutic relationship (e.g., "The patient feels free to say what he likes") (p. 241). Correlations among therapists were significant at the .01 level. Typical ideal characteristics of the fourteen found are an empathic relationship, good patient-therapist relations, ability of the therapist to stay close to the patient's problem, and mutual trust.

A second study found that lay persons who had never been in therapy described the same type of ideal relationship, suggesting that it would be desirable in daily life.

Both studies revealed that expert counselors representing different approaches were more alike than experienced and inexperienced counselors representing the same point of view.

Combs and Soper (1963) studied the perceptual organization of twenty-nine counselors in training and found that those rated best by instructors differed from the less effective counselors on twelve perceptual dimensions at at least the .05 level. Some of the dimensions are the internal frame of reference (concerned with how others see things), friendliness (sees others as positive and nonthreatening), confidence of ability to cope with problems. As the raters in the study represented a single approach (client-centered), Combs and Soper raise the question whether different results would have been obtained with raters of other orientations, but refer to Fiedler's study to support the position that a recognition of the importance of a good relationship transcends schools of counseling and psychotherapy.

Truax (1963) reported a series of studies that gave evidence of the importance of high levels of accurate empathy, positive regard, and self-congruence in the helping relationship, and of the negative effects of low levels. A number of other studies also deal with therapist-offered conditions (referred to as techniques in this chapter). The study by Carkhuff and Alexik (1967) is an example. A coached client varied the level of self-exploration with counselors who had been providing either high or low levels of empathy, positive regard, congruence, and concreteness (emphasis on specific rather than vague and general feelings and experiences). The counselors who had been providing low levels of the helping conditions were less effective than the high-level counselors when manipulated by the client, i.e., when the client deliberately reduced the level of self-exploration.

The extensive study by Rogers and Dymond (1954) found that clients in client-centered therapy increase congruence between real and ideal selves, and demonstrated more mature behavior (Rogers 1954, pp. 416–423). The difficulty of research on human subjects involving a helping process is illustrated by criticisms of the design, e.g., not placing individuals who need immediate attention in the "wait control group" (Meltzoff and Kornreich 1970, p. 126).

The central question is whether or not counseling and

psychotherapy work. Some reports have been negative (Eysenck 1952). But careful research comparing spontaneous recovery rates and results achieved in controlled studies show that it does help (Brown and Herrnstein 1975, pp. 596–599; Meltzoff and Kornreich 1970, p. 177; Tyler 1969, pp. 236–237). The critical question is not whether it works, but what approach is most effective with what counselees, for what counselors, with what kinds of problems, and under what circumstances (Brown and Herrnstein 1975, p. 599). The answers to these questions will indicate which particular psychotherapeutic approaches are suitable for use in schools. For example, what approach would work best with a minority-group pupil who resists counseling and is not used to expressing feelings? How will it resemble or differ from that which would be effective with the highly verbal, middle-class pupil who expects counseling to be beneficial? The school counselor is faced with these and similar questions every day.

EXPERIENCE

COUNSELING POINTS OF VIEW

Each member of the class (or of a smaller group in the class) selects one of the counseling points of view described here for treating a pupil described as follows: "Has problems getting work completed on time. Always late for class, misses appointments, and seems to be going around in circles, getting nowhere. Feels need to change, but self-help has not worked." Choose the counseling approach that you would prefer for help with this problem and explain why you feel it would be the best one.

EXPERIENCE

MATCHING APPROACHES AND PERSONAL CHARACTERISTICS

As you read over the brief descriptions of counseling approaches, list five words for each that reflect your feeling about it. Then list five words that describe your personal characteristics. See which approach provides the best match, i.e., which list of words describing an approach most closely resembles the list of words you use to describe yourself.

OBJECTIVES

1. To become familiar with the counseling points of view that could be used by the school guidance worker. Name the three most useful and three least useful points of view for the school counselor, in your judgment, and give a one-sentence reason for your choices.

The answer will depend on your choice. The reason may involve the degree of comfort you experience with each approach. For example, you might choose developmental as most useful because it emphasizes the strengths of the individual and choose Gestalt as least useful because you do not like to urge others to face unpleasant situations.

2. To test out points of view to determine the one(s) best suited to your personality. Select one to four points of view that allow you to be yourself in counseling.

The objective is somewhat like the previous one but with one essential difference—the emphasis is on the point of view serving an extension of your personality rather than merely a process you can feel comfortable with. For example, you might like the eclectic approach and feel comfortable about its assumptions. But in actually working face-to-face with another person, you may prefer to have a consistent point of view to follow (e.g., client-centered).

3. To be aware of how points of view apply to specific individuals. Which would you recommend for the following pupils?
— **Pupil 1: High school junior. Is making good progress in school, but uncertain about what to do after graduation.**
— **Pupil 2: High school sophomore. Lonely, unhappy, and has very poor opinion of self. Has been skipping school lately.**

Pupil 1 appears to be a good prospect for counseling designed to help with planning and choosing (e.g., developmental, decision making). Pupil 2 appears to need a type of help that emphasizes an accepting relationship and facing negative attitudes (e.g., client-centered, transactional analysis). All points of view could be used with either case, however, as each has the objective of helping the counselee work through the presenting problems.

TECHNIQUES OF COUNSELING

Techniques or skills in counseling are somewhat analogous to the mechanics of writing—spelling, punctuating, and organizing material into logical units. These skills are used in all sorts of writing; they make it possible for an author to put ideas across. Thus, most counseling techniques may be used with any of the points of view, although some are more closely related to one approach than another.

An example of the relation of a technique to a counseling approach is reflection of feeling in client-centered counseling. It is a major technique in this approach, but many others also utilize it, too. Interpretation has more limited use; it is heavily used in psychoanalysis, for example, but would not be appropriate for client-centered counseling and similar approaches. Information about careers and other areas of choice is used in decision-making counseling, but would not be part of the therapeutic approaches such as Gestalt and TA. But many techniques cut across all or most approaches and are the counselor behaviors that help to implement theory.

Techniques may be classified in various ways. Typical methods include arranging them on a spectrum from directive to permissive or from cognitive to affective. Techniques are also classified on a spectrum from verbal to nonverbal. Additional dimensions can be used (e.g., interpretative to reflective), but most are similar to the first two. For example, interpretation is a relatively directive technique.

Examples of counselor responses illustrate differences. Suppose the counselee says: "I'm feeling so low that I don't want to talk today." How would you respond? The reply of a directive counselor, indicating how the counselee should proceed, might be "What has happened today to get you down?" The counselor is structuring the counselee's response by indicating what to talk about. This response is also cognitive; the counselor does not actually respond directly to the feeling expressed.

A more permissive response would be "Would you care to talk about it?" This reply, too, is more cognitive than affective, but it does not specify how the counselee should respond as clearly as the first one.

A more affective and permissive response would be "You're really hurting." Here the focus is on the feelings expressed by the counselee, and there is no indication of what the counselee should say next.

The directive-to-permissive classification is one of the most useful and interesting. At one end we have responses like questions and suggestions that represent control on the part of the counselor, who is directing what the counselee will do. Responses like "uh-huh" and others that acknowledge counselee responses are toward the permissive end; they do not affect the direction of the interview (unless, of course, they reinforce the counselee to keep going in the same direction). At the permissive extreme are responses that are based on what the counselee is thinking or, more particularly, feeling. The counselor reflects the counselee's expressed or implied feelings and goes along when the counselee proceeds; no direction is provided. A counseling approach that places most responsibility on the counselee makes extensive use of techniques on the permissive end of the continuum.

The classification from cognitive to affective is of somewhat the same type. A cognitive technique is more directive; an affective one is more permissive. The similarity is not total; the counselor may use affective responses in a very directive way, e.g., insisting that the counselee talk about a traumatic event. But cognitive responses tend to prompt a certain kind of counselee response (e.g., naming siblings, estimating grades), while affective ones shift responsibilities to the counselee for both direction of the interview and depth of feeling expressed.

Verbal and nonverbal techniques involve both counselor responses and the utilization of counselee behavior. For example, the counselor may smile, nod, lean forward, or look expectantly at the counselee. But the counselor may also direct attention to nonverbal responses of the counselee, for example, if the counselee clenches her hands while discussing her home situation, and the counselor comments that the topic evokes strong feelings.

Facilitative conditions such as empathy, positive regard, genuineness, concreteness, and immediacy represent techniques, even though these are pervasive conditions involving the counselor's pattern of relating. They are generated by specific as well as general counselor behaviors, are used in a number of counseling approaches, and can be assessed with some degree of reliability.

These core facilitative conditions have been extensively studied and scales have been developed to assess the degree to which counselors provide them (Carkhuff 1969, pp. 315–327). Empathy can range from no awareness of counselee feelings to sensitivity to both surface and deeper emotions. Positive regard or respect ranges from a low or no regard for the counselee to communication of deep respect and concern. Counselor genuineness may be at a level where feelings and communications are quite unrelated to the counselor's inner experience to spontaneity arising from actual emotions. These types of counselor behaviors are important for any helping relationship, whatever its purpose.

The status of techniques has varied considerably over the years; the summary of the history of guidance in Chapter 4 gives the background for differing levels of interest. In the early development of the profession, they were considerably emphasized. Then the focus shifted to the counseling relationship, and techniques per se were downgraded. Now, however, there is a revival of interest brought about by new ways of teaching skills and results of research on effectiveness (Ivey 1974). Microcounseling has been effective for building skills in specific techniques such as attending behavior, using open-ended questions, selective listening, and interpretation (Ivey 1974; Ivey and Gluckstern 1974). Dyer and Vriend (1975) highlight techniques like questioning, giving information, and establishing connections. There seems to be substantial agreement that counseling techniques deserve serious consideration, that they help to deepen the relationship, and that counselors, regardless of preferences for approaches, need to master them.

Techniques reflect the counselor's philosophy and theory; they put into effect attitudes and beliefs about human nature and the helping process. A counselor can start with a preferred theory and decide on appropriate techniques for implementation (along the lines the theory sections of this chapter suggest) or work the other way around, starting from preferred techniques and searching for reasons for having chosen them so as to infer theory. For example, if the counselor uses reflection to help the counselee bring out and face feelings, the emphasis appears to be on a theory that gives importance to the counselee's perceptions of self.

OTHER TECHNIQUES AND APPROACHES   There are some exotic techniques or approaches that have received considerable visibility in newspapers, magazines, and TV. Some hold considerable promise; others are of questionable value. Transcendental meditation is a method for self-improvement that has recently received wide publicity. Self-help programs abound (see Rosen 1976). Hypnosis is a technique that has been used in helping procedures (see Hilgard 1973). Biofeedback enables the individual to control bodily processes (see Schwartz 1973; Lazarus 1975). Primal therapy is aimed at enabling the individual to release the infantile pain that causes emotional problems (see Brown and Herrnstein 1975, pp. 620–622). There are others, and new ones are certain to emerge. Potential value to the school counselor varies; it is good to maintain both an open mind and healthy skepticism.

EXPERIENCE

COUNSELOR RESPONSES

Pair up with another student and try out the following exercise.

One student playing the counselee begins by describing a recent experience in a sentence or so. The other student, playing the counselor, responds in a directive way. (The response may consist of a statement or question that determines what the counselee will say next as in this sample exchange):

Counselee: I was crossing the street and a car came so close that it almost hit me. Some crazy driver!

Counselor (directive): Were you in the walk lane? (Note that counselor is controlling the counselee's response by emphasizing facts and content.)

Next, use a permissive response, recognizing the affect in the counselee's statement (e.g., "It really made you mad!"). Here the counselor is responding to emotions rather than content.

Reverse roles.

Next, have both players give reactions to counselor responses.

Use somewhat the same procedure in small groups. Have one member say something he or she considers personally important. Then have each member respond in a given way, for example: first member, directive; second member, permissive; third member, interpretative (i.e., "interpret" the reasons for the statement). Ask the member playing counselee to give reactions to the different types of response.

EXPERIENCE

EVALUATING COUNSELOR TECHNIQUES

In the following brief excerpt, select the response which as a counselee you would prefer. Give reasons for your preference.

Counselee: I don't usually talk to people about things that bother me. Nobody wants to listen anyway.
Counselor 1: That's what I'm here for. To talk about those things.
Counselor 2: I think you'll find that others are really interested.
Counselor 3: It's not easy to talk about personal things.

Counselee: I used to think I could tell my parents, but they say "Oh, that's not that big a thing." I feel like they think it's sort of silly and childish.
Counselor 1: They mean well. They just don't want you to worry.
Counselor 2: How did you approach them? Maybe they thought you weren't really worried.
Counselor 3: You felt they didn't really hear you.

If small groups are used, compare preferences and discuss reasons for similarities or differences.

EXPERIENCE

AFFECT V. CONTENT

Keep a tally for a day of your responses in important interactions with others according to the following two criteria:

— Affect: you respond to the feelings someone expressed.
— Content: you respond to the factual content of what another person said.

Results will depend on both your way of responding and the types of comments made to you (if, for instance, others make mostly factual comments, it will limit the types of replies you can make).

How do you feel about your response style? Does it convey what you want to communicate to others?

OBJECTIVE

1. To be able to identify major dimensions of counseling techniques and classify examples. Name two dimensions of techniques and give examples that illustrate the opposite ends of the dimensions selected.

The major dimensions given in the text are:

— permissive to directive
— cognitive to affective
— verbal to nonverbal

In an illustration at the permissive end of the permissive-to-directive dimension, the counselor reflects the feeling expressed in the counselor's statement:

Counselee: I feel like an outcast in this school. I'm going to get out as soon as I can!
Counselor: It really gets to you.

The response does not direct or control the interview; the counselee can move in to any topic from this point.

A directive response that could have been used is "Do your parents know that you're leaving as soon as you can?"

In this statement, the counselor is establishing what the counselee will talk about and thus directing the interview.

ADDITIONAL READINGS

Carroll, Marguerite R. "Introduction." *School Counselor* 20, no. 5 (1973), p. 333.

A special issue on psychological education containing five articles describing new approaches to implementing the counselor's role in the school.

Corsini, Raymond, ed. *Current Psychotherapies.* Itasca, Illinois: F. E. Peacock, 1973.

One of the major references on theories, covering 12 different points of view, and providing illustrative case material. Reading may be selected according to preferences.

Egan, Gerard. *The Skilled Helper* and *Exercises in Helping Skills.* Monterey, California: Brooks/Cole, 1975.

This book and the accompanying training manual illustrate counseling techniques and provide exercises for practice. Both publications are interesting and easy to understand.

Ewing, Dorlesa Barmettler. "Twenty Approaches to Individual Change." *Personnel and Guidance Journal* 55, no. 6 (1977), pp. 331–338.

An extremely helpful review of major approaches to counseling. The author's system of grouping theories adds much to a reader's understanding.

Guidance for Education in Revolution. Boston: Allyn and Bacon, 1971, pp. 453–491.

The theory and practice of the change agent's role for school guidance workers. A comprehensive review of theory, and description of useful strategies.

Meyer, James B., and Meyer, Joyce K. *Counseling Psychology.* Boston: Allyn and Bacon, 1975.

Approaches and techniques for handling actual cases are presented. An excellent reference for an in-depth look at some typical counseling interventions.

Patterson, C. H. "A Current View of Client-Centered or Relationship Theory." *Counseling Psychologist* 1, no. 2 (1969), pp. 2–25.

Patterson gives an up-to-date and lucid explanation of the client centered point of view. Each issue of this journal deals with a specific topic; various theories are covered, and contributors take positions pro and con.

———. *Theories of Counseling and Psychotherapy.* 2d. ed. New York: Harper and Row, 1973.

Contains summaries of many of the counseling points of view discussed in this chapter. One of the major references on the subject. Select sections according to interests.

Poppen, William A., and Thompson, Charles L. *School Counseling.* Lincoln, Nebraska: Professional Educators Publications, 1974.

Particularly useful in connection with this chapter for an expanded coverage of theories. The review of techniques is also valuable reading.

Stefflre, Buford, and Grant, W. Harold, eds. *Theories of Counseling.* 2d ed. New York: McGraw-Hill, 1972.

A standard reference on theories, including an excellent discussion of the use of theory in counseling. The book emphasizes school counseling; Chapter 2, "Counseling theory and practice in the school," is particularly relevant.

CHAPTER EIGHT
ADAPTING GUIDANCE
TO SPECIFIC NEEDS

Group activities are an important part of the counselor's helping services. In fact, the use of groups is one of the most significant trends in school guidance. Among the approaches used are small counseling groups, affective education, and guidance groups for information giving. Under these general types, groups for pupils, parents, and teachers are used for a wide variety of purposes. This chapter provides an overview of the major types of group procedures used in school counseling, classified under the headings of counseling, guidance, or a combination of the two. No type is exclusively affective or cognitive. In processing information, both affect and cognition are involved. Doverspike's GUICO (Guidance and Counseling) approach (1971) is an example of synthesizing the best features of counseling and guidance and brings both feelings and cognition to bear on activities in groups large and small.

Finally, counseling needs of special groups are covered to emphasize the need for flexibility in helping and for knowledge of group characteristics. There is a common core of attitudes and techniques for counseling all individuals, but special groups require assistance adapted to their needs.

GOALS

1. To be aware of the types of group work that are used in schools and other institutions.
2. To appreciate the potential of groups for expanding the impact of guidance.
3. To become aware of your feelings about working with groups.
4. To understand the guidance needs of minority and other special groups.

GROUP COUNSELING APPROACHES

Groups are usually made up of ten or less, and the emphasis is on affect, exploration of feeling, and group-selected topics.

Group Counseling   Groups are small enough for extensive interaction. (Group counseling is discussed more fully later in this section.)

Encounter and Sensitivity Groups   Major emphasis is on expression of feelings and developing an awareness of others. Marathon groups using these approaches may last for a day or longer. The differences between the two types have been blurred by everyday usage. Originally, sensitivity training referred a small group process designed to develop an awareness of human interaction. The encounter group emphasizes the growth of each member through expanding awareness of self and others. (More is said about these types of groups later in this section.)

Group Therapy   This type of group deals with unconscious motivations causing emotional problems. Treatment is intensive and relatively long term.

Family Counseling or Therapy   A variety of counseling approaches involving the whole family. One version, family group consultation, is used with parents to help them learn to show positive feelings toward each other and develop openness in communication. Keebler (1976) refers to family counseling as a profusion of methods and lists seven different variations.

GROUP GUIDANCE APPROACHES

Groups may be either large or small, but are often class-size. The emphasis is on cognitive materials and learning of content; a teaching approach may be involved, and topics are usually leader-selected.

Group Guidance   A group may be large or small, but it usually runs to 15 to 20 members (about class-size). Much of the emphasis is primarily cognitive, for example on subjects like information getting, orientation, how to study.

Orientation   This type of group activity is primarily information giving and may be large-scale as in orientation to first grade or entry into middle or high school. Orientation includes group meetings such as career days, college days, and career fairs.

Games and Simulations   These methods, utilizing either large or small groups, provide an opportunity for participants to make simulated decisions for others, for example in planning the life of an imaginary person.

Moral Education   The emphasis is on how to make moral decisions rather than learning a particular moral point of view.

Parent Groups   A variety of approaches may be used to help parents understand and communicate with children. Groups provide a consulting, teaching, and therapeutic experience.

COMBINATIONS OF GUIDANCE AND COUNSELING APPROACHES

Combinations bring together many of the strengths of both guidance and counseling, and embrace newer strategies that can provide help on a school-wide scale.

Psychological Education   This is more a collection of affective techniques than a specific approach. The aim is to promote self-understanding, communication, and positive behavior. Peer counseling may be used to facilitate understanding of psychological principles of growth and development.

Affective Education   This approach is in some ways similar to psychological education, but it is usually employed with classroom-size groups and concentrates on the development of the emotional aspects of the individual's life such as learning to experience and express emotions.

Assertiveness Training   These are groups that help individuals develop confidence in asserting their own point of view and to regard themselves as significant and worthy of respect.

This list does not represent all of the group approaches but includes many that counselors may use in treating pupils, parents, or teachers. It gives some idea of the tremendous range of possibilities and clearly illustrates why the school counselor needs to be competent in group methods. New approaches are developing constantly. A sampling of applications recently listed by a college counseling program includes:

— *Women in transition.* For those experiencing major transitions, e.g., reentry into the labor force.
— *Couples enrichment groups.* For dating and married couples, to facilitate improved relationships.

— *Couples communications groups.* For couples, to achieve new patterns of interaction.
— *Students' problems with alcohol.*
— *Women's sexual enrichment.* Learning to be more open to sexual experiences and how to deal with guilt.
— *Gestalt-oriented growth groups.* To promote growth of the whole person.
— *Dating skills interaction groups.* To develop meaningful relations in dating.
— *Interpersonal growth groups.* To improve communication skills.
— *Male sexual and social roles.* For exploring the male role in society.
— *Assertiveness training groups.* To enhance self-awareness and effectiveness in personal relationships.

Another college program offered family communication groups, relaxation groups, gay groups, and groups for the overweight.

These programs illustrate how group procedures, involving both counseling and guidance techniques, are structured to meet needs of particular populations. While these groups are for the college level, the same needs-meeting approaches can be used in the school.

APPLICATIONS OF GROUP PROCEDURES

The bases for these group approaches come from points of view of counseling and therapy, psychology of group action, and theories of personality. Many of the counseling approaches described earlier are used for group work (e.g., client-centered, Gestalt, decision-making). The unique feature of group application is the interaction among members, the leader's role as facilitator, and the roles that members play in the social situation. Regardless of the type of group (with the exception of an information-giving format), the emphasis is on providing a growth-producing setting where members can learn to understand themselves, experience the reactions of others, and develop more effective life-styles.

Group counseling is growing rapidly in the school setting. Often the purpose is to facilitate developmental tasks, e.g., establishing group relations with peers, improving communication, developing social skills, enhancing the self-concept, and many others. While the underlying rationale may differ from group to group, the emphasis is on a counseling-type of relationship. The group is small enough to provide for intimacy and extensive participation. The leader is typically a participant-facilitator who enters into the activities, helps members express feelings, models techniques such as feedback, and in further ways works to generate a growth-producing climate.

Counseling groups tend to go through stages. In the initial period members get to know each other. Some trust may be established, but anxiety is high. As trust is developed, a group feeling emerges. Expression of feeling increases. In later stages, the group is characterized by intimacy, trust, and cohesiveness. Group counseling generally runs to eight or ten meetings.

Psychological education is a relatively new concept, bringing together a number of techniques and procedures in which the counselor takes the "initiative in deliberately teaching aspects of mental health to larger groups" (Ivey and Alschuler 1973b, p. 589). It draws heavily on psychology, and involves both cognitive and affective experiences; the counselor's role is therefore expanded considerably. It may involve such features as peer counseling (Carroll 1973b, p. 357), moral education (Ivey and Alschuler 1973a, p. 593), values clarification (Simon 1973), or communications training (Gray and Tindall 1974). Developing teachers' skills is given high priority so as, in effect, to "give away school counseling" (Pine 1974, p. 94). The detailed description of one working program (Mosher and Sprinthall 1971, pp. 3–82) includes activities such as peer counseling, improvisational drama, and pupil participation in child-development seminars. This approach, emphasizing long-term personal learning, strategic timing of activities, multiple techniques, and changes in the school itself (Ivey and Alschuler 1973a) has great potential for spreading the counselor's effect throughout the total institution.

Affective education deals with the emotional aspects of learning, such as feelings of competency, acceptance, attitudes towards school (Stillwell 1976). Teachers utilize prepared programs in the classroom to facilitate affective responses. The counselor's role includes demonstrating techniques for the teacher to use, and supplementing the program with group and individual counseling.

Encounter and sensitivity groups involve 10 to 15 members who wish to deepen experiencing, reduce defenses, and develop new behavior styles (Eddy and Lubin 1971). Sensitivity training provides for interactions to help members become more aware of themselves, and to experience interactions with others more accurately (Eddy and Lubin 1971). Encounter and sensitivity group therapy are designed to increase the quality of personal experience, improve interpersonal competency, and free potential; they do not attempt to reduce severe emotional conflicts.

Assertiveness training is becoming popular, particularly with women. It is designed to help counselees overcome a submissive, withdrawn style of interacting with others and facilitate positive, expressive, outgoing behavior. The counselor or therapist offers encouragement and otherwise attempts to get the group members to engage in new patterns of behavior to achieve a more rewarding life-style (Rathus 1975). Typical activities could include coaching another group member to be assertive, using a

planned episode to obtain new responses, or keeping a diary of both assertive and unassertive behaviors (Cotler 1975).

The range and scope of group activities is so extensive and growing so
rapidly that such a discussion can barely scratch the surface. Little has
been said about effectiveness, specific techniques, and clientele, all of
which must be examined for a full understanding of the potential of group
work for schools. Evaluation, particularly, is of critical importance. Brown
and Herrnstein (1975, pp. 611–619) summarize evaluations of the effects
of a large number of encounter groups. Their results revealed very modest
success and some harmful effects. The user needs to select with care.
Meltzoff and Kornreich (1970, pp. 401–402) point out that results are
often not as positive as enthusiastic advocates state.

EXPERIENCE

HELPING RESPONSES

Using groups of three to six persons ask each to relate a positive
experience in up to three minutes. After the initial presentations,
have each member comment about someone else's experience.
While making comments, speakers will look directly at the person
addressed, use that person's name, and indicate their own feelings
about what the person said.

Do not explain or describe the other person's feelings or motives,
but say only what you feel or think about the experience. For example, if one person says, "I got the job I didn't expect to," you might
say, "It seems to me that you felt really competent," but would not
say, "You thought you wouldn't get it."

At the end of the exercise, ask members to describe feelings in
this type of communication.

EXPERIENCE

GROUP ROLES

In small groups (4 to 6 members) begin by having all members
introduce themselves and suggest one way the group could help
identify personal values. Then have the group appoint a leader,
agree on one of the suggestions, and deal with it for a few minutes.

At the end of the group activity (about ten minutes) discuss the
following questions:

— What was the major difficulty in choosing a topic?

— Who helped resolve the difficulty?
— Who was the synthesizer (helped to get those with different points of view together)? What did this person do to help the group?
— Who was the scapegoat (someone blamed for the group's difficulties)?
— Who was the facilitator (helped the group to move forward with its task)?
— Decide which of the following behaviors were present or absent in the group:

1. General conversation
2. Advice
3. Expressions of feeling
4. "I" statements (about one's own thoughts and feelings)
5. "You" statements (in which one member "interprets" the meanings of another)
6. "Should" statements (in which one member suggests what the group ought to do).

Which of these factors helped and which hindered group progress?

EXPERIENCE

GROUP PARTICIPATION

Join a group counseling program offered on campus or by a community agency. Keep a diary of your reactions to meetings, emphasizing new insights about yourself or others.

RESEARCH

SOME SAMPLES OF STUDIES OF GROUP COUNSELING

Group counseling has been used in schools for educational, career, and personal-social problems. Results have not been uniformly positive, but overall the approach seems to be productive.

Baymor and Patterson (1960) compared the effectiveness of client-centered group counseling, individual counseling, and a one-session motivational-encouragement meeting for 32 underachieving eleventh graders. No significant improvements were found in study habits and grades, although pupils counseled individually and in groups taken together showed improvement at the .05 level on personal adjustment when compared with the one-session motivational group and the control group. The small number of subjects and the need to use pupils with vacant periods for groups may have reduced the probability of significant results.

Benson and Blocher (1967) studied the effects of group developmental counseling on low achievers in the tenth grade. Two groups of six pupils each met for eighteen 55-minute periods. The groups, led by the same counselor, moved over the course of the counseling from guidance informational activities to exploration of feelings. Results showed that grades and feelings of adequacy improved significantly (.05 level or better). Disciplinary referrals and dropping out were reduced to a degree that had practical significance for the school. The authors point out that this was a limited study, but it does suggest that group counseling may be a useful strategy for low achievers.

Hansen, Niland, and Zani (1969) investigated the effectiveness of model reinforcement with elementary school pupils who had low sociometric status. Fifty-four low-social-acceptance pupils and eighteen high ranking ones participated. The eight meetings used in the study emphasized getting along with others and developing social maturity. Results (from p. 743) were as follows:

t-VALUES FOR DIFFERENCES BETWEEN COUNSELING TREATMENTS

Treatment	t
Model reinforcement v. reinforcement	2.16[a]
Model reinforcement v. control	2.44[a]
Reinforcement v. control	0.08

[a] $P < .05$

Not only did group members with social models improve significantly in sociometric ratings, but a follow-up two months later showed that improvement had been maintained.

The study by Thoresen, Hosford, and Krumboltz (1970) investigated the effects of peer social models with eleventh graders. With information-seeking behavior as the criterion, pupils in low-, medium-, and high-success groups were exposed to videotapes showing a counselee at different levels of social, academic and athletic success. Part of the tape showed the counselee developing a strategy for collecting information for future planning. For the four schools used, results varied, and no support was gained for the social-power hypothesis. In some cases, high-effective models did stimulate a significant amount of information-seeking behavior. Overall it appears that the reinforcing power of the counselor is an important variable.

Harris and Trujillo (1975) used self-management through behavior modification and group discussion techniques to help junior high school pupils improve study habits. Both treatment groups differed significantly from the control group, though not from each other. However, the self-management group reported better study habits (e.g., having a time and place to study).

OBJECTIVES

1. To learn about group approaches to counseling and guidance. Name three group approaches that you would like to use and give one reason for each choice.

The text identifies three major types of group approaches, and twelve specific methods. Personal choice is based on elements that appeal to you, e.g., the small number of members in group counseling, and the opportunity to interact on a personal level.

2. To identify potential benefits of group approaches in guidance and counseling. Name five ways that groups could contribute to pupil growth.

The following are among the major potential benefits:

— They provide the opportunity for peers to interact.
— They may be focused on developmental needs and problems.
— They may be used to promote positive and productive behaviors.
— They provide counselees with an opportunity to learn how others see them.
— They provide a relatively safe place to learn new interpersonal skills.

NEW APPROACHES AND NEW TECHNOLOGY

Very remarkable developments are taking place in counseling, with respect both to new ways of helping and sophisticated uses of technology. Many of the new ways (e.g., psychological education) have been covered in the previous section; Chapter 9, which deals with providing information, includes further discussion of new technology, but specific contributions to group counseling and guidance merit recognition here.

NEW APPROACHES TO COUNSELING AND GUIDANCE Standardized, field-tested kits for administration by counselors, teachers, and support personnel are a major new development. There are also self-administered guidance techniques for the counselee. Peers and other paraprofessionals (discussed in Chapter 12) carry out specific face-to-face helping activities with kits and free the counselor for services requiring full professional skills.

Two of the best known programs are DUSO (Developing Understanding Self and Others) and VEG (Vocational Exploration Group), the latter put out by Studies for Urban Man, Inc., Vocational Exploration Group, Tempe, Arizona. DUSO is available for two levels: kindergarten and lower primary, and upper primary and grade 4. The materials can be used by the classroom teacher and involve children in actively dealing with developmental problems. Tapes, hand puppets, and similar materials are used.

The VEG is a sequence of career guidance activities and makes extensive use of group interaction designed to further counselees' self-knowledge and to help them relate knowledge to job demands and satisfactions. The program, which is available in both a short and long version (two hours or about four hours), ends with an individual plan to be implemented after the group session is concluded. The program is particularly appropriate for the high school years, but has also been used with college students and adults.

There are numerous other programs, some taped with learning aids, some described in books. A well-known one is PET (Parent Effective Training) which is the name both of a book (Gordon 1970) and of a course offered by persons with special training provided by Effectiveness Training Associates, Pasadena, California. Dinkmeyer and McKay's, *Systematic Training for Effective Parenting* (STEP), distributed by the American Guidance Service, is another widely used program for helping parents develop positive relationships with children.

Three how-to-do-it life-skills books prepared by Robert Carkhuff (1973, 1974) cover helping, problem solving, and program development. For counselees, the one on problem solving is particularly useful; it goes through the process step by step, from exploring all aspects of the problem to incorporating the entire problem-solving process in handling day-to-day situations.

Counselors can turn to many well-developed programs. The ones mentioned have been tested and evaluated in research studies and help the counselor considerably in implementing guidance practices in the school.

The SDS (Self-Directed Search) (Holland 1972, 1973) is a self-administered career-guidance instrument that enables the counselor to expand services. Its results show relative strength of interests in six general areas; a separate booklet is designed to expand career options by listing a large number of jobs for each interest area. The instrument is appropriate for grades 7 and 8 on up through high school and adult levels.

THE CONTRIBUTIONS OF NEW TECHNOLOGY TO COUNSELING   The major technological aids for the counselor are computer guidance systems, computer search systems, and programs using materials such as microfiche cards to provide information. These and other systems are described more fully in the next chapter but are mentioned here because of the part they play in extending the effectiveness of counseling and guidance.

Technology is advancing rapidly, and, logically enough, the question has arisen whether computers could be used to "counsel" pupils, either individually or in groups. At one time many counselors seemed concerned—could they be replaced by computers? The fear was not totally unrealistic. Computers can provide information, e.g., about occupations and educational programs. They can interact with users to "suggest" occupations in line with aptitudes, values, and related factors. They could even help pupils learn how to plan career strategies and improve planning skills. However, using these computer capabilities frees the counselor for relationship activities, which, for example, may help the counselee make personal use of what has been learned from the computer. The trend is for computers to be integrated in a counselor-directed program, involving individual and group counseling.

Other technological aids depend even more on the counselor. While it is true that some pupils may need only the kind of limited information obtainable from a computer, microfiche reader-printer, or slide-tape program, many can profit from counseling help to make effective use of it. Everyone using a technological source of information, particularly the computer, should also have some personal contact with a counselor.

PUPILS WITH SPECIAL NEEDS

Some of the problems identified in the descriptions of schools in chapters 1 and 2, relate to needs of particular groups of pupils. Guidance models discussed in Chapter 6 provide strategies for the counselor to assess school-wide needs as well as needs of special subpopulations requiring assistance tailored to their particular situations. To provide effective help it is necessary to understand both group characteristics and individual group members, and to develop appropriate strategies for assistance.

Exceptionally bright pupils should be included in any definition of students with special needs.

There is an increasing acceptance of the point of view that guidance (and all of education) should attend to the needs of specific populations. This trend in no way lessens the concern for the needs of all pupils, as is apparent from the recent emphasis on pupils' rights—in the home, at school, morally, and legally (Rotter and Crunk 1975). But the needs of special groups—such as women, minorities, the disadvantaged, the hand-icapped, those with crisis problems, and pupils in special education—have recently been gaining a major place in the guidance picture.

To point out the rights of children may seem surprising in our culture—we are characterized as a youth-centered society. Youth is highly prized; there are a multitude of programs and techniques available to help parents with child raising. But in spite of the professed interest and concern, practice falls far short of the ideal. Many children do not live in a two-parent family. Many are subjected to psychological and physical abuse. It is not unreasonable to say that every child has a right to a loving, happy, safe home with parents skilled in making it a place for full development of potential (Bell 1975), and that the school should be aware of a child's right to learn, participate in meaningful activities, and develop skills and independence (Van Hoose 1975). This awareness of the rights of all pupils goes hand in hand with the growing concern for rights and needs of special groups and widens the responsibilities of guidance workers.

WOMEN   The special needs of girls and women confront counselors with new problems regarding attitudes and practice (Lewis 1972). To some extent barriers to personal development, identity formation and equal legal status have been removed, but personal and social stereotypes prevent many females from achieving in line with their potential (Hansen 1972). Educators, particularly counselors, tend to promote traditional careers for girls, although many profess to see women as having the potential for a much wider range of roles. The critical issue is not whether a homemaking or career role is best but whether the girl knows her options, understands her potential, can get help dealing with personal and societal views of women's roles, and has freedom to choose for herself. Many of the messages they receive from family and counselors hinder rather than help in achieving such insight (Matthews 1972, pp. 23–27).

MINORITY GROUPS   Blacks make up the largest minority group, but there are others, such as Hispanic Americans, American Indians, Puerto Ricans, and Vietnamese. Each group has preferred values and cultural characteristics, but relying too much on descriptions of these patterns leads to stereotyping. It is important to recognize individuals as unique, whatever their background (Banks 1977).

Blacks   To understand black counselees and provide a helping service, the prospective counselor needs insights from personal association as well as from reading and study. Research typically focuses on lacks, difficulties, and deprivation, and much of it does not successfully avoid the dangers of stereotyping. Frequently the terms "disadvantaged" and "black" are used together so as to suggest that all blacks are disadvantaged. Differences-oriented research has tended to suggest that blacks are different from whites in family structure, communication styles, and self-concepts, but less attention has been paid to the critical factors (racial, political, and socioeconomic) in society that have an impact on these aspects. A catalogue of specific black characteristics and specific helping strategies is less useful to the counselor than personal contacts that reveal unique individuals—not members of a group that is different and requires special treatment, but individuals dealing with social pressures, demands, and barriers of which the counselor might not be aware. Helping calls for less emphasis on special techniques and more concern for changing the special conditions that limit or block development (Banks 1977; Smith, 1977).

Hispanic Americans   As with other minorities, group descriptions can easily blind the counselor to personal individuality and lead to a stereotype of Chicanos (Palomares 1971a). But it is still important to be aware of attitudes, problems, and customs to help understand members of this subculture, the second largest minority group in the United States. Palomares (1971b) describes the essential attitude behind the popular slogan "Viva la raza," as the determination to gain an identity and a place of status in this culture, and recounts the difficulties and defeats that have marked the lives of many Americans of Mexican descent. It is critical for the counselor to be aware of the status of members of the subculture within the larger culture as well as to appreciate personal customs and mores.

There are other significant Latin groups besides Mexican Americans, as Ruiz and Padilla point out (1977). The total of about 9 million in the United States live mainly in cities and tend to remain in areas near their former home countries; most ex-Cubans live in Florida. It is important for counselors to understand and appreciate the history and subtle characteristics among subgroups of the total Latin culture. For example, many misconceptions about Latin cultural characteristics arise from literal translation of Spanish phrases into English without proper consideration of their significance to a native speaker. The concept of Latin fatalism is due in part to the implications in English of the typical expression "Lo que dios desea"—whatever God wills (Ruiz and Padilla 1977, p. 403).

Asian Americans   Until recently little attention has been paid to the needs and problems of Asian Americans. In fact, the group, with its high educational level and low delinquency rate was generally thought to be very successful. But as Sue and Sue (1973) point out, an unrealistic belief in Asian success has masked problems of educational and career deficiencies and cultural conflicts. An underlying cultural barrier against self-disclosure, which prevents a child from making a request of the teacher or being assertive in social situations. (Sue, S. 1977). As in other cultural minority groups, many young Asian Americans are beginning to question middle-class American values and are seeking meaning in their own cultural heritage (Kagiwada and Fujimoto 1973). This situation highlights the need to look below surface manifestations, to understand cultural patterns and values, and to interact with individuals who are members of the culture.

American Indians   Members of this subgroup are often mistakenly stereotyped as silent, inscrutable survivors from the days of the wild West. Counseling has usually failed with Indians because of lacking recognition of their special needs, ignorance of their culture and its contributions, and handicaps in communication (Spang 1971). Stereotyping is one major barrier to understanding. Enormous cultural differences in values, social structure, and life-styles between their own and the majority culture lead to pressures it is very hard for an Indian boy or girl to deal with. Counselors need to be aware of this "caught between two worlds situation" (Spang 1971, p. 99).

Other culturally different groups have needs as great as the ones discussed. Much work remains, but little is being done to improve the situation. Needed steps include relating both counseling processes and goals to life-styles and values of different cultural groups (Sue 1977).

The Disadvantaged   Individuals from any racial and subcultural group may fall in this category; cultural, economic, educational, and vocational deficiencies are not limited to any one group. But in minority groups, the percentages of disadvantaged people are disproportionally high. Poverty limits opportunities for development and is a major factor. Racial and cultural factors may contribute if language, customs, and attitudes interfere with adapting to school and preparing for work (Gordon 1974, pp. 452–453). To plan remedial strategies, both environmental factors contributing to disadvantaged status and the nature of the specific individual deficiencies need to be understood. Assessing pupil status is not enough; once lacks are understood, steps should be taken to promote development and to help individuals acquire coping skills.

The Handicapped   Even though there are special school programs for the mentally retarded and community guidance services for the physically handicapped counselors can expect increased responsibility for work with pupils with physical and psychological handicaps. If there is to be a well-rounded program, elementary school counselors must share in working with special-education pupils. Counseling at all school levels should emphasize long-range planning to help the retarded become as self-sufficient as possible (Heath 1970, pp. xi, 53). The counselor is in a key position to keep this goal before the school and to work with community agencies when the pupil is ready for their services.

Care needs to be exercised in classifying pupils as retarded; the counselor can help to establish diagnostic procedures that are not racially, nationally, or otherwise biased. Both direct treatment and curriculum planning are based on understanding the total pupil, especially with respect to learning and communication abilities. For the school counselor, the mentally retarded have been to some extent an isolated group; counselors and special education teachers have typically done little collaborative work. But the picture is changing. Counselors should include the mentally retarded in needs studies and school-wide strategy planning.

Counselors are also becoming increasingly involved with pupils with emotional disabilities. Individual and group counseling have been used as therapy, but special classes and programs are being set up for pupils whose emotional difficulties require a special learning environment for part of the school day. Pupils in this category need understanding, assistance, and the opportunity to develop new effective ways of behaving in home, school, and community. The counselor at any school level is in the key position to assess needs, plan helping strategies, and actually implement many of the therapeutic approaches, both for individuals and groups. Effective work with the emotionally handicapped, as for other exceptional pupils, involves cooperative relations with the home. Family counseling, which school counselors are using increasingly, is one way to involve the home in treatment.

CRISIS NEEDS OF PUPILS Those facing emergencies or crises constitute a special group with unique needs. Drug users are an example (Ognidene and Riccio 1973). The counselor needs to know not only the effects of drugs, but must also understand the reason people use them and the gratifications they provide. Battered children make up another special crisis group (Forrer 1975). The counselor can help identify mistreated pupils, provide assistance to counteract damaging effects, and initiate legal action to remedy their situation. Pupils faced with death make up still another crisis group (Clay 1976; Hawener and Phillips 1975). Death is one of the taboo areas typically treated with silence in our society, but openness, honesty, and recognition of feelings are more therapeutic and helpful (Nelson and Peterson 1975).

Other emerging crisis needs in the schools will also demand attention from the counselor. Some of these will be identified by needs studies; others will be detected by more subtle means (e.g., in confidential counseling situations). Pregnancy and abortion are areas where pupil problems are growing more frequent. The counselor must consider both humanitarian and legal aspects in helping unmarried pregnant girls seeking information about abortion. Conflicts experienced by gay pupils who are considering coming out of the closet present counselors with particularly challenging problems involving the individual, school, parents, and the community.

Working with individuals in any of these groups (particularly in the crisis category) involves the counselor's values. But regardless of personal philosophy, if help is to be provided, the counselor must understand the needs of pupils, and be open to whatever values and attitudes they present. Often pupils' values run contrary to those of the counselor; though not value-neutral, the counselor does not force personal viewpoints on counselees, but helps them to understand their own situations and options, and to make personally satisfying decisions. Different opinions about the role of women provide an example. It may be easy for the male counselor to recognize intellectually that women should be afforded equal opportunity in occupational, educational, and social affairs, but it is quite another matter to accept this attitude at the emotional level. In the area of sexual counseling strong value conflicts often emerge. Picture the counselor who believes that premarital sex is wrong working with an unmarried pregnant teenager or dealing with the problems of an unmarried couple living together.

Recognizing and meeting the needs of special groups is one of the counselor's major challenges. But these processes should not result in setting a group apart as "different" nor should they get in the way of perceiving the unique individuality of each pupil in the school.

EVALUATING RESULTS

The ultimate test of the value of counseling and guidance services is how much they help pupils. An approach may be thoughtfully designed, utilize theory and techniques adapted for the individuals served, and be carried out by well-prepared professionals or carefully trained paraprofessionals. But if it does not make a difference in the lives of those served, it cannot be justified.

But impact is only one part of the picture. Relative effectiveness of strategies must also be considered. If a counselor has eight one-hour meetings with pupils and achieves the same results as in a single one-hour group, obviously the group procedure is preferable.

Effects are the critical test, but they are difficult to assess (see Chapter 15). Most of the carefully designed research has been done in psychotherapy and in nonschool settings; much of it may apply to school counseling, but in most cases the correspondence has yet to be established. There seems to be a trend toward accepting the results of psychotherapy as applicable to school counseling; perhaps this is to some extent justified since counselors often use methods that are classifiable as psychotherapy. But as Meltzoff and Kornreich (1970, pp. 335, 394, 402) point out, many claims of positive effects have not been substantiated. On the other hand, Brown and Herrnstein (1975, pp. 594–598) show that critics who assert that therapy has zero or negative effects have not reviewed all of the relevant literature; there is evidence that the overall effect is at least slightly positive.

The issue of evaluation is an important one. Under the pressure of accountability, counselors and guidance workers are finding it essential to determine effects. Both research and evaluation are needed. Research gets at the relative effectiveness and costs of approaches; evaluation deals with results. Unfortunately, many of the available studies are flawed in one way or another, are not generalizable, or have failed to obtain results that are significant from both a statistical and a practical standpoint.

ADDITIONAL READINGS

Carroll, Marguerite R. "Special Feature: Training Models in Communication." *School Counselor* 22, no. 2 (1974), p. 93.

This issue, on psychological education, gives a variety of programs for implementing this approach to school guidance.

Gazda, George M., ed. *Basic Approaches to Group Psychotherapy and Group Counseling*. Springfield, Illinois: Charles C. Thomas, 1968.

Gazda makes a distinction between counseling and therapy, and covers a number of group approaches related to the theories of counseling and psychotherapy discussed in this chapter. Chapter 1, covering definitions and heritage, is a good starting point.

———. *Group Counseling*. Boston: Allyn and Bacon, 1971.

Primarily a guide to group counseling, this book gives a complete and easy-to-read description for counselors at all school levels. Definitions of all types of group work are covered in pages 7–14.

———. "Group Approaches—Problems and Prescriptions," *Personnel and Guidance Journal* 49, no. 8 (1971), p. 592.

A special issue on group work including counseling, guidance, and psychotherapy. Select articles according to preferences.

Ivey, Allen E., and Alschuler, Alfred S., eds. "Psychological Education Is . . ." *Personnel and Guidance Journal* 51, no. 9 (1973), pp. 588–589.

A special issue on psychological education that provides a comprehensive view of theory and techniques.

Kristal, Helen F. *The Role of the School in Child Abuse and Neglect*. Washington, D.C. American School Counselor Association, 1977.

A valuable reference for counselors on what can be done about mistreatment of children, including a review of children's legal rights and relevant legislation.

Larson, A. William. *Student Rights: Relevant Aspects for Guidance Counselors*. Washington, D.C.: American School Counselor Association, 1977.

For those who want to get an understanding of the emerging concerns for pupil rights, legal bases of policy, and productive strategies for the counselor, this is an extremely valuable reference.

Lee, James L., and Pulvino, Charles J., eds. *Group Counseling: Theory, Research and Practice*. Washington, D.C.: American Personnel and Guidance Association, 1973.

A collection of outstanding articles on groups from journals of the American Personnel and Guidance Association. The school level is well represented.

Smith, Paul M., Jr. "Get Together Now!" *Personnel and Guidance Journal* 48, no. 9 (1970), p. 706.

This special issue on guidance for blacks is the first of a number that deals with special groups and types of problems. Each is a valuable reference in learning to work with cultural, ethnic, or other groups.

Zimpfer, David G., "Some Conceptual and Research Problems in Group Counseling." *School Counselor* 15, no. 5 (1968), pp. 326–333.

The lead article in a special issue on group counseling. An excellent reference on theory, research, and applications.

Weinrach, Stephen G., "Reviews," *Personnel and Guidance Journal*, vol. 55, no. 9, 1977, pp. 556–559 and vol. 55, no. 10, 1977, pp. 612–618.

Reviews of many of the best known packaged group techniques, including some that are briefly mentioned in this chapter, for example, PET, values clarification. Comments of evaluators, many of whom took part in group leader training, and responses of originators of the techniques are extremely helpful in understanding purpose and effectiveness of those new approaches to group work.

CHAPTER NINE

PROVIDING INFORMATION:

THE COUNSELOR'S ROLE

School counselors need to have up-to-date information about educational and training opportunities and about areas of personal and social concerns. They need to know what types of information are available, where to get it, how to evaluate it, and how to provide it to others. Sophisticated technological instruments, group and individual counseling, large-scale guidance procedures, and regular classes are the major methods and settings for dissemination.

In deciding on an occupation, selecting a school, or sorting out personal and social problems, many types of information are needed. Pupils ask questions like, What does an architect do? Where can I get training to be a machinist? What effects do drugs have? What do I do in a job interview? The need for information is universal. The school should have all sorts on hand in easily accessible form.

GOALS

1. **To develop an awareness of the importance and need for information in the guidance program.**
2. **To learn about the major types of information the school counselor uses.**
3. **To help conceptualize a model for an information service.**

Minimally, information about occupations, educational and training opportunities, and personal-social areas should cover the following points:

Occupations
— What one does in the occupation.
— Requirements for employment (including training, education, experience, and psychological and physical factors).

— Remuneration (including fringe benefits).
— The relation of school subjects to the occupation.
— How to locate jobs, how to apply, and how to participate in employment interviews.
— Trends in the occupation, particularly numbers of persons needed compared with the number being prepared.
— Opportunities for advancement.
— Relations among occupations and groupings of similar occupations.
— The life-styles that go with occupations (the social climate, the sociological characteristics of the work setting, the life and career patterns of workers).
— Local full-time and part-time opportunities.

Educational and Training Opportunities
— Data about programs, entrance requirements, costs, housing, and degrees or certificates.
— Relation of training and education to occupations.
— Information about financial assistance, e.g., scholarships, fellowships, loans, and part-time work.
— Characteristics of students in the institution.
— Climate of institutions, particularly colleges and universities (academic, professional, social).
— Information about value derived from various educational or training programs (cultural values, occupational preparation, etc.).

Personal-social Information Needs here run the gamut from self-understanding, home and family relations, and peer relations to drugs, sex, values, maturity, and physical and psychological development. New needs are constantly emerging as previously taboo subjects like abortion and homosexuality are being discussed more frankly. An almost endless variety of materials, differing in format, medium, and content, is available to meet these needs. The limited number of examples identified in this chapter illustrate the sources the counselor can turn to.

THE PERSONAL-SOCIAL-CAREER INFORMATION CENTER

Ideally, the information center should make data readily available to pupils, teachers, and others. This concept seems to be well accepted at the high school level, especially in terms of career information. But the center should also provide access to social and personal information, and such facilities are needed also at the elementary and middle school levels (Handel 1973). With an increased emphasis on career education, the elementary school should have an organized, up-to-date collection of career information for use both by pupils and teachers. Shertzer and Stone

(1976, p. 302) state that both elementary and secondary schools need all the information they can get to help with social, academic, and career decisions.

The information service brings together all types of media and techniques, including community resources. Data sources range from individual booklets on single occupations to computer memory banks with information about hundreds of occupations. Community resources are listed in a card file of persons who will talk with pupils interested in their line of work or of establishments where pupils can observe jobs or get part-time exploratory work experience. A counselor or paraprofessional may give group or individual help. Outreach programs are often provided in the form of large-scale group procedures such as career days and career fairs. Pupils with special needs may be helped by group sessions (e.g., those designed to teach effective participation in employment interviews). Packaged techniques (such as vocational exploration groups) may be used for those who need help making choices.

Establishing the service involves assigning responsibility, assessing need, designing the system, selecting materials, testing the system, instructing both pupils and counselors how to use it, and follow-up and evaluation. The public schools in Newton, Massachusetts have developed a complete career information center, including a library, job placement facilities, and follow-up services (Campbell, Walz, Miller, and Kriger 1973, pp. 125, 127–128).

The information-center concept will no doubt be increasingly accepted, and school counselors will be expected to be knowledgeable in this method of guidance delivery. One supporting factor is the U.S. Department of Labor Program to help states and local school systems set up occupational information centers (Stern 1975). Furthermore, the concept makes possible systematic planning and evaluation, thus following an important trend in contemporary guidance.

RESEARCH

EVALUATION OF INFORMATION CENTERS

In 1972, Jacobson described information-center plans in four California schools; he emphasized the value of bringing sources of information together and the necessity of using paraprofessionals so that centers can be staffed at all times. He later evaluated information centers in California and found that they tend to fall in four levels: those just being organized; those providing information; those emphasizing career development; and those providing a full services program with professional staff and extensive integrated services (Jacobson 1975, pp. 5–7).

Pupil evaluations of each center's services include the following positive results (p. 75):

	Number of Visits to Career Center					
	None	1–2 Times	3–4 Times	5–6 Times	7 or More Times	F Lin Ratio
Receiving enough career guidance	2.20	2.66	3.01	3.35	3.57	80.63
Assistance in exploring careers	1.87	2.10	2.50	2.68	2.96	48.00

The results of only the two above items from the extensive data collected, show (in the F test for linearity) that there is a significant increase in pupil satisfaction with guidance assistance the more the service is used. In addition, pupils in schools with no information centers give an average response of 2.25 to the first question ("Are you receiving enough career guidance?") — a rating of 2 means "not enough."

The complete findings show that career centers are needed in schools, that they should concentrate on encouraging pupils to make regular visits, and should help them learn how to utilize information and make decisions (Jacobson 1975, p. 115).

EXPERIENCE

VISITING AN INFORMATION CENTER

Make an informal survey of local school and college information centers by visits or phone calls. First, find out if these institutions have such centers at all. Then ask what they consist of and who uses them. Compare these facilities with what you would consider an effective, well-organized center.

EXPERIENCE

AWARENESS OF INFORMATION NEEDS

In a small group ask members to think about an important career or educational decision they are making or expect to make in the future. Then have each person briefly present the decision and identify the three most important types of information needed to make it. The others note whether they agree or disagree with the stated priorities. After the presentation, have members give feedback to each other about agreement or disagreement with priorities.

In conclusion, discuss what members have learned about the utility and the relative importance of various types of information in decision making.

OBJECTIVES

1. To be able to identify the types of information about occupations pupils need. List five questions that should be considered in choosing an occupation.

Questions could include: What does one do? How much education or training is needed? What school subjects are related to the occupation? What are the trends? What are the financial and other benefits?

2. To be aware of questions pupils should ask about educational and training opportunities. List three questions that the counselor might raise with pupils when programs are being considered.

A pupil should be able to answer the following questions (among others) before choosing an educational or training program: How long does it take? How much does it cost? What are the abilities and preparation required for admission?

3. To understand the scope of personal-social information. Identify three areas of pupil concern that should be provided for by this type of information.

Home and family relations, peer relations, and drugs are among the most important.

4. To understand the benefits of having a school information center. In one sentence, state the major reasons for having this type of facility.

The major reason is that it brings together all types of information in a systematic way for easy access.

A FRAMEWORK FOR THE USE OF INFORMATION   The decision model discussed in Chapter 7 provides a framework for information-giving strategies. As the counselee begins to identify options, there is an essential need for exploratory information. For example: What school programs are available and what are their requirements? To what types of occupations or advanced training do they lead? As preliminary decisions narrow the range of choices, more detailed information is needed. A counselee who is beginning to consider engineering as a college major needs to know such

specifics as what institutions offer programs, costs, admission requirements, types of students that attend, the course programs, types of work
to which programs lead, and employment trends in engineering occupations; throughout the process the counselee also needs to consider information in terms of personal interests, values, abilities, and achievements.

The use of information in the decision process is based on the counselee's grade level and maturity. For example, career information for third
graders would be quite different from that appropriate for middle school
pupils or high school seniors. But decision processes would be the same.

The overall rationale for the use of information indicates that information should be fed into the guidance and counseling process when needed
to facilitate decision making. This process calls for an extensive and readily available supply of up-to-date and accurate information. Examples in
the next section indicate popular items. Technological aids described later
facilitate the delivery of information to pupils in usable form.

RESEARCH

DECISION STRATEGIES USED BY PUPILS

Jepsen (1974) used 59 female and 59 male high school pupils from
eleven Wisconsin high schools to study decision strategies used by
non-college-bound pupils.

Results showed a total of twelve different strategy types. The two
with the larger memberships were:

Strategy type 6: Active planners — These were described as active, knowledgeable, and self-aware. They were involved in planning, engaged in more school-community activities, named more
friends, and provided more self-descriptions than other pupils. They
had considered more occupational alternatives than the average
pupil, and had explored information sources more thoroughly.

Strategy type 3: Singular fatalists—Members of this type sought
little career information, concentrated on a narrow range of goals,
and did not see current actions as related to plans.

The author describes this as an exploratory study involving only a
small number of pupils. Even so, the evidence suggests that not all
pupils can obtain and use information with equal effectiveness.

In other research Jepsen showed (1975) that even among a group
with similar objectives pupils over the high school years engage in
more complex information search about occupations and feel more
confident about preferred occupational choices. Pupils tend to have
more reasons and to bring more self-knowledge to bear on choices,
and to show an increase in number of rewards expected.

A SURVEY OF RESOURCES   To understand the counselor's task of setting up and maintaining an information service, a rundown of some of the more widely used materials and technologies is helpful. Admittedly the area is complex; not only are resources extensive and of widely different types, but specific materials quickly go out of date; ongoing maintenance is needed. Local information such as that obtained directly from workers and employers is often the most useful. For example, it may be interesting to know that the need for carpenters nationwide is increasing, but the boy who is considering this work in his community needs to know his chances for getting a job in local construction when voc-tech training and apprenticeship are completed. Both local and national information are integral to a complete information service.

Reference Works   When the counselor begins to build an information center, a good first step is to obtain one or more indexes to help locate needed data. Three well-known reference works are *Vocational Guidance Quarterly, Inform,* and *Counselor's Information Service.* The first is the journal of the National Vocational Guidance Association (APGA, 1607 New Hampshire Avenue, N.W., Washington, D.C. 20009); it regularly contains a section on career literature and frequently includes a section on films. Both briefly describe and evaluate materials. *Counselor's Information Service,* a quarterly publication describing all sorts of information, may be obtained from B'nai B'rith Career and Counseling Services (1640 Rhode Island Avenue, N.W., Washington, D.C. 20036). *Inform* is issued ten times a year by the American Personnel and Guidance Association (address above) and provides sources of current career information and bibliographies on particular work areas such as science and public service.

A center typically includes books describing occupations. The best-known is the *Occupational Outlook Handbook* (U.S. Department of Labor 1976) which covers more than 850 occupations and 35 major industries; at $7, it is the best buy in the field. Another well-known set of books is the *Encyclopedia of Vocational Guidance* (3rd ed.; Garrett Park Press, Garrett Park, Md. 20766), covering data on 650 fields of work and related information. A new fourth edition of the *Dictionary of Occupational Titles* (U.S. Department of Labor 1977) to replace the widely used third edition published in 1965 provides valuable planning assistance to pupils and counselors. Occupational definitions and information about worker traits and occupational groups are provided. A separate publication of the new edition is specifically designed for work with high school pupils. There are many other books on occupations that can be used in the information service. The indexes provide an efficient way to locate them.

Much information is available in pamphlets and booklets, but such materials must be used with caution. Some are accurate and unbiased,

A good information center provides personal-social information — but there are limits.

but many of them, particularly free materials, are designed for recruiting purposes.

No one can begin to remember all the details pupils and parents request. But guides and directories to educational and training institutions make up an important part of the information service. Lists of publications may be found in Norris, Zeran, Hatch, and Engelkes (1972, pp. 212–218) and Tolbert (1974, pp. 109–110); current information about the most recent editions should be obtained from publishers. Users of the information service also need to know about opportunities for financial aid. This information is difficult to obtain, but college and training institution catalogues are of some help. The service should include the most recent catalogues and other publications of community and four-year colleges, universities, trade and technical schools, apprenticeship programs, and other types of information of potential interest to pupils.

The Informational File The basic information service resource is the occupational file. Even with computers and other technological aids, it is a standard aid. The counselor decides on the type of file and selects or institutes a plan for building and maintaining it. File folders are set up in some useful way (e.g., alphabetically). The most practical plan is to purchase a ready-made system such as those described in Hoppock (1976, pp. 55–62) or Norris, Zeran, Hatch, and Engelkes (1972, pp. 385–394). Files come complete with materials, and some publishers offer subscription services to keep files up to date.

Films, Filmstrips, and Related Materials The media have moved into the guidance field with a wide range of well-made and effective materials. Films, filmstrips, videotapes, and slide-sound programs cover the whole range of pupil needs—careers, education and training, social and personal questions. The American Personnel and Guidance Association's twelve-film series, WERC (Why Not Explore Rewarding Careers?), is an excellent example of information about careers that do not require a college degree. For preschoolers a sixteen-film series on career awareness, "The Kingdom that Could Be You," helps develop a sense of the importance of work (Ralston 1974). The sound filmstrips prepared by Guidance Associates (757 Third Avenue, New York, N.Y. 10017) cover all areas, and offer complete programs of series of sound filmstrips on topics such as drug abuse. Locally made films, slides, and audiotapes can be valuable supplements to the information service and have a special relevance for the particular school and community. For example, one counselor recorded a series of interviews with local workers for pupils to use in learning about community jobs.

Information Systems There are a number of what might be called "systems" for information, utilizing various media and equipped with instructions for use, that do not involve complex technology. The Guidance Associates drug program mentioned above is one example. Career Wheels, marketed by the American Personnel and Guidance Association, are relatively simple pupil-oriented devices for educational and occupational information; the pupil can dial information about occupations in five major areas, such as social science. The *Career Data Book* (Flanagan, Tiedeman, Willis, and McLaughlin 1973) gives profiles of aptitudes, abilities, interests, and other variables for a longitudinal study of high school pupils in various work groups (e.g., engineering, business). A second volume, *Using the Talent Profiles in Counseling* (Rossi, Bartlett, Campbell, Wise, McLaughlin 1975), explains how to use the profiles. A good way to learn about these programs and materials is to look through issues of *Vocational Guidance Quarterly* for brief reviews before contacting publishers. These materials are often expensive, and it is wise to request a preview before purchasing.

Informational techniques utilizing moderately complex technology are illustrated by the VIEW (Vital Information for Education and Work) system (Tolbert 1974, pp. 126–128). It consists of microfiche cards containing both national and local information about work and necessary preparation and a microfiche reader-printer that allows users to read and make personal copies of information. At a related level of complexity are programs in which the pupil operates a sound slide show using a special type of audiotape slide projector (Hansen 1970, pp. 88–97).

Information services often include simulation materials and games. *Job experience kits* (Krumboltz 1970) are an example. Following directions in the kit and working with materials provided, pupils, individually or in groups, learn about the work of, for example, a carpenter or accountant.

Computer guidance systems are the most sophisticated, complex, and expensive of all, but they offer the greatest potential for improving guidance. Picture the pupil sitting down at what appears to be a large typewriter keyboard with a screen like a TV beside it. Using the keyboard, the pupil asks about occupational areas that relate to interests and abilities. Suggested areas appear on the screen, along with comments about which ones look best. The pupil selects one or two and types questions about suitability. The screen shows comparisons and points out unrealistic goals, whether too high or too low. Detailed information about the work itself (e.g., opportunities for employment, remuneration) are available instantly. The pupil may spend only one or two hours at the computer terminal, but receives more information about occupations, educational opportunities, and how his or her personal qualities compare with those of workers in fields under consideration than a team of experts could have collected and provided in several days!

Computer guidance systems may be classified as "indirect inquiry systems," "direct inquiry systems without monitoring," and "direct inquiry systems with monitoring" (Harris 1972*a*, pp. 4–7). This classification does not include test reporting systems that compute scores and sometimes provide interpretive printouts. Systems have been developed in each of these categories, and are operational in schools.

The first category, involving *indirect inquiry,* usually operates on the basis of questions. Typically a system of this kind will store answers on a questionnaire, and hold them until enough data have been collected to return a report. For example in college selection the pupil fills out a questionnaire about geographical preferences, grades, interests, test scores, and other data, and after an interval, receives a report on suitable colleges to apply to. Another example used in college placement centers is a system of matching seniors with employers.

In the second category, involving *direct inquiry without monitoring,* the pupil can obtain information directly from the computer, for example by using a terminal keyboard to ask questions about occupations, educational institutions, and other areas. It is, as Harris says (1972, p. 7), similar to using an automated library for instant information. The individual interacts with the computer, but it stores no personal data. Another example, the *Guidance Information System* (GIS), formerly known as the *Interactive Learning System* (ILS), is in use in over 1,400 career information centers in twenty-six states (Time Share n. d.). Now owned by Houghton Mifflin, this system provides occupational, educational, and financial-aid information and directs the user to other multimedia resources that are part of the total program.

The third category, involving *direct inquiry systems with monitoring*, is the most significant model for counselors. This is the type illustrated at the beginning of this section. The key features are: data banks with information about occupations and educational and training programs; data about the individual; data about interactions; and the capability to relate all of these. The computer, with the aid of a visual display, can answer questions about how the individual compares with those working in an occupation, evaluate decision-making ability, and suggest various options. It is somewhat like a "counseling" situation, although attempts to have computers actually counsel have not been successful (Super 1970, p. 4).

There are several systems of the third category serving pupils. CVIS (Computer Vocational Information System) is in operation at Willowbrook High School, Villa Park, Ill., and in approximately 375 other sites, serving junior high schools, secondary schools, and community colleges (Harris 1972 *b*; Rabush 1976). ECES (Educational and Career Exploration System) is in operation in Genesee Intermediate School District, Genesee County, Mich. (Mallory 1972). This system has been incorporated in a counselor-computer plan for more effective help to pupils and has generated positive counselor attitudes toward computer capabilities (Mallory and Drake 1973, pp. 19–27). *Discovery*, a new system in the development stage (Harris-Bowlsbey 1975), forecasts a new generation of computer guidance systems. Some of the seven components, which range from self-concept clarification to implementing a career plan, require counselor, teacher, and community support; the system cannot stand alone. Discovery has been field-tested with pupils in grades 7–12 at all achievement levels and with college students. Results have shown it to be suitable for this entire range of subjects (Discover, n. d., p. 2).

The computer-guidance field is relatively new but is developing rapidly. Harris predicts major new advances that will increase visual capability; offer users the opportunity to simulate occupational, educational, and personal experiences; enhance decision-making processes; and permit group interaction through computer terminals (1972*a*, pp. 10–11). Evaluation shows that operational systems are well accepted by users, do as well as counselors on certain tasks, increase vocational maturity, and are reasonable in cost (Harris 1974).

EVALUATION OF INFORMATION   The task of evaluating information falls to the counselor, and since the amount, complexity, and cost of information are accelerating rapidly, this responsibility is becoming more critical. But well-developed criteria for evaluation are available. In addition to the ratings of materials in the *Vocational Guidance Quarterly*, the National Vocational Guidance Association has published *Guidelines* (1972) for printed materials, films, and filmstrips. Weinrach (1974) used these guidelines in preparing a complete and convenient evaluation form that takes into account such critical factors as date, coverage, authors' qualifications, format, and content. Hill's earlier checklist (1966) is still useful, and Norris, Zeran, Hatch, and Engelkes (1972, pp. 193–200, 244–245, 286–287) give criteria and procedures for evaluating career, educational, and personal-social information.

RESEARCH

SOME RESULTS OF COMPUTER GUIDANCE SYSTEMS AND DECISION-MAKING-SKILLS TRAINING

The use of the ECES (Educational and Career Exploration System) combined with counseling and a decision-making curriculum showed the following results:

— 79% of a group of eleventh graders felt that decision-making-skills training and ECES gave them skills they could continue to use in career planning.
— 97% of another group, comprised of tenth and eleventh graders, felt that decision-making-skills training and ECES skills would continue to be helpful in their career planning.

Counselors rated students using ECES decision-making-skills training significantly higher (<.01) in their preparedness for making career decisions than students who did not use ECES or did not have skill training (Mallory and Drake 1973, p. 22).

RESEARCH

BIAS IN OCCUPATIONAL MATERIALS — A FACTOR IN EVALUATION

Lauver, Gastellum, and Sheehey (1975) analyzed photographic illustrations in the *Occupational Outlook Handbook* in terms of sex, age, and ethnic origin of workers on different jobs. In one occupational category, scientific and technical workers, results are as follows:

Sex —
    female: 8   total: 40   percentage female: 20
Age —
    twenties: 2 thirties: 11 forties: 9 fifty and over: 6
Ethnic Origin —
    minority: 5 total: 32 percentage minority: 16
Minimum Educational Requirements —
    8th grade and below: 0 above 8th grade: 31

The authors point out that the representation in illustrations does not match occupational distributions; women make up 37 percent of the work force. Illustrations are thought to exert a subtle force on the reader ("A picture is worth a thousand words").

Overs (1975) argues that photographs should reflect the actual rather than a biased or idealized distribution, even if an explanatory note details differences between percentages in given jobs and percentages of workers in the labor force by sex, age, and minority-group status.

Bias is one of the chief factors to consider in evaluating all information, including that dispensed by computers and other technology. Others are accuracy, clarity for the intended consumer, comprehensiveness, and relevance.

OBJECTIVES

1. To be able to identify useful types of materials for the information service. Name five specific items.

A number are listed in this chapter. Indexes, as included in *Vocational Guidance Quarterly, Inform,* and *Counselor's Informational Service* are needed. Current editions of *Occupational Outlook Handbook* and *Dictionary of Occupational Titles* are also essential items.

2. To be aware of the potential of technology for providing information. Name two types of technology useful in the information service and identify one unique contribution of each.

Microfiche viewers—store a large amount of up-to-date information in a small space.

Computer guidance systems—assist pupils with information and predictions for decision making.

3. To appreciate that information usually has affective as well as cognitive meaning for the pupil. Recall a fact that you considered in planning your college major. Was affect involved?

You may, for example, have learned that a certain test score was required for admission, that jobs would be plentiful, or that financial aid was available. Did those or other similar factors influence your feelings about the choice?

4. To be able to identify new developments in technology and materials that facilitate the work of the counselor. Name three types of developments and explain in one sentence how each helps the counselor.

— Prepared programs—The counselor can easily train others to use them.
— Self-administered guidance instruments—The counselor can reach a larger number of pupils.
— Computer guidance systems—The counselor is relieved of the task of collecting and providing information.

COUNSELING ACTIVITIES IN PROVIDING INFORMATION

Methods of providing information range from one-to-one counseling to large-group activities, which the counselor directs or coordinates. The most important factors are the meaning of information to counselees, how they feel about it, and what is appropriate at given stages of development. Thus, providing information involves career-development, counseling, and learning theory, and dealing both with affective and cognitive aspects of development. With the broadened concept of career as life-style (Hansen and Gysbers 1975), career information, educational information, and personal-social information merge, but enough differences remain that special attention must be paid to each type.

PROVIDING INFORMATION THROUGH INDIVIDUAL COUNSELING The essential conditions for effective communication of information are the counselee's own awareness of need and expressed desire to receive it. The counselor may make use of a variety of materials and techniques (Krumboltz and Baker 1973), including job simulation, the occupational file, the *Occupational Outlook Handbook,* or homework involving viewing a film or slide-sound program, or interviewing a worker. The important factor is that the counselee participate actively in the process and assume responsibility for carrying out exploratory activities (Herr and Kramer 1972, p. 224).

PROVIDING INFORMATION THROUGH GROUPS   The group situation has the double advantage of economy and interaction, and is the ideal setting for providing information. Whether the method is simulation, films, talks, interviews, modeling, or some other procedure, all members can learn at the same time. The interaction among members enhances the meaning and personal relevance of information.

Groups are usually more than strictly information-giving sessions; they combine personal exploration with the dispensing of factual material within the framework of a developmental theory. Healy's developmental group procedure (1973) is an example. Five sessions are used to explore personal concerns; learn about potentially suitable occupations; assess personal potential; plan a course of action; and implement the plan. Interaction is used throughout the process to encourage and support exploration and planning. Evaluation of the model showed positive results in terms of increased confidence in making a choice and willingness to engage in planning (Healy 1974).

The group approach provides an effective, interesting, and economical way for the counselor to expand the essential information-giving function. The benefits of face-to-face contacts both with counselor and peers are realized, and the personal meaning of information is enhanced. Programs like VEG and Deciding exploit the advantages of learnings that accrue from interactions among counselees. Resource persons—e.g., local employers—can meet with groups to present material and discuss opportunities. Groups have been used effectively to increase awareness of career options in sixth-grade girls (S. Harris 1974). Pupils in small schools can meet in group sessions to process information obtained in community visits to employers; this procedure contributes to the school career education program and enhances positive school-community relations (Stillwell and Collison 1974). In one junior high school, the language arts curriculum was used to help pupils explore interests and abilities through simulation materials and studies of occupational clusters, and thus greatly facilitated career development (Winter and Schmidt 1974).

Groups can effectively take advantage of learning theory and technology in promoting the use of information. Several types of reinforcement in group sessions motivated high school and college counselees to seek out more career information than those who did not receive this kind of stimulation (Krumboltz and Schroeder 1965; Fisher, Reardon, and Burck 1976). Groups have been used to enhance the effects of computer guidance systems (Cassele and Mehail 1973; Mallory and Drake 1973). Other types have been used to motivate truants to return to school (Grala and McCauley 1976).

Many methods of providing information are aimed at classes rather than small groups, particularly in elementary school. Activities include drawing pictures of jobs and discussing them, reviewing educational preferences, and discussing workers pupils know (Jefferies and Spedding 1974). Sequential team-building projects such as communication exercises, taking on work roles, and engaging in small-group career projects have also been tried (Wubbolding and Osborne 1976). Career units using a multimedia approach to study related occupations (Washburn and Schmaljohn 1975) and job placement for in-school helping positions (Elleson and Onmink 1976) are other new and innovative approaches. Sustained career development activities in junior high school have been shown to increase students' occupational knowledge (Perrone and Kyle 1975).

School-wide information programs have in some cases been incorporated in career education programs, though in many schools counselors have no significant role in this new educational model. Mesa, Ariz. (McKinnon and Jones 1975), has a system that uses guidance units with all types of information for K–12, and counselors here have played an active part. The guidance program has become an integral part of the total career educational model. The Detroit Developmental Career Guidance Project, a K–12 program for disadvantaged youth (Leonard and Vriend 1975), brings school and community together in a cooperative program, which utilizes classroom activities by teachers and counselors and provides a wide range of informational activities, e.g., films, career games, field trips, and work experience. A unique feature of the program is the heavy involvement of parents. It is an excellent example of a well-planned system that utilizes both school and community resources.

The Life-Career Development System (Walz and Benjamin 1974) is an example of a program for high school and adult populations. Nine modules, each consisting of several sessions, help participants develop the understanding and competencies for a successful and rewarding life. Emphasis is on applying learning to one's personal situation and on practicing new skills. This program illustrates a new generation of carefully planned developmental experiences for which leaders need to participate in preliminary training programs.

Placement has had a checkered past (Campbell, Walz, Miller, and Kriger 1973, p. 202) but is emerging as an important school service, particularly in career education (see Ch. 13). The information service has a responsibility to help individuals learn about occupations, make decisions, and develop ways to implement them. It ties in with both educational and occupational placement. Exploratory work experience, an excellent way to obtain occupational information, involves placement; pupils planning to go to work after high school rate it the best method (Jacobson 1975, pp. 68–71). Placement is coming to be accepted as a school responsibility emphasizing community linkage, development of pupil competence in getting jobs, and follow-through to provide additional help if needed (Odell, Pritchard, and Sinick 1974).

RESEARCH

METHODS OF PRESENTING OCCUPATIONAL INFORMATION

Johnson, Korn, and Dunn (1975) employed three methods for presenting occupational information to 58 high school pupils, ages 15–17, classified as reluctant learners. The three methods were printed word, audiotape, and slide-tape presentation; a control group received no treatment. A test was used to assess the amount of information learned, and preferences were obtained by a questionnaire. Differences among groups were significant at the .01 level, both for amount learned and preferences for methods. The slide-tape presentation was the most effective and the most widely preferred.

The authors point out the practicality of homemade information. Researching and producing the 32 slides and interviews took a total of 5.5 hours and cost less than $50. They suggest this approach for meeting the informational needs of special target groups.

EXPERIENCE

YOUR OWN NEED FOR INFORMATION

Take five sheets of paper and write one of the following statements at the top of each:

— Who am I?
— What do I want out of life?
— What can I do best?
— Where could I do it?
— What additional preparation do I need?

Take a few minutes to write answers to each question.

Then go back and underline items that call for information. Do the results give you any new insights about the importance of information?

EXPERIENCE

KNOWING OPTIONS

Imagine that you have won a lottery that will pay you $1,000 a week for life. Would you continue doing what you are doing now? If not, what would you do? Is your decision based on preferences or a lack of information about alternatives?

Raise the same question with a small group, and go around for answers.

EXPERIENCE

REWARDS OF OCCUPATIONS

Interview someone in the line of work you plan to enter. Ask for the one most desirable aspect of the work. Compare this with what you consider to be the most attractive feature. Are they the same? Does the response have any effect on your plans?

EXPERIENCE

HOW IMPORTANT IS INFORMATION?

This activity can be carried out in an individual interview or a small group. The purpose is to identify points in one's life when lack of information (or inaccurate information) resulted in unsatisfactory action.

Ask members to recall an important educational or career decision and have them identify the most significant information that was used, or needed but not available. (Often another individual will have been the source of such information.)

Then go around the group and ask each individual briefly to answer these questions: In light of what I know today, was any essential information lacking? What would I have done if I had known then what I know now?

EXPERIENCE

FINDING INFORMATION

This activity can be carried out by an individual or a small group.

Make a list of five specific areas about which counselees may need information (e.g., college admissions, pregnancy clinics, job openings). Then rank them according to ready availability in specific community sources you can name. (Do not list college catalogues for college admission information, but places in the community where such catalogues are available.)

What does your ranking show about your knowledge of sources? How can you upgrade your knowledge if improvement is needed?

OBJECTIVES

1. To become aware of individual and group methods the counselor uses to provide information. Name three settings in which information can be provided.

In one-to-one counseling, in small groups, and in the classroom.

2. To understand the importance of placement as a guidance service. Ask three persons how much they knew about finding a suitable educational program or job the last two times they made a change. Ask yourself the same question.

Maybe no difficulties were experienced, but chances are that people you talk to (and you) were more or less at a loss about how to go about making a change, wasted a great deal of time, missed some good opportunities, and experienced some anxiety. The need for placement services is obvious.

ADDITIONAL READINGS

Isaacson, Lee E. *Career Information in Counseling and Teaching*. 3rd ed. Boston: Allyn and Bacon, 1977.

A definitive text on career information and its use in guidance and counseling. Part 5, on occupational information materials and techniques, is particularly useful in connection with this chapter.

Norris, Willa; Zeran, Franklin R.; Hatch, Raymond N.; and Engelkes, James R. *The Information Service in Guidance*. 3rd ed. Chicago: Rand McNally, 1972.

Almost any section of this book provides background for topics in this chapter. Pages 27–36 define types of information needed; Part 3, pages 157–287, is a comprehensive review of the many types available. Local occupational surveys (not covered in this chapter but an important type of community information) are described in Chapter 8.

Pietrofesa, John J., and Splete, Howard. *Career Development: Theory and Research*. New York: Grune and Stratton, 1975.

Chapter 8 on decision making helpfully discusses how information can facilitate the guidance process. Other sections of the book deal with all the chief aspects of career development, and provide a useful foundation in this area.

Super, Donald E., ed. *Computer-Assisted Counseling*. New York: Teachers College Press, 1970.

A series of reports on computer guidance systems providing a comprehensive view of developments, problems, and guidelines for users. Although it is several years old, it is the most comprehensive publication available.

Tolbert, E. L. *Counseling for Career Development*. Boston: Houghton Mifflin, 1974.

Information systems are discussed in Chapter 4; group methods are reviewed in Chapter 7.

Walz, Garry R.; Smith, Robert L.; and Benjamin, Libby, eds. *A Comprehensive View of Career Development*. Washington, D.C.: American Personnel and Guidance Association, 1974.

This contemporary review of promising trends and practices emphasizes career guidance, but also discusses various types of information systems.

CHAPTER TEN
CONSULTATION:
EFFECTING
SYSTEM-WIDE CHANGE

One of the major new directions of guidance today is consultation—working with others who will in turn help pupils. This process spreads the effects of guidance. If, for example, a counselor spends one hour assisting a teacher in responding to feelings, as many as 150 or more pupils may benefit! If a few hours with administrators bring about positive program changes, results can affect the entire school. Consultation provides a means to serve as a change agent, modify the environment, and build system-wide developmental programs.

Models for program development discussed in Chapter 6 make extensive use of the consulting approach. The cube model (Morrill, Oetting, and Hurst 1974) includes consulting as an intervention method. Shaw (1973, p. 94) considers consultation a major strategy in the indirect approach. In the services models, consultation is being used increasingly to enhance the impact of guidance throughout the school.

GOALS

1. To understand the consulting function.
2. To understand one's own attitudes toward it.

DEFINITION AND IMPORTANCE
OF THE CONSULTING FUNCTION

Any good definition of consultation should compare and contrast this activity with counseling. McGehearty does so lucidly and completely:

> The philosophical base is similar—both processes move toward helping a person help himself. One of the major goals of the consultant is to help the consultee to recognize his own strengths and weaknesses and the ways in which he as a person may interact constructively with another person. This other person may be a parishioner, student, law-breaker, or ordinary citizen.
>
> The major difference in the actual technique of consultation (as narrowly defined—there are many other varieties of consultation) is that it focuses the interview on a third client, rather than on the consultee himself. The professional brings with him a body of knowledge, and the consultee has at his command a different body of knowledge from a different discipline. The sharing of knowledge is a very real part of the process, and the result is a genuine sense of peer relationship. As with counseling, the consultant is listening with his "third ear" to the consultee tell about his case. The consultant exercises every particle of the professional skill at his command to evaluate the person in front of him and to understand his phenomenological world. He tries to move into the frame of reference of the consultee and see the world through his perceptual framework (1968, pp. 259–260).

Thus helping skills as described in Chapter 7 are essential to consultation; the aim is to help a third party solve personal problems, and teaching is an acceptable aspect of the process.

Role statements for school counselors at all levels emphasize the consulting function. The American School Counselor Association Statement of Policy and Guidelines (ASCA 1965) states that the counselor helps all members of the staff to understand pupils and the effects of the school program on pupils, and works with parents to assist them to facilitate children's development. Specific consulting responsibilities are identified, e.g., sharing pupil data with staff members, helping teachers to identify pupils' problems, providing in-service training. A later statement for the secondary level (ASCA, 1974b) further outlines responsibilities to parents, teachers, administration, and the community, for example, working closely with the administration to build a positive atmosphere in the school.

The situation is the same in middle school and particularly similar in elementary school. One of the major functions of the elementary school counselor (ASCA 1974c) is consulting with teachers, other staff members, and parents. At the middle and junior high school levels (ASCA 1974d) the point is made that the counselor must share his or her knowledge and expertise with teachers, administrators, and parents through conferences and in-service meetings. Other professional publications, too, emphasize the importance of the consulting function. *Elementary School Guidance and Counseling Journal* (Carlson 1972) devoted a special issue to the topic. The APGA reprint series on the consulting process covers a wide range (Carlson, Splete, and Kern 1975). Gerler (1976) found that a large number of articles in guidance journals suggested that the work of counselors is generally some form of consultation. He concluded that consultation and training are widely considered the most appropriate means for delivering counseling services, particularly in times of budget cutbacks and more demanding standards of accountability. The report of the Vail Conference, dealing with issues of social control v. impact on society, suggests that counselors must deal with factors causing problems in society rather than serve as social control agents with the goal of making counselees adjust to negative conditions (Ivey and Leppaluoto 1975).

The consulting role, however, does not seem to be very well understood. Counselors have not been getting their functions across to administrators, teachers, and others. Particularly administrators lack a clear perception of the consulting emphasis; counselors understand it much better than teachers (Buckner 1975). It is possible that administrators tend to see the counselor consultant as a member of the supervisor's staff rather than as a helper providing direct services to pupils. This misapprehension, if widespread, would greatly diminish the counselor's effectiveness.

Consultation today includes much more than working one-to-one with a counselee on the subject of a third person. Newer strategies involve a wide variety of methods for institutional change; working with parents; and helping teachers, pupils, and administrators. Consulting now includes such features as helping peer counselors become facilitators; it reflects contemporary needs and trends such as "giving counseling away" and using expertise to promote human welfare (Miller 1969). Accountability has required that counselors help others perform more effectively by serving as learning development consultants (Stilwell and Santoro 1976).

EXPERIENCE

BEING A CONSULTEE

One way to experience consultation is to serve as consultee, seeking help for a third person. A real problem of a friend, college student, or high school pupil, should not be difficult to find, but a hypothetical one will do. Ask a counselor to help you help the third person. (Explain that this is "practice" for you.) Note particularly the focus of the conference. Is it on the third person? Does it include your needs and attitudes?

What are your feelings about being a consultee? (Do you, for example, feel involved, subservient, threatened, secure?) What would you do differently if you were the consultant?

RESEARCH

WHAT JOURNAL ARTICLES SAY ABOUT CONSULTATION

Gerler's study of four guidance journals for the years 1970–74, referred to above, involved locating comments about accountability and cutbacks and identifying practices to help counselors cope with threatened staff reductions. Results showed the wide acceptance of consulting as a way to deliver services efficiently:

ARTICLES RECOMMENDING CONSULTING

Strategy	Number
Work with individuals and small groups	34 (of 206 total)
Increase in counselor intervention with associational groups (groups based on interests or needs)	129
Increase in counselor intervention in institution/community	116
Using consultation/training as a method of intervention	116

Gerler interprets the results as strong support for a consultation approach to meeting needs and justifying support of services (Gerler 1976, pp. 249–250).

OBJECTIVES

1. **To understand attitudes of professional organizations toward consultation. What is the position of the American Personnel and Guidance Association and Divisions on the function?**

Positive. All role statements emphasize its importance.

2. To become aware of the potential extent of the use of consultation. Name groups with whom the counselor could consult.

Teachers, administrators, pupils, parents, other community members.

3. To be aware of problems that may arise because of the consulting role. How might misunderstandings on the part of the principal affect the role?

As counselors become more active in consultation, principals may come to perceive them as part of the school management staff. Loss of effectiveness in work with both teachers and pupils would result.

TYPES AND LEVELS OF CONSULTATION

The third party focused on in consultation may be an individual, an institution, or a situation an individual is facing. Recent adaptations of consulting include psychological education, teaching, preparation of peers for helping activities, and other similar procedures. In some processes, the difference between consultation and teaching fades; the two terms seem at times to be used interchangeably when teaching concentrates on personal aspects of development rather than subject matter. For example, if a group of pupils is "taught" to improve communication with parents, in a sense the counselor is serving as a consultant to the group.

Consultation may operate at different levels; Caplan (1959, pp. 121–126) describes three. The first is initiated by the consultee in need of assistance who requests it from the counselor. If, for example, the teacher (consultee) is having difficulty with a pupil, the counselor (consultant) may suggest helpful procedures. In Caplan's second level, the counselor and consultee work together in a close relationship that provides support for new behaviors. With rapport established, the teacher may gain the necessary confidence to try out new techniques in the classroom and the consultant can feel free to suggest new approaches. The third level is more or less a counseling relationship with the teacher. For example, the consultant may help the teacher understand and accept hostility toward the pupil as well as plan new strategies.

Opinions differ on whether the counselor should or can counsel colleagues in the school setting. The first and second levels are appropriate, but the counseling level is not advisable with a colleague. Everyday counselor-teacher relations in the school could be hampered by having teachers as clients. It is more suitable to refer staff members to counselors in other schools.

Two other concepts of consultation illustrate innovative approaches to spreading the effects of guidance work. Lister (1969) suggests full-

Consulting is no longer limited to discussing the problems of a third person.

time professional consultant-counselors to help counselors upgrade skills and gain self-understanding and greater proficiency. Counselors have reacted favorably to this type of consulting, and school administrators express positive attitudes to the position description, particularly in larger school systems (Tolbert 1971). Berdie proposes the new counselor role of "applied behavioral scientist" (1972), designed according to principles from behavioral sciences, to help individuals and institutions; were Berdie's proposal implemented, the role would largely be a consulting function. More recently Stilwell and Santoro (1976) have further conceptualized the role of the learning-development consultant.

Community mental health agencies provide a relatively new type of consultation in the school (Passons 1976). Potential consultees include administrators, counselors, parents, and teachers. Having someone to discuss cases with is only one of the valuable services such facilities can provide to counselors. Another way they supplement the school guidance program is by making available services the counselor may not have the time or preparation to institute (e.g., family counseling). Out-of-school consultants can also help counselors deal with intraschool communication problems, but their greatest contribution is providing additional staff to give the hard-pressed counselor more time to deal with inschool needs.

Consultation has the potential to improve both the school learning environment and the community. Teacher and counselor working together can foster pupil development by agreeing on goals that are "intellectually rigorous and respectable, and that are humane and centered around concern for the growth and dignity of the individual student" (Blocher 1977, p. 355). There need be no conflict of different roles. In the community counselors can act in cooperation with others to assess needs, coordinate resources for help, assist others to develop facilitating skills, and serve as advocates for those who lack power to protect their own rights (Lewis and Lewis 1977).

RESEARCH

A LOCAL STUDY OF REACTIONS TO THE COUNSELOR-CONSULTANT

Twenty-nine enrollees in an advanced level year-long NDEA Institute on consultation served in schools as consultants to counselors (Tolbert 1971). Consultants worked closely with counselors and others to help them define roles, upgrade skills, and make maximum use of potential, but approximately one fourth of their time was spent in working directly with individual and groups of pupils. Seventeen counselors in elementary and high schools served by counselor-consultants rated the assistance they received by written responses to open-ended questions and comments in tape-recorded group meetings. Of 187 responses, 139 were very positive about the value of consultants; 41 were neutral, and only 8 were negative.

A sample written comment reads: "I think that this was the most important thing that could have happened to me being a new counselor and by myself in a school situation, having someone that I knew would be there that would sit down and talk with me about my problems."

RESEARCH

A BRIEF SURVEY OF SCHOOL ADMINISTRATORS' ATTITUDES ABOUT CONSULTANTS

One hundred thirty-eight school superintendents from large to small school districts across the country were asked whether counselor-consultants (as described above) were needed in schools and if they would employ them if available. Partial results follow:

Size of school district	Consultants Needed		Would Employ	
	Yes	No or no response	Yes	No or no response
Up to 1,000	8	52	18	12
1,000–5,000	26	42	21	13
5,000–10,000	40	30	22	13
10,000 and over	40	38	22	17

Results show that there is substantial acceptance of the role, and that the larger the system the more positive the attitudes (Tolbert 1971).

EXPERIENCE

ADMINISTRATORS' AND TEACHERS' ATTITUDES ABOUT THE NEED FOR CONSULTING

Do a mini-survey of teachers' and counselors' views on the value of consulting. Ask the following questions:

— What is your definition of consultation?
— Do you think the school counselor should provide consultation to staff members?
— If "yes," what percentage of the counselor's time should be devoted to this responsibility?

What do the results say about the function? How do you feel about the reactions?

OBJECTIVE

1. To understand the similarities and differences between counseling and consultation. Name one important similarity and one difference.

In consultation, concern is primarily about the third person, while in counseling it is about the counselee. Similarity involves the nature of the relationship—in both activities it is accepting, open, and reflects interest.

HOW CONSULTATION FITS INTO THE TOTAL PROGRAM

Consulting should be given a high priority on the counselor's list of responsibilities. Making the service known to teachers, parents, and administrators helps, but it takes an active approach to get others involved. Level one consultation, in which the teacher comes to the counselor with a request for help, will work in many cases. More often than not, however, the counselor will need to meet potential consultees more than halfway to make consultation a vital part of the program. Examples show how this has been accomplished in several school settings.

Building good relations with teachers is a productive way to begin. Dent (1974) describes a program in which counselors and teachers were members of a guidance team and worked closely together in handling problems relating to classroom guidance, career education, and communication. At first teachers were apprehensive about a guidance responsibility, but acceptance improved considerably with improved communication between teachers and counselors, and through cooperative activities such as developing career education units and building skills in values clarification. Engelhardt, Sulzer, and Alterkruse (1971) describe how a counselor worked out a reinforcement schedule with a teacher to strengthen positive behavior of a disruptive child. After establishing a baseline for the disruptive behavior, the reinforcement schedule was carried out and the undesirable behavior was sharply reduced. Kuzniar (1973) describes an approach in which a teacher requesting help was first sent to visit other classrooms to observe different classroom climates. The consultant and teacher worked together to develop lists of desired classroom activities, strategies for implementing them, and ways to reward pupil progress. The consultant started where the teacher was, avoided devoting too much attention to negative aspects of her work, and supported her in trying out new experiences. The teacher's changes in classroom management procedures reflected a change in the teacher herself.

Another strategy for bringing consultation into the school program consists of gaining administrative support in the initial stages. Working with groups of teachers is the next important priority. Administrative help is needed to set up teacher groups on a regular schedule. Dinkmeyer (1973) suggests the "C-group" learning-experiential process; it involves collaboration, consultation, communication, and consulting with parents in groups.

Consultation with parents is an important aspect of the counselor's work. Strategies for reducing disruptive behavior often involve parents as well as teachers. The step-by-step process used by Macaluso (1976) involves conferences with teachers, observation in classrooms, planning strategies with teachers, and conferences with parents to assess home climate and to work out plans to assist the child. Helping also includes conferences with the child to explore feelings and plan activities such as the *magic circle*. Parent consultation can take place in conferences with one or both parents of an individual child, in parent groups set up to help parents understand and promote growth in children, or in family groups in a counseling-type program to help with family relationships and school adjustment. Sauber (1975) describes several models in which counselors work with three or four complete families to achieve greater intrafamily harmony and promote an understanding of the school program. In this approach, the boundary between consulting and counseling practically disappears.

Consultation with parents has been shown to have positive effects, but much of it tends to be remedial; more emphasis needs to be put on developmental programs with specific objectives. The most successful approach appears to be the combination of relatively long-term consulting with pupil counseling, with attention to parent-child communications and to relationships between parent and pupil behavior. Positive reinforcement in the home is an essential component (Warner 1974).

The same method can be aimed at the school program or the total system. Psychological education (Ivey and Alschuler 1973b) is one of the newer approaches to using consultation in the curriculum, and has been employed, for example, for values clarification in the classroom. Consultation with school staff members may be used to improve the climate and operation of the institution (Murray and Schmuck 1972). In such a strategy, the organization is taken to have the problem; consultants use their special skills to improve communication, effect structural changes, and modify norms to lessen dissonance.

Stiller's version (1974) of the consultant's role is along the lines of the model described earlier by Lister (1969). As an outside, nonevaluative expert, the consultant works with counselors to help them upgrade competencies, learn new approaches, solve local problems, and combat obsolescence. The use of the visiting consultant and institutions change agent described by Murray and Schmuck (1972) constitutes a similar approach. All these experts see the need to make the whole school an environment more hospitable to growth.

More extensive consulting services have been developed to make possible a greater impact on the total institution. The Center Satellite model (Malcolm 1974) is designed to prepare professionals who can change the system, provide cooperative consultation and in-service education to schools, and foster community participation. All those involved in and affected by changes participate in the process. Roles are flexible; a school guidance worker, for instance, may serve in the satellite program and learn from it, but also bring in the school's point of view. Malcolm describes this as a bold new attempt to improve education at a time when positive results are especially needed. It also illustrates a systematic approach to staff development, one of the new strategies in consultation.

The trend in consultation is for counselors to use a variety of approaches, somewhat along the lines of the cube concept (Morrill, Oetting, and Hurst 1974) or of the approach proposed by Shaw (1973). "Giving counseling away" is another current strategy (Pine 1974). The counselor has already moved into the significant environments of pupils—the classroom, the school, the home, and the community. The profession needs counselors with the requisite understanding, competencies, and constructive attitudes for making environments more positive and growth-producing. Such workers will be able to extend services in keeping with contemporary needs and make the most of available financial resources. But preparation for this expanded role of consultation is a critical factor. Stilwell and Santoro (1976) suggest a LDC (Learning-Development Consultant) model. Individual and group counseling is still important, but is only one of the strategies to be used (Ivey 1976). The LDC model calls for a school guidance team constituted according to strengths and preferences of personnel. This team will use multiple strategies to assess pupils' status in terms of affective, academic, and career development and thus to gain a comprehensive understanding of every member of the school population. Team members will go on to formulate objectives in terms that are meaningful to pupils, teachers, and parents. Next, strategies will be selected; past successes form the basis for choosing most effectively. The LDC model provides a particularly innovative follow-up to ensure that staff, parents, and pupils maintain improved achievement levels. This often neglected aspect requires extensive use of the consulting function. Stilwell and Santoro's well-designed change-agent model uses consultation as the major strategy. It obviously must be managed by a competent team leader who believes in the consulting approach.

There is wide agreement today on the value of the counselor-teacher role (Authier, Gustafson, Guerney, and Kasdorf 1975). Ivey (1976) summarizes the current trend, saying there is no question whether counselors should engage in consulting, teaching counseling skills to others, and psychological education; the question is how to carry out these tasks.

RESEARCH

CONSULTING WITH PARENTS

Forty-five parents of rural sixth through eighth grades took part in a study of the effects of a three-week mini-course (six hours of meetings; four of actual group work) on "Communication with Your Teenager" (Guzzetta 1976). Thirty-seven of the group were mothers; fathers, therefore, were not included in the statistical analysis.

The study involved three treatment groups and a control group. Each group of parents received structured learning in empathy; their children participated as follows:

— Group 1: Children did not participate.
— Group 2: Children participated separately.
— Group 3: Children participated with parents.

Results were as follows:

— All three treatment groups were significantly higher (.01 level) than the control group on two measures of empathy.
— The treatment groups were identical in terms of transfer of training, although parents whose children participated in the training with them, and whose treatment situation therefore most closely resembled real life, attained higher levels of empathy. Guzzetta points out, however, that display of empathy in role-playing episodes designed to measure transfer may not accurately reflect what would happen in the home.

Other evidence supports the value of consulting with parents. Shaw (1968a) found that parents show very positive attitudes toward group consulting and demonstrated good attendance at meetings. Frazier and Matthes (1975) compared two parent-consulting methods and concluded that both affected parents' behaviors and attitudes. The behaviors of children with parents in treatment and children with parents in a control group, however, showed no differences.

RESEARCH

USING CONSULTATION TO CHANGE PUPIL BEHAVIOR

Palmo and Kuzniar (1972) include findings from many studies done at the elementary-school level in which either group counseling or parent or teacher consulting were used to help pupils with adjustment problems. Their study, however, compared three treatment methods involving group counseling, consulting and counseling, and consulting alone:

1. Twelve sessions of group counseling for pupils, three at-home consulting sessions with parents, and twelve consulting meetings with teachers.
2. Twelve sessions of group counseling for pupils.
3. Three sessions of at-home consulting with parents and twelve consulting meetings with teachers.

A control group met with a counselor but did not engage in counseling activities.

Based on your knowledge of counseling, which group would you expect to have improved most in classroom behavior? Would you expect all treatment groups to be the same?

Compared with the control group, all treatments groups improved significantly (.05 level). The group that showed the greatest improvement was the parent-teacher consulting group (No. 3). The difference was significant at the .05 level.

EXPERIENCE

PRACTICE CONSULTING

Role play a situation in which one person serves as a counselor, another as a consultee, and a third as the "third person." The consultee and third person first decide on the problem. Next, the consultee asks the counselor for help.

If possible, record the consulting session.

After about five minutes, have all three persons review the session. Use these questions as guides: Did the counselor try to understand the circumstances surrounding the problem? How well did the consultation focus on the third person? Was a plan of action formulated?

EXPERIENCE

PROMOTING CONSULTATION

One of the major tasks in implementing the consulting approach in the school is building trust and positive attitudes in teachers and administrators. The following exercise is designed to bring out some of the attitudes that may arise.

Designate a team to prepare a strategy to acquaint teachers with consultation and to generate support. Have them present the approach to the school (played by the class).

At the conclusion of the simulation, discuss feelings evoked. How did the role-playing teachers respond to the offer of consultation? Would the "counselors" use the same approach again?

OBJECTIVES

1. To become aware of new approaches that enhance the consulting function. What is the major theme of new developments in this area?

Helping others (e.g., teachers, parents, and pupils) to learn and apply helping skills and attitudes.

2. To become aware of approaches to consultation which may be used in day-to-day work. Give three examples of providing consultation help.

A number of examples are given in the text, e.g., helping the teacher use a reinforcement schedule to reduce disruptive behavior. The total school system may also be the target in consultation.

3. To help you assess your attitudes about the consultant's role. List your views of the major features of the consultant's function and give each a personal-preference grade of A, B, C, D, or F. What is the average?

The major features will depend upon your point of view. One might be the need to have a good background in helping principles and the characteristics of special groups or situations. Another could be helping others to provide direct assistance. Your average grade may give an indication of how much you would like the function. Talking to counselors about consulting will give additional background for making the ratings.

4. To test your preference for strategies in handling consulting cases. A teacher says that he is having difficulty with several pupils; they are not interested in the class, wander around the room, and complain that the teacher doesn't understand them. The teacher asks you to either take over the pupils and see what you can do with them or to help him deal with the situation. Which strategy would you prefer?

You know very little about the situation from this brief description, but it offers an opportunity to try consultation in fantasy. You may be tempted to have the pupils referred to you so that you can demonstrate your expertise. But serving as a consultant is not only likely to be more effective but could also gain support for the guidance program.

ADDITIONAL READINGS

Caplan, Gerald. *Concepts of Mental Health and Consultation*. Washington, D.C.: U.S. Department of Health, Education, and Welfare, 1959.

A well-known reference on consultation and the source of many concepts currently in use in schools. Chapter 8 is particularly useful reading in conjunction with this chapter.

. *The Theory and Practice of Mental Health Consultation*. New York: Basic Books, 1970.

Pages 32–34 describe four types of consultation that provide useful models for the school counselor. Additional sections may be selected according to interests.

Carlson, Jon; Splete, Howard; and Kern, Roy, eds. *The Consulting Process*. Washington, D.C.: American Personnel and Guidance Association, 1975.

A book of reprints of outstanding articles from journals of the American Personnel and Guidance Association. An excellent source of readings covering all aspects of the function.

Fullmer, Daniel W., and Bernard, Harold W. *The School Counselor-Consultant*. Boston: Houghton Mifflin, 1972.

A useful reference on the need for and nature of consultation in the schools. Chapter 5 gives background on the development of the concept and discusses work with teachers and parents. Consideration is also given to the counselor as a change agent.

Munson, Harold L. *Foundations of Developmental Guidance*. Boston: Allyn and Bacon, 1971.

Chapter 8, "The Consulting Function," gives a well-balanced, comprehensive picture of consulting in the school. One of the most useful references for the school counselor.

CHAPTER ELEVEN
THE NEED TO ASSESS

You have probably at one time or another taken tests, completed inventories, filled in forms, or given information about your abilities, interests, and hobbies. You were being assessed. As a counselor, you are on the other side of the fence; you are in the position of having to assess pupils. You need to know how it is done, the strengths and weaknesses of different procedures, issues and criticisms, and prospects for the future. You also need to explore your attitudes about this aspect of the counselor's responsibility; it is a function that generates strong feelings pro and con.

GOALS

1. To learn how assessment fits in and contributes to the school guidance program.
2. To gain insight into your feelings about using assessment procedures with counselees.

PURPOSES OF ASSESSMENT

In guidance assessment — with or without testing — is carried out to help the pupil gain self-understanding, make plans, and make decisions. Data about aptitudes, achievements, and interests facilitate these counselee tasks. Results may also be used in the instructional program, to determine progress of pupils, to identify areas of strengths and weaknesses, and to plan instructional programs. Administratively data are used in admission and placement, particularly for special school programs, colleges, and other post-high-school institutions. Recent concern with accountability has given assessment new importance; it is necessary to determine how much progress has been made in an institution toward meeting goals and objectives.

Despite important similarities, there are fundamental differences between such functions as testing and evaluation and assessment. Assessment is a broad concept involving testing and other methods to determine an individual's characteristics, qualities, or achievements. Assessment of mechanical ability, for example, might involve a test, an evaluation of work experiences, and proficiency in using materials. Testing utilizes a specific standardized technique to determine the individual levels of performance. A test of mechanical ability, for example, might determine the pupil's ability to answer fifty questions about mechanical principles. A test attempts to measure an individual's maximum performance. An inventory taps preferences, attitudes, or beliefs. Pupils might be asked, for example, whether they like to work with tools. There is no right or wrong answer; results show something about individual attitudes. Evaluation is quite similar to assessment—it is a broad term covering different techniques to determine the results of a program, or to build relatively complete personal descriptions. For example, you could administer a test to measure a specific mechanical aptitude, such as understanding how mechanical devices work. To assess mechanical ability, however, you would use as much data about the individual as possible—hobbies, work experience, school courses, and test results.

TYPES OF TESTS
AND NON-TEST TECHNIQUES

Instruments for assessment may be classified according to what they measure, number of persons assessed (individuals or groups), types of data considered (paper-and-pencil responses or performance), and time limitations. The first classification is the most useful; it has practical value for the counselor planning ways to help the counselee.

MENTAL ABILITY   Terms such as "mental ability," "intelligence," or "academic aptitude" refer to the ability mentally to manipulate verbal, quantitative, and other abstract symbols. Tests may be designed for individual or group administration (typically used in the school). Items are related to school learning (e.g., vocabulary), and correlate with success in academic types of tasks. The Stanford-Binet and the Weschler scales—

e.g., the WAIS (Weschler Adult Intelligence Scale) and the WISC (Weschler Intelligence Scale for Children)—are among the best-known individual intelligence tests. Widely used group tests are the California Test of Mental Maturity and the Otis Lennon Mental Ability Test.

ACHIEVEMENT TESTS   This type measures how much has been learned, how far skills have been developed, or what competencies have been acquired. A paper-and-pencil test may be used to measure learning in social studies, but a work sample demonstrating a skill also represents achievement. Test items are usually selected to represent the content of a course; thus this is a major type of test used to demonstrate accountability. Results may be used diagnostically (to determine strengths and weaknesses in a subject area). Results of past achievement are among the best indicators of future progress; tests therefore can be used for prediction. There are a number of well known achievement batteries, among them the California Achievement Tests for grades 1–14, the Stanford Achievement Tests for grades 1–12, the Sequential Tests of Educational Progress (STEP) for grades 4–14, and the College Board and Graduate Record exams.

APTITUDE TESTS   These are designed to estimate potential for future performance. Intelligence and achievement tests can be used for this purpose, but the term is usually applied to tests of vocational aptitude. A battery of tests is often prepared so that a profile with comparable scores for different aptitudes can be made up for the individual. One of the best known is the General Aptitude Test Battery (GATB) used in state employment services. (A nonreading edition is also available.) Work evaluation, such as the Singer Vocational Evaluation System (Cohen and Drugo 1976), involves handling materials and tools and has begun to incorporate methods of evaluating work personality. One of the best-known aptitude tests is the DAT (Differential Aptitude Test) which gives nine scores, including a composite score of verbal and numerical abilities similar to typical intelligence tests. A career-planning questionnaire for use in conjunction with the test is also available.

PERSONALITY INVENTORIES   These questionnaires gather information on pupils' preferences, attitudes, or problems. Results are stated by comparison with a given group, e.g., a sample of high school pupils. Some inventories are lists of problems which counselees check to portray their own situations. A limitation of such instruments is that results may be faked, but some have scales to detect efforts to present a favorable picture. Other instruments are projective—the individual responds to unstructured material such as ink blots, ambiguous pictures, or incomplete sentences. Such stimuli evoke responses that reveal personality needs and organization; they require specific preparation to administer and interpret. Widley used personality inventories are the Minnesota Multiphasic Personality Inventory (MMPI), the Edwards Personal Preference Schedule, and the Myers-Briggs Type Indicator. The best known projective tests are the Rorschach and the Thematic Apperception tests.

CAREER INTEREST Interest inventories get at pupils' career preferences by asking questions about preferred jobs, hobbies, and other activities. Responses are compared with those of others (e.g., a general group, or people successful in a particular occupation) to determine high and low interest levels. Intra-individual comparisons are also made; results might show, for instance, that a pupil likes mechanical activity more than literary work. But interest inventories do more than measure occupational likes and dislikes and may even be viewed as personality measurements (Holland 1973, p. 7). The major inventories in use today are the Strong Vocational Interest Blank (SVIB), and the Kuder Preference Record, which has several forms that are scored in different ways.

CAREER DEVELOPMENT MEASUREMENTS This type includes both tests and inventories and gets at the individual's attitudes toward work, knowledge of occupations, and ability to use information in decision making. Results indicate the individual's status with respect to career development (Westbrook 1974). This is a relatively new area of measurement, but instruments incorporate the same type of content as achievement tests, and personality and career-interest inventories. Those in use today include the Career Development Inventory (CDI), the Career Maturity Inventory (CMI), and the Cognitive Test of Vocational Maturity (CTVM).

NON-TEST ASSESSMENT TECHNIQUES A few of these are listed here to illustrate the value of the general approach.

Anecdotal Records These are brief statements of actual behavior recorded by a teacher or counselor. The factual description gives a picture of how the person actually behaves in various sorts of situations. Interpretations, if any, are kept separate from the behavior description.

Ratings and Other Observational Techniques These procedures involve an observer's ratings of characteristics such as motivation, empathy, or attending behavior. The same techniques may be used for self-rating.

Autobiographical and Other Self-Reports Unless the instructions are quite detailed, this approach includes some projection. Reports may briefly treat such topics "My most positive experience," or "What I would like to be," or they run to lengthy autobiographies of several pages. Probably because much time is needed for preparation and analyzing results, the technique is used infrequently. But it does offer a helpful glimpse of the individual's inner world.

Time Schedules These are very rarely used except in how-to-study instruction. A time schedule shows how a pupil spends time, and is often a necessary first step in planning a more effective and balanced time distribution.

In addition to these major assessment devices and techniques, there are interesting variations the counselor should know. The individual can use the self-administered guidance technique, Self-Directed Search (Holland and Nafziger 1975), to arrive at career choices. The assessment approach of the staffing conference can determine students' progress and difficulties (Kelly and Dowd 1975). The High School Characteristics Index (Tolsma, Menne, and Hopper 1976) measures pupils' perceptions of the climate of the institution (Walz and Miller 1969). A more exotic technique one reads about from time to time in the journals is the Ertl Index (Kappan Interview 1972; Ertl Machine 1973). It is a technology for measuring neural efficiency to assess potential for intellectual development without the effects of educational experience; results to date have not been unequivocally persuasive.

ISSUES IN TESTING

Testing has always had strong advocates and strong detractors. Recently, however, and for several reasons, it has increasingly come under fire. Chief factors include charges of cultural and sexual bias, debates about the heritability of intelligence, lack of accurate predictions, and misuse of test results.

Culturally, test items tend to favor the middle-class-American group, and to work against minorities, particularly the disadvantaged and blacks (Williams 1970). The suggestion has been made to impose a moratorium on testing until better tests are constructed. But Messick and Anderson (1970) uphold the value of testing to show the current status of an individual, regardless of previous deprivation. Eliminating tests would result in more subjective assessment methods (Ebel 1975). Attempts to construct culture-fair or culture-free tests have not been successful (Wesman, 1968). Cultural factors do seem to affect knowledge of items, attitudes toward taking tests, and feelings of competence about test taking; some

Test results alone do not reveal the whole person, although they can provide accurate clues.

resulting inequalities may be reduced by exercises and practice and some by remedial work.

Sex bias in tests and inventories, particularly career interest inventories, is another recent concern. Standards for interpretation and use of inventories (American Psychological Association, *Standards for Educational and Psychological Tests* 1974; National Vocational Guidance Association, *Career Development* 1973) suggest ways to prevent bias in test use but have had limited effects (Tanney 1975). Relatively little sex bias has been found in general interest inventories (Johansson 1975), but enough to call for such remedial action as establishing checklists for determining the amount of sex fairness and sex bias in career interest inventories (Diamond 1975). Sex bias in computer guidance systems utilizing interest inventories has also been investigated (Harris-Bowlsbey 1975, "Sex Bias"). Little has been found, but suggestions have been made for future use, such as analyzing and making necessary revisions in the storage of occupational information. The issue of sex bias is not settled; some argue that it can only be eliminated at the cost of reduced usefulness of tests and inventories (Standardized Tests 1975).

Another difficulty that must be faced is the problem of prediction, which requires that test results be compared with results of a specific relevant population. If, for example, a woman is considering an engineering program in college, test items have to take into account characteristics of the male-dominated field. But care must be taken to eliminate test items that do not relate directly to professional success. If workers in a given occupation tend to have a certain characteristic (with respect, for example, to race, sex, or socioeconomic level) that does not actually affect proficiency in essential tasks, a test showing high validity on this characteristic would be biased in favor of the status quo.

The difference between achievement and aptitude tests poses further recurring problems. Since both, in a sense, measure the same thing— previous learning—deprivations of various sorts in school and home can result in low scores in both.

Much of the recent controversy over utility of tests in counseling was touched off by Goldman's statement (1972b) that tests and counseling made up a "marriage that had failed," and his contention that tests do not predict accurately enough to be helpful in counseling. Wesman (1972) and others take issue with this point of view and assert that tests supply needed information about counselees that is particularly useful in planning remedial help for the culturally deprived. Goldman himself has recommended developing new kinds of tests that would not only tell where a person stands, but also provide ways to improve deficiencies (Goldman 1972a). Steps have been taken in this direction. For example, in the new system of multicultural pluralistic assessment (APA *Monitor* 1976, vol. 7, no. 5, p. 13), an individual's test scores are compared with those of others with similar social and cultural backgrounds.

Tests, regardless of predictive validity, do in any case provide vital information that may not be obtainable in any other way, or only at great difficulty and expense. It is true that tests make predictions only for groups (e.g., 50 percent of pupils with a given score will earn grades of C or better in college), not for specific individuals. Moreover, predictions usually have a large "error." On the basis of a test, a counselor might be able to tell a high school student: "Chances are two out of three that your college marks will fall between a C minus and a B plus." Quite a range! What is more, the counselor cannot be sure that the counselee will be competing with a group similar to the one on which validity and norms were originally computed.

RESEARCH

SEX BIAS IN TESTS AND COMPUTER GUIDANCE SYSTEMS

Studies of interest inventories and computer systems have revealed sex bias to an extent calling for remedial action (Association of Measurement and Evaluation in Guidance Commission 1973; Diamond 1975). CVIS (Computer Vocational Information System) data show such examples of subtle bias as (Harris-Bowlsbey 1975, p. 190):

Home Economics	. . . many graduates work for a time before marrying, then leave to raise their families . . .
FBI Agent	. . . and wear business suits . . .
Boiler Operator	. . . most men in the field . . .
Cameraman	. . . all engraving may be done by one man . . .
Production Manager, Advertising	. . . many successful advertising men . . .
Pilot	. . . most men begin as copilots . . .

EXPERIENCE

OPINIONS ABOUT TEST BIAS

Talk with several members of minority groups. Ask for their opinions of standardized testing programs in schools and for the source of information on which they base their opinions.

Also ask what they think should be done about testing programs. Should they be dropped, modified, or kept as they are? Can they suggest alternatives to testing?

A fourth major criticism concerns misuse of tests and test results. Such problems usually arise because of a lack of understanding of tests on the part of counselors or teachers, the tendency to categorize individuals as if test scores were precise and unchangeable, and the failure to recognize factors (e.g., native language, cultural background) that cause tests to give misleading results. The main difficulty is that those who use test scores are inadequately prepared; the remedial strategy is to make sure they acquire a thorough understanding of the theory and construction of tests.

In spite of limitations, testing is here to stay. Tests are a widely accepted feature of our culture, and they are being improved. Counselors will continue to be involved in the selection, administration, and interpretation of instruments in the schools, and to work with pupils who face testing for admission to educational programs and jobs. Controversies will continue to arise on the subject of test bias, and the counselor will be called upon for an expert opinion. Personal enthusiasm will vary, but it is realistic to anticipate a high level of involvement in testing in day-to-day work.

EXPERIENCE

CULTURAL TEST BIAS

In the class, set up four groups, each representing a different culture, as follows:

— *Urban*. Lives in a city environment.
— *Mountain*. Relatively isolated in a mountainous area.
— *Rural*. Has lived exclusively in a farming area.
— *Island*. Has never communicated with others off the island.

Ask each group to make up a five-item "intelligence test" relevant to their culture. (It may be necessary to do some research to prepare relevant and difficult items.) Have each group in turn administer its test to the class. Compute scores, and discuss reactions to taking tests based on a different culture.

OBJECTIVES

1. To understand the meaning of the terms "testing," "evaluation," and "assessment." Give examples of situations in which each procedure would be used.

Tests obtain information about a particular skill, ability, or quality, e.g., intelligence.

Evaluation determines effects of a group procedure, e.g., the impact of a verbal-skills program on pupils' communication abilities.

Assessment estimates individual qualifications, e.g., for entering college; it might include such features as tests, analysis of school grades, and interest inventories.

"Appraisal" and "assessment" mean approximately the same thing.

2. To become aware of the different types of test and non-test techniques. Name and identify two techniques in each category.

Types listed in this chapter include tests of mental ability, achievement, and aptitude. Career-interest and personality measurements are most accurately called "inventories," since they do not "test" the individual, but gather responses, attitudes, and preferences typical of specific groups. Ratings, autobiographies, and time schedules are non-test instruments. These identifications can be based on descriptions in this chapter.

3. To become familiar with major issues in testing. Identify three.

There are several. Cultural bias, sexual bias, and lack of predictive efficiency are major ones.

4. To gain insight into your own feelings about issues in testing. List the major issues and give three terms that reflect your feeling about each.

Your responses concerning feelings indicate how well you reach this objective. On the issue of cultural bias, for example, a response such as "unfair" reflects a feeling, but "haven't seen any" does not. You can react affectively on the testing issue without being an expert.

TESTING IN THE GUIDANCE PROGRAM

Schools usually have an ongoing testing program, grades 1–12, to monitor achievement and mental ability; in the upper grades, career interest and personality inventories may be added. Programs differ considerably from school to school, but one common practice is to give mental-ability and achievement tests every other year, using similar types to obtain comparable scores. Recently, accountability requirements have given rise to programs designed to measure pupils' status before and after the year's work.

The underlying rationale for school testing at the local level derives from the goals and objectives of the local school program. Tests are used to gather data that is otherwise difficult or impossible to obtain. Quite often, however, a testing program is established county-wide or even state-wide; while local objectives may be very well covered by such measurements, the school does not expressly select such tests on the basis of them.

The counselor's participation in the testing program should be limited to helping with planning and coordination, instructing others in methods of administration and interpretation, and setting up ways to put data to use. Clerical tasks of the testing function have often fallen to the counselor, however, and the obtaining, distributing, and collecting involved have taken an inordinate amount of time, and it has been hard to get rid of these chores.

Counseling use of testing emphasizes direct help, e.g., helping an individual understand abilities before choosing a program. Instructional use estimates learning acquired and identifies areas needing special attention; this use is mainly a concern of the teaching staff. Used for administrative purposes, tests may provide information needed for setting up special classes, evaluating the status of pupil learning in the school, and allocating of resources; such use concerns the school administration and supervisory staff. The guidance function suffers if the counselor becomes too heavily involved in all these areas.

School-wide testing programs provide the counselor with helpful data. Results summarize pupil progress. Analysis of scores can be used in planning new teaching methods, courses, and objectives; the counselor participates in this process as a consultant. Secondly, the results, which are entered in the student's record, may be used directly in counseling and guidance.

Tests are also increasingly used in demonstrating accountability. Some programs represent a very serious misuse of tests. To evaluate the status and progress of a class or even a school without background information about differences among pupils is unwarranted, and it can only alienate teachers and others on the subject of tests. Tests that tap only a narrow part of course objectives often give a biased report of learning that is taking place and thus can encourage teachers to concentrate on "teaching the test."

Today parents are coming into contact with tests more than ever before. Expanded test reports, accompanied by explanatory material that is supposed to make results easily understandable, are in many cases given to pupils to take home and discuss with parents. New legislation allows parents to inspect their children's school records (Worzbyt 1976; Wilhelm and Case 1975); these developments require school personnel who use tests, particularly counselors, to be knowledgeable about interpretation. The same legislation that opens up records to parents or guardians also requires their permission for running certain types of tests on their children (Burgum and Anderson 1975, pp. 82–83). The counselor must exercise caution not only in administering and interpreting tests; other types of data in the cumulative record, such as comments and evaluations, may be used in libel suits if not handled with care. Adhering to the APGA's ethical guidelines for the use of tests (Ethical Standards, Appendix C, Section C, "Measurement and Evaluation") should lessen the likelihood of legal problems.

School assessment services often include college-admission testing, such as the College Board and American College Testing programs; typically such tests are administered by an out-of-school agency, but the school receives the results for its records. The National Merit Scholarship Program and others like it test candidates for scholarships. The College Level Examination Program (CLEP) enables high school pupils to obtain credit for college course work. American College Testing (ACT) provides schools with a career guidance assessment package in addition to the well-known college admission test. The Career Planning Program for grades 8–11 assesses abilities, interests, and experiences, and provides for exploration in six basic career clusters. This last type of prepared program, which combines well-designed measurements with strategies for planning and decision making, is particularly valuable for guidance and counseling.

USING ASSESSMENT IN COUNSELING

Criticisms stressing the inadequacies both of tests and counselors have been leveled against the use of assessment in counseling (Goldman 1972b), but tests can and do help in planning and decision making, stimulating exploration, developing self-understanding, and establishing life goals in career, educational, and personal areas. Tests particularly selected for counseling and those that are given in the school testing program and go into the pupil's cumulative record can be employed in these ways (Kirk 1969). Such utilization requires an understanding of technical aspects of tests, and skills in helping pupils—individually or in groups—to use results.

Information about tests to be adopted or already in use is available in several forms. Buros' *Mental Measurements Yearbooks* are the best single source of critical reviews and bibliographies of research studies. Reviews in journals such as *Measurement and Evaluation in Guidance* are also valuable. Test manuals (particularly their technical sections) can be used. The section on *Use* in the APA booklet on standards (American Psychological Association 1974) provides a helpful set of guidelines.

To make use of test evaluations and reviews, and to make personal analyses, the technical aspects of instruments need to be clearly understood. Reliability, validity, norms, and scores are essential concepts. Reliability indicates the stability of the test score. Validity shows how accurately the test measures what it is supposed to measure, e.g., success in school. There are other types of validity; it is important for the counselor to apply them in accordance with the use to which a particular test is put. Norm groups are another important factor; comparisons between individual pupils and groups should have bearing on the individuals' own choices or plans. The counselor therefore needs to be aware of the makeup of groups on which norms were established, and the difference between norm-referenced and criterion-referenced tests (Popham 1976; Hambleton and Novick 1972). Scores, too, are complex; to interpret them, the counselor must understand how they are derived. Even the simplest types (e.g., percentiles, ratios) are likely to mystify a counselee. These terms are defined in the glossary, but an example may help clarify their importance to the counselor. Suppose you have a test of forty questions measuring mechanical ability. Each question shows a picture of a tool, and the pupil is asked to check one of four choices indicating its use. If the test has been given to 1,000 high school seniors to establish score levels, these 1,000 pupils make up the norm group. If you give them the test twice and compare scores, you are assessing reliability (test-retest type). If you compare scores with grades in industrial arts you are establishing a type of validity (predictive). Now, suppose you compare John Smith's score with the scores of the 1,000 pupils in the norm group, and he ranks near the top. You are using a norm-referenced approach to evaluate his performance. But if you decide that at least half the questions should be answered correctly to indicate success in industrial arts, you are not concerned with the scores of others, but only with whether John scored high enough to complete his program successfully. You are now using a criterion-referenced approach. (See the glossary for definitions of scores and additional types of validity and reliability.)

Actual face-to-face interpretation of test data involves the application of counseling procedures. Much research has been done on how to use results with counselees (Sharf 1974), but there is not sufficient evidence to single any one approach out as the best. Kirk's strategy (1969), which includes the counselee in the test-selection process, is highly recommended. Participation is as valuable in test selection as in other aspects of the counseling relationship; interpretation, in which the counselor and counselee explore reactions to results, is also a cooperative enterprise.

Test use in counseling has changed with the development of self-explanatory answer sheets or computer printouts with detailed discussions of the meaning of the scores (Sharf 1974). These printouts save the counselor a lot of time, but do not replace the counselee's interaction with a counselor. Computer guidance systems, which provide somewhat the same type of data, may go further by furnishing the counselee with predictions based on test scores. Many school programs routinely provide comparisons of results from state, national, and local testing programs, thus providing large amounts of helpful information that can be used with counselees. The counselee needs help in using any of these data; the amount of assistance depends on the individual, but none of the results from test-data systems "stand alone."

The interpretation in counseling may involve one or more of Goldman's three bridges (1971): the norm bridge, the regression bridge, and the discriminate bridge. Each is useful; Prediger (1971) describes how the discriminate bridge, which provides a measure of the counselee's similarity to specific groups, facilitates exploratory behavior and promotes a sense of how the counselee would feel as a member of each group. The counselor has detailed information about the various groups, and can thus plan with the counselee the steps to be taken to attain the proficiencies required to be accepted and successful in a chosen group. This approach provides necessary assistance without exaggerating the potential benefits of tests. It brings together all sorts of data and helps the counselee form a well-rounded picture of choices and options.

RESEARCH

USING TEST RESULTS IN COUNSELING

Two related studies with college students, by Tuma and Gustad (1957) and Gustad and Tuma (1957), are examples of well-planned research on differential effects of counselors and methods on counselee learning. The first study compared: counselor-client similarity, three methods of test introduction, and four methods of test interpretation. The three methods of introducing tests were:

— Client-motivated
— Counselor-originated (Client selects tests.)
— Counselor-directed (Counselor assigns tests.)

In the four methods of interpretation test scores were:

— Presented in general terms
— Presented in specific terms (e.g., percentiles)
— Compared with clients' previously completed self-estimates on traits measured
— Compared with clients' previously completed self-estimates, with client keeping the written comparison for further study

The earlier study by Gustad and Tuma (1957) had shown no influence of different methods of test introduction and interpretation on client learning; this one revealed that if counselor and client had very similar personalities, clients learned more. Gustad and Tuma call for further research to assess the effects of different approaches to counseling and other variables (such as the counselor's sex) on client learning. (This research used only one counseling approach.)

Fernald and Makarewicz (1967) investigated the degree of accuracy with which college students could identify real v. fake descriptions of personal characteristics. Results showed subjects to be correct in most choices. Thus the authors conclude that personal validations of test results by the counselee may be a helpful approach. These results obtained with college students may apply to the high school level.

Some studies have been done on secondary school pupils. Carey (1968), for example, used ninth and eleventh graders to compare the effects of oral v. written summaries of test results. Results showed that ninth graders who received written summaries along with counselors' oral interpretations learned more and were better satisfied; no differences were found for eleventh graders. Carey suggests several reasons for the differences at the ninth grade level; testing was more recent, for example, and pupils were in a group guidance program at the time he conducted his study.

EXPERIENCE

HAVING A TEST INTERPRETED

If a university testing-center is available, ask to take an interest inventory. When the results are interpreted, note the methods used. Did you feel anxious, threatened, comfortable? Did you understand the personal meaning of the results?

EXPERIENCE

INTERPRETING TEST RESULTS

Role play the following situation: A counselee is coming to a counselor to discuss test results for admission to the graduate program. The counselee knows that scores will determine admission or rejection. Before seeing the counselee, decide by the flip of a coin (not a good admissions procedure!) whether the results will be suitable or not, but do not tell the counselee the choice.

Spend three to four minutes giving results to the counselee.

How did you feel about using test results in this way? Did you try to put the counselee at ease? What were the counselee's reactions?

Rotate roles and discuss reactions.

EXPERIENCE

FEELINGS ABOUT TESTS

Ask each person in a small group or class-size group to give three descriptive words about testing experiences they have had. Are the majority positive or negative? Could anything have been done to make the negative situations positive?

EXPERIENCE

COMPLYING WITH REQUESTS FOR TEST DATA

Assume that the following fictitious test data and scores are in a twelfth grader's record:

Absolute Intelligence Test	90 (low average)
Super-Subject Achievement Tests	math: 50 (average)
	English: 25 (bottom quarter of the school)
	social studies: 20 (bottom fifth of the school)
My Choice Interest Inventory	unskilled labor: 95 (very high)
	academic: 15 (very low)
	mechanical: 50 (average)
	leisure time: 80 (high)

The pupil's parents have requested to see the test results. (They have the legal right to do so; you cannot prevent it.) Moreover, they have high ambitions for their son, and want you to help him gain admission to a competitive college.

What are your feelings about the situation? What would you say to them?

In a group situation, ask members to give the comments they would make to the parents.

OBJECTIVES

1. To understand how tests are used in the guidance program. Identify three uses.

For college admission, to determine status of pupils in school courses, to plan remedial programs, and to modify courses and teaching methods.

2. To understand how test and non-test data may be used to help the counselee. Identify three counseling situations in which assessment would help counselees reach their goals.

When there is a need to explore abilities and attitudes; when planning and decision making depend on data on potential and preferences; when there is a need to identify areas for remedial work.

3. To understand factors to consider in selecting tests to be used in guidance, and to be aware of sources of needed data. Name and briefly describe factors to consider, and identify two major sources of test information.

The following factors should be considered:

— Goals of the educational program. Does the test cover important ones?
— Norm group on which the test has been standardized. Is it similar to pupils with whom the test will be used in your school?
— Validity. Does the test measure what it is supposed to measure?
— Reliability. Can you depend on results to be consistent?
— Ease in interpretation. Are commonly used scores employed rather than exotic, complicated ones that are difficult to figure out?

Other factors, such as cost, ease in administering, and attractiveness of format should also be considered.

Data can be found in Buros' *Mental Measurements Yearbooks,* and in individual test manuals and technical reports.

ADDITIONAL READINGS

American Psychological Association. *Standards for Educational and Psychological Tests.* Washington, D.C.: American Psychological Association, 1974.

The major guide for technical aspects of tests and use of results. Pages 56 – 73, particularly "Interpretation of Scores" (pp. 68 – 73), are useful in the context of this chapter.

Anastasi, Anne. *Psychological Testing.* 4th ed. Riverside, N.J.: Macmillan, 1976.

A comprehensive and lucid text covering the basic information a counselor needs. Useful supplementary material covers topics such as ethical standards; guidelines for evaluation as well as lists of tests and test publishers are also included.

Association for Measurement and Evaluation in Guidance. "The Responsible Use of Tests: A Position Paper of AMEG, APGA, and NCME."

Measurement and Evaluation in Guidance, 5, no. 2 (1972), pp. 385–388.

A statement by several concerned professional organizations on how to improve the use of tests and respond to increasing criticisms of testing.

Cronbach, Lee J. *Essentials of Psychological Testing*. 3rd ed. New York: Harper and Row, 1970.

A major text on tests and measurements covering all aspects of the subject, this volume belongs in the counselor's personal library as a valuable reference.

Goldman, Leo. *Using Tests in Counseling*. 2nd ed. New York: Appleton-Century-Crofts, 1971.

A comprehensive reference on the use of tests in counseling. Chapter 2 on the purposes of testing is an excellent introduction to the subject.

Shertzer, Bruce and Stone, Shelley C. *Fundamentals of Guidance*. 3rd ed. Boston: Houghton Mifflin, 1976.

Chapters 8 and 9 cover tests and non-test appraisal methods. Comprehensive and timely, these sections provide valuable background to topics introduced in this chapter.

Tyler, Leona E. *The Work of the Counselor*. 3rd ed. New York: Appleton-Century-Crofts, 1969.

Chapter 7, "Surveying Possibilities in the Self by Means of Tests," is an excellent discussion of the use of tests in counseling, and includes an extensive summary of research on the values of tests to counselees.

CHAPTER TWELVE
SUPPORT PERSONNEL
AND EXPANDED SERVICE

Delworth said it in 1974; paraprofessionals aren't coming, they're here. They're here in all types of settings—schools, community agencies, colleges, hospitals; they go by names like "aides," "human service workers," "guidance assistants," and "support personnel." Their training ranges from brief on-the-job orientation to one or two years of specialized preparation in a formal program.

GOALS

1. To understand how support personnel can contribute to the guidance program.
2. To gain insight into feelings about working with support personnel.

TRENDS IN THE USE OF SUPPORT PERSONNEL

The relatively young movement to use support personnel began in the 60s and was almost immediately embroiled in controversy. Project CAUSE (Counselor Advisor University Summer Education), which trained counselor assistants for work in the U.S. Employment Service, alarmed the profession by implying that trainees would be accorded professional status after a brief period of training and on-the-job experience (Tolbert 1974, p. 227). Even so, the concept of paraprofessionals has enjoyed strong support by the American Personnel and Guidance Association, which issued a policy statement in 1966 (APGA, "Support . . ." 1967). Since that time a comprehensive study of status, preparation, roles, and issues has been published by Zimpfer, Frederickson, Salim, and Sanford (1971), *Personnel and Guidance Journal* has devoted a special issue to paraprofessionals (Delworth 1974), and guidelines for paraprofessionals have been published (American School Counselor Association 1976, pp. 282–284).

There has been some confusion, however, in identifying the counselor's role and responsibility in relation to paraprofessionals. Even counselors who express enthusiasm for the services of paraprofessionals may fail to realize their full potential if they are apprehensive about competition (Zimpfer, Frederickson, Salim, and Sanford, 1971, p. 32). The American School Counselor Association (1976) provides some clarification in stating that counselors have specific responsibilities in working with paraprofessionals (e.g., selection and supervision).

There are many types of support personnel. Peers, probably the most numerous, are pupils trained to work with classmates and younger pupils. Parents too serve in school guidance programs, both in volunteer and paid capacities. Retired persons often perform as volunteer paraprofessionals. Paid helpers are more numerous in community agencies, mental health programs, drug centers, and outreach programs for the disadvantaged, but are also utilized in schools for specific functions such as working with groups, maintaining the information service, placement, clerical work, and assisting in the testing program.

RATIONALE
AND PROFESSIONAL GUIDELINES

As in any profession, specific functions in guidance can be readily performed by a minimally trained worker with very little supervision. The counselor operates at peak competence helping the counselee engage in self-exploration of feelings, understand strengths and limitations, and make decisions; but some aspects of guidance do not require the counselor's personal participation. It is possible, for example, to specify what types of information—personal, social, occupational—should be provided to counselees and how it should be given.

There are three basic requirements in working with paraprofessionals. First, a professional with sound background in theory, competencies, and evaluative skills must set up all activities. Second, paraprofessionals must be trained to carry out specific functions (e.g., communication skills); following training, the activity of paraprofessionals must be supervised by such means as staff meetings or individual conferences.

Finally, work should be evaluated, feedback provided, and additional training set up as needed.

APGA (1967) guidelines break paraprofessional activities into *direct* helping (such as obtaining interview information from an individual), and *indirect* helping (such as administering a test). Many current practices may even exceed the limited responsibilities outlined in policy statements. The extent of direct-helping responsibility described in guidelines seems to be limited to helping the counselee be at ease and ready for counseling, but examples show paraprofessionals not only performing such initial preparation, but actually providing help in identifying and resolving problems.

The report by Zimpfer, Frederickson, Salim, and Sanford (1971, pp. 34–46; 56–62) suggests three stages of paraprofessional competency in four areas—people, data, knowledge, and autonomy. The work of first-level paraprofessionals with people would involve gathering information about individuals. At the second level, paraprofessional work could involve supplying the counselor or counselee with information about people obtained directly from the individuals, prepared or collected under counselor direction. The third and highest level of responsibility might include activities such as talking with pupils or teachers to collect information and providing information to individuals or groups utilizing procedures established by the counselor.

The ASCA position statement (1976) spells out guidelines for the effective use of paraprofessionals to free counselors for counseling and other demanding professional functions. Well-prepared and carefully selected paraprofessionals are used

— *for clerical work* (maintaining pupil records, helping pupils to complete information forms, etc.).
— *as resource persons* (e.g., to make contacts with community agencies, build the informational file, prepare materials for counselor use, and operate technological equipment).
— *as helpers in assessment* (e.g., carrying out the arrangements for administering and scoring tests).

Paraprofessionals should be interested in working with pupils, sensitive to their needs, and aware of how the guidance program works.

Counselors should help in the selection of paraprofessionals, and provide training and supervision. Counselors and the professional organization should take steps to establish effective training programs. The well-prepared paraprofessional should be competent in

— Secretarial skills
— Use of multimedia equipment and materials

— Practical evaluative procedures
— Human relations skills
— Group testing
— Making ethical judgments
— Building home-school relations

The ASCA position statement makes clear that the paraprofessional must have specific noncounseling skills, and that all paraprofessional work is done under the close supervision of a professional counselor.

ISSUES, PROBLEMS, AND OPPORTUNITIES

Two major issues confront the employment and use of paraprofessionals today. The first is the attitude of counselors toward their utilization on significant tasks (Zimpfer, Frederickson, Salim, and Sanford 1971, p. 32; Delworth 1974). Understandably, school counselors sometimes feel defensive about untrained persons taking over guidance tasks. It has been implied in some instances that paraprofessionals can replace counselors; this situation sets up barriers against effective use.

The second problem concerns the attitudes of paraprofessionals toward supervision. As beginners among highly trained professionals, they may find it difficult to establish an identity and feel like important members of the institution. An agency-type problem, which also arises in the school, is pressure on support persons to conform to institution policies and rules, although their own backgrounds might help them discover new ways to work with individuals, particularly within their own subgroups (Delworth 1974; Gartner and Riessman 1974).

Much of the current writing and research that deals with the community agency applies more or less directly to schools. One problem, generally due to poor planning, is the tendency for initial overenthusiastic acceptance of a program and great expectations followed by the phasing out of positions (Grzegorek 1976). Often evaluation is not included or not well designed, so that it is difficult or impossible to judge whether a program is effective.

The paraprofessional movement emerged in part from dissatisfaction of minority groups with helping services, a recognition of the need for helpee participation in the guidance process, and emerging concern about the status of minority groups (Banks 1977), but practice has fallen short of expectations. Difficulties have resulted for many reasons: lack of meaningful and challenging work, lack of adequate orientation, lack of preparation for understanding the organization and operation of the service, and lack of attention to the importance of the paraprofessional's initial job supervisor. Moreover, the paraprofessional's concern for status, prestige, and advancement greatly affects job satisfaction. As skills develop, individuals begin to look for increased responsibility. Those in bridge-type roles (i.e., who come from the population they serve), tend to grow less effective as they become more a part of the agency, and must learn skills for new kinds of work (Feild and Gatewood 1976). If and when these conditions are remedied, the problem of competition with counselors will call for particular attention. It is likely, for example, that providing a career ladder or more meaningful work for paraprofessionals could make counselors perceive them as threats to their own positions.

Training is a major factor in effective utilization of paraprofessionals. Both preservice and in-service training are needed; the latter type offers a vehicle for supervision and for growth by both counselor and paraprofessional. The counselor can learn a great deal from the paraprofessional, particularly if the paraprofessional belongs to a minority group with which the counselor has had little personal contact. Cooperative working relationships and a supportive, enhancing climate for paraprofessionals are extremely important and should set the tone for the whole program (Zimpfer, Frederickson, Salim, and Sanford 1971, p. 42).

The content and approach of training programs have been the subject of considerable study, and productive models have been developed. Emphasized areas include human relations and clerical, media, and guidance services (e.g., how to administer an interest inventory). But the greatest attention has gone to human relations. Danish and Brock (1974) break the category down into six competencies: understanding oneself, using nonverbal behavior, using verbal behavior, using self-involvement, understanding others, and building helping relationships. They point out that teaching methods are critical; failure can result from lack of a delivery system as well as from deficiencies in the trainer's skills. Manuals for leaders, workbooks for trainees, visual materials, and use of consultants are used to ensure success (pp. 301–302).

A further breakdown of training areas (Zimpfer, Frederickson, Salim and Sanford 1971, p. 42) illustrates the types of skills that should be developed.

Human Relations Skills
— Listening
— Observing
— Articulating
— Intrapersonal dimensions
— Interpersonal dimensions
— Person to person via technology

Clerical-Audiovisual Skills
— Typing
— Duplicating
— Letter writing
— Recording information
— Telephone procedures
— Filing
— Audiovisual-equipment operation

Guidance Center Skills (Sample)
— Collection and display of occupational information
— Dissemination
— Test technology
— Recording student data
— Job-application procedures
— Follow-up procedures
— Structuring interviews with parents
— Class scheduling
— Coordinating visits of college representations

How well do paraprofessional programs work? Research evidence, although in some instances lacking in rigor, is very positive. Support persons themselves are enthusiastic. Statements like these give the flavor of reactions: "I love my work!" (Potter 1974), "It's exciting to learn something . . ." (Donovan 1974), "I see the paraprofessional as a viable resource . . ." (Brasington 1976).

RESEARCH

WORK VALUES OF SUPPORT PERSONNEL

Quesada-Fulgado (1975) investigated attitudes of a group of disadvantaged paraprofessionals in a New York City Manpower Development Program regarding their need to work. Subjects rated three needs: human relations, activity, and livelihood.

Which of these needs would you expect to be greatest for this group? (College students ranked activity first, followed by human relations, and livelihood.)

The rank order given by the subject was: human relations, work as an activity, and the need to earn a livelihood. The human relations need was higher at the .01 level of significance, but the other two were about equally important. There were no differences by sex. This hierarchy gives an important insight to counselors who work with support personnel.

RESEARCH

COUNSELOR ATTITUDES ABOUT FUNCTIONS OF PARAPROFESSIONALS

A survey of a five-percent random sample of ASCA members, including both elementary and secondary school workers, revealed counselors' views on what functions are appropriate for paraprofessionals. The study covered six clusters of activities. The following table from Zimpfer, Frederickson, Salim, and Sanford 1971, p. 30 shows cluster averages in percentages; average ratings are based on a four-point scale.

Cluster	Percentages of Counselors				
	Strongly disagree	Disagree	Agree	Strongly agree	Average rating
1. Interview-type activities	8.0	24.3	56.1	11.6	2.71
2. Group-discussion activities, e.g., on information resource	5.3	27.4	55.2	12.1	2.74
3. Indirect-help activities, e.g., testing, obtaining job information	1.7	11.2	50.4	36.6	3.22
4. Referral assistance activities	7.3	36.5	44.9	11.2	2.60
5. Placement and follow-up activities	1.3	11.5	58.3	28.8	3.15
6. Program management activities, e.g., making reports	2.0	11.5	52.3	34.3	3.19

The survey shows substantial differences of opinion about the suitability of each of these functions for paraprofessionals. It also shows that indirect helping activities are favored over those that bring the paraprofessional face to face with pupils and referral resources.

RESEARCH

EFFECTS OF A HELPER TRAINING PROGRAM

Using the Danish and Haver program with both professionals and paraprofessionals in training (undergraduate students, some planning to enter professional schools), a study was made to determine if facilitative helper responses could be increased (Danish, D'Augelli, and Brock 1976, p. 263). Ten training sessions were used, with groups of twenty subjects. The training method involved defining, explaining, and modeling the skills, followed by intensive practice and evaluation. Results are as follows:

Category	t Tests for Changes from Pretesting to Post-testing	
Content — *reflects* the content of prior statement	16.72[a]	(increase)
Affective — *reflects* a feeling counselee has not yet identified	11.27[a]	(increase)
Advice — suggests to counselee other attitudes or behaviors	3.79[b]	(decrease)
Influence — makes statements to change counselee's attitude	4.08[b]	(decrease)
Open questions — cannot be answered with "yes" or "no"	.78	(no change)
Closed questions — can be answered with "yes" or "no"	17.60[a]	(decrease)

[a] $p < .001$ [b] $p < .01$

These results show that helpful responses (e.g., content and affective) increased significantly. On the other hand, closed questions, advice, and influence decreased, also significantly. There was an overall increase in helper responses emphasizing affect and greater ease on the part of the counselee in continuing discussions. Responses that directed the interview and those that tended to stop interaction decreased.

There was no control group and no follow-up, so the study does not take into account maturational effects or stability of the changes. It does provide evidence, however, that systematic training can help paraprofessionals develop effective interview techniques.

What types of responses do you think you tend to give? Role play a brief interview and have a third person count your responses by category. (The reflection type will be the most difficult to identify, but reviewing the examples in Chapter 6 will help.)

EXPERIENCE

SUPPORT PERSONNEL'S PERCEPTIONS OF COUNSELORS

Talk to one or more support persons about their work. Ask these questions:

— What are the most positive and negative aspects of paraprofessional work?
— What kind of supervision do they receive?

What do the answers tell you about ways to work with support personnel?

OBJECTIVES

1. To understand the major trends in the use of support personnel in guidance. Identify two aspects of the contemporary situation.
Rapidly increasing use. Growing variety of types of persons used.

2. To become aware of the types of individuals who may serve as support persons. Name three types.
Peers. Volunteer parents. Paid helpers.

3. To understand which types of functions support personnel can carry out. Name three types and indicate the amount of supervision needed.
Types include working with data, people, and objects. (Services may also be classified as direct or indirect. For all activities, close counselor supervision is needed.)

4. To understand contemporary issues about the use of support personnel. Identify the major ones and give a one-sentence explanation of each.

We have discussed two issues: counselors' attitudes about effective use, and support personnel's difficulty in accepting role limitations. Counselors have been resentful and suspicious of possible encroachment on counseling functions. Support personnel may feel defensive about lack of professional background.

5. To understand the role of preparation in enhancing the effectiveness of support personnel. Name two approaches to preparation and give a one-sentence statement of the unique value of each.

Preservice—helps the individual feel prepared for new responsibilities.

In-service—provides opportunity for close working relationship between supervisors and paraprofessionals.

6. To understand the potential of supervision for both counselor and support person. Name one value that each could derive.

The counselor can learn more about the support personnel's subgroup. The support person can upgrade skills and utilize potential more effectively.

EXAMPLES OF PROGRAMS

The following descriptions illustrate the types of program that can be set up at each school level and the potential uses of paraprofessional help.

IN THE ELEMENTARY SCHOOL   Peer counseling programs have been developed and shown good results. Three sixth-grade classes in Dryden Central School, New York (McCann 1975), took part in a peer-counselor training program. Pupil helpers were selected by class sociograms. The counselor discussed the program with sixth-grade teachers and then met with classes to talk about helping and the work of peer counselors. Eight volunteers were selected, evenly divided by sex; all but one elected to continue after learning more about what was involved. In eight one-hour primarily experiential training sessions, pupils were trained to listen, notice nonverbal communication, talk to others about problems and feelings, reflect feelings, develop options for problem situations, and demonstrate caring. After training, they worked in a drop-in center under the counselor's supervision. Results showed that both peer counselors and counselees

A paraprofessional could ease this counselor's work load by providing clerical assistance, helping in assessment, and being a resource person.

benefited. Counselees expressed positive attitudes toward the program; peer counselors learned helping skills and developed positive attitudes toward being of service to others.

Other types of paraprofessionals work in the elementary school. Carlson and Pietrofesa (1971) describe a three-level organization. At the first level paraprofessionals perform routine clerical duties and build school-community relations. The middle level consists of guidance workers who concentrate on activities other than counseling. The Deerfield, Ill., project (Carlson, Cavins, and Dinkmeyer 1969) utilized guidance assistants who had more training than the typical paraprofessional. Pasco County, Fla., used five occupational specialists in elementary career-education to develop and present career-oriented materials in

Project CHOICE (Comprehensive Humanistic Oriented Implementation of Career Education); although college preparation is not required for the occupational specialists, all had bachelor's degrees.

An impressive use of paraprofessionals to improve career guidance for disadvantaged youth, grades K – 12, is demonstrated by the Detroit Developmental Career Guidance Project (Leonard and Vriend 1975). Evaluations have shown that the work of community aides as liaison between school, home, and community is one of the major reasons for success of the program.

IN THE MIDDLE/JUNIOR HIGH SCHOOL Much paraprofessional work in the middle school years is performed by peers and parents. Ehlert started a peer-counseling program with three seventh-grade "kid counselors" (1975, p. 260) who were trained to help fellow students. A typical task consisted of assisting a boy with no friends to develop social skills. Peer counselors derived personal benefit from the program and the counselor gained new insights about junior high school pupils. Gray and Tindall (1974) used a training program with ninth graders and found that pupils who participated improved significantly in communication skills over controls who did not. Anecdotal evidence too, such as teachers' comments on pupil behavior, revealed that trained pupils functioned effectively as helpers and showed marked personal growth.

HIGH SCHOOL LEVEL Varenhorst (1974) describes the long-term, extensive peer-counseling program at Palo Alto, Calif., that involved precounseling training and in-service supervision. Both junior and senior high students trained together in groups of ten or twelve in an eighteen-hour course covering communication skills, decision making, counseling strategies, and ethics. Initially, peer counselors were assigned tasks, usually at the request of teachers or counselors. Later, they chose assignments in line with preferences and estimated capabilities, often starting out with elementary pupils. This program has the unique feature of regular practicum supervisory meetings. Specially trained leaders come from all sorts of backgrounds and include parents and secretaries; many of them are paraprofessionals themselves. Varenhorst points out the difficulty of obtaining evidence of benefits to pupils, but subjective data on effects were positive, and there are plans to offer peer counseling as a credit course.

Many other programs illustrate the wide use of support personnel. SPICE (Sex Peer Information Center for Everyone), a pupil-operated information center, is part of pilot program of the Student Family Living

Sex Information Project in New York City. The pupils who staff the project centers have undergone extensive training in sex information, self-understanding, and communication skills; the program has had to anticipate and overcome many objections (Welbourne 1975). Volunteers as well as peers are widely used in career information centers (Jacobson 1972; Jacobson 1975) to help pupils find information, maintain information files, and attract pupils to the service. The occupational specialist, a position established by the Florida legislature (Panther 1972), has no graduate preparation, but may take the place of counselors. There are occupational specialists in about two thirds of the counties in the state (Raney 1975). Evidence suggests that the program produces positive results and shows it to be well accepted (Myrick and Wilkinson 1976).

SUGGESTED APPROACHES FOR PRODUCTIVE UTILIZATION

The experiences of those who have managed programs and analyzed the paraprofessional movement provide guidelines for building new services. The four steps suggested by Grzegorek (1976) ensure both effectiveness and viability. First, there should be an assessment of needs, including those met by existing services. Second, support should be sought and resources should be identified. In the school it is particularly important to promote faculty backing and interest. Third, an effective skill-training program should be developed and implemented. Preservice preparation is needed so that paraprofessionals can provide quality services as soon as they begin work with pupils; in-service training too is needed, both to maintain quality and provide for the personnel growth. Finally, paraprofessionals should gain a sense of identity, participate in goal setting, and learn organizational skills. Communication is particularly important; deficiencies can build barriers, generate misunderstandings, and give rise to a counterproductive climate of suspicion and hostility.

The program should include evaluation procedures to determine effectiveness in meeting needs. Eventually, these data will be required when decisions are made about continuing the service.

Delworth (1974) offers other suggestions for the effective utilization of paraprofessionals. He warns of the danger of "cooling out" individuals who might develop new and even radically different approaches to providing services. The ideas and subgroup connections of a support person should be valued for the fresh look at traditional practices and roles they offer. Moreover, support persons should be given opportunities for additional training and advancement.

RESEARCH

EFFECTIVENESS OF PEER FACILITATORS

Cooker and Cherchia (1976) compared a group of high school pupils prepared by an eight-hour program based on Carkhuff's communication model and an untrained control group on their ability to respond effectively as peer facilitators. Results were assessed by a communications questionnaire, role-playing ratings by trainers, and pupil evaluations in group sessions. Peer facilitators worked with practically the total high school population in three one-hour small-group meetings.

Results showed there were differences, significant at the .05 level, between the trained and untrained peer facilitators on written and role-playing evaluations; the differences favored the trained group.

The results for trainers' and peers' ratings in group work with high school pupils are shown below (from p. 466):

| Group | Trainers' ratings | | Peers' ratings | |
	Mean	Standard Deviation	Mean	Standard Deviation
Trained	2.64	.66	3.08	.41
Untrained	1.82	.56	2.76	.58

Schweisheimer and Walberg (1976) trained high school juniors selected by sociometric ratings as peer counselors for group work with freshmen. The counseled pupils were educable mentally-handicapped and others classified as potential dropouts. Peer counselors were trained in a thirty-hour program, and two peer counselors per group worked with pupils for a total of twenty hours.

Results showed that attendance for the experimental group improved significantly; decisiveness (as seen, for example, in the intention to complete tasks) was also significantly higher (both at the .05 level). No differences were found in fourteen other variables. The authors attribute this finding partly to the newness of the program and to organizational problems.

A number of new peer counseling programs are being developed (Bell 1976; Cunin 1976), and pupils show strong support for this approach to guidance (Williams 1976).

RESEARCH

CAREER-GUIDANCE SUPPORT PERSONNEL IN THE HIGH SCHOOL

The support function of the occupational specialist, legislatively mandated for Florida schools in 1970, has been evaluated several times (Mobley 1976). Two evaluations were carried out in 1973, and one in 1976.

Results of the two 1973 evaluations revealed the following:

— Occupational specialists are successfully carrying out responsibilities (helping pupils with career guidance and placement, and serving as career information resource persons in schools).
— Administrators support the program.
— Pupils rate it as valuable.

In 1976, there were over six hundred occupational specialists, distributed through practically every county in the state.

The most recent evaluation, including reports from forty-two counties, is shown in part below. Other activities such as teacher/administrator conferences, pupil follow-up, and career guidance totaled 493,914.

Number of pupils helped	
Total	700,000
Per month per specialist	375
Number placed in alternative programs (e.g., vocational technical, adult)	27,500
Number placed in jobs	13,253
"Counseling" activities	
Total	226,369
With potential dropouts	29,202
With actual dropouts	11,702
With other pupils	179,594
With parents of potential dropouts	5,871

EXPERIENCE

USE OF SUPPORT PERSONNEL

Findings from a survey of school counselors (Zimpfer, Frederickson, Salim, and Sanford 1971, p. 32) revealed that "counselor preferences will tend not only to separate support personnel from counselees, but also to separate counselors from support personnel."

How do you feel about this attitude? How do you think support persons feel about it?

Role play a situation in which the support person protests against this situation to a counselor.

EXPERIENCE

WORKING WITH SUPPORT PERSONNEL

As a counselor in the school, you have been assigned two support persons to help you in your work. Both have had a brief preparation program in communication skills, administering group tests, and leading group discussions. Their previous experience includes completing high school and some miscellaneous work. They are in their early thirties. One is male (white), the other female (black). Both are anxious about acceptance and do not feel very competent to handle expected tasks. They want helpful supervision and in-service preparation.

Role play your first meeting with your new support persons. After about five minutes stop and review the session, covering the following questions:

— What were your feelings while talking to the support persons?
— Did you respond to their needs? (e.g., anxiety about acceptance by school staff and pupils, lack of confidence in abilities, desire for on-the-job training.)
— How much responsibility did you give them?
— What would you do differently the next time?

Rotate roles and repeat.

If support persons are available, include them in the role play, both as themselves and as counselors.

EXPERIENCE

WORKING AS A SUPPORT PERSON

Find a campus or community setting that uses volunteer help. (Usually a community information center can help locate volunteer opportunities.) Offer your services as a volunteer worker. The experience will give you the opportunity to see the work from the support person's point of view.

OBJECTIVES

1. To become aware of examples of programs utilizing support personnel. Briefly describe a type of program at each school level.

Several programs are described in the text, e.g., peer counseling, adult support personnel in the elementary school.

2. To become aware of ways for increasing the effectiveness of support personnel. What one process or technique would you recommend to accomplish this task?

Of those suggested in the text, a planned program beginning with needs assessment and ending with evaluation of success should be the most beneficial. Others are listening to and utilizing suggestions of support personnel, and providing opportunities for advancement.

ADDITIONAL READINGS

Brown, William F. *Student-to-Support Counseling*. Austin: University of Texas Press, 1972.

This book is about the college level, but describes adaptations of the study-skills and academic-motivation approach to the high school level on pages 156 — 179. Discussion of Upward Bound pupils is also included.

Delworth, Ursula, ed. "The Paraprofessionals Are Coming!" *Personnel and Guidance Journal*, no. 4 (1974).

A special issue on support personnel. Rationale, roles, and programs are covered. An excellent reference to gain an understanding of the current status and major trends of the movement.

Morgan, James I., ed. *Paraprofessional Training: Functions, Methods and Issues*. Gainesville: Psychological and Vocational Counseling Center, University of Florida, 1976.

While the emphasis is on college and community agency settings, the series of articles and studies on function, training, and issues will be of value to anyone working with support personnel.

Zimpfer, David; Frederickson, Ronald; Salim, Mitchell; and Sanford, Adelphus. *Support Personnel in School Guidance Programs*. Washington, D.C.: American Personnel and Guidance Association, 1971.

A monograph of the APGA Guidance and Counseling Series providing the most comprehensive review available of support personnel in schools. Particularly useful on the concept of levels of personnel. Highly recommended.

CHAPTER THIRTEEN
NEW EDUCATIONAL MODELS

Guidance is a part of the changing educational institution and must develop new methods, techniques, and strategies to keep abreast of new developments in schools. Moreover, guidance workers should be involved in the change process both to infuse guidance concepts in the institution and to build relevant and effective services for new models.

Our country is only a little more than two hundred years old. The first public school supported by direct taxation was started in 1639; the first locally elected school board came three years later. These two innovations were established no more than a hundred years before the American Revolution. In the period shortly after the Revolution, it was not generally accepted that formal education should be provided to all (Pierce 1975). But less than forty years after the beginning of the Republic, public education of one sort or another had been instituted in practically all the States. The rate of change illustrates the dynamism of the enterprise of education.

GOALS

1. To become aware of some of the new educational models.
2. To understand the part the counselors may play in new approaches to education.
3. To understand personal attitudes about working in new and evolving settings.

If one looks at the three basic forces that have shaped public education in this country since its inception, it is easy to see why changes are taking place today at a rapid rate, and why we can expect further change in the future. These forces—political, economic, and social—emphasize the types of understanding needed to participate in a democratic form of government, the ability to cope successfully in an urban-technological society, and the attitude of acceptance needed for various cultures to live together (Pierce 1975). An idealistic, humanistic theme has pervaded education throughout history, but the political factor has been paramount in the shaping of our system. Education in our country will continue to come up against the pressures and demands of society; it must be forward-looking and in touch with major trends.

New educational models emerge in response to criticism and dissatisfaction with schools as they are, or through efforts to maintain the best existing features while introducing new concepts and practices. Accountability is a recurring theme. This is the time of the active, assertive consumer. Public opinion polls assess voters' preferences, purchasers' reactions, and TV-viewers' choices. Major decisions in countless areas depend on poll results. Education is no exception. The annual Gallup educational polls (Gallup 1975, 1976) give clear indications of the public's expectations.

Discipline is the major problem; it has led the list in seven of eight national surveys. Almost half the persons surveyed feel that pupils are given too many rights, and about half (more than half for high school) do not believe schools require pupils to work hard enough. The general attitude is further emphasized by the finding that the majority would prefer to send their children to schools with strict discipline and rules. There is a preference for practical education that will help pupils get jobs, and overwhelming support for job training for unemployed young persons not attending school. Fewer than half of the respondents give schools a grade of B or above. Even so, schools fared better in public-confidence ratings than Congress, the Supreme Court, organized labor, and big business.

But taking a broad perspective, schools over the past two hundred years have met society's expectations with amazing success (Tyler 1975b), and it is apparent that education for tomorrow will be shaped by society's demands and expectations today. The first demand is that education reach all, irrespective of differing home and subcultural experiences, and deal with the total range of pupil needs. Second, education should foster an orderly, peaceful, constructive transition from childhood to productive and satisfying adult life. Third, education must provide occupational preparation, particularly for those who lack skills and do not readily take part in training opportunities. Fourth, education must emphasize character development; the urgency of this demand has increased dramatically as the influence of home, church, and community have lessened. Fifth, there must be a strong link between schools and other major community institutions; educational facilities must be opened up to the community and local resources brought into the schools. Sixth, schools must make fuller use of the findings and developments of science and technology.

These positive, forward-looking demands reflect response to criticisms that arise from widely diverse quarters. Career planning by high school pupils needs to be improved (Flanagan 1973b). Pupils need to develop ways of coping with the "future shock" changes and proliferation of opportunities (Hoffman and Rollin 1972). New methods of productivity must be found to keep costs in line with available resources (Abert 1974). The effects on schools and on pupils of increasingly limited budgets need to be examined and ways found to ensure a positive impact on pupils (Robinson 1972; Noeth, Roth, and Prediger 1975). The community must be restructured to build a productive total educational environment. In this restructuring the schools must play a part (Tyler 1975b).

NEW MODELS, APPROACHES, AND TECHNIQUES

Some critics advocate doing away with schools entirely and replacing them with different processes; others favor giving education a new orientation (Ginzberg 1972; Marland 1972). Many recommend alternative types of schools (Smith 1973), and some call for a return to the fundamentals (Gallup 1975, 1976). Many new concepts have been implemented. Schools available to Pasadena youth, enumerated by Neill (1976), run the gamut from alternative to fundamental. Riles (1975) describes California's new statewide approach to early childhood education, which features cooperative community development of a needs-based program, individualized instruction, diagnosis of pupil status, and participation of parents and aides in classroom instruction.

Career education and community education are two new approaches with profound implications for the way guidance workers will function and the number of them that will be needed. A third new model, called PLAN, utilizes technology, flexible organization, and competency-based units of instruction (Dunn 1972). Cooperative Education (Bostwick 1972; Hampson 1975), alternative schools, and life-long education are other emerging patterns. Voucher plans and performance contracting, while not new models, constitute strategies for providing or utilizing educational services.

This section briefly defines each of these new plans; the three major ones — career education, community education, and alternative schools—are discussed in greater detail later in this chapter.

Career Education   This approach includes all learning experiences in the whole context of a way of life (Hoyt 1975a). Career education covers the life span, from preschool years, and includes acquiring values and competencies, and setting goals for both in- and out-of-school experiences. The spread of this new concept has been rapid. It is being implemented in every state, and most states have held conferences on it for further study (Worthington 1974, abstract). Its status in 1974–75 is summarized in a report of a national survey:

> Less than five years later (after its introduction) career education is now permeating educational programs thinking throughout the nation. More significantly, after four and a half years career education is *still* of concern in a field where fads have often erupted with brilliant oratorical support and then quietly faded away (McLaughlin 1976, p. 12).[1]

Critics, however, find that the concept is based on unwarranted assumptions (Grubb and Lazerson 1975; Kroll, 1976), primarily regarding the availability of challenging and suitable work for all in a free-enterprise, technologically advanced society.

Community Education   This model achieved national visibility in a little over one decade (Minzey 1972). There are all sorts of definitions (e.g., school programs for adults), but the term has assumed much broader meaning today—it is a utilization of all resources in the community for the benefit of its members (Seay 1974, p. 11). The emphasis is on community needs; the concept is in line with current trends to bring school, community, and local resources together in a cooperative effort to meet these needs.

PLAN   The PLAN approach, grades 1–12, makes extensive use of modern technology to individualize instruction and maintain complete, up-to-date records on progress. A large number of learning units incorporate instructional objectives, evaluation strategies, and testing materials. Guidance is built into the local program, which might include, for example, units for grades 1–4 introducing the world of work. Teachers use the computer to help plan the program best suited to the individual pupil, but the pupil takes responsibility for checking materials out and returning them. The program is currently in operation in a number of school systems.

---

1. It should be mentioned, however, that the quotation is not generally representative of the findings presented in the report. For example, much needs to be done to expand program implementation, evaluate outcomes, and increase teacher and counselor involvement. But recommendations given in the report emphasize the potential contribution of well developed and adequately funded career education programs.

Cooperative Education This is not a new model; schools have had work-study programs for many years. Recently, however, more attention has been given to this concept, which now includes such features as plans for alternative paths to high school graduation (Hampson 1975). The classroom is not necessarily a profitable place for all young people, and many need to spend at least part of their time earning money in purposeful work in an adult work setting (Ginzberg 1972).

Alternative Schools Early in the 70s, many communities began to recognize that a single-standard school would not meet the needs of all pupils. Special schools, such as the Bronx High School of Science, had been established earlier, but the movement is only now becoming widespread. Frequently used plans are: schools without walls, learning centers, continuation schools, multicultural schools, free schools, and schools within a school (Smith, Burke, and Barr 1974, pp. 9–11). (These types are illustrated later in this chapter.)

Apprenticeships offer a wide range of training for high-school and post-high-school age pupils, but they are not widely used in this country. Cole (1975) describes how eleven European countries use apprenticeships to teach occupational skills and personal competency and attributes the low juvenile-delinquency rates of these countries at least in part to the quality and high-status occupational training these programs provide to young people.

RESEARCH

IMPLICATIONS OF SURVEYS FOR NEW EDUCATIONAL MODELS

A 1976 Gallup poll of attitudes toward the public schools indicates desired changes. The following excerpts from survey results are examples; some are already implemented in new models.

Public schools were rated with letter grades:

A	13%
B	29%
C	28%
D	10%
Fail	6%
Don't Know	14%

Actions to Improve the Quality of Public Education	National Percentage in Favor
Devote more time to teaching basic skills	51
Emphasize career education and developing salable skills	38
Require pupils to pass a standard nationwide competency test to receive a diploma	65
Give more emphasis to careers and career preparation in high school	80
Include information about jobs and careers in the elementary school curriculum	52
Give courses to parents to help them help their children in school (51 percent would be willing to pay additional taxes to support the program. 83 percent of those 18–29 years of age support the program.)	77

EXPERIENCE

DESIGNING A NEW MODEL FOR EDUCATION

Assume that you can start from scratch to develop an entirely new system of public education. There are no limits — you do not have to have school buildings, schedules, credits, or any of the traditional procedures or regulations.

Prepare one- or two-sentence answers to the following questions:

— What would my school do?
— Who would do it?
— What would be the most important attribute of an 18-year-old in this school? (*Note:* Eighteen need not be the age for terminating the program.)

If you are working with others, have group members discuss which school they would send their own children to. Which would they agree to pay taxes to support?

OBJECTIVE

1. To become aware of major forces shaping public schools. Name three.

Major forces are political, social, and technological. Others include accountability and criticisms of schools.

CAREER EDUCATION MODELS The term "career education" has a unique meaning and goes far beyond preparation for a career. The concept involves a restructuring of American education, grades K–12. It is a developmental process; its major ongoing purpose is to make all educational experiences—curriculum, guidance, teaching methods—enhance the individual's ability to cope successfully in a technological society, and to impart a full appreciation of the importance and dignity of work. It features appropriate activities at each grade level and throughout one's lifetime (U.S. Dept. of Health, Education and Welfare 1971, pp. 2–3). The concept has recently been spelled out in detail (Hoyt 1975c, pp. 3–4). The key elements are these: education consists of all learning experiences; and one's career includes work experience throughout one's life. Career education, therefore, involves the whole spectrum of personal experience—school, hobby, part-time work, social life—that enables the individual to learn about work, achieve self-understanding, plan for the future, decide on alternatives, implement choices.

The origins of career education may be traced back to the early stages of education in this country. Its underlying principles have now and then been prefigured in federal legislation (Herr 1974). But data released by Commissioner of Education S. P. Marland, Jr., showing ineffectiveness in education really launched the concept in 1970–71. His report indicated that approximately 2.5 million individuals left the educational system without adequate preparation for a career. Of these, 850,000 were elementary and secondary school dropouts; 750,000 took the "general high school program which did not prepare for work or higher educational programs. Of those entering college, 850,000 dropped out before completion of their programs." (U.S. Dept. of HEW 1971, p. 4). The 1976 Education Amendments have authorized additional support for career education, guidance, and development programs for all ages. There are special provisions for counselors to learn about business and industry, and for representatives of employers to come into schools as advisers. Funds are available to states to be used for career education planning. Florida, for example, expects to have some form of career education for all pupils by 1980 (Florida . . . 1977, p. 34). Much of the support for career guidance and career education provided by federal bills stems from the American Personnel and Guidance Association's efforts to acquaint members of Congress with the need for services. More recently, Congress has shown substantial support for the concept. House bill HR7 was passed, authorizing almost $300 million for career education, K–12, over a five-year period. Senate action has not yet been completed, however.

There is widespread optimism that career education will provide a much-needed response to some of the major problems facing education today. It is generally recognized, however, that the concept is still not well understood. A great deal must be done to marshall the efforts of teachers, parents, counselors, and administrators to make career education work. If funds are provided by Congress, career education should have the needed stimulus.

The concept has caught on with phenomenal success. States have expended large sums on program development. Federal support too has been extensive and includes funding for research centers to design and test models. Seven major test sites have been set up in six city-systems: Atlanta, Ga.; Hackensack, N.J.; Mesa, Ariz.; Lakewood, Colo.; Los Angeles, Calif.; and Pontiac, Mich. Many other programs are being tested (Hewett 1975; Worthington 1974, pp. 19–24). While less than one third of the seventeen thousand school districts in the U.S. have received federal funds for career education, over five thousand have established programs, and most states have employed a career-education coordinator (Glickman 1975).

Visibility in professional literature is another indication of the concept's significance. Both *Personnel and Guidance Journal* (Hansen and Gysbers 1975) and *School Counselor* (Carroll 1973a) have published special issues on the subject. An important book of readings, *Career Education and the Counselor* (Pietrofesa, Leonard, and Giroux 1975), has appeared recently, and the total number of publications is enormous and growing rapidly.

There are four models being field-tested, three of them outside the school. One of them is an employer-based/experience-based model. The school-based model previously mentioned is by far the most extensively tested and has the greatest potential for implementation in school guidance work, but all four illustrate a wide range of innovative approaches to education. A large number of research and development studies are in progress (Education and Work Group 1977).

The variety of school-based implementations and field tests is wide and exciting. Three school districts in California joined to establish the Orange County Consortium Career Education Project (Hamilton 1975). Starting with a needs assessment of education K through community college, the program directors, assisted by teachers and counselors, introduced career-education activities and concepts into the curriculum. Materials were developed for the fifteen occupational clusters identified by the U.S. Office of Education (broad groupings of occupations such as business, clerical, and construction.) Teachers were paid incentive stipends to develop units, and part-time "facilitators" were set up in each school to help teachers obtain materials, establish resource centers, and provide career education experience. Counselors have been active in the program from the start and have been quite effective as resource persons. The Skyline Center in Dallas (Marland, Lichtenwald, and Burke 1975) divides its curriculum into twenty-eight clusters, each including several career families, e.g., business and management technology, aeronautics. Pupils' programs, consisting of a balance of academic and occupational education, are based on needs. School policy on curriculum is flexible, enabling pupils to change from one cluster to another and to proceed at their own pace.

Model II, employer-based/experience-based, is an innovative approach currently being offered in four sites to high school sophomores through seniors who for one reason or another do not profit from a traditional school program or who want more experience related learning. Pupils participate in an individualized program that merges the worlds of work and school; they are based either in their own schools or in community learning centers. Pupils also participate in non-paid work experiences in real-life settings to prepare for adult life (EBCE 1975; National Institution of Education 1975). The primary setting for learning is the community. An EBCE student may conduct biological research and experiments (for science credit) while exploring a possible career in ecology (for career development credit). Student accountability and performance evaluations are given high priority; results so far are quite positive (National Institute of Education 1975; EBCE 1975, pp. 10–11). The potential for new guidance roles is evident in a program that engages pupils in real-life experiences and helps them determine personal meaning in their activities (Baron 1975). As stated in the National Institute of Education Bulletin, *The Community is the Teacher* (1975), "EBCE is an attempt to take the subject matter that the students normally study, add many new ingredients (about people, jobs, self and the way communities work) and let high school students learn about them out in the community through direct experience with adults in all walks of life." The four educational laboratories selected to develop and test pilot-programs are: Far West Laboratory for Educational Research and Development, Oakland, Calif.; Research for Better Schools, Inc., Philadelphia, Pa.; Appalachia Educational Laboratory, Charleston, W.Va.; and Northwest Regional Educational Laboratory, Tigard, Ore., outside Portland.

The future use of the approach may involve use in alternative school programs or the adoption by school systems of parts of the model. The Office of Education, National Institute of Education, and Department of Labor are conducting studies at the national level to determine the feasibility of EBCE for work-study and similar training programs. More than sixty educational agencies in forty-six states are operating or planning to institute EBCE programs (Update 1977).

Model III, the home-community based model, is being tested only at one site—Providence, R.I. Initiated in 1972, the program is unique in its focus on the career-development needs of home-based adults (Career Counseling . . . 1975, p. 3). The clientele consists of persons not engaged in full-time work or training, and so far has included more women than men, ages 16 to 70. Continuous community-needs-assessment serves as the guide for priorities, and evaluation is built into the program through systematic follow-up. The major strategy is outreach, using radio, TV, and other media to reach prospective clients. Counseling is carried out by telephone. Paraprofessionals help clients assess present status, capabilities and limitations; provide them with information; help with decision making; and assist in carrying out plans. The third component, the resource center, contains information about occupations, trends, and opportunities. An information unit supports the counseling service by developing local information for specific client needs. Finally, the evaluation component provides feedback about the service's effectiveness. Results show that clients make and carry out plans, and that their response is almost unanimously positive. A recent report (Career Counseling . . . 1975, p. 3) indicated that over five thousand men and women have used the service.

Compared to other career education models, this one is characterized by "an impressive clarity of purpose" (Career Education Task . . . 1973, p. 99). But the problem that it confronts may not merit high priority support since it has not been demonstrated that the home-based unemployed or underemployed need help with career planning and placement (Career Education Task . . . 1973, pp. 99–100). Now that the research and development phase has been completed successfully, NIE funding has ceased, but the state will continue to operate the service.

Model IV, rural/residential career education is the most expensive per client. It is a total intervention plan, aimed at helping the unemployed, problem-ridden rural family become economically self-sufficient. The family receives counseling, training, and other services in a residential center. After completing the program, the family will presumably function effectively and be economically independent in everyday society (Career Education Task . . . 1973, pp. 103–107; Worthington 1974, p. 28).

One field-testing site, serving 200 families at a time, has been set up by the Mountain-Plains Education and Economic Development Program, Inc., at Glasgow, Mont. The program appears to be very expensive, but could be cost-effective *if* actually successful in rehabilitating families. Even if the model is not in its entirety practical for local communities, it provides a laboratory for testing strategies to help families and accentuate impact through the use of a completely coordinated group of family services (Career Education Task . . . 1973, pp. 105–106). An estimated 2.3 million families, or a total of approximately 11 million individuals, are eligible for family-centered residential career education programs of this type. (Bale, Park, and McMeekin 1976, p. i).

As mentioned earlier, career education is not uncontroversial. Peterson and Park (1975) point out the critical place of values in career education—career education, though helpful in bridging the gulf between adolescence and maturity, may emphasize the values of the industrial system to the neglect of humanistic ones. Agne and Nash (1973) throw out four cautions: the concept of career education is basically conservative; it overemphasizes the status quo; it promotes an uncritical acceptance of the importance of work to maintain the system; and it develops work skills rather than the person. The concept is under suspicion of serving to divert capable blacks from attending college and exploit them as a labor pool for business and industry (Kearney and Clayton 1973). Labor has received many aspects of the concept with enthusiasm (Sessions 1975; Institute . . . 1973, pp. 14–43), but has expressed concern over narrowing opportunities, viewing individuals only as economic producers, and forcing them into premature occupational choices. Model II, the employer-based model, was particularly negatively received by labor; the name has been changed to "experience-based" to avoid the implication that employers take over the function of the schools.

RESEARCH

THE VALUE OF CAREER EDUCATION

Evidence shows that career values emerge in the elementary school (Cooker 1973); that by the end of the fifth grade sex stereotyping has taken place and later becomes increasingly difficult to change (Leonard, Sather, Sheggrud, and Handel 1973); and that career education can raise the level of career maturity (Clapsaddle 1973).

Edington (1976) tested the effects of three methods of developing career awareness — the first level of career education — in kindergartners. Using an interest center, class visits, and field trips, ten occupational groups were studied. Career awareness was checked at the end of the study and three months later.

Partial results are as follows:

Treatment	Post-test Means	Three Months Later
Control group	2.97	3.67
Field trip	7.56	7.02
Classroom visitor	5.88	5.27
Interest center (models and taped messages)	4.63	5.21

Differences were significant at the .01 level.

While there were some initial differences favoring the field-trip group, the results show that career awareness can be developed and the field trip appears to be the more effective approach.

Edington advises, however, that personal characteristics of the field-trip group may account for the higher score.

Omvig, Tulloch, and Thomas (1975) investigated the effects of career education on career maturity in sixth and eighth graders. Teachers implemented the concept in the classroom after attending a summer workshop. The time between pretest and post-test was about six months.

Results showed that for the six variables compared at each grade level, three were significant at the .05 level. They were:

Variable	Career Education Group (mean)	Non-career Education Group (mean)
Occupational information (sixth grade)	11.81	10.64
Planning (sixth grade)	10.97	9.29
Planning (eighth grade)	11.91	9.83
Attitudes (eighth grade)	32.21	30.37

All other differences except one favored the career education group, but not at the significance level (.05) set for the study. Emphasis on career education did not adversely affect progress in academic areas. Positive though not significant increases in both achievement and attitudes favored the career education group.

EXPERIENCE

COUNSELING AND GUIDANCE IN CAREER EDUCATION

Assign small groups to work on the first two career education models. Give about 10–15 minutes to complete the following tasks:

— List two guidance objectives you as counselor would recommend for the model, and explain how you would assess them.
— In no more than three or four sentences, describe the role you would choose in the program.

Follow up reports with discussion of attitudes about working in the assigned setting.

EXPERIENCE

NEEDS —
ONE YEAR AFTER GRADUATION

A recent survey (Survey Yields . . . 1977, p. 12) of renewal and updating needs of more than nine hundred practicing counselors revealed that among the top twenty-five areas "Career Education: Concepts and Implications" ranked as the twenty-third area of priority.

Assume that you have been on the job for a year. Think about the setting in which you hope to work. Then rank career education in top, middle, or lower third for updating priority.

Next, give the ranking you would assume your future clientele would assign it. Explain similarity or difference.

If a small group is used, have each member give and comment on the two rankings.

OBJECTIVES

1. To learn about some of the new models for public education. Name two that in your judgment seem viable and two that do not, and give reasons for your choices.

Your answer depends upon your judgment. One considered view is that career education and community education meet needs and expectations of society, while alternative schools and the extreme fundamental approach do not appear to have staying power.

2. To understand the major features of career education. Describe three major characteristics of career education, allowing one sentence for each.

Three major points are that career education prepares individuals to cope in a technological society; involves a restructuring of education; and emphasizes the dignity of work. There are several others of equal importance.

3. To be able to identify the major career education models. Name and identify the four models.

School-based, employer/experience-based, home/community-based, and rural/residential-based. (See text for characteristics.)

COMMUNITY EDUCATION This concept has attracted nationwide attention. Major support has come from the Mott Foundation, which lists centers in 47 states and identifies over 970 school districts which have been helped to build programs (Centers for . . . 1975). A number of brief but vivid descriptions are given in "Community Educational Vignettes" (1972), and Nierman (1972) describes the development of the Flint, Mich., Community Education Center Demonstration Project, a new type of school to deal with the total educational-, health-, and social-service problem in an elementary school setting. Guidance and counseling play significant roles in the program, and the program has introduced the innovative function of the home-school counselor who provides a link between school and family (Campbell 1972).

Community education is for all members of the local area. As Piotrowski points out:

> Community education is defined as a series of activities through which community members interacting together identify individual needs, common problems and concerns, and available resources. The community members make use of those resources to generate alternative methods for meeting needs, solving problems, and resolving concerns. The purpose of this interaction is to gain a greater sense of influencing what goes on about them as well as gain greater control over themselves. It is the sense of community which creates a learning atmosphere where all those who participate can benefit from the utilization of available resources (1975, no pagination).

Unfortunately, however, the role of guidance in community education is seldom mentioned, possibly because of the belief that counselors, who offer a highly specialized service, would not be amenable to roles suggested by others. But counseling and guidance services at various levels are vital to community education. The professional counselor provides individual and group therapeutic/developmental help; the paraprofessional dispenses information, furnishes instruction, and refers those needing specialized help to the counselor. Outreach is particularly important; those needing help may, for a number of reasons, fail to take advantage of available services. One of the counselor's major responsibilities in this setting is the coordination of all the helping services and agencies. Carrying out these responsibilities requires the counselor in a community-education program to keep in close touch with the evolving needs of the population served, and to evaluate systematically the results of services (Martinson and Seay 1974, pp. 261–281).

ALTERNATIVE SCHOOLS The concept of the alternative school emerged when communities realized that a single type of institution could not meet the needs of all pupils. Changing economic and social conditions, the increas-

New educational models include using the community as a classroom. In this setting, counselors may organize helping services.

ing percentage of school-age children and young people actually attending, efforts to help the disadvantaged, and technological advances have made any single type of school inadequate. The realization was slow in coming, but it has finally arrived (Smith, Burke, and Barr 1974, pp. 6 – 7).

The number of alternative schools is increasing. In 1973 Vernon Smith reported that several hundred communities in over thirty states were providing these types of schools. Figure 13-1 vividly portrays the rapid growth of alternative institutions. These schools, existing in several forms, reflect community efforts to meet crisis needs rather than a national educational program. Regardless of the type, they tend to have the following commonalities (Smith, Burke, and Barr 1974, p. 12):

— They are open to anyone in the community.
— They reflect the makeup of the community population.

— They are more responsive to specific educational needs than the traditional school.
— While addressed to specific needs, they also have broad goals, such as helping to improve pupils' self-concept and coping skills. Major emphasis is on personal development.
— They are more flexible and more likely to change in response to feedback and evaluation than traditional schools.
— They are smaller in size, have fewer rules, and involve less bureaucracy than traditional schools.

Open Schools   Individualized learning experiences utilizing learning or interest centers in the school. Interest in this type has been growing because of new developments in the psychology of learning and the popularity of open schools in England. One example is the St. Paul Open School, housed in a former warehouse, enrolling 500 pupils, K–12 (Smith, Burke, and Barr 1974, p. 9).

Schools Without Walls   The community serves as the setting for learning, and there is considerable interaction between the school and the community. One example is Chicago's Metro High School. It holds classes in a number of business and other community settings. Courses include ethnic cooking and dramatics taught by community persons, as well as traditional offerings (Crabtree 1975). Walden III in Racine, Wis. (Johnson and Parker 1975), is an alternative school for eleventh and twelfth graders. It places a strong emphasis on the maturity, importance, and trustworthiness of pupils and involves them in administration. The community serves as the learning environment. Evaluation of the program shows excellent results, even though pupils had high failure rates in previous schools.
The EBCE model previously discussed shows another alternative approach to secondary school.

Learning Centers   In this type, resources in one location draw pupils from throughout the community. Magnet schools, educational parks, and career education centers are examples. The more traditional community vocational schools also fall into this classification.

Continuation Schools   These schools provide for pupils whose education has been interrupted or who would be unable to attend the traditional school. Street academies, dropout centers, pregnancy-maternity centers, and adult high schools are examples.

Multicultural Schools   The emphasis here is on cultural pluralism and awareness of ethnic and racial characteristics and mores. The Agora

School in Berkeley is a multicultural school for blacks, Chicanos, and whites (Smith, Burke, and Barr 1974, p. 10).

Figure 13–1. The growth of alternative public schools, 1964–72. Based on information from 276 alternative public schools.

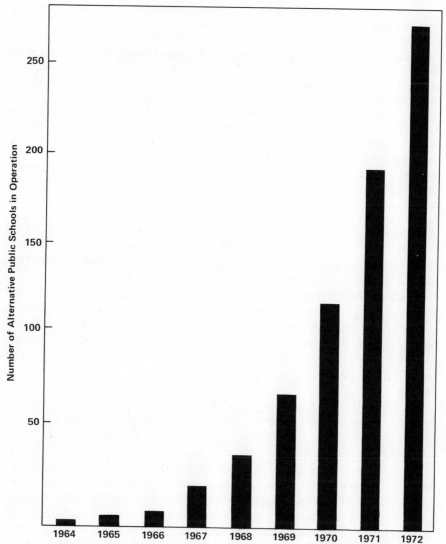

Source: From Vernon H. Smith, ed., *Alternative Schools* (Lincoln, Neb.: Professional Educators Publications, 1974), p. 15. Reprinted with permission.

Free Schools Greater freedom for both teachers and pupils to set up and engage in learning activities is the major identifying characteristic. The following brief conversation in the Southeast Minneapolis Free School portrays the climate:

She strolls in, wearing her purple velvet beret and eating an apple. She sits on the table, all bare feet and soiled jeans and teen-age insouciance. Is she listening to the introduction? Yes. She corrects it: "Chairperson, not chairman." Brief smile.

Then Christine tells us how the Southeast Minneapolis Free School is run. Student control? Not entirely. "The principal can sometimes veto us."

"But Mr. Britts," I said afterward, "what will happen to this young woman when she tries to get a job? No employer will tolerate that casual, flippant attitude, even when he discovers she can think circles around him. Especially when he finds she can think circles around him. Why don't you teach her some manners?"

"Oh, but you're wrong. She is already holding a responsible job after school. She knows the amenities. She plays whatever role the situation requires. She's playing the ' free school ' role now. She has to work because, like 46% of the other kids here, she comes from a single-parent family. You should have seen her five years ago when we opened this school. Insolent, truant, bored stiff. A traditional school soon forces this kind of youngster into a correctional institution." (Elam 1975, p. 226).

Schools Within Schools This type, which can coincide with other forms already mentioned, involves a small number of teachers and pupils who have elected to participate in a learning experience which differs from that of the parent school.

There are other types of alternative schools. Smith (1974, p. 18) identifies one that makes use of *behavior modification* in Grand Rapids, Mich. Neill (1976) describes the Pasadena (Calif.) Fundamental Schools, which involve conservative social regulations and place a strong emphasis on formal academic work; they are not "alternative" in the strict meaning of the term, but they offer parents one special educational option.

The attitude toward guidance and counseling in alternative schools appears to be largely negative; their services tend to be seen as more remedial and corrective than developmental and preventive (Franklin 1977). Moreover, the typical counselee load is far too great for the type of help envisioned by alternative programs. Different roles have been devised for the counselor, who may, for example, serve as student advocate or defender of the school program when others question its value. In some small schools, the counselor can maintain a one-to-one relationship with pupils. In other settings a teacher-counselor role is used, making extensive use of group and individual support services. In this type of program, group facilitative skills are extremely important (Glatthorn 1975, pp. 142–146).

One approach that follows the group-work emphasis is ALPHA (Alternative Learning Program for the High School Age) in Livonia, Mich. (Sparks 1977), which uses *psychological education* as the major strategy. For example, workshop sessions with 20 pupils focus on communication skills, values clarification, and facilitative listening. The Street Academy of New York (Franklin 1977) makes primary use of personal counselors who are well versed in the relevant youth culture and the language of the street. Dropouts make up a large number of the pupils in this school, and one guidance focus is understanding the "culture of formal education" (Franklin 1977, p. 420). Much work goes into the task of preparing pupils to deal with societal attitudes about testing, as well as that of mastering subject content.

IMPLICATIONS FOR GUIDANCE WORK

This review of new educational programs and procedures covers only some of the major models, but gives an idea of the new directions and even revolutionary changes in public education. With the proliferation of knowledge, the acceleration of change, and the complexity of new social and technological organizations and systems, guidance workers are hard pressed to keep up with their own specialty. But the school is part of the specialty, and counselors can contribute most to the total institution as well as to their own effectiveness by keeping up with trends that vitally affect practice.

Some counselors prefer to think of their specialties as narrowly defined, and so unique and sophisticated that they should be accepted and respected by school staff and parents. There is merit in this point of view. As guidance has become more professional, the role of the counselor has gained status. It should not be bent or squeezed to fit every new educational plan that comes along. Counselors can, however, devise new ways of helping, such as outreach, psychological education, and "giving guidance away." Rather than diluting the role, new models enhance it.

Two major approaches are used with new educational models. One emphasizes the contributions of guidance; the other examines the positive and negative aspects of the new approach to education. In the case of career education, publications have focused on applicable guidance policies and techniques. For example, the APGA book, *Career Education and the Counselor* (Pietrofesa, Leonard, and Giroux 1975), the special issue of the *Personnel and Guidance Journal* (Hansen and Gysbers 1975), and the NVGA/AVA position paper (National Vocational Guidance Association 1973) all deal with ways career guidance can contribute to career education. The second very important activity deals with the philosophy and approach of career education; it is illustrated by a special issue of the *School Counselor* (Carroll 1973*a*) analyzing the hazards and potentials of the new educational model. This too is an essential function. Counselors should be concerned (not all are!) about this new model and the place of guidance within it.

Both approaches are essential. Guidance workers should develop new approaches and techniques that will enhance new educational models. Counselors should provide critical input to ensure that the form of a new model itself embodies guidance concepts. Further efforts along the lines of the *School Counselor* article, "Teacher-Counselor Working Relationships in Career Education" (ASCA Position . . . 1976, p. 282), should be made to spell out in detail how the counselor can participate. Hopefully, such guidelines will be incorporated in counselor-education programs so that counselors can move into new educational plans without a costly and frustrating period of trial and error.

EXPERIENCE

INVESTIGATING NEW MODELS

Check your community to see if any of the models discussed here are in operation. (A good place to start your search is in the school district office.) If possible, visit the program(s) and look especially for the following:

— Attitudes of pupils and teachers.
— Role of the counselor in building and providing the program.

If a visit is not possible, talk with the director by telephone.

Compare the counselor's activities and responsibilities with what you feel they ought to be in the program. (If a counselor is not on the staff, ask about provisions of guidance: Who does it? What do they do? How?)

OBJECTIVES

1. To be aware of the rationale for community education. What is the one major purpose of this approach?

It is based on community-wide needs. While it involves a coordinated use of all resources in and outside of the school, the emphasis on meeting needs is its most distinctive feature.

2. To gain insight into your feelings about building a counseling program into new educational programs. After reading over the model descriptions, pick the one you would prefer to work in and list three rewards you would expect.

Identifying the rewards will help you gain awareness of your feelings about working in the program. The counselor's place in these new types of models has not been clearly established; assess your feelings about trying to convince others of the value of what guidance can contribute.

3. To be aware of strategies for demonstrating the value of guidance in new educational models. What would be the first three steps you would take to demonstrate its value?

First, study the model. Next, make a needs assessment. Third, specify what you expect to accomplish and describe how it will be assessed.

ADDITIONAL READINGS

Carroll, Marguerite R. "The Current Issue." *School Counselor* 21, no. 2 (1973), p. 89.

Appears in a special issue on career education. This article is particularly useful in analyzing pros and cons of this new plan for public schools.

Elam, Stanley M. "Secondary Reform: An Idea Whose Time Has Come." *Phi Delta Kappan* 56, no. 9 (1975), p. 586.

Appears in an issue containing several articles about school innovations and alternative schools.

Evans, Rupert N.; Hoyt, Kenneth B.; and Mangum, Garth L. *Career Education in the Middle/Junior High School.* Salt Lake City: Olympus Publishing Company, 1973.

A lucid explanation of career education and applications to the middle years of the public schools. The introductory chapter is useful background reading, and future projections about schools (pp. 311–316) are provocative and stimulating. Examples of counselor participation are given on pages 78–86.

Hansen, Lorraine Sundal. "A Different Approach to Career Education." *Personnel and Guidance Journal* 53, no. 9 (1975), p. 636.

Appears in a special issue on career guidance and education. An excellent summary of contemporary theory and practices.

Hoyt, Kenneth B. *An Introduction to Career Education.* Washington, D.C.: U.S. Government Printing Office, 1975.

The first comprehensive definition of career education by the U.S. Office of Education. The counselor's role is clearly identified.

Magisos, Joel H., ed. *Career Education*. Washington, D.C.: American Vocational Association, 1973.

A complete review of all aspects of career education, from historical development to applications at all levels of education. Hoyt's definition (pp. 15–29) is a good starting place. The models are described on pages 239–280, and the counselor's role is discussed briefly on pages 374–383.

Marland, Sidney P., Jr. *Career Education*. New York: McGraw-Hill, 1974.

Written by the originator of career education, and one of the most helpful publications on the concept. Select readings according to interest.

National Commission on the Reform of Secondary Education. *The Reform of Secondary Education*. New York: McGraw-Hill, 1973.

Chapter 1, "Rationale for a New Examination of Secondary Education," and Chapter 2, "Recommendations for Improving Secondary Education," point out problems and needs that have given rise to new models. Other chapters cover career education, alternative schools, and other innovations.

Pietrofesa, John J.; Leonard, George E.; and Giroux, Roy F. *Career Education and the Counselor*. Washington, D.C.: American Personnel and Guidance Association, 1975.

An excellent collection of articles from journals of the American Personnel and Guidance Association.

Seay, Maurice F. *Community Education: A Developing Concept*. Midland, Michigan: Pendall Publishing Company, 1974.

Reviews the community education movement and describes programs. The counselor's role is discussed on pages 259–281.

CHAPTER FOURTEEN
GUIDANCE
AS A PROFESSION

This chapter is about the guidance profession. Up to this point, the em-
phasis has been upon roles, techniques, historical development, and
foundations. Now the focus shifts to other factors that have an impact
upon the profession: preparation, legal status, certification and licensing,
and ethical standards. Organizations and resources for keeping up-to-
date are discussed. The work of colleagues in other settings and other
countries is reviewed; they share many of our domestic concerns.

GOALS

1. **To become aware of the professional concerns of the counselor.**
2. **To begin to build a professional identity through applying profes-**
   sional standards and guidelines.

THE MEANING
OF A PROFESSION

The guidance worker needs to develop a sense of unique personal identity,
and with it an awareness and appreciation of the meaning of a profession
with all the specific guidelines, regulations, and policies that define the
practice of the specialty. When one analyzes the definition of the term
"professional," the importance of the aspects covered in this chapter is
clear.

The major identifying characteristic of a profession is its knowledge base. Theory and research are organized to guide practice. Guidance, drawing on the disciplines of psychology, sociology, economics, and others, meets this criterion.

A second characteristic is a code of ethical practice. The counseling profession has for many years been concerned with ethical standards, and the American Personnel and Guidance Association has formulated a comprehensive and well-designed statement. But it is up to the individual practitioner to observe standards voluntarily. Employers such as school systems may use the APGA's ethical standards as guidelines, but often look to the local standards and ethics of the teaching profession when questions of improper conduct arise.

The control of preparation and practice are two further factors that help define a profession. Through establishing admissions standards for preparation programs and specifying what these programs should accomplish, the guidance profession does exercise some control. But the role of the profession is largely advisory; its recommendations have considerable influence but do not set the standards for all employers.

A fifth characteristic of professional identity is personal autonomy in the provision of service; the individual counselor exercises independent judgment, makes decisions, and provides help. Counselors may have considerable freedom in the way they practice their profession, but little control over allotment of time for specific activities. Even so, there is adequate autonomy for the counselor to utilize professional expertise.

A final professional characteristic involves the function of service to others. Counseling and guidance qualify as a profession by this criterion more fully than by any other. There is room for improvement in the applications of standards for preparation and practice; but professional status is justified in all crucial respects.

PREPARATION

The American Personnel and Guidance Association has taken the lead in formulating standards for preparation for guidance at the elementary and secondary levels. The guidelines are clear-cut, specific, and constitute excellent models. The secondary school standards have been more extensively studied, reviewed, and developed than those for the elementary school; but the current guides (which appear in this volume as Appendix A) cover all counselors regardless of educational level.

Before the most recent standards were adopted in 1973, an earlier set of guidelines (APGA 1967) had been widely used by counselor-education institutions and accrediting organizations for self-study and program improvement. A manual was also prepared to help counselor education staffs prepare for evaluations (ACES 1967). The new revision brings together existing guidelines for all levels in a unified and comprehensive report. The Association for Counselor Education and Supervision (a division of APGA) carries on the development of standards as a continuous process; new revisions will be forthcoming.

The introduction to the new standards reflects many contemporary trends. First, it spells out the need for students to demonstrate competencies. Second, it assumes differential rates of student progress; some may take longer to acquire proficiency than others. Third, it considers various models that extend graduate preparation beyond a single year; one such program, for example, combines an undergraduate major in guidance with a year of graduate study.

The four major sections cover objectives; the program of studies and supervised experience; responsibilities concerning students in the program; and support for the counselor-education program, administrative relations, and institutional resources.

The opening section on objectives sets the stage for the program. The major emphases are on explicit, cooperatively planned objectives evolving from input of those involved—counselor educators, students, and practitioners. Objectives show sensitivity to needs, problems, and trends in schools; they are regularly revised and updated.

The program of studies calls for academic and practical work to enable students to move to increasing levels of competence and responsibility. There are opportunities for observation and involvement in guidance. Responsibility for working face-to-face with individuals and groups comes as competence is developed. Along with increasing competence in helping activities, the program fosters a spirit of inquiry, ethical sensitivity, and skill in self-evaluation. The practical-work component is given specific emphasis; in a one-year period, 60 hours should be spent in face-to-face individual or group work.

The third section deals with selection, retention, endorsement, and placement of students. It speaks to student rights, pointing out the need for making clear the criteria and procedures for admitting students, and retaining or separating them from the program. It also indicates the program's responsibility for endorsing and placing graduating students.

The final section covers institutional support for programs in guidance. Emphasis is on cooperative relationships with other college or university departments for courses, and with school settings for practical experience. It specifies a minimum full-time staff of three members and spells out the necessary professional qualifications for those working with students. These standards, which describe what the program should provide and define the professional competencies to be mastered, are of great significance to the beginning students.

The APGA standards require preparation to cover all levels of the profession; added emphasis on specialized work settings is to be provided through courses and practical work. For example, students preparing for elementary school counseling would concentrate particularly on courses and practical work designed for this educational level. Preparation for career guidance and participation in career education would feature added emphasis on these areas (Bradley 1973; Hoyt 1974, 1975a, 1975b).

Current standards are oriented to competency, as are several contemporary preparation models. The system-based approach (Zifferblatt 1972) and HRD (Human Resources Development) (Carkhuff 1972), for example, emphasize specific competencies, systematic means of achieving them, and evaluation in terms of counselor effect on counselees. The ACES standards (Appendix A) emphasize that programs are to be evaluated in terms of competencies of each student. Such competencies would be illustrated by specific items such as supervised practice in working with groups. Zifferblatt discusses the systems approach, in which specific skills are learned (e.g., nonverbal communication), and students are recycled until they reach an acceptable level of competency (1972, p. 15). Another illustration shows specific and measurable characteristics of many competency approaches in terms of the student's growing self-awareness:

> Given two hours with a group of fellow trainees, the trainee must be able to make five self-observation responses, the validity of which can be confirmed by a majority of group members (Bernstein and LeComte 1976, p. 32).

Among other strategies recommended in preparing counselors is an experiencing-growing-sharing process between counselor educators and students, which stresses individual development (Arbuckle 1975).

There is certainly no dearth of models (Stilwell and Santoro 1976), which is a very positive sign. The future of those now in use, however, is not clear. Kennedy (1976) describes problems that could cause the competency model to fade from the educational scene; it may not be feasible, for example, to keep students in the program until competencies are mastered. Programs must, despite limited resources, prepare counselors to meet new demands for services and demonstrate effectiveness.

EXPERIENCE

PUTTING THE STANDARDS TO WORK

Make up a brief checklist of the major items of the Standards in Appendix A. Have members in a small group give their thoughts, based on this list, about the strongest features of the program you are in. Ask members to state, in one sentence each, what they would like to see done to make the program more effective.

OBJECTIVES

1. To understand the characteristics that identify a profession. Does counseling qualify as a profession?

Yes. The prerequisites for professional status are discussed in this chapter.

2. To understand the type of preparation needed for the competent practitioner. What major topics are covered in preparation standards?

Major sections cover philosophy and objectives; program of studies; student admission, progress, and job placement; and institutional support for the program.

3. To appreciate the comprehensiveness of the preparation program. After reading the discussion of preparation in this chapter and the Standards in the appendix, list any important topics not covered.

The response depends upon your own goals. The Standards are so thorough that you may very likely have no further topics to add.

LEGAL STATUS, CERTIFICATION, AND LICENSING

These areas are among the most controversial and ambiguous in the counseling profession; they are of major concern to anyone planning to enter the field. Potential legal problems revolve around malpractice, right to privacy, serving as defendant in criminal action, encouraging an illegal act, or involvement in civil disobedience (Burgum and Anderson 1975). Certification poses fewer potential problems. Your program will probably meet requirements, but you should know not only the standards in your own state (which you will have the responsibility of meeting), but also those of any other state you may wish to move to. Licensure is of recent concern. Previously it was critical only for counselors in some nonschool settings, but it is now emerging as an issue for school counselors too. Currently the employees of an educational institution are given sanctions to practice by virtue of their employment status; the institution authorizes their activity and assumes responsibility for performance. This may not be true in the future.

LEGAL STATUS   An understanding of legal factors is essential both for day-to-day practice in conventional types of service, and for anticipating problems that may arise with changing conditions. For example, a counselor may feel existing laws and regulations are harmful and ought to be challenged but must know the consequences of disregarding them and share this information with others who might need to know, particularly pupils. The processes one chooses to bring about changes are to some extent a function of one's political convictions. (Drapela 1974; Adams 1973). Counselors are entitled to their own views, but there are harsh realities to consider when changes involve committing illegal acts.

Counseling today has no specific legal status. It has only recently come to be recognized as a formal part of school programs. Few court cases have dealt directly with school counseling, and even fewer statutes specify legal obligations and responsibilities. The status of counselors must be clarified in the light of the few existing cases and statutes, and on the

An understanding of the legal pitfalls in counseling could prevent an undesirable interruption in a counselor's practice.

application of the law to people in general. Enough data are available to spell out some guidelines and to alert counselors to their responsibilities and limitations (Burgum and Anderson 1975, p. 7).

Increasing professionalization has generated rising concern about legal issues. Counseling today amounts to a service of therapeutic intervention in the pupils' lives. With the responsibility this implies, it is sometimes uncertain just how the counselor can offer most help to the counselee without violating civil and criminal law. As Burgum and Anderson point out, counselors have no general immunity from criminal law and are subject to civil law. Moreover, while statutes give some general guidelines, state and local laws vary enormously (Burgum and Anderson 1975, pp. 7, 12).

These are some of the questions a practicing counselor might encounter on a perfectly routine day: Can I assure the counselee of confidentiality? How about in group work? Can I be held liable for malpractice? Am I likely to become involved in a civil suit for carrying out my assigned responsibilities? Are there counseling activities that might lead to criminal charges?

Questions about confidentiality are the most frequent of all. Can counselors assure counselees of confidentiality? Except in a state that has privileged communication statutes, the answer is no. Some states do have such statutes (Litwack 1975), but policies are hedged with restrictions. There is no general privileged communication for counselors, although Burgum and Anderson suggest the federal courts could extend it to them through interpretations of rules of evidence (1975, pp. 17–20).

Regardless of national statutes, however, state and local precedents should be examined before assuring counselees of confidentiality. When the counselor has determined these legal limits, they should be explained to the counselee. In general, these principles are helpful (Nasman 1977, pp. 20–21):

1. If the counselee is a clear danger to self or others, the counselor cannot maintain confidentiality. Steps should be taken to protect others if they are in danger.
2. Generally the counselor respects the rights of others to confidentiality.
3. If a counselee is the victim of a crime, there is no privileged communication.
4. School counselors in most states do not have privileged communication. Where they do, laws may cover only certain types of information. (See Nasman 1977, pp. 53–80 for a summary of state laws and a model bill.)
5. For school use the term "privileged communication" can be defined as information shared with the counselor by the counselee, which the counselor cannot release without the approval of the counselee.

6. An individual may subpoena personal case material in college files for use in other actions. In the Bates College case, for example (Creel v. Brenann 1968; Ware 1971), the court upheld the plaintiff's request to view information he thought was hampering his admission to other colleges. The more recent Buckley Amendment (see p. 288) deals more completely with the question of access to records.

The counselor must also be concerned with the right to talk to others about the counselee without danger of legal action for libel and slander (Burgum and Anderson 1975, pp. 76–77). Usually if the counselor makes comments about pupils, sends reports to parents, etc., believing the reports to be true, acting without malicious intent, and communicating only with individuals entitled to such information, legal action for libel and slander would not be successful.

EXPERIENCE

HOW FAR DOES CONFIDENTIALITY GO?

Assume you are working with a pupil who threatened violence against a teacher and/or another pupil. You have the information, but the pupil will not give you permission to release it. What would you do? Could you be sued by the victim if violence actually took place?

Formulate your answer before reading the note below. If a small group is used, go around for responses from each member.

In the case of Tarasoff v. the Regents of the University of California, the California Supreme Court ruled that the therapist should take steps to save human lives over all other considerations. In this case the therapist, who knew of a threat by Prosenjit Poddar, subsequently carried out, to kill Tatiana Tarasoff, was held liable for failing to warn and protect the victim (Whitely and Whitely 1977).

Civil liability was an issue infrequently raised in past years, but it is a problem causing concern today. There is no sure way to judge what could be construed as counselor malpractice. If, however, the counselor follows the ethics and standards of the profession, malpractice liability would likely not be incurred, even if counseling has not been successful. A key requirement is that the counselor makes a referral when a problem becomes too difficult to handle. Group counseling involves the same responsibility, except that the probability of malpractice increases—there are more counselees to observe and understand. Some problems are more likely than others to raise the civil-liability issue, particularly those involving sexual relations and abortion (a counselor who dispensed oral contraceptives, for example, would be guilty of practicing medicine without a license). According to Burgum and Anderson (1975, pp. 27–35), advice about abortions, including possible medical and psychological complications, are beyond the counselor's competency. Even so, counselors must deal with these problems every day.

The case of Bogust v. Iverson (Burgum and Anderson 1975, pp. 29–31) illustrates the extent of the counselor's liability. A counselor in Wisconsin worked with a girl, Jane Dunn, on career, educational, and personal problems for a period of six months. When he felt that she had made all the progress she could, he terminated the case. Six months later, she committed suicide. Her parents sued the counselor, but the court ruled that he was not liable for failure to inform parents of her condition, and in fact, his training did not make him competent to make a judgment about danger to herself. The six months interval also weighed against placing liability on the counselor. If the counselee had become emotionally very upset at the termination of counseling, very likely the counselor would have been held liable.

With respect to libel, slander, and other areas of possible civil liability, the counselor has no special privilege. It is true that the counselor can talk or write about a counselee to those who are entitled to the information (e.g., parents, teachers, prospective employers) without liability for legal action. But giving information to those who are not entitled to it, or doing so with harmful intentions, could result in a defamation suit. The same principles apply to student records; the safest course of action is to include only factual information. Unverified damaging information may make one liable for a civil suit (Burgum and Anderson 1975, pp. 78–80, 85–87). Since parents can examine records, control release of information, and challenge the contents (Burcky and Childers 1976; Wilhelm and Case 1975; Worzbyt 1976), civil liability can easily be incurred. Professionally, though not legally, it is the counselor's responsibility to make sure that all school personnel understand the meaning and use of data (Worzbyt 1976).

Although it is unlikely, a counselor can, with the best of intentions, become a defendant in a criminal case. Burgum and Anderson list four possible types of charges (1975, p. 88):

— Accessory to a crime after the fact
— Encouraging an illegal abortion
— Coconspirator in civil disobedience
— Contributing to the delinquency of a minor

Reading their discussions of each of these situations (1975, pp. 69–70, 105, 113–115) will add depth to your understanding of guidelines for practice.

Burgum and Anderson also describe an illustrative case relating to criminal liability (1975, pp. 94–99) in which the school counselor, who had developed a good relationship with a boy in the custody of the juvenile court, inadvertently helped him avoid arrest. The boy, with two companions, robbed a service station and then, realizing the gravity of his actions, went to the counselor for help. The counselor convinced the boy that he should turn himself in, but it was late at night, and they agreed he would go to the police the following day. Meanwhile, however, the counselor committed a series of acts that could make him guilty of being an accessory to a felony. He denied to police that the boy was in his house. He gave the boy money, which was found in the youth's possession when he tried to skip town the next morning rather than reporting to the police. The counselor would have been well advised to report the matter to the boy's juvenile office, which would have been in his favor in a trial.

Another area of local concern to the counselor relates to the rights of pupils. The Gault case (Nasman 1977, pp. 8 – 10) brought about full guarantees of due process for minors. Counselors can help pupils by making them aware of their legal right to due process in education, free speech, and property ownership. Rights of the handicapped are emphasized by due process provisions of PL 94-142. As Nasman points out (1977, pp. 9–11), due process is not satisfied by establishing a standard procedure including such steps as informing the individual of charges and providing for a hearing, but rather it demands protection of pupils' rights under the Constitution, just as if they were adults involved in legal charges. Due process should fit the situation and protect the pupil from arbitrary, unfair, and autocratic rules and policies.

The Buckley Amendment, already mentioned, deserves special attention. This law restricts the use of information in personal records; enforcement involves the denial of federal funds if violations are allowed to occur (Nasman 1977, pp. 22 – 31). In the past, school records were not treated with respect for the individual's rights of privacy, nor have parents and pupils had access to most of the information contained in them (Russell Sage 1970). The Buckley Amendment (Burcky and Childers 1976) has given parents and pupils of legal age the right to inspect records, including letters, comments, and recommendations. (It is not a violation, however, to maintain a file of personal notes which does not fall under the access regulations of this law.) Besides opening up records to pupils and parents, the law restricts access of others to these data. In general, parents must give consent for information in records to be released. Nasman discusses the regulations in detail (1977, pp. 22–31). The complete law appears in the *APGA Ethical Standards Casebook* (Callis 1976, pp. 93–109).

Parts of the Buckley Amendment (The Family Rights and Privacy Act of 1974 and the Buckley Amendments to the Act) with specific applicability to counselors' use of student records are as follows:

Each educational agency or institution except as may be provided by 99.12 [confidential information placed in the record prior to Jan. 1, 1975] shall permit the parent of a student or an eligible student [usually 18 years of age] who is or has been in attendance at the agency or institution, to inspect and review the education records of the student.

The parent of a student or an eligible student who believes the information contained in the education record of the student is inaccurate or misleading or violates the privacy or other rights of the student may request that the educational agency or institution which maintains the records amend them.

Since the passage of the Buckley Amendment, counselors must make previously confidential files accessible to students and their parents.

The legal status of counseling is being established through new laws, statutes, and court decisions. While relatively few cases directly affecting counseling have gone through the courts, more can be expected as counseling achieves greater status and visibility as a helping service.

CERTIFICATION   All states regulate the practice of counseling through certification, licensing, or endorsement on a teaching certificate. Certification requirements of counselors in different states are more striking for uniqueness than for similarity (Dudley and Ruff 1970), and certification standards are changing both in scope and nature.

The most innovative development is the competency-based program. Dudley and Ruff's survey (1970) included only one suggestion of this approach, and only one program of this type was reported in the literature (Brammer and Springer 1971). Now 50 percent of the states have, or are planning a competency-based program, while only about 7 percent are not considering it. Over two thirds of the counselor preparation programs intend to convert to this approach, even though only about 7 percent have actually done so (Jones 1976). The Washington program (Shoemaker and Splitter 1976) started in 1971 is an example. Behavioral objectives were established through input of teachers, pupils, administrators, and counselors. Counselors have been certified at three levels of competency: preparation, initial, and continuing. The initial-level competencies are the type developed in a masters-level program. Six areas of competency are specified; major ones are counseling, information service, and placement. Deficiencies in any of the competencies must be remedied according to procedures spelled out in guidelines of the certification program.

Program accreditation is closely related to certification of individuals; it also gives students an important indication of the quality of a program (Dickey 1968) and enhances job-getting potential. If evaluation for accreditation is performed, it conforms to the counselor preparation standards already discussed. Shertzer and Stone (1976, p. 474) envision a national system of accreditation by an organization such as the Association for Counselor Education and Supervision or an educational accrediting agency such as NCATE (National Council for Accreditation of Teacher Education). There is no national accrediting system in operation today, but there are indications that one may eventually be established.

LICENSURE   This topic is relatively new for counselors, although psychologists have been active in formulating state licensure policies for at least two decades (Sweeney and Sturdevant 1974). School counselors have been concerned mainly with certification and have only recently become aware of the potential importance for their work of developments in licensure (Cottingham 1975).

There are important differences between certification and licensure. Each provides a service to the users of counseling by indicating the adequacy of practitioners. Certification laws regulate the use of the title "counselor" and specify the amount and type of training required for practice. Licensing goes beyond regulating the use of the title and indicates the unique services and practices that fall in the domain of the profession (Sweeney and Sturdevant 1974; Cottingham and Swanson 1976). The term "credentials" is often confused with certification. "Credentials" refers to the degree or other certificate the individual has been awarded; the term is also used to indicate competence for a job (e.g., an individual certified as a counselor has the "credentials" for the work).

Up to now, licensure has been a concern of counselors in community settings such as mental health agencies and private practice. To date only one state (Virginia) requires licensing for personnel and guidance workers. But recent licensure laws have alerted counselors to the potential for state regulation of some or all of their work. In Ohio, for example, licensing laws on the practice of psychology have been interpreted to limit the use of tests by a counselor in off-duty hours. In the case, City of Cleveland v. Cook 1975, a counselor who was not a licensed psychologist was arrested for testing (the use of psychological tools). The court found in favor of the defendant; Ohio counselors are contesting this interpretation of the law. The APGA Model Licensing Law (Appendix B) specifies the points favored by the counseling profession, including exemptions for those employed as school counselors. But as the situation now stands, school counselors who plan to enter private practice in states with this type of regulation come under the licensing laws for psychologists (Cottingham 1975).

The implications, however, may go far beyond off-duty activities or future career plans. As Sweeney and Sturdevant point out, the Ohio law and other similar ones specify that helping types of activities using psychological principles are regulated by licensing. Besides, licensure and privileged communication give school psychologists more freedom and prestige than school counselors. Sweeney and Sturdevant see "the right for school counselors to practice at all as being challenged" (1974, p. 578).

Only one state actually licenses counselors, and most experts do not predict that other states will soon follow suit (Jones 1976). But the situation may change; both the American Psychological Association and the American Personnel and Guidance Association are actively promoting licensing laws. If counselors do not establish their own licensing criteria and procedures, others will do it for them. The American Personnel and Guidance Association aims to ensure that counselors are represented on licensing boards and that licensing requirements are designed for counselors (Appendix B, 1976; Virginia Licensing 1976).

Licensure gives every indication of becoming a major issue. Congress and federal agencies are showing increasing interest in occupational licensing. Present methods of licensure testing can be unfair to qualified persons; some, for example, do not perform well on standardized tests. Licensure can affect employment opportunities, status, and legal bases of counseling.

Effective and well-designed licensure laws can enhance the counseling profession, protect the public, and open up new work opportunities; restrictive and unfair ones will interfere with the contributions of many potentially well qualified to offer others assistance. Sweeney and Sturdevant (1974) and Cottingham (1975) recommend that counselors keep up with what is happening in licensure and support favorable alternatives. Their advice points out a responsibility of all members of the profession.

ETHICS   One mark of a profession is a code of ethics. It serves as a guide for providing services and ensures legality in carrying out these services. The counseling profession has a comprehensive, well-developed code, as well as special guidelines for work in schools.

School counselors have two major ethical statements and several other aids to use as guides. The first, "Ethical Standards" (APGA 1974) of the Personnel and Guidance Association, is the result of several revisions of the first statement published in 1961, and is designed for counselors in any setting. The second, the statement of the School Counselor Association (American School Counselor Association Code . . . 1973), covers the counselor's ethical responsibilities in the school. The American Psychological Association's ethical standards (APA, "Ethical . . ." 1968) are useful as supplementary reading to help develop a broad perspective. Three casebooks, one by the American Personnel and Guidance Association (Callis 1976), a second by Stude and Goodyear (1975), and a third by the American Psychological Association (APA 1967) give examples of ethical problems and recommend solutions. Another publication of the American Psychological Association, *Ethical Principles in the Conduct of Research with Human Participants* (1973) is a standard reference for designing research studies.

The 1974 APGA ethical standards in Appendix C includes a preamble and six major sections: general; counselor-counselee relationships; measurement and evaluation; research and publication; consulting and private practice; and personnel administration. Each section gives general principles that apply to any situation the counselor may face.

To understand fully the implications for professional practice the complete ethical standards must be read, but a brief summary will indicate emphases. The general, introductory section covers such topics as responsibilities to counselees and employers, and for ethical behavior of other counselors. The second section on the counseling relationship makes clear that the primary concern is for the welfare of the counselee whether in individual or group situations. Confidentiality is the rule; variations take place only if there is a clear and present danger to the counselee or others requiring immediate action.

The main points of the section on measurement and evaluation are that the counselor should understand tests, be particularly cautious about their applicability for minority groups, and present or interpret results in keeping with test validity. The section on ethical standards for research and publishing identifies the welfare of the individual as the primary factor to be considered; the counselor should make every effort to avoid harmful effects of research and should take action to reduce or eliminate such effects if they occur.

The section on consulting and private practice deals more with the activities of the private consultant, although much of the counselor's work with teachers, administrators, and parents would be based on consultation principles. The section on personnel administration covers organizational and administrative responsibilities in the school counselor's work setting, particularly the need to establish mutually agreed upon goals with administration for major aspects of the job (e.g., counseling relationships, confidentiality, work load, and accountability).

The final section deals with preparation standards and their importance to the beginning student.

The school counselor code of ethics (ASCA 1973; Appendix E) is uniquely helpful for the elementary and secondary levels in that it identifies responsibilities to self and those with whom the counselor works—pupils, parents, faculty, staff, the school, and the community. In all relations the counselor respects pupils' dignity, individuality, and right to self-direction. Responsibilities to pupils and parents follow the APGA ethical standards closely, but those relating to staff, community, self, and profession give additional guidelines for cooperative work with colleagues and community agencies, for self-development, and for implementing a contributing role in the profession.

In the experiences that follow problems are presented for discussion and solutions. Additional examples may be drawn from personal experience and from the casebooks already listed.

EXPERIENCE

ETHICAL ISSUES IN THE COUNSELOR-COUNSELEE RELATIONSHIP

Either individually or in small groups, evaluate the actions of the counselor with a plus if in accord with ethical principles and a minus if contrary to them.

Identify the ethical principle involved, using the standards in Appendix C.

1. A distressed student rushes into the counselor's office to report a clash with a teacher. The counselor allows the student's criticism of the teacher to be stated and "hears him out." He permits the student to explain the damage to his ego caused by the teacher and accepts the responsibility for helping the student work through the conflict situation.
2. Jim comes to the junior high school counselor to express criticism of a certain teacher. After Jim talks out his problem, the counselor feels that things could be best remedied by the counselor talking to the teacher. He asks permission from Jim, but Jim feels that he would be singled out if the counselor made this contact. The counselor still thinks that talking to the teacher would be best and that Jim does not fully comprehend the situation; therefore, the counselor contacts the teacher. The teacher expresses surprise and some irritation that Jim has gone to a counselor. The counselor is unable to get any suggestions across to the teacher concerning her relationship with Jim. Subsequently the counselor sees Jim several times, but the boy expresses no interest in returning for any further discussions (Callis 1976, pp. 22–23).

Do not look at the paragraph below until after completion of the exercise.

The ethical principle involved is in section B.1 of Appendix C on the counselor-counselee relationship.

"The member's primary obligation is to respect the integrity and promote the welfare of the counselee(s), whether the counselee(s) is (are) assisted individually or in a group relationship. In a group setting, the member-leader is also responsible for protecting individuals from physical and/or psychological trauma resulting from interactions within the group."

The first description is in accord with this ethical principle; the second is not.

EXPERIENCE

ETHICAL ISSUES IN REFERRAL

The following case description and discussion from Stude and Goodyear (1975, pp. 26–28), present a problem that calls for the counselor to make an ethical decision. Read over the case description, decide what you would do, and identify the ethical principles involved (see Appendix C). Then compare your decisions with those that follow. If you are working with a small group, have members give brief answers and compare them with the discussion at the end of this box.

Situation: A counselor feels that one of his clients needs psychiatric treatment . . . (A psychiatric evaluation by a psychiatrist supports the counselor's feelings. Since the client is a minor, the counselor discusses the recommendations for psychiatric treatment with the parents.) The parents actively reject the recommendation and refuse to even consider the possibility of psychiatric treatment (Christianson 1972, p. 202).

— What are the issues involved?
— What ethical standard is involved?
— What would you do?

Ethical issue involved: One can expect this kind of problem when dealing with highly emotional situations such as referral for psychiatric treatment. [The] situation highlights two separate ethical issues. First, what are a counselor's obligations if a minor client's parents refuse to follow through on a recommended referral? Second, when a counselor realizes the client's problems are beyond his personal capabilities what ethical obligation does he have to continue to work with the client if the client's family refuses suggestions to seek more qualified professional assistance?

The APGA Code indicates that [Appendix C]:

If a member is unable to be of professional assistance to the counselee, the member avoids initiating the counseling relationship or the member terminates it. In either event, the member is obligated to refer the counselee to an appropriate specialist . . . In the event the counselee declines the suggested referral, the member is not obligated to continue the relationship.

Discussion:

In applying these guidelines to the above situation, the following should be considered. Although the counselor's primary responsibility is to the client, *he must* realize his own professional limitations and capabilities. When situations arise that are beyond his abilities he has an obligation to make an appropriate referral. Consequently, the counselor was following acceptable ethical practice by providing for further evaluation of the client's problems and attempting to initiate a psychiatric referral.

However, the question that needs to be looked at is did the counselor approach the parents regarding the need for psychiatric treatment in the best possible manner? Did he request permission from the parents before obtaining the psychiatric evaluation? Since the client is a minor, the counselor should have obtained prior permission of the parents before arranging the psychiatric evaluation. If he did not obtain permission he may have already acted unethically. In the event the parents did agree to the psychiatric evaluation initially, why are they now rejecting efforts for further help?

Given the parent's active rejection of the recommendation, the counselor may want to schedule a joint conference of the parents, client, and psychiatrist. This would give the psychiatrist and counselor an opportunity to discuss with the parents the client's need and how therapy might benefit him. In the event that this suggestion is also rejected, the counselor should attempt to open better communication with the parents within a reasonable length of time and effort.

It should be made clear to the parents that if the counselor continues working with the client without referral, his actions may be detrimental to the client's well-being. Should the parents still refuse the recommendation, the counselor would be ethically obligated to terminate services. If the client, in his current condition, is detrimental to himself or others, the counselor may, within the guidelines and approval of his agency, refer the problem to appropriate authorities that have the power to intervene for the ultimate well-being of the client.

EXPERIENCE

LEGAL DECISIONS

What are your answers to the following questions? Each is directed to a counselor and each involves a legal principle.

In a small group, have each member give an answer, and take a few minutes to try to reach a consensus.

Questions:

1. "Mr. Snyder, if I tell you something, will you promise not to tell anyone?"
2. "Mrs. Goodyear, can you help me get an abortion so that my parents won't know?"
3. "Mr. Herrman, I'm Officer Gallant and I'd like to see Sam Powers for questioning."[a]

Answers: (Do not read this section until completion of your group discussion.)

1. Mr. Snyder can't promise not to tell anyone, but he should know and relate to the counselee the situations where he must tell someone.
2. Mrs. Goodyear can refer her counselee to someone who will provide abortion information, if it is legal in her state. Unless specifically required by district policy, she would not have to notify the parents;

but she should be aware that any routine record of the interview may be subject to discovery and disclosure.

3. Officer Gallant can see Sam if he insists, but Mr. Herrman or a school administrator should make immediate effort to delay the interrogation until she/he can notify Sam's parents and give them an opportunity to be present or arrange for counsel.[a]

[a] Source: Nasman (1977, p. 32).

OBJECTIVES

1. To be aware of legal factors that are important for the counselor's work. Name three areas of legal concern and rate degree of significance for the counselor.

Malpractice; right of privacy; licensure. The second is extremely important. The other two are becoming important.

2. To understand the meaning and importance of certification and licensure. In one sentence each, indicate the key difference between the terms, and rate the importance of each for the school counselor.

Certification regulates the use of the title, while licensure regulates both use of the title and practice. At present, certification is a major concern for counselors; licensure is less important, but may become critical in the future.

3. To understand the importance of ethics in counseling. List and rank in order of importance three important principles from APGA's Ethical Standards. (Use both the discussion in this chapter and Appendix C.)

The answer depends on your own preferences. Typical ones could be emphasis on welfare of the counselee and confidentiality. To make choices, familiarize yourself with Ethical Standards.

ORGANIZATIONS

Professional organizations provide counselors with support, facilitate professional development, bring together colleagues with similar interests, offer opportunities for active participation in leadership roles, and provide placement services. Counselors can help themselves by building a strong organization. Representatives of the profession are active at national, state, and local levels to promote favorable legislation and to obtain funds for improved services.

Participation can begin during preservice preparation. The American Personnel and Guidance Association, a federation of thirteen divisions, is the most important and best-known organization for counselors. APGA offers student memberships at reduced rates, and students can attend APGA national conventions and take part in programs. (A history of APGA appears in Chapter 4.)

The American School Counselor Association (ASCA) is the APGA division for school counselors, but others too relate directly to work in public educational settings. These are: National Vocational Guidance Association (NVGA); Association for Humanistic Education and Development (AHEAD); Association for Measurement and Evaluation in Guidance (AMEG); Association for Non-White Concerns in Personnel and Guidance (ANWC); Association for Specialists in Group Work (ASGW); National Catholic Guidance Conference (NCGC); and an affiliate, International Association of Counseling Services (IACS). The five remaining divisions deal with particular work settings such as college, university, and employment service. Appendix D contains a list and brief description of each special-interest division. There are also fifty-two state branches offering the opportunity for participation at the sate and local levels.

APGA and each of its divisions publish newsletters and journals covering current developments in the field, research, practices, legislation, and sources of information and materials. *Personnel and Guidance Journal* and the newsletter *Guidepost* are distributed to all APGA members. The American School Counselor Association is the only division that publishes two journals, *The School Counselor* and *Elementary School Guidance and Counseling,* in addition to a newsletter. Other periodicals are listed in Appendix D.

Many other useful materials are available from APGA. Program abstracts, published at the time of the national convention, give summaries of presentations. Educational aids ranging from brochures, reprint series, and books to cassettes and films, may be obtained at reasonable cost. APGA publications include Hosford and de Visser's book *Behavioral Approaches to Counseling* (1974) and an accompanying series of eight films keyed to units in the book. The organization also offers a seven-unit interviewing and communication skills development program, *Influencing Human Interaction,* which includes films, cassette tapes, filmstrips, and books.

Students and counselors alike can participate in APGA by contributing to its many professional journals. Editors urge members who have something to say to submit material for publication (Carroll 1975b; Sue 1975). Journal staff members give helpful and detailed advice on how to prepare articles for publication, explain common faults that result in rejections, and describe the step-by-step process of editing and publishing a professional journal (Wall 1974; Alexander and Wall 1975). Articles that pass the editor are given blind reviews (i.e., the author's name is removed), and evaluators' comments are passed on to the author. At regular intervals each journal prints guidelines for authors specifying length, format, number of copies of manuscripts to be submitted, and other such details.

COLLECTIVE BARGAINING Counselors, like their teaching colleagues, are using collective bargaining to obtain better salaries, improved working conditions, and other benefits. Humes and Kennedy (1970) view the process as a means to gain a power base for achieving professional status in the school and a full voice in decision making. Creange (1976) believes that building a strong, broad-based national organization is one of the most critical issues facing school counseling today. But the American School Counselor Association (ASCA) has found little interest among counselors in collective negotiation (Negotiations . . . 1975a,b). Many counselors are concerned with the question of professionalism v. collective negotiations; thus there is a search for a strong organizational base to advance the status of the profession, to protect job security, and to ensure a voice in determining professional roles and responsibilities.

COLLEAGUES IN NON-SCHOOL SETTINGS

Counselors are employed in educational institutions, community agencies, business and industry, hospitals, and clinics. In their comprehensive monograph on employment opportunities, *Careers in Counseling and Guidance* (1972), Stone and Shertzer identify eighteen settings: vocational and technical schools; community and junior colleges; colleges and universities; vocational rehabilitation; U.S. Employment Service; Veterans Administration; programs for the disadvantaged; correctional and penal institutions; community mental health clinics; family service agencies; child-guidance clinics; Jewish Vocational Service; Urban League; marriage counseling; business and industry; adult education; pastoral counseling; and private practice. The divisions of APGA identify settings other than public schools such as colleges and universities; rehabilitation services; employment services; and correctional and penal settings. Another listing of opportunities in the counseling profession (Goldman 1973) includes business and industry; employment; and higher education. To these could be added counseling older persons (a rapidly emerging area), and a variety of services in consulting firms (this usually is considered private practice and offers opportunities for a small number of counselors).

These lists show mixtures of settings, programs, and specialties. This reflects the situation with actual job opportunities; counseling older persons, for example, may be done in colleges, businesses, and community settings (Blake 1975a). In each setting, however, the basic competencies, ethical standards, and legal guidelines apply. Priorities vary, however. There may, for example, be more responsibility in one setting for face-to-face work, while in another higher priority goes to coordinating services. The focus of the work may also differ; career and program planning may consume most of the counselor's time in one institution, while in another personal therapeutic help may be the major emphasis.

Counseling takes on somewhat different forms in such post-high-school educational setting as voc-tech centers, community and junior colleges, and four-year colleges and universities. In vocational and technical centers emphasis is typically on career planning and placement; the master's degree may be adequate qualification. The role and function statement for the voc-tech setting (ASCA 1974) resembles the statement for the high school. Community and junior-college counseling more closely resembles counseling at the college and university levels. Emphasis is developmental, but career planning and placement are particularly important for students in terminal occupational-preparation programs. The work of community-college counselors ranges from therapeutic and developmental programs to programs emphasizing career guidance, counseling, placement, testing, and a variety of administrative duties.

The college and university level typically offers two major types of work roles—one in the counseling-center setting, the other in general student personnel (e.g., housing, placement, financial aid). The counseling center provides individual and group counseling and is moving toward functions of influencing student life and intervening in the campus community (Magoon 1973). Placement offices, which in the past have emphasized interviews with prospective employers for graduating students, are now becoming involved in career development and guidance and may offer services to entering students. Student-personnel work is putting increasing emphasis on student development, establishing living-learning centers on campus, and outreach and consultation, and counselors are finding new areas to apply their skills and expertise.

Community agencies and services offer a wide variety of occupational opportunities for counselors. Interest in these settings and private practice is reflected in the increasing concern about licensure. Counselors work in community mental-health agencies, family-service agencies, crisis-intervention centers, halfway houses, drug-counseling centers, and a host of programs set up for special populations, such as minorities, the disadvantaged, and the unemployed (Stone and Shertzer 1972, pp. 114–118, 123–136; Gellman and Murov 1973; O'Brien and Lewis 1975; Goodyear 1976). Each of these services typically involves some counseling, particularly those that deal with interpersonal conflicts and emotional problems. Those for work problems may put more emphasis on placement and training.

Working with older persons is one of the major new opportunities for counselors. The need is apparent ("Millions . . ." 1976). Few services exist (Schlossberg 1975). Counselor-preparation programs have done very little to develop competencies (Salisbury 1975), but interest is increasing (Blake 1975b; Counselors want . . . 1975). The reasons for growing concern are not difficult to understand. It is predicted that by the year 2000 one half of the U.S. population will be over 50 years of age and one third will be over 65 (Salisbury 1975, p. 237). Also, there is increasing emphasis on providing counseling over the entire life span (Sinick 1976).

The Federal-State Employment Service is one of the largest employers of counselors in the country. Under the Comprehensive Employment and Training Act of 1973 (CETA), many special programs for guidance and training were taken out of the Employment Service, but its major function has not changed. There is a trend to provide more counseling to job seekers and to upgrade the qualifications of counselors (Fantaci 1973). The CETA program emphasizes placement for work and/or training, and thus is mainly concerned in helping individuals to understand their abilities and interests and to make decisions.

Rehabilitation counselors offer assistance to a wide range of handicapped individuals. Typically the master's degree is required. Work is making increasing use of a counseling approach rather than job finding and physical restoration, and its major aim is to increase the effectiveness of rehabilitation and job placement (Sinick 1973). Preparation is comparable to a school counselor's, with the addition of courses on medical aspects of disability, rehabilitation procedures, and agencies. Since the major emphasis is to get the handicapped individual into a suitable job or preparation program, the assessment of potential through tests and medical examinations is a major function. In helping the handicapped individual move into the new setting successfully, the counselor must know a great deal about environments and utilize counseling to deal with attitudes that could interfere with success.

Opportunities for counselors are also growing in correctional settings. Penal institutions offer jobs in which counselors serve as links to the community, and work with delinquents (Ivey 1974a; Lee 1975). This setting has expanded enough in recent years to merit a special feature section in the *Personnel and Guidance Journal* (Dye and Gluckstern 1974) and the establishing of a separate APGA division. Programs aimed at upgrading the skills of correctional staffs make use of counseling methods and offer a new consultation-training role for counselors in the correctional setting (Gluckstern and Wenner 1974a; Brodsky 1974; Wittmer, Lanier, and Parker 1976). In this approach, counselors use group methods to help correctional officers learn more effective ways to deal with inmates.

Business and industry employ relatively few counselors despite widespread use of management programs based on counseling theory. Programs for employees tend to be mainly informational. While there is an increased interest in federally supported programs for alleviating emotional problems, negative work attitudes, and low productivity, there does not appear to be a trend to employ counselors to implement them (Kunze 1973). Examples of innovative programs suggest, however, that jobs can be developed. Benedict (1973) served as an outreach counselor in a trucking firm and in a twelve-month period had contact with almost one third of the employees. Strategies included serving as a communications-skills teacher, referral agent, troubleshooter, and human-relations mediator. The results of Emener's communications training for industrial supervisors (1975) showed that supervisors improved in communications skills and felt the program to have been beneficial. Hopson's career development program in industry (1973) provided counseling to employees, "gave away" counseling skills to staff members, and instituted career-development workshops for employees.

Work has also been done to help counselors in training learn about occupations and work climates within business and industrial settings (Patterson, Hayes, and McIntire 1974; Bertotti, Sweeney, McIntire, and McManus 1975). These programs illustrate cooperative relationships between counselor education and industry, but they do not directly lead to counseling positions in industry.

The Veterans Administration began providing counseling services during World War II in the late 40s and now employs a sizable number of counselors, most with doctoral-level qualifications. They work in two departments: Veterans Benefits, and Medicine and Surgery. In the medical setting, counseling psychologists carry out therapy and other services aimed at helping the hospitalized veteran return to civilian life. Counselors in the Department of Veterans Benefits emphasize career and educational counseling. The required level of preparation is high; the doctorate is preferred, but two years of academic work plus appropriate experience is acceptable. Many states require licensing for classification as a psychologist. At present, it may be difficult to meet licensure provisions if the degree was not obtained in a psychology department. Private practice offers some opportunity for counselors, but here too licensure is a major concern, and the same difficulties can arise as for VA counselors. Furthermore, it is risky to rely on private practice as a sole source of income.

INTERNATIONAL ASPECTS

Learning about guidance in other countries can provide valuable concepts for counselors in the U.S. and help develop a new perspective on what we do (Goldman 1974). Bingham (1976) notes the tendency of American counselors to be uninformed about work in other countries and notes that visitors find room for improvement in our practices. Comparative guidance as an area of study has gained only moderate visibility (Drapela 1975), although it offers the opportunity to broaden one's understanding of cultural diversity and can suggest new ideas and insights.

Interest in international guidance has fluctuated over the years. One highlight was the appearance of Keller and Vitales' classic, *Vocational Guidance Throughout the World*, in 1937. Today we are witnessing a definite rise in concern about what others think of our practices and what colleagues in foreign countries are doing. The APGA International Education Committee has gained organizational support and publishes a regular newsletter. An organization of field representatives in this country and abroad has been set up by the committee to collect material about foreign programs and personalities, and to arrange tours. A textbook on guidance in other countries is in use in comparative-guidance courses in several institutions (Drapela 1977).

We can gain valuable insights about ourselves by seeing our work through the eyes of foreign visitors (Goldman 1974b). We are not particularly noted, at present, for our interest in the work of our foreign colleagues (Christie 1974), and are widely thought to be picking easy tasks that will show favorable results for purposes of accountability (Deen 1974). The need for various types of groups appears to some foreign observers to reflect the effects of a materialistic society (Harris 1974). We are criticized for our overenthusiasm for what is new and anti-intellectualism (Ziv 1974). Watts' analysis (1973), containing his reactions after an extended stay in this country, points to the excessive amount of time given over to administrative tasks, principal concern for able and middle-class pupils, and an extremely therapeutically oriented approach. While not always complimentary, these perceptions help clarify our own thinking.

Despite a rather casual interest in what others in the profession are doing around the world, there have been a substantial number of programs at APGA conventions on guidance in such other parts of the world as the Middle East, the Philippines, and the Netherlands (Patouillet, Drapela, and Karayanni 1975; Ravelo 1975; Deen 1977). Wrenn's study (1976) of changing values in sixteen countries reveals that counseling changes in relation to changes in values, and that, conditions permitting, counseling tends to become more humane. An analysis of career guidance in eight countries describes a number of models that have implications for domestic programs in such areas as community information and counseling services, relations with parents in occupational planning, and emphasis on flexible training programs (Tolbert 1976).

Learning about guidance in other countries and getting involved in exchange of information is getting easier. Besides the publications already mentioned, which give some background, foreign journals like the Canadian *School and Guidance Worker* (Editors 1973b) and the *British Jour-*

nal of Guidance and Counselling (Editors 1973*a*) describe programs and practices. Recently the Canadian journal published a review of guidance in other countries. The International Association of Vocational and Educational Guidance holds biennial meetings and can provide addresses of persons in other countries to visit or correspond with (U.S. National Correspondent, IAEVG, 70 Frost Avenue, East Brunswick, N.J. 08816). The International Round Table for the Advancement of Counseling also brings together counselors from all over the world for biennial meetings (Livingston House, Livingston Road, London, E152LL).

APGA is active in building international communication. There is a Committee for International Education and a regular newsletter on activities, research, and foreign programs. The International Association of Counseling Services is an APGA affiliate.

THE ACTIVE PROFESSIONAL

The Ethical Standards help identify the life-style essential for the active, growing professional (ASCA 1973, pp. 139–140). The ASCA Standards recommend contributions to professional organizations, participation in research, keeping abreast of new developments, and maintaining competency. Moreover, career-development skills enable the counselor to move into positions that utilize abilities, to advance, to change positions if desirable, and to progress in settings that foster personal development. The counselor who is active, interested, and growing is able to be a stimulating model and an effective helper.

Development begins with an effective, challenging preservice program that gives the prospective counselor a solid foundation in theory, techniques, organizational and programming skills, history, legal guidelines, and ethical standards. But this is only the start; the real test of self-motivation comes when the counselor begins with full-time work.

Each individual has a unique pattern of personal and professional development; but there are some major resources that facilitate growth. Professional organizations and professional meetings are two of the most important. Participation is critical; being a member and attending with some involvement helps develop a feeling of identity. Contact with others in the same type of work, describing your activities, and hearing about the accomplishments of others make one aware of being a part of an important profession.

Involvement in research is a second major activity for professional development. Much research takes the form of ongoing evaluation (checking the effectiveness of procedures), but research to test out ideas, look for better procedures, and discover new models can be among the most exciting of all activities.

These involvements, plus writing and wide-ranging interests beyond the boundaries of the profession, help make a well-rounded professional. Counselors with this approach to professional development do not think they "have all the answers." A "comfortable" position soon becomes a rut. It is frighteningly easy to become like the teacher who bragged of ten years of experience who in fact had, as one observer pointed out, one year of experience ten times!

The careers of the great leaders of guidance are marked by continuous professional growth. Recent issues of the *Personnel and Guidance Journal* illustrate this point with brief, vivid biographies of E. G. Williamson (Ewing 1975), Esther Lloyd-Jones (Smith 1976), and Robert Hoppock (Conyne and Cochran 1976).

EXPERIENCE

ESTABLISHING A PROFESSIONAL ORGANIZATION

Assume that you work in an area not included in the APGA interest areas, e.g., community mental health. Present your reasons for establishing a new division to the "Board of Directors" (role-playing students). Ask for feedback on the persuasiveness of your presentation.

How does it feel to be an outsider trying to establish a professional "home"?

Note: This relates to a situation that has frequently occurred in recent years when individuals have wanted to found an organization to meet their specific needs. In the future you may be in a position to promote the establishment of such a new organization.

EXPERIENCE

LEARNING ABOUT OTHER COUNSELING SPECIALISTS

This can be an individual experience, but it will be more effective in a small group.

Interview someone in a non-school counseling specialty. If possible, spend several hours observing the daily routine. What positive and negative aspects would these activities feature for you? Describe these aspects to other group members and explain the reasons for your reactions.

At the conclusion of the group discussion, ask each member to rank the occupations described in terms of their attractiveness for them.

EXPERIENCE

PERSONAL DEVELOPMENT

In a small group go around with each member giving two areas of strength (personal/professional) and one in which improvement is desired. Next, have each member in turn offer suggestions for steps to facilitate development in the weaker area and give their impressions of personal resources they perceive as supportive to such growth.

At the conclusion of the discussion, ask each member to write for personal use three things to do in the next month to facilitate development in the area identified as needing improvement.

EXPERIENCE

GOALS FOR THE FUTURE

This can be an individual or group experience. Small groups are recommended.

Write the following headings at the top of separate sheets of paper:

— Goals at graduation
— Goals five years later
— Goals ten years later

On each sheet write your three major goals for each period in order of importance. If working in a small group, go around with each member giving the top goal in each period and explaining in a sentence or so why it is important.

An alternate group procedure is to have each member give the single most important goal for all periods and have other members give about a minute's feedback assessing the likelihood of the speaker's success in reaching the goal.

OBJECTIVES

1. To become aware of the professional organizations for counselors. List three that you feel will meet your needs.

Major organizations are listed in the text and in Appendix D. Your choice should reflect personal interests and career goals.

2. To become aware of the settings in which counseling is practiced. Name five settings for counseling other than the public school.

Colleges and universities; vocational rehabilitation agencies; employment services; penal institutions; community agencies.

3. To become aware of the value of learning about counseling and guidance in other countries. Identify two ways in which knowledge of this kind can contribute to the counselor's professional development.

To learn potentially useful guidance procedures; to gain a fresh perspective on principles and practices in this country.

4. To understand ways to engage in an active professional career. Name three ways the counselor can maintain a program of self-development.

Set career goals; participate in professional organizations; write for professional journals.

ADDITIONAL READINGS

American Psychological Association. "Ethical Standards of Psychologists." *American Psychologist* 15, no. 5 (1968), pp. 357–361.

A useful set of ethical standards for counselors. The most recent revision in the *APA Monitor* (6, no. 11 [1975], pp. 18–19) is more up-to-date, but the publication may not be available.

———. *Ethical Principles in the Conduct of Research with Human Participants.* Washington, D.C.: American Psychological Association, 1973.

Pages 1–2 give a brief summary of important principles for guidance and counseling research involving human subjects. Other sections provide elaborations and illustrations of principles.

Banikiotes, Paul C. "Personal Growth and Professional Training." *Counselor Education and Supervision* 15, no. 2 (1975), pp. 149–152.

Discusses the nature of a growth-producing preparation program.

Burgum, Thomas, and Anderson, Scott. *The Counselor and the Law*. Washington, D.C.: American Personnel and Guidance Association, 1975.

A valuable reference during preparation and when legal problems and issues arise on the job. Chapter 1 gives an excellent overview of the legal status of the school counselor.

Callis, Robert. *Ethical Standards Casebook*. Washington, D.C.: American Personnel and Guidance Association, 1976.

A revision of the widely used 1965 casebook, containing examples of appropriate and inappropriate counselor actions. An effective aid for learning to apply ethical standards. The Buckley Amendment is included as an appendix.

Forster, Jerald, "What Shall We Do about Credentialing?" *Personnel and Guidance Journal* 55, no. 10 (1977), pp. 572–576.

This is the lead article in a special feature section on licensure and certification. All of the articles will add to the reader's understanding of the development and current status of this critical issue.

Lindenberg, Steven P. "Attention Students: Be Advised . . ." *Personnel and Guidance Journal* 55, no. 1 (1976), pp. 34–36.

A thought-provoking look into the next decade discussing possible developments in the licensure of school counselors.

Moore, Marv. "Counselor Training: Meeting New Demands." *Personnel and Guidance Journal* 55, no. 6 (1977), pp. 359–362.

A stimulating discussion of how the preparation of helpers can and should change to meet needs and give the profession increased viability.

Nasman, Daniel H. *Legal Concerns for Counselors*. Washington, D.C.: American School Counselor Association, 1977.

An excellent and lucid review of the legal aspects of the counselor's work. Includes several valuable appendices, including information on the status of individual states on privileged-communication legislation.

Peterson, Donald R. "Is Psychology a Profession?" *American Psychologist* 31, no. 8 (1976), pp. 572–581.

A discussion of the characteristics of a profession with profound bearing on counseling.

Stone, Shelley C., and Shertzer, Bruce. *Careers in Counseling and Guidance*. Boston: Houghton Mifflin, 1972.

An excellent survey of settings where counselors are employed.

———. *Fundamentals of Guidance* 3rd ed. Boston: Houghton Mifflin, 1976.

Chapter 6, on the school counselor, is an excellent survey of professional topics and issues.

Stude, E. W., and Goodyear, Don L. *Ethics and the Counselor*. Fullerton: California Personnel and Guidance Association, 1975.

A valuable aid to understanding the use of ethical standards in practice.

After ethical problems are presented (see example in this chapter), relevant principles are identified and the issues involved are discussed. The book also contains a review of legal guidelines and several complete formulations of ethical standards.

Tolbert, E. L. "Guest Editor's Introduction." *Vocational Guidance Quarterly* **24, no. 4 (1976), pp. 294–297.**

A special issue devoted to career guidance in other countries. The emphasis is on services for high-school-age youth.

Wall, Judy. "Getting Into Print in P and G: How It's Done." *Personnel and Guidance Journal* **52, no. 9 (1974), pp. 594–602.**

This article removes the mystery from preparing and submitting an article for publication. A must for those starting out, and equally valuable for most of us who can use all the help we can get.

Wrenn, C. Gilbert. *The World of the Contemporary Counselor.* **Boston: Houghton Mifflin, 1973.**

Pages 270–287 give Wrenn's views on the meaning of the counselor's role and help the reader clarify the purposes of the profession.

CHAPTER FIFTEEN
EVALUATION, RESEARCH, AND ACCOUNTABILITY

The three closely related concepts, evaluation, research, and account-ability, are of major significance to guidance workers. Accountability is the most important. Accountability incorporates both research and evaluation in strategies designed to establish how well guidance is meet-ing its goals and objectives, and gives every indication of gaining a firm foothold. Guidance workers in all settings will have to deal with it. If we do not define our own accountability and take steps to find ways to demonstrate it, others surely will. The task will not be easy. Demands of legislators, administrators, and parents will make for a difficult and chal-lenging assignment. But the profession will benefit if we take advantage of the positive aspects of accountability.

"Research" is a broad term covering any systematic effort to discover facts about a problem or the principles that govern it (English and En-glish 1965). It does not necessarily aim to assess program effectiveness; results do not have to have a practical application at all. Evaluation, on the other hand, is carried out to determine the effects of an activity, to estimate success in reaching goals, and to help in decision making. Combining the two in "evaluative research" gives the best answers to the question whether counseling and guidance make a difference (Warner 1975a) and whether a given program is accomplishing the purposes for which it is accountable.

GOALS

1. To develop an understanding of accountability.
2. To understand how accountability can benefit the guidance profession.

3. **To become aware of personal feelings about working in a setting that requires accountability.**
4. **To understand the typical procedures used in research and evaluation.**
5. **To understand the potential value of research and evaluation to your own work.**

ACCOUNTABILITY AND ITS RELATION TO EVALUATION AND RESEARCH

Accountability is the ability to answer for performance. How well does a given service meet its goals and objectives? To satisfy the demands of accountability for reliable and relevant data, evaluation utilizes many techniques and principles adapted from research. It provides a frame of reference for examining the effects of guidance and counseling, and for improving the design and delivery of services.

THE MEANING OF ACCOUNTABILITY Being held responsible—"accountable"—is not new. But the term "accountability" has only recently emerged on the national scene. Barro, commenting on its rapid assimilation by both educators and school critics, suggests that utility rather than novelty explains the wholesale adoption. Conditions giving rise to the concept are: emphasis on evaluation of school systems by the federal government; the trend to compare educational output with costs; the need to provide education for the disadvantaged; and the trend to make education responsive to local communities (Barro 1970); it is part of a general societal trend for greater accountability in all public affairs (Kaplan and Stoughton 1974, p. iv).

For the purposes of decision making, accountability has a widely accepted commonsense meaning of relating resources and procedures to results (Lieberman 1970). The description by members of the Cooperative Accountability Project is representative of current usage:

Educational accountability serves to explain the results that are being achieved by public elementary and secondary schools. It provides a basis for developing understanding of the relationship between quality in education and available resources in order to make educational improvements (Bettinghaus and Miller 1973, p. 1).

Accountability in education seeks answers to three questions:

— What is happening in the schools?
— How much does it cost?
— Is it effective?

No one disputes the need for accountability. As Robinson points out, "Few would deny the general premise that teachers and other school people should be 'accountable, liable, and responsible.' " But beyond such general agreement, opinions diverge widely. Robinson continues:

But to say for a particular child it is more desirable in a particular year to seek to improve his measurable reading skills than to strengthen his self-concept and his ability to relate to others is open to question, as is the assumption that the teacher's responsibility for this improvement can be fairly identified and compared for salary purposes with the results obtained by another teacher with other children (Robinson 1970, p. 193).

PURPOSES OF EVALUATION Accountability has forced the counseling profession to articulate clearly and fully the rationale for evaluation. The major purposes are: judging the effectiveness of programs; strengthening weak functions; revising elements; justifying continuation; obtaining financial support; and assembling information for public relations.

Program effectiveness is the key issue. It has always been the guidance worker's deep concern, but the pressure of day-to-day activities has left little time for a systematic assessment of results. Besides, until relatively recently, there was a general and uncritical trust in the value of guidance. But the question must be asked: Do counselors make a difference? From the ethical point of view, evaluation is an essential activity; if help is not effective, we must change our methods to make the most of the available resources.

Results must also be considered in terms of costs. Evaluation makes possible a comparison of costs and results, and can thus help suggest ways to achieve the same goals at a lower price. With the fierce competition for available funds, guidance services will have to marshal hard evidence to demonstrate the benefits it claims to deliver.

Evaluation should be built into all aspects of the school guidance program. Counselors can make systematic evaluations of their work individually. Services—counseling, testing, providing information, orientation, and placement—can be assessed. The cumulative results summarize program accomplishments.

The trend in evaluation is to use techniques that provide counselors with up-to-the-minute information on the effectiveness of all aspects of a program. Pine (1975) recommends discrepancy evaluation; standards set up at the beginning of a program are used at each stage to assess performance in terms of design, installation, process, product, and cost. Discrepancies between the set standard and actual performance give the staff data on which to base needed adjustments.

RESEARCH APPROACHES Research methods provide the counselor with a variety of evaluation techniques, ranging from simple to complex and from small- to large-scale. Standards for identifying needed data are also based on research principles. If we are to be held accountable for effects of counseling and guidance, we want to be certain that judgments are formed on the basis of dependable evidence.

Adequate criteria — data by which to measure success — are essential in any evaluation plan. Pine (1975) identifies the criterion problem as the single most critical one in evaluation. But it often gets only cursory or superficial treatment; criteria may be stated vaguely or not at all (Warner 1975a). Solid criteria are tremendously difficult to prepare. Suppose, for example, that attitudes toward school are used as a criterion. What do we mean by attitudes toward school? How will they be demonstrated? How will we measure them? How will we know changes are due to the guidance program? As the following illustration shows, "success" can be a problematic criterion: A withdrawn, compulsive pupil becomes more outgoing and healthy as a result of counseling; achievement drops and assertive behavior increases; results of counseling appear negative by the criterion of academic achievement, but the pupil is much improved from a mental health point of view (Pine 1975).

The number of fundamental research strategies varies according to authorities. Shertzer and Stone (1976, pp. 436–438) identify three: survey, experimentation, and the single case. Pine's more extensive list (1975) gives nine:

1. Experimental
2. Tabulation
3. Follow-up
4. Expert opinion
5. Client opinion
6. External criteria (using a "yardstick" of effective practices as a basis for evaluation)
7. Opinion surveys (e.g., of teachers)
8. Descriptive approach
9. Case-study approach

In guidance, research most generally takes an experimental approach. Essentially, this involves administering a deliberate treatment to pupils and measuring its effects. Controls — pupils who do not receive treatment — should be used for comparison; conditions should be kept constant; and the test group should constitute a representative sample. The approach has its limitations. It restricts the counselor's daily work and gives results of effectiveness only after termination of the study, and does not provide early input that can be used for improving programs (Pine 1975).

The survey approach is quite similar to the public-opinion poll; a representative sample of pupils, parents, teachers, former pupils, or others are contacted for opinions, attitudes, and similar evaluative data. The needs survey is an example of this technique. Follow-up studies of former pupils are one of the more widely used survey-type evaluations. The tabulations method (a type of survey) consists of counting facilities, personnel, and procedures, and provides a quantitative evaluation. Standards for accreditation and program evaluation are usually of this type (Shertzer and Stone 1976, p. 437; ACES Manual . . . 1967).

The descriptive approach resembles survey and tabulation methods; for example, the organization of the program may be described, indicating who does what, when, and with what preparation. Usually little or no information is obtained that can attribute effects directly to activities.

The status of the case study as a research and evaluative approach has had varying degrees of status over the years. Recently, however, the $N = 1$ design has gained new popularity. It is the choice of the clinician (Spence 1973) and is particularly suitable when the counselor is trying to understand the causes of a pupil's behavior (Miller and Warner 1975). The single-case type of evaluation can be made reliable and valid with the use of a base rate (describing typical behavior) and by checking inferences with the individual (Frey 1973).

In later sections of this chapter, examples of accountability utilizing research and evaluation procedures will illustrate how all contribute to the overall goal of assessing results and improving services.

POINTS OF VIEW
ON ACCOUNTABILITY

Counselors and other educators see accountability in different ways. To some it implies a focus on specific types of cognitive learning, to others a broad approach to human development. Still others view it as a method of organization, while in some cases it means reporting results to those who finance the program. There are also divergent opinions on the appropriateness of accountability within an educational enterprise.

The question of broad v. narrow applications is the major issue for guidance. It is easier to identify and measure specific behaviors (e.g., number of occupations one can describe, number of positive self-evaluations one checks) than it is to assess competencies such as adaptability to new situations or decision-making skills. The problem is put into sharp relief by Kaplan and Stoughton:

Schools are concerned with people, with complex human attributes, such as values and attitudes, and with personal and social goals that can be measured only over a long period of time (1974, p. iv).

While there is no consensus on the desirable makeup for a guidance-accountability system, all points of view include a series of steps similar to the following:

1. Decide where you want to go (in terms of goals, which are broad, and objectives, which are reachable subsets of the goals.)
2. Find out how far you are from reaching these objectives.
3. Decide what steps you should take (programs and strategies) to close the gap between where you find you are and the objectives you want to reach.
4. From time to time, measure your progress toward the objectives (through assessment and evaluation).
5. Calculate how much it has cost to make that progress.
6. Report your findings to those who will make the decisions about how best to strengthen the program's effectiveness the next time around (feedback and recycle) (National Forum . . . 1975, p. 6).

Step 6 is particularly important. A planned program of communication—involving the determination of what a program does, to whom, how, and with what results—is needed. The message should be adapted to the audiences, particularly key groups who are critical to the program's success (Bettinghaus and Miller 1973, pp. 6, 8–9).

The question of what to assess is difficult. Cognitive objectives are important (e.g., knowledge of occupational requirements); affective ones (such as self-understanding), however, are the most relevant and the most difficult to assess (Wight 1975). Many guidance objectives take time to achieve and are long-term compared with short-term cognitive goals. Wight sums up the issue:

The message should be quite clear—we do not have educational accountability if we neglect the affective goals and objectives. As educators it is our responsibility to make whatever changes are necessary to give each individual student, regardless of background and circumstances, the best possible preparation to live his life productively, creatively, joyfully, responsively, and in harmony with society (1975, p. 7).

A second problem is identifying the persons to whom counselors are accountable. One cause of difficulty are differing perceptions of the counselor's task (Buckner 1975). If counselors are assigned duties not in keeping with the counseling role and involve outcomes over which they cannot have any substantial effect, the problem of responsibility is accentuated. For example, the counselor may be assigned disciplinary responsibility; this would determine to whom he or she is accountable, but would also make the counselor responsible for an aspect of the school over which little real control could be effected. But once objectives are clearly stated, it is relatively easy to specify the groups to whom the counselor is accountable, e.g., administrators, teachers, pupils, or parents.

While accountability approaches have been carefully planned and extensively analyzed, little evaluation of the strategy itself has been done (Elam 1974). An assessment of the well-known Michigan Accountability System revealed some negative factors (House, Rivers, and Stufflebeam 1974). Teachers were evaluated by the results; objectives were established at the state level without much local input. While some findings in the evaluation have been questioned (Kearney, Donovan, and Fisher 1974), there are indications that accountability systems may arise in response to legislative pressure and may be used in ways that reduce the effectiveness of the educational process and threaten personnel.

RESEARCH

DO COUNSELORS KNOW ACCOUNTABILITY RESPONSIBILITY?

Buckner's study (1975) approached the question of accountability from the standpoint of counselors' awareness of the profession's position on responsibilities.

Respondents to a list of functions based on ASCA-ACES guidelines included 36 counselor education students, 37 secondary education pupils, 25 secondary school counselors, and 25 public-school administrators, all from Utah.

Of a total of approximately 50 role and responsibility statements, there was disagreement of 20 percent or more between respondents on only 12 items. Other results showed that:

— Teachers, pupils, and administrators agree with the ASCA-ACES standards as much as practicing counselors.
— Practicing counselors assume responsibility for enjoyable tasks, but do not choose those that would make them controversial.
— Counselors do not inform administrators about unique skills nor insist that they have the opportunity to use them.
— Counselors appear to be unaware of professional responsibilities; in some cases administrators were better informed.

EXPERIENCE

ATTITUDES ABOUT ACCOUNTABILITY

Using a small group, go around with this question.

As a counselor in the school setting of your choice, what are the three major things you would prefer to be accountable for? (Your salary and tenure will be based on end-of-year evidence of accomplishments.)

At the conclusion, compare the ratio of affective to cognitive elements.

EXPERIENCE

ATTITUDES ABOUT ACCOUNTABILITY (ANOTHER APPROACH)

Using the same organization as above, have each group take a specific area of counselor responsibility:

— School-community relations
— Work with teachers
— Individual and group counseling
— Change agent

As in the previous experience, identify the three major things you would prefer to be held accountable for.

At the conclusion, compare the ratio of affective to cognitive elements. Which type will be easier to measure?

OBJECTIVES

1. To understand why accountability has recently gained visibility. Give two reasons for current prominence.

Comparing educational output with costs, and making education responsive to local communities are major reasons.

2. To understand major differences in definitions of accountability. Which definition appears to be more appropriate for guidance work?

The major difference involves a narrow cognitive approach for specific behavioral objectives v. a broad one utilizing affective as well as cognitive objectives. The latter is more appropriate, although more difficult to implement.

3. To be able to identify the major techniques of evaluation. Name the most useful and the least useful types for the practicing counselor.

Choices are based on your judgment. Typical ones given in the text are survey, single-case, experimental, and follow-up studies.

A LOOK AT THE POSITIVE ASPECTS OF ACCOUNTABILITY   While accountability may be seen as a threat to professional autonomy, it can have significant benefits. Kaplan and Stoughton (1974, p. v) argue that identifying target population and clarifying what is to be accomplished can bring pupil personnel and guidance services into the mainstream of the educational program. Krumboltz (1974) predicts increased support, improved public relations, enhanced professional status, and personal satisfaction. Accountability enables counselors to make a strong case for concentrating efforts on functions they are best prepared to carry out, and on targets that have the greatest need. Accountability has also provided the motivation for counselors and other educators to look for more effective ways to achieve results.

There is a strong current of positive thinking about the potential values of accountability to the guidance profession, the capability of guidance workers to provide valid data, and its place as a logical and needed feature of guidance. It enables counselors to achieve responsible freedom and to prove their value within the total educational process. By pinpointing objectives and developing effective assessment procedures, the counselor can demonstrate the value of guidance services (Hays 1972a). In times of critical scrutiny of all expenditures and priorities in education, accountability "may well save the day for guidance" (Humes 1972, p. 25).

A final word about the positive potential comes from Leon Lessinger, often referred to as the "Father of Educational Accountability."

> We can do magnificent things if we can agree together that we want to find out what's going on for the purpose of getting where we want to go. That's called quality control. It is a systematic attempt to get where you want to go.
>
> Without that notion, accountability will never be accepted. It will be sabotaged, which it is; it will be struck against, which it is; and we shall have the unlovely notion of a great profession flying in the face of common sense . . . 'cause there ain't no way you can strike against accountability (Cooperative Accountability Project 1975, pp. 19–20).

THE NEGATIVE SIDE   Pressure from outside to adopt an accountability system is the most negative aspect, particularly since emphasis has been on the business model emphasizing short-term, tangible output which can be relatively easily assessed (Kaplan and Stoughton 1974, p. iv). While there is little research on the benefits of accountability, legislators and others are going ahead enthusiastically with adoptions—by 1973, 33 states had passed legislation or resolutions favoring some form of accountability. There sometimes is a hidden agenda — e.g., punish teachers and other educators when pupils do not learn. In this climate, counselors can expect to have a difficult time providing the public with data to show that they are getting "more bang from a buck" (Elam 1974, p. 657).

In spite of the national surge toward accountability, there are heated debates about whether the strategy is fundamentally and philosophically sound. Bundy (1974) sees accountability as avoiding what are the real issues today: dehumanized and bureaucratic education and the monopoly that schools exert over formal learning. To restore public confidence, radical change is needed in the educational establishment; accountability is not the solution.

SUGGESTIONS FOR GUIDANCE WORKERS

We can make three assumptions: (1) accountability in some form or other is here to stay; (2) the future of the guidance movement depends upon how effective professionals are in establishing workable accountability approaches and gathering evaluative data; and (3) it is possible to state guidance objectives so that they meet accountability requirements. The best strategy is to move as quickly and effectively as possible into the accountability mainstream.

The first step calls for learning about accountability. It helps to read in the references given and others, and to visit programs that have been developed or are in the process of being developed. Guidance workers also need to define their roles, first, for themselves, in keeping with standards and policies of professional organizations, and then for others— administrators, teachers, community persons, and legislators.

The steps that follow are essentially those outlined by Kaplan and Stoughton (1974, pp. 1–6) and used in most other accountability models.

1. The first is to develop a statement of goals representing the needs and desires of those involved in the school system —pupils, teachers, administrators, parents and other community persons. It is not necessary to spell out all possible goals at the outset; supplementary ones can be added as the program develops. The important point is that a number of important priority-ranked goals be established, so that the development process can continue.
2. The next step is to specify objectives for each goal in terms that make assessment possible. This is the most difficult task; it is necessary to describe what pupils will accomplish, how it will be assessed, and the level that represents success. Kaplan and Stoughton (1974, p. 3) recommend beginning with a relatively small number of objectives (e.g., five for each goal), and adding others later.
3. Establishing the program and functions to achieve objectives is the next step. Quite often functions are mistakenly listed as objectives (e.g., "group counseling [a function] will be provided"). This stage

utilizes capabilities in terms of staff, facilities, and other resources. If, for example, a counselor has a load of five hundred pupils, scheduling a conference with each one each term would consume most of the working hours. Keeping in mind the time required to reach objectives, staff, and facilities should be used in the most effective ways possible.

4. Evaluation is carried out to determine whether or not the program has accomplished the results for which it is held accountable. The statements of objectives contain the guides needed for evaluation. Two purposes are served—to estimate how well the job is being done, and to identify areas that need to be improved. If evaluation is used to rate personnel for salary, promotion, or separation, it will produce resentment and anxiety, and generate a host of ways to "play the game" and distort results. Methods must be devised to reward those who do outstanding work, but the emphasis of the evaluation is on helping individuals understand how well they are performing and what they can do to remedy deficiencies.

The use of evaluative data for feedback to improve the program merits special attention. Both costs and effectiveness data are used. For example, if test interpretation can be done just as efficiently in small groups as individually, the group method would be less expensive. If the group method were somewhat less effective, however, a comparison would have been made of relative benefits of the more costly method compared with those of the less expensive one.

ACCOUNTABILITY — SMALL SCALE STRATEGIES

Much of what has been said either implies or states explicitly that accountability is large-scale—school-wide, district-wide, or even statewide. But it can take place on an individual basis, in which individual counselors evaluate their own work. On a slightly larger scale it can involve one aspect of a program (e.g., how well the information service performs its function). The counselor's evaluation of each case is particularly helpful; it not only provides data on effectiveness, but also serves as an approach to professional development.

GUIDANCE WORKER'S PERSONAL SELF-EVALUATION Counselors can evaluate the effectiveness of their own work by relatively simple and brief procedures (Tolbert 1972, pp. 376–380). Written records should be kept showing the problem, counselor actions, expected effects, and actual results as ascertained in a follow-up by interview, telephone, or letter. The

procedure is somewhat like the systems approach. First, needs are identified. Second, objectives are established (the counselor and counselee
decide what should be accomplished). Next, the helping activity is carried
out with continuous feedback for revision and correction of plans. The
results are compared with goals: further adjustments in helping are made
if needed.

Values accrue to both counselor and counselee through this informal
self-evaluation. The systematic checking of inferences with reality sharp-
ens the counselor's ability to observe, synthesize, and hypothesize. The
counselee benefits through a flexible mode of helping attuned to needs, an
opportunity to return for more assistance, and the support of awareness
that the counselor cares enough to see what happens.

Another approach consists of a survey to obtain needed data about
questions such as how pupils see the counselor and sources of help they
use (Weinrach 1975). An example is the survey of Heilfron (1960) to investigate pupils' perceptions of types of problems appropriate for counseling.
This survey does not fulfill evaluation needs of the total guidance program, but does provide valuable input to help counselors improve the
quality of their work.

A concept that can be incorporated in the counselor's personal evaluation has recently attracted considerable attention. The N = 1 research
plan provides a framework (Frey 1973). The counselor uses bits of data,
including base rates of behavior, to learn about the individual. As these
are synthesized, an understanding of the person emerges. The longitudinal nature of the process makes it possible to gather data about the effects
of counseling, to determine whether to continue the same treatment, or
to vary the treatment.

The N = 1 approach does not replace research involving groups nor
does it necessarily explain why behavior changes (Nòrdberg 1975). Other
influences in the counselee's life may have made the difference.
Moreover, it may be difficult to identify the specific actions or characteristics of the counselor that resulted in the effect.

EVALUATION IN SCHOOL-WIDE ACCOUNTABILITY   Before discussing school
accountability programs, we will look at the essential aspects of the
evaluation process. It will be helpful to review the models given in Chapter 6, which provide the framework and process for a school-wide accountability program. The systems approach (Miller and Grisdale 1975; Stufflebeam 1968), for example, begins with the determination of needs and
continues until evaluation results are obtained. At the conclusion, the
cost-effectiveness of each objective can be determined.

Four types of evaluation are included in the systems approach: context,
input, process, and product (CIPP). Each of these involves an important

type of evaluation and each provides data for planning the next step as well as improving previous steps (Jones, Tiedeman, Mitchell, Unruh, Helliwell, and Ganachow 1973, p. 3-2). Context evaluation indicates target population needs for formulating goals and objectives. For example, in your school you might identify, in addition to the needs of the major pupil population, the needs of several other groups such as minorities, transfers to the institution, and potential dropouts. These needs constitute context evaluation.

The next type, input evaluation, assesses the personnel, facilities, existing programs, and other resources that may be used to achieve the goals and objectives of the guidance program.

The third type, process evaluation, assesses the effects of implementing programs and determines how well parts are working. This stage may involve transactional evaluation to estimate effectiveness of communication during periods of stress and change. Formative evaluation is a similar process and measures success in getting the program into operation. For example, you may have decided on the basis of needs, objectives, and resources that group career-counseling should be provided to juniors and seniors. Process evaluation indicates success in setting up the group counseling program, but not the actual extent of help that these groups provide to pupils. Finally, product evaluation indicates results of the guidance program, establishing, for example, whether pupils do make progress in school, establish good relations with others, or choose suitable occupations. This is the most significant type of evaluation for the purposes of accountability; results have more meaning to the public than any other type of data. Results are also more important to the clientele because they indicate how well needs are being met.

The first three types—context, input, process—are often included under the single term "process evaluation." Thus, evaluation may be described more simply as process and product. The latter type is the most critical for accountability.

Wellman's proposal (1967, pp. 169–172) gives a useful and innovative look at secondary school guidance objectives for the purposes of evaluation. Figure 15-1 shows the framework for objectives. The reference groups are those of importance in pupil development. The developmental dimensions are those areas in which secondary school pupils would be expected to show progress and for which, as for the environmental dimensions, criteria for judging achievement would be established. Wellman defines the three levels of objectives as follows:

LEVEL I. Perceptual Objectives. These objectives include the acquisition of information and knowledge, the development of skills and the clarification of attitudes and values so that the individual becomes more aware of, and is able to differentiate more accurately, those aspects of his new environment related to developmental choices and adjustment, as well as his own personal attributes. For example, occupational groups can be differentiated on the basis of the type and level of training required for entry. A perceptual level objective for the student might then be to differentiate occupational groups in this manner, and the criterion measure would attempt to determine the accuracy of such differentiation following the application of process. It should be noted that the objective relates to student output rather than process, which in this case might be to provide and interpret information relevant to occupational training requirements. Objectives at this level will tend to be expressed as more immediate types of outcomes and will be act-oriented to a greater extent than those at the higher levels.

LEVEL II. Conceptual Objectives. Objectives at this level reflect the formation of concepts by relating perceptions of self to specified environmental perceptions. These objectives infer the personal meanings that the individual places upon perceptual relationships. The concept of the various environmental roles and their relationship to normative values is inherent in these objectives. Outcomes at this level should relate to the accuracy, consistency and reality of choice behavior and role performance. For example, a conceptual objective would be to make a tentative vocational choice consistent with the individual's predicted potential for completing needed training. The criterion measure could include self and counselor evaluation of a tentative choice. The conceptual objectives include both immediate outcomes and conations for future outcomes, hence the outcomes of reality testing in the form of valuing and corresponding increase in behavioral tendencies become more significant.

LEVEL III. Generalization Objectives. Generalization objectives reflect purposeful action, adjustments within normative tolerances, and consistent and enduring modes of behavior. Objectives classified at this level include the more global performance outcomes, such as the accommodation, satisfaction, and mastery criteria suggested by Tiedeman (1963), and the long range outcomes investigated by Campbell (1965). The systematic and consistent application of a value hierarchy in both internally expressed evaluations and external manifestations, as well as commitment to purpose, would typify generalization objectives related to value formation. Within the vocational development area, one generalization level objective might be to obtain and sustain employment in a position which affords continuing personal satisfaction, and where the individual can consistently meet the employer's performance standards. Two criterion measures of the achievement of this objective might be production output and expressed satisfaction. At this level, a combination of act-oriented and global objectives and criteria will probably be more manageable than at the two lower levels, where behavior development is more fluid and perhaps less integrative (Wellman 1967, pp. 170–171).

Wellman argues that this framework will be useful in developing meaningful outcome criteria. The model offers a way of establishing evaluation procedures that represent the impact of guidance in major environments and relationships and of ordering these objectives according to level of complexity. Moreover, it illustrates for the prospective counselor the elements that need to be considered in establishing guidance objectives.

Figure 15 – 1. Basic dimensions of guidance objectives and outcomes.

DEVELOPMENTAL DIMENSIONS	ENVIRONMENTAL DIMENSIONS					
	Reference Points			Reference Groups		
	Educa-tional	Voca-tional	Social	Family	Peers	Signif-icant Others

Level I.

1. Perceptual
   a. Awareness ___ ___ ___ ___ ___ ___
   b. Differentiation ___ ___ ___ ___ ___ ___
2. Role Identity ___ ___ ___ ___ ___ ___

Level II.

1. Conceptual
   a. Relationships— meanings ___ ___ ___ ___ ___ ___
   b. Concept formation ___ ___ ___ ___ ___ ___
2. Role Concepts
   a. Acceptance ___ ___ ___ ___ ___ ___
   b. Evaluation—adequacy ___ ___ ___ ___ ___ ___
   c. Normative values ___ ___ ___ ___ ___ ___
3. First Order Integration ___ ___ ___ ___ ___ ___

Level III.

1. Generalization
   a. Action—pursuit of purpose ___ ___ ___ ___ ___ ___
   b. Accommodation ___ ___ ___ ___ ___ ___
   c. Satisfaction ___ ___ ___ ___ ___ ___
   d. Mastery ___ ___ ___ ___ ___ ___
2. Role Performance
   a. Adjustments—norma-tive tolerances ___ ___ ___ ___ ___ ___
   b. Commitment to purpose ___ ___ ___ ___ ___ ___
   c. Value formation ___ ___ ___ ___ ___ ___
3. Integration ___ ___ ___ ___ ___ ___

Source: From J. W. Whiteley, ed., *Research in Counseling: Evaluation and Refocus* (Columbus, Ohio: Charles E. Merrill Pub. Co., 1967), p. 171. Copyright 1967 Central Midwest Regional Laboratory, Inc., St. Louis, Missouri. Reprinted with permission.

RESEARCH

THE QUALITY OF EDUCATIONAL RESEARCH

Since the quality of research/evaluation studies is the foundation of accountability, it is important to be aware of how well these studies are designed and carried out. Some evidence is provided by Wandt's report of the evaluation of 125 articles from 41 educational and psychological journals, including *Personnel and Guidance Journal* and *Journal of Counseling Psychology*. A partial summary of results is as follows (1969, p. 5):

Characteristic	Mean Ratings		
	All Articles	81 Articles in Educational Journals	44 Articles in Related Professional Journals
Problem is significant	3.59[a]	3.31	4.09
Research design is appropriate to the solution of the problem	3.03	2.65	3.67
Method of sampling is appropriate	2.97	2.85	3.23
Conclusions are substantiated by the evidence presented	3.11	2.63	3.95

[a] 5 = excellent, 4 = good, 3 = mediocre, 2 = poor, 1 = horrible example.

"Related journals" included such publications as *Journal of Counseling Psychology* and *Journal of Educational Psychology*.

In addition to the above ratings, research evaluators in the study would have accepted only 19 of the total of 125 without revisions.

While the studies evaluated are not specifically on the topic of accountability, the results indicate that the application of effective research methods often falls short of a desirable level. As an evaluation for accountability, some of the results could have been misleading.

EXPERIENCE

HOW TO START AN EVALUATION

Assume the following situation:

There has been no evaluation in your school, and there is a general feeling that none is needed because staff and program are very effective. You, as counselor, believe that there are a number of unmet needs and would like to make a systematic evaluation. You do not sense resistance to the idea, but you are sure that many teachers and counselors will be surprised by the suggestion, and some will feel threatened.

What would you do?
If you decide against taking further steps, describe your feelings about the decision in a role play with two other "counselors" who have agreed with you about the need for an evaluation.
If you decide to go ahead, what would be your first step? Designate persons who would be involved and role play the situation.

EXPERIENCE

DO SCHOOLS USE EVALUATION?

Check several local schools to find out if evaluations of any type are being made or have been made in the past. (Look over reports if they are available.) Ask the following questions.

— Why was the evaluation made?
— What type was it (e.g., process, product)?
— What use was made of results?

What conclusions do you arrive at about attitudes toward evaluation?

OBJECTIVES

1. To understand how accountability can help the guidance profession. State two potentially positive aspects.
Accountability makes possible the specification of reasonable objectives and provides data for public relations.

2. To understand the negative aspects of accountability. Name two aspects that could reduce the effectiveness of guidance.

Counselors may be put on the defensive by being held accountable for conditions beyond the scope of their responsibility. There may be pressure for immediate, easily measurable results.

3. To understand steps guidance workers can take to make the most of accountability. List two initial steps and two later ones.

First, learn about it and define roles. Later, evaluate results, and provide information to others about effectiveness.

4. To be able to plan for self-evaluation of one's work. Give three factors to include in this type of evaluation.

Objectives of the assistance; the helping approach; and effectiveness of intervention.

EXAMPLES:
IMPLEMENTING THE POSITION

A number of school systems have planned or actually instituted accountability programs that utilize some or all of the steps given in preceding sections. The Arizona plan, which has been referred to repeatedly above, is an example of a district system (Mesa, *Toward* . . . n.d.). The Grossmont Union High School District (Jacobson and Mitchell 1975) modeled on the California plan for career guidance (Cunha, Laramore, Lowery, Mitchell, Smith, and Wooley 1972) is another example that demonstrates the results of careful planning for accountability. The Minnesota Program of Outcome Management applied to pupil-personnel services is a third that illustrates accountability in action (Mease and Benson 1973). A brief, illustrated brochure outlines an accountability program developed by the Michigan School Counselors Association (1974). Two of these exemplary programs are discussed in detail below.

The Mesa, Ariz., Public School Career Education Accountability model is aimed at life goals and thus actually illustrates an approach for the total guidance program. Seven steps were carried out in building the program, from identifying target groups to setting up evaluative procedures. Counselors, with administrative support, with resources provided by special funding, and with the help of consultants, initiated the program with a needs assessment of all groups affected. Pupils, teachers, parents, community members, and employers were contacted. Questions and techniques for collecting needs information were prepared, and data were collected from representative samples in small group meetings by sort cards in four areas of pupil needs: intrapersonal, interpersonal, academic learning, and educational-vocational.

The next step was an assessment of the present guidance program resources. Counselors kept records of how time was spent and purposes of activities; results indicated priorities and provided data with which to compare needed and current emphases. When completed, this resources inventory described what was being done, who was doing it, how effective it was judged to be, and what facilities were available.

Following the collection of needs and resource data, a comparison was made to determine how well current practices matched need priorities. When discrepancies were found, goals were formulated to eliminate them. For example, the resources survey found that only about 5 percent of the counselors' time was spent in helping high school pupils get along better with others although this was one of the top priority needs given by pupils. The discrepancy was therefore the basis of a goal statement that set aside at least 20 percent of a counselor's time to deal with needs such as solving problems with parents, learning how to accept criticism, learning to be a better listener, and developing confidence and the ability to be at ease with others. All of these goals came under the general heading of learning how to get along with others.

The next step was to structure the guidance program; select target groups, materials, and procedures; and disseminate information about the program to pupils, parents, teachers both to inform and obtain input.

After goals and objectives were formulated, translating them into a program was the next major task. Group sessions were used by counselors to identify ways to achieve goals. Useful materials and procedures already available were located and adopted. Small groups of counselors then undertook to plan for the accomplishment of each goal and its objectives. The general strategy adopted was counseling-learning units keyed to objectives. Flowcharts were developed for each goal, showing level of learning (comprehension, application, and analysis) and thus facilitating the most productive ordering of objectives. These preliminary steps provided the bases for constructing units.

Field-testing was done at elementary, junior-high, and senior-high-school levels. An English course, "English and Careers," was used as the setting. Counselors taught units the first semester; teachers took over the second semester, during which period evaluations were carried out. The guidance center provided counselors to monitor progress, lead groups, and help individuals. The units enabled pupils to move at their own rates, and teachers and counselors served as resource persons and consultants, providing help, counseling, and materials.

Evaluation took place at all stages of program development. The formative evaluation included context evaluation for planning, input for structuring, and process for implementation. During implementation, it was possible to begin on product evaluation (i.e., the summative evaluation) to assess outcome. A variety of evaluative techniques were used to compare treatment and control groups, including criterion-referenced tests, pupil self-reports, and unobtrusive measurements (pupil requests for the next course). Very positive results were obtained for most of the evaluation, although in some areas (e.g., knowledge outcomes), it did not come up to expectations. Outcomes, particularly those indicating achievement below expectations, were used in formative evaluation to revise materials and procedures for the next program trial.

Future plans call for improving and expanding the program by bringing in additional departments, and enlarging the work-observation, experience, and placement program to tie into career guidance.

The Grossmont Union High School District plan for guidance also emphasizes career guidance and counseling while serving total guidance needs (Jacobson and Mitchell 1975, pp. 6–8). It illustrates involvement of those counselors who will actually implement the program and systematic step-by-step procedures, beginning with consideration of guidance models and needs assessment and ending with plans and budget estimates for implementation.

Significant school and community persons were involved in each step of the planning. Each school had a parent and business advisory panel. Each also had a reviewer/reactor panel representing students and teachers, and involved guidance personnel, administrators, and others in a reviewer/reactor role. This strategy provided continuous evaluation and feedback for formative evaluation.

Having developed a general model from a review of others in use, a needs survey of forty questions based on the content of the model was given to pupils. Card sorts and sampling were used to get at pupil needs.

An assessment of the current program was also conducted to determine the extent and effectiveness of practices. Input was collected from pupils and parents on how well objectives were already being reached. Competencies of counselors were inventoried to determine staff development needs, and the current program was analyzed to determine what was already being done by teachers and counselors to achieve objectives.

Next, several strategies were developed for reaching each objective so that schools could choose the most suitable one for their purposes. Criterion measures were also developed for each of the objectives; at the start of the program they were used to collect baseline data.

Guidelines were prepared for making the most effective use of staff to achieve goals and objectives. Because of budgetary and other constraints, innovative staffing procedures were needed, including adult volunteers, pupils, and community resources. Cost-effectiveness studies will be carried out to identify programs that give the greatest payoff.

A STATE-LEVEL EVALUATION PROGRAM   Wysong's evaluation package used in Ohio (Objectives . . . 1974) emphasizes assistance to pupils as the primary objective of the program. Secondary objectives are services to teachers, administrators, parents, and counselors so that they in turn can better assist pupils.

This well-developed program includes a self-study evaluative criteria which may be used by school staffs for self-evaluation, and a series of instruments for assessing pupil and teacher attitudes about guidance, knowledge of services, and utilization of helping activities. Additional materials describe the steps for preparing for the visit of the evaluation team. The procedure is cooperative and involves state guidance consultants, school staff, and the visiting team. A follow-up is conducted after a year by staff of the State Division of Guidance and Testing.

A study of the effects of the evaluation program by O'Connor (1973) showed that in the twenty schools studied nearly one third of the visiting team's recommendations had been put into effect a year later. Another one third were in the process of being implemented, and the remaining third had not been acted upon. Lack of financial resources and time were the chief reasons for not making recommended changes. Schools reported that the evaluation had provided data which could be communicated to various publics, and the total evaluation procedure had helped the school staff develop a better understanding of guidance services and objectives.

THE CONTRIBUTION OF TECHNOLOGY TO ACCOUNTABILITY The computer has made possible detailed analyses of evaluation data and continuous monitoring of effectiveness of programs. Needs data, allowing weighted responses and analysis by sex, grade levels, and other factors, require extensive manipulation that computers can easily handle. For example, the computer makes it possible to organize thousands of pupil responses about needs, rank them in order of priority, and summarize them by specific groups. Studies that would have been practically impossible because of clerical time and costs can be carried out with ease. Computers can "evaluate" pupils' decisions about educational programs and careers and progress in programs. Most are capable of the three data processing functions mentioned by Cramer, Herr, Norris, and Franz (1970, p. 165): (1) storing large amounts of data for relatively simple analysis, e.g., test scores, school grades; (2) relatively more complex analyses of masses of data, e.g., correlating test scores with grades; and (3) highly complex analyses of smaller amounts of data, e.g., statistical analyses of experimental data. Computer guidance systems, however, are not usually programmed to provide formative and cumulative evaluations, but computer handling of data can be useful for evaluation. For example, pupil choices of programs can be compared with ratings of success.

The computer is being used more and more in research and evaluation. New technology will undoubtedly open new possibilities. Small hand-held computers, for example, can be programmed to do various sorts of data analyses. Project Talent (Flanagan 1973) has provided analyses of the impact of various factors on effectiveness of guidance programs; psychological profiles of a nationwide sample of high school pupils graduating in 1960–63 (Flanagan, Tiedeman, Willis, and McLaughlin 1973; Rossi, Bartlett, Campbell, Wise, and McLaughlin 1975); and attitudes about education, work, personal and family life eleven years after school for more than 100,000 individuals (Wilson and Wise 1975). The PLAN system (Program of Learning in Accordance with Needs) makes use of the computer to monitor pupils' progress and assists in planning individual learning programs (Flanagan 1971). Another large-scale research and evaluation study was done by Jencks (1972) on the effects of schooling. He used data from a number of other reports, and found, among other things, that school achievement does not predict work performance very accurately (p. 192). The National Assessment Program (*NAEP Newsletter*, vol. 9, no. 4, pp. 1; 3–4), starting in 1964, is a large-scale national census-like survey of the knowledge, skills, understandings, and attitudes of individuals at ages 9, 13, 17, and young adults between 26 and 35. The total sample is about 80,000. These types of evaluation studies greatly expand the data base for accountability planning, and also illustrate techniques schools can use in their own accountability programs.

AFTER EVALUATION: PUTTING THE RESULTS TO WORK

Evaluations at all stages of program planning are used to improve, revise, and modify what is done. For example, in program development, new data suggest that some current goals are inappropriate—new ones are needed. But there may be a vested interest in the old ones. Besides, it can be threatening to be required to change from old, familiar goals to new ones that cause drastic modifications.

Making changes in a school program is not an easy task. Consultation is the critical skill needed all through the evaluative process. Practical experience, maturity, sensitivity, and a tolerance for ambiguity enable evaluators to work effectively with staff and others and to gain respect and cooperation (Oetting and Hawkes 1974).

The ability to communicate effectively with the various publics who need to know results of current or future programs and who are instrumental in putting results into action is essential (Oetting and Hawkes 1975). For example, a report that would be understandable to other evaluators might not be suitable for parents, and a summary for presentation at a service club would not contain the detailed information needed by counselors.

Accountability has become a significant tool in objective self-assessment by counselors.

A number of problems face the counselor in translating results into action. An overcommitment to the existing program may make it difficult to be objective (Warner 1975b). It is possible for a new program to be so highly regarded that the institution decides to implement it even before there is an evaluation; in these circumstances an objective scrutiny cannot be afforded (Campbell 1969). Organization and management skills in relation to the particular institution are needed if results are to be incorporated in the program (Glaser and Taylor 1973). High-level research skills are required; errors can creep into interpretations when there is a need for immediate action, which often happens in social research and evaluation (Wortman 1975). One of the most vivid illustrations of overenthusiastic acceptance is described by Glass in his article "Educational Piltdown Men." He gives examples of faulty research and evaluation that produced results eagerly snapped up by professionals and lay persons, just as readily as the discovery of Piltdown man was accepted as proof of Darwin's theory of evolution. This is a manifestation of the "wishful will to believe" when a miraculous solution is claimed.

The evaluator thus has a change-agent function, steering a course between overenthusiastic acceptance and rigid, ossified opposition. Moreover, involvement with the program must not result in attempts to oversell on the basis of faith, even though evaluative data do not warrant support.

Dustin's Five Principles of Change (1974) provide guidelines for the evaluator who seeks to implement results. They are:

1. *Outside pressure comes first.* Examples are plentiful—student unrest during the 60s and 70s, the demand for accountability, the career-education movement. The evaluator needs to be aware of and utilize these forces.

2. *Change comes from the top down.* Administrative support is essential in every aspect of program development and evaluation. This principle is borne out by the evaluative reports summarized, and emphasizes the need for the evaluator to work closely with administration to effect change.

3. *Change takes place within the institution.* Those who will be responsible for carrying out changes should participate in evaluation. "Members most affected by a change should be brought into the change process" (Dustin 1974, p. 423).

4. *Change tends to be superficial.* This is particularly true when outside evaluators come for a short time, arrive at some sweeping conclusions, and leave. Surface changes may take place, but soon erode. New and expensive materials are bought or prepared, and end up stored in a closet. New techniques fade, and in-service preparation is neglected for new staff. If an evaluation is to have an impact, the evaluator needs to set up a system for continuous monitoring, establish school-based resource persons and coordinators, insure systematic preparation for new staff, and involve the regular staff.

5. *Extensive change may follow unsatisfactorily superficial change.* Pressure builds up with ineffective changes, and institutional directors eventually realize that extreme steps are needed to satisfy the public. Dustin suggests that the change agent's role at this stage is to build support through effective relationships, which enable the evaluator to introduce and support changes.

RESEARCH

PROBLEMS IN INTERPRETATION
OF EVALUATIVE RESEARCH STUDIES

One major problem in interpreting the significance of studies has to do with the chance to detect differences among programs if they actually exist. Suppose, for example, two counseling methods are compared, and one is actually more effective than the other. Does the statistical test detect this difference?

Haase (1974) analyzed sixty research reports published in *Counselor Education and Supervision* 1968–71, and arrived at the conclusion that in many cases differences would not have been likely to be detected even if they existed. The results indicate that researchers need to design studies with particular attention to statistics used and sample size to avoid "stacking the statistical deck against themselves (p. 129)."

While this is a statistical concept that might not appear to be directly related to accountability, it has important implications for anyone evaluating the effectiveness of programs. Suppose, for example, you found that pupils were low in career maturity and you set up groups to help them improve in this area. At the end of the program you found that there was some improvement over baseline data but that it was not statistically significant.

You are about to drop the group program because it has not had the desired effects. Part of your job responsibility is to facilitate career development of pupils, so you look for other strategies.

But your statistical analysis may have failed to indicate results that were actually achieved. For example, if an expected improvement were in the medium range, and you had used statistical analysis in approximately the same way as employed in 40 percent of the studies analyzed, you would have had less than three chances in ten of finding a difference *even* though it existed. That is, even if your group procedures helped pupils improve career maturity, you would not have realized it in many cases.

EXPERIENCE

HAVE YOU PARTICIPATED IN AN EVALUATION?

Have you ever been contacted to give your reactions to your high school or college program? If so, did you feel that there was an interest in obtaining your input for evaluation?

Ask several other students if they have been followed up after high school graduation.

What do you conclude about the school's or college's interest in the evaluation?

Would you suggest any changes?

EXPERIENCE

WHAT WOULD YOU DO?

As a counselor in a school you have been carrying out an evaluation of the guidance program. Results show that the present program has a number of shortcomings. Major ones are:

— It concentrates on the 30 percent planning to go to college.
— Most of the counselors' time is taken up with administrative tasks.
— Counselors are used to administer discipline and to urge problem pupils to drop out.

The principal and many of the staff are very proud of the guidance program and are pleased with the way it is operating. Besides, the current emphases are in line with both the principal's and superintendent's policies.

What will you do with your evaluation study?

In a small group, have each member give a strategy.

Role play a meeting with the principal.

EXPERIENCE

IMPLEMENTING RESULTS OF EVALUATION

A visiting expert has arrived at your school to study and make recommendations about several problems such as absenteeism, vandalism, and poor achievement. The visitor asks you to make suggestions about strategies to ensure that the findings will be given serious consideration and appropriate strategies will be implemented.

What would you advise?

EXPERIENCE

LOCAL USE OF ACCOUNTABILITY

Ask counselors or principals in one or more local schools the following questions:

— What do you think of accountability?
— What use, if any, do you make of the concept?

Compare findings with the point of view in this chapter.

OBJECTIVES

1. To understand how a total school program can be evaluated for accountability. List steps that should be taken.

Several examples in the text illustrate effective ways to evaluate a program. Use one of these, e.g., the Grossmont Union High School District program, as a guide for identifying steps.

2. To understand how to use results of evaluation to improve practices. What are two major problems often encountered in implementation of changes?

The institution is committed to established procedures. Overenthusiasm for immediate action.

3. To use evaluation in day-to-day counselor-preparation activities. Identify several ways that this can be done.

One way would be to think of tasks, assignments, and participation in terms of objectives ("What specifically do I hope to gain?"). Another way could be to begin to develop projects—which might be suitable to meet course requirements—utilizing an evaluative approach (e.g., follow up a sample of graduates to obtain opinions about the program). A third would be to compare your program with the counselor-education standards in the appendix.

4. To understand personal attitudes about accountability. List five words that the term evokes.

Reactions will indicate your attitudes. Negative words in a projective exercise of this type imply opposition to the concept; positive words show support. The objective is reached if feeling words are used.

ADDITIONAL READINGS

Bettinghaus, Erwin P., and Miller, Gerald R. *Keeping the Public Informed: Accent on Accountability*. Denver, Colo.: Cooperative Accountability Project, 1973.

A guide to the very important function of public relations and building support for educational programs by disseminating accountability evaluations.

Buckner, Eugene T. "Accountable to Whom? The Counselor's Dilemma." *Measurement and Evaluation in Guidance* 8, no. 3 (1975), pp. 187–192.

This article, on which parts of this chapter are based, illustrates one reason why counselors are having problems with accountability.

Burck, Harman D.; Cottingham, Harold P.; and Reardon, Robert C. *Counseling and Accountability: Methods and Critique*. New York: Pergamon Press, 1973.

A useful discussion of aspects of research and evaluation with analyses of fourteen studies in counseling and guidance.

Cooperative Accountability Project. *Accounting for Accountability*. Denver, Colorado: 1975.

A report on two accountability conferences giving a vivid account of pros and cons.

Cramer, Stanley H.; Herr, Edwin L.; Morris, Charles N.; and Frantz, Thomas T. *Research and the School Counselor*. Boston: Houghton Mifflin, 1970.

An excellent guide for research and evaluation of the types of research the counselor carries out most frequently.

Glass, Gene V. "Educational Piltdown Men." *Phi Delta Kappan* 50, no. 3 (1968), pp. 148–151.

A revealing look at what can happen if research and evaluation reports, especially ones that promise needed remedies, are accepted uncritically.

———. "Primary, Secondary, and Meta-Analysis of Research." *Educational Researcher* 5 (1976): 3–8.

A provocative proposal of ways to increase the value of large numbers of individual studies by a systematic evaluation and synthesis of results. It is interesting to compare this view with Goldman's.

Goldman, Leo. "A Revolution in Counseling Research." *Journal of Counseling Psychology* 23, no. 6 (1976), pp. 543–552.

The author discusses weaknesses and limitations of current research approaches and offers new strategies both to improve designs and facilitate implementation of results.

———. "Toward More Meaningful Research." *Personnel and Guidance Journal* 55, no. 6 (1977), pp. 363–368.

This article, very much like the one listed above (1976), reports the author's candid look at counseling research, and concludes that new approaches are needed to help the practitioner and theory builder. Both of these articles have important implications for accountability.

Hays, Donald G., and Linn, Joan K. *Needs Assessment: Who Needs It?* Washington, D.C.: American School Counselor Association, 1977.

This monograph deals with needs assessment and illustrates how resulting data are translated into goals and objectives and used for program improvement. The easily understandable discussion and examples of programs make this a particularly valuable guide for the school counselor. Forms for local adaptation are included.

Kaplan, Louis, and Stoughton, Robert W. *Pupil Personnel Service Guidelines for Introducing and Developing a Program of Accountability*. Princeton: National Association of Pupil Personnel Administrators, 1974.

An excellent brief guide describing the process of setting up a practical program at both the school and the district level.

Krumboltz, John D. "An Accountability Model for Counselors." *Personnel and Guidance Journal* 52, no. 10 (1974), pp. 639–642.

One of the most useful references for counselors on what accountability means, how it can be implemented, and how it can help identify cost-effectiveness of services.

Lasser, Barbara R. "An Outcomes Approach to Counseling Evaluation." *Measurement and Evaluation in Guidance* 8, no. 3 (1975), pp. 169–174.

A helpful discussion of the importance of goal setting and evaluation in counseling. The model is particularly useful for carrying out a self-appraisal of one's effectiveness, and for changing techniques to achieve greater impact.

Mease, William, and Benson, Loren L. *Outcome Management Applied to Pupil Personnel Services*. St. Paul, Minn.: Department of Education, 1973.

An interesting and useful booklet describing the Self-Other Outcome Management (SOOM) approach to accountability.

Michigan School Counselors Association. *Reaction to Action Guidance*. Kentwood: Executive Board, Michigan School Counselors Association, 1974.

Humorous illustrations make this brief mimeographed discussion easy to understand. In spite of its brevity, it contains a great deal of valuable information on accountability.

National Forum on Educational Accountability. *Striving Toward Dialogue*. Denver, Colo.: Cooperative Accountability Project, 1975.

The report of a national forum on accountability, vividly illustrating different views of the concept.

Peters, Herman J., and Shertzer, Bruce. *Guidance Program Development and Management*. 3rd ed. Columbus, Ohio: Charles E. Merrill, 1974.

Approaches to accountability are covered in pages 538–547; the classification system differs from the one in this chapter.

Rothney, John W. M. *Adaptive Counseling in Schools*. Englewood Cliffs, N.J.: Prentice-Hall, 1972.

Chapter 6 gives an excellent review of evaluation by one of the major authorities in the field. Problems are discussed, and practical methods are described.

Shertzer, Bruce, and Stone, Shelley C. *Fundamentals of Guidance*. Boston: Houghton Mifflin, 1976.

The chapter on evaluation, pp. 428–452, gives a comprehensive review of research and evaluation approaches, problems, and use of results.

Sullivan, Howard J., and O'Hare, Robert W., eds. *Accountability in Pupil Personnel Services: A Process Guide for the Development of Objectives*. Fullerton: California Personnel and Guidance Association, 1971.

A comprehensive guide for building an accountable program, particularly useful for the many examples included.

Tolbert, E. L. *Research for Teachers and Counselors*. Minneapolis: Burgess Publishing Co., 1967.

A brief review of research approaches, with examples of action research and counselors' personal applications of results.

CHAPTER SIXTEEN
THE FUTURE: ISSUES, TRENDS, AND PROSPECTS

This final chapter is mainly about the future—what guidance will be like in the years ahead. Predictions about the coming years imply or explicitly state the nature of contemporary problems and issues in the profession and how they will be resolved. Much has already been said about current disagreements, needs, and challenges. The contribution of history to identifying directions has been assessed. Now it is time to take a broad view of the prospects for guidance and counseling in the next two or three decades.[1]

There will be changes; the major thrust will be to enlarge the scope and enhance the quality of services. My own optimistic stance allows no room for predictions that the tremendous progress of the past half century or so will be swept away by a tide of conflicts, frustrated demands, and financial crises.

GOALS

1. To appreciate the essential role that guidance will continue to play in our society.
2. To understand probable societal trends and their implications for guidance services.
3. To become aware of the importance of a close relation between guidance and social problems.
4. To realize the need to look into the future and to anticipate relevant programs and services.

1 In this final chapter, objectives, and research and experience boxes are omitted. It is time to take an unstructured look into the future.

NEED FOR GUIDANCE

The conditions that support the need for guidance have been highlighted all through the preceding chapters. It is inconceivable that any of them will fade away; recent events in social, economic, and political life show that problems and needs will become more complex and pressing.

The viability of guidance as a major helping service depends not only on the profusion of societal problems, complexities, and needs; it must be seen as an effective response. The many publics—pupils, parents, legislators, the community at large, and educators—must view guidance as a profession that provides a needed service, available from no other source. Two factors determine whether or not this will occur. The first is the sensitivity and perceptiveness of guidance workers in discerning the *real* problems and needs, particularly those of which the general public is only dimly aware. The second is the effectiveness in communicating goals and results to this same public.

Obviously something positive has to happen in the lives of those who come in contact with guidance. Identifying needs and publicizing results will not alone accomplish the task of ensuring the support of guidance services. But guidance already has the means to ensure that it has a significant impact, and the dynamic nature of the profession, documented throughout this book, practically guarantees that it will enlarge and improve on present approaches and techniques.

Thus, the question needs to be faced, Will the guidance profession be able to respond effectively to the two major tasks? My position is that it will; the motivation, competency, and imagination of those who will do the job are already plentiful. In fact, a recurring theme in earlier chapters is the inventiveness guidance workers have repeatedly demonstrated not only in dealing with current needs but in anticipating emerging or hidden ones. Failure will come only if enthusiasm falters, and pressures and challenges are allowed to cause a futile search for security through ingratiatingly taking on a myriad of insignificant and irrelevant tasks in the attempt to become indispensable rather than be professional.

OUR FUTURE
AND IMPLICATIONS FOR GUIDANCE

Predictions are hazardous but necessary. The task is made easier by the post-Bicentennial climate of taking stock and looking to the future. A positive orientation towards the future is essential in the midst of the present confusions and dilemmas:

America is wallowing in a period of disappointment and disillusion. The idea of progress is still alive, but it is not well. There is an emerging 'new pessimism,' not only in foreign policy but in domestic affairs. Government is viewed as, inevitably, bumbling and corrupt. Other social institutions are considered obsolete and ineffectual (Elam 1976, p. 3).

But, Elam's view is not one of long-term pessimism. Hopeful signs both of society in general and schools in particular can be drawn from the position that ours is a "self correcting society" and the schools are "a major instrument in shaping the future" (1976, p. 3).

The bases for optimism are substantial. Resources are being depleted, but there are avenues available utilizing selective growth and alternative energy resources that can, if used fully and promptly, head off disaster. The nation's collective ingenuity can find new ways to cope with destructive trends. Scientific and social innovations and breakthroughs have served to improve the quality of life in past years and have the potential for equal or greater success in the future. We are only beginning to use our intellectual potential for progress on all fronts; education, especially, stands to gain enormously from new developments in both the cognitive and affective areas (Shane 1976). But we may need to experience a "socioquake" (Harman 1976, p. 135)—and thus arrive at new ways of viewing man in relation to the environment rather than patching up the old perceptions and practices.

With an assumption of constructive and positive changes, what are major directions for the next several decades? A review of even a handful of the significant themes requires a look at political, economic, social, and educational aspects (Shane 1976).

There is a continuity in the international political alignments among power blocs, even as new nations strive for status and recognition, and energy resources modify relations among countries. International politics will be based on power balances and energy resources, but there will be a greater recognition and acceptance of the concept of interdependence of nations. The related worldwide problems of growth, crowding, and inadequate resources will be faced; cooperative efforts will be made to slow down the population explosion, increase worldwide food production, and enhance the self-sufficiency of third-world countries.

Economic problems, primarily inflation, and unemployment, will continue to cause hardships for individuals, while increasing both the cost of services and the need for them. Cooperation among nations will be emphasized, while reduced energy resources and needs of undeveloped countries heighten economic problems in this country.

The trend of a rising median population age will continue, and the effects will be felt in every aspect of life. Not only will there be a shift in the emphasis of guidance and counseling, but retirement policies and benefits, education, housing, medical care, and the world of work will be dramatically affected.

Work and the work setting are changing in ways that will have profound effects in the years ahead. There will be an increased demand for job security as protection against the fluctuations in the economy. At the same time, however, more humane and stimulating working conditions will be sought. The work week and work day will be shortened, and variations such as splitting jobs and self-selected work hours will be tested. The increasing age of the labor force and the steady trend for more female participation will affect the workplace in many ways not yet known to us.

Changes in education will range from introducing new financing plans to establishing programs for lifelong learning. As the proportion of school-age individuals decreases, the cost of public education rises, and the needs and political power of older persons become more visible, we may see a higher quality of schooling. It seems certain that there will be provisions for lifelong easy entry and exit in educational and training programs (Asimov 1976). New school models will merge education and life—family, community, and work—in ways that will make education more significant. Wirtz predicts that "some kind of provision for interspersing the earning and learning of a living, for interweaving employment and self-renewal, is going to have to be recognized as the essential condition for an effective career as worker, citizen, or human being" (1976, p. 129).

A host of trends are encompassed by the need Shane describes as "how to remotivate youth to feel that life is good, that it is worth living, and that it can bring enduring satisfaction" (1976, p. 81). Many of the problems of today stem from the lacks this statement implies; some young people seek solutions in fads, cults, drugs, or deviant life-styles. The educational institution will play a significant part in building new values and purpose, but the next several decades will be marked more by questions and searching than by answers and solutions.

If we translate the societal trends into guidelines for counseling and guidance, a general picture of increased pressure for services emerges. The need to make the most use possible of human and material resources leads to a greater concern for individual awareness of potential and opportunities. Material resources will be carefully used by those who are sensitive to the needs of others and are aware of the importance of sharing rather than thinking only of themselves.

The increasing interdependence among nations could enhance concern for problems that are common to different cultures and bring guidance workers in different countries closer together to pool strategies and techniques. Developing and underdeveloped countries can profit from learning about what is done in other areas if they have the opportunity to adapt principles and strategies for local use. It would be well to avoid an attitude that what is done in technologically advanced countries is best for others. A cooperative approach to unique needs of each culture would be a true implementation of the spirit of guidance.

Economic trends appear to guarantee that new life-styles will be adopted and that individuals will have to tap their personal resources to find satisfying and challenging ways to cope with changing conditions. Many of the cutbacks that appear to be inevitable will very likely cause disruptions in established patterns of travel, recreation, and day-to-day living. New modes may actually be growth-producing—there may, for example, be less dependence on commercial entertainment—but the changes may call for difficult adaptations.

The changing age of the population has obvious and important implications for guidance. Not only will there be a shift to include expanded services for those in their middle and later years, but new types of help will be needed, e.g., assisting mid-life and older persons with educational and work planning (Entine 1976; Quirk 1976).

The changing world of work offers some of the most direct implications for guidance and counseling of any aspect of life. Even though efforts are being made to adapt work to individuals and to develop new patterns of work hours and sharing jobs, the central problem of finding meaning and fulfillment will demand increased attention. Perhaps a combination of meaningful leisure activities and income-producing work will be needed. Whatever the eventual solutions, it seems that some kind of human development services both in the workplace and in the community will be needed.

The increasing need for accountability and making the most productive use of resources will make education give additional emphasis to helping all pupils understand and utilize their full potential. Questions are being raised about the assumed benefits of large schools (School consolidation . . . 1976; Chaffee 1976), and there is a shift emerging that emphasizes compulsory education, not just compulsory attendance (Ross 1976). These and other trends imply that help will be needed to make the school a place for learning and development attuned to the needs of the individual and the community.

The task of helping youth to find challenge, meaning, and stimulation in school programs, work, and productive community life is made even more demanding by the changing social and economic conditions. This is a school-community problem that demands the best efforts of practically everyone, but it is one in which guidance personnel have a unique opportunity for effective leadership and service.

A brief and general review of major trends slights a multitude of specific issues, problems, and directions of critical significance for guidance workers (e.g., licensure, ethics, preparation, and affirmative action), but it gives the backdrop against which they will be worked out. Moreover, the major trends contain an affirmation of an increasing need for guidance and counseling for helping all individuals in lifelong growth and development and to give guidelines for dealing with the specific questions and problems.

THE NEED
FOR NEW APPROACHES

A major point of this book is that new strategies, techniques, and technology are vital to effective delivery of services today. The future will make even greater demands on the creativity and inventiveness of guidance workers. Two factors support this prediction—accountability and financing. From the counselor's point of view, the major reason is to provide better-quality help to more people; improving the quality of life ranks above the demand for hard evidence of effects and adjusting to cope with financial limitations. But the realities of the situation require a consideration of the most effective use of personnel and material resources to achieve desired goals. Tomorrow may usher in strategies that are unknown today.

The past few years have witnessed a proliferation of approaches, technology, and strategies. Some are destined for a brief meteoric life before falling into oblivion. Others are sure to become major styles of guidance in the future. The problem that counselors face is how to tell the difference. There is no quick or easy way; research and evaluation provide the most valid answers. Intuition may seem a trusty guide, but it is often so entangled in personal commitment to an approach or enthusiasm for a cause that its value is doubtful.

Moreover, the attitude that what is new is good and what is old is bad leads to a distorted view that inhibits a thoughtful and perceptive selection of the most effective means. This naive position, coupled with a tendency to partially try out and quickly dispose of new approaches, not only creates discontinuous development but often relegates to the scrap heap potentially valuable methods and materials. There is much faddishness in U.S. guidance, abetted by an affluence that permits spending of enormous sums on new developments that are discarded even before rigorous testing can be completed. This luxury is fast disappearing. It will take careful evaluation and use of both the old and new to fashion the guidance of the future.

Productive elements that will gain additional use in the years ahead are reflected in earlier chapters. Consultation is one. Together with psychological education and "giving guidance away," it represents a new strategy that pulls together diverse helping approaches that have been taking shape for many years. Paraprofessionals and computers also have great potential. The needs survey, a new label for holding guidance close to what the public wants, is obviously here to stay. It has never disappeared since the concept of guidance first surfaced at the turn of the century, but since then it has fallen on hard times. Accountability is of course not new; the only surprising thing is that it took so long to emerge as a major consideration in the helping services. A number of other strategies have been endorsed in the preceding pages; the movement toward lifelong learning and guidance, and integrating the school with the community and workplace are the most significant. The separate elements are not new, but the synthesis brings into being a strategy of tremendous importance.

One front along which the profession advances does not involve large-scale movements nationwide in scope—it is in the day-to-day work of the counselor who may, for example, develop a better way to help a counselee explore goals, make decisions, and carry out plans, or devise a new mode of working with groups of pupils or parents. It could be any of the multitude of things the counselor does. Shared with colleagues, these activities have a ripple effect that eventually makes a difference in school guidance.

Reflections on programs naturally lead to speculation about the practice of guidance five, twenty, or thirty years ahead. What will it be like? Is it possible to look into the future with any certainty?

GUIDANCE IN THE NEXT FIVE YEARS Some trends appear to be fairly clearly indicated by current developments. One of these is licensure. There almost certainly will be some type of widespread provisions for licensure, which will have an impact on school counselors. Effects will be felt more definitely by those in non-school settings, however, as it is predicted that employment in an educational institution will enable the counselor to practice regardless of licensure status.

Accountability will be given more attention in all settings. Evidence of positive effects will be needed to ensure the continued existence of school guidance services as well as to maintain support for programs in other settings. Moreover, counselors will be expected to expand services with little additional financial support.

The counselor's role will be more clearly defined, partly because of accountability and partly because of the use of new strategies such as outreach and psychological education, which give the work a visible structure and purpose.

Increasing attention will be given to the needs of special groups, e.g., mid-life and older persons, minorities, the handicapped, and women. Moreover, we will see at least the beginnings of the implementation of lifelong learning and school-community cooperative approaches.

Changes in public education, particularly the expanded infusion of career education, will make the school a more dynamic and realistic learning environment. At the same time the "basics" will be increasingly emphasized. All of these changes will offer counselors opportunities to serve in new ways and to build a solid position in education.

More processes and personnel will be utilized to expand the reach of guidance services. Paraprofessionals are one example, particularly peer counselors. After their slow start in the past decade, computers will be used with increasing frequency.

As school budgets are examined, questions will be raised about the necessity for guidance services. The predicted outcome, however, is that there will be an increase in the support for services because they offer ways to deal with the most pressing school and community problems.

GUIDANCE IN TWENTY YEARS The impact of the social, economic, and political trends described on pp. 342–345 will have a more pronounced effect on guidance and counseling than in the immediate future. It is predicted that more definite patterns of those trends given for the next five years will have emerged, e.g., licensure regulations will be crystallized, career education will be the major mode in public education, and guidance roles will be more clear-cut and more widely understood. Computer technology will be used, and counselors will have much more time to devote to the personal, affective, and decision-making needs of youth.

Lifelong education and school-community cooperation will be realities, and counselors will work with all ages in both school and community. There will be increases in the number of counselors needed; preparation standards will provide for differential staffing, with high levels of technical and human-relations competency for those in supervisory positions. At the same time there will be increased attention to prevention of problems and the provision of easily available community-wide services. School counselors will be regarded as logical persons to coordinate all school-guidance and pupil-personnel services, and will provide leadership for community-wide coordination strategies.

GUIDANCE BEYOND THE YEAR 2000 Disregarding the gloomy projections of those who question the likelihood of civilization lasting into the 21st century—such apprehension would have been equally appropriate in any epoch of recorded history—it is not only possible but essential to look ahead to try to discern a reasonably accurate, if tentative, outline of the shape of guidance. Leaders in the field, such as Berdie (1972), Harris (1968), Morgan (1974), Tyler (1972), and Walz (1975), show a substantial consensus about major developments in the future.

What will the year 2000 bring? A ten-hour work week? Longer life spans?
Androids? Will there be a need to counsel those with leisure time? The
elderly? Androids? Options may change, but the problem of choice will remain.

Four characteristics stand out. First, the counselor will go where people
are; outreach will be a major strategy, and there will be considerable use
of support persons. Marple (1972) describes a thought provoking fantasy
of the future in which "Friendship Centers" alter the lives of people
nationally and internationally. But typically, no clear-cut definition of the
arrangement of such a center is given; but the implication is that location
and type of housing will be of less importance than what happens in the
community.

The second major prediction is that services will be available lifelong;
the school-age emphasis will have disappeared. Guidance will be provided
over the whole range of individuals and groups; no social strata or subcul-

ture will be favored over any other. Along with this breadth, helping agencies and institutions will collaborate far more than they do today, and guidance workers will have a more comprehensive knowledge of, and better working relationships with, colleagues in other settings.

Much of the counselor's work will emphasize prevention; while crisis help will be provided, the major thrust will be the change agent's task of reducing or eliminating destructive features of the environment that generate problems.

The counselor's increased versatility will require a sound background in theory, research, and techniques; the quality of preparation will rise. Facilitating personal development, building effective working relationships, and gaining an in-depth understanding of various cultures will be given higher priority. Preparation programs will utilize input from the school, the community, and the working world, and measure student progress on the basis of competency.

Other aspects of the role in the years ahead involve legal status, ethical practices, professional organizations, and counselors' supply and demand. Prospects are good for increased professional status and the attendant legal and ethical responsibilities. Professional organizations will attain the prestige to induce employers to upgrade hiring standards. Some form of licensure will be in operation; counselors will participate in setting qualifications and examining applicants. It is very probable that counselors will be completely in charge of this process.

Expansions in the directions predicted here—lifelong service, and broad applications in life areas—will mean that the demand for counselors will exceed the supply. Notwithstanding changes in support at the federal and state levels, and increased competition for available funds, the need for counselors will be so apparent and the efforts of guidance so well documented, that ample financing will be forthcoming and opportunities for employment will be plentiful.

ADDITIONAL READINGS

Elam, Stanley M. "Without Hope, the People Perish." *Phi Delta Kappan* **58, no. 1 (1976), p. 3.**

A special Bicentennial issue of the *Phi Delta Kappan* that reviews the country's past and present and predicts the future. A number of articles give penetrating analyses of what the next twenty-five years will bring in all aspects of American life.

Harris, Philip R. "Guidance and Counseling in Year 2000." *Counselor Education and Supervision* **7, no. 3 (1968), pp. 262–266.**

A perceptive look into the future, which suggests a number of developments similar to those discussed in this chapter.

Morgan, Lewis B. "Counseling for Future Shock." *Personnel and Guidance Journal* 52, no. 5 (1974), pp. 283–287.

> The author recommends guidance and counseling responses to the onrushing changes predicted by Toffler in his book, *Future Shock*.

National Commission on the Reform of Secondary Education. *The Reform of Secondary Education*. New York: McGraw-Hill, 1973.

> The specific recommendations on pages 13–22 give a brief overview of likely developments in secondary education. Other sections contain indepth analyses of the recommendations.

Shertzer, Bruce, and Stone, Shelley C. *Fundamentals of Guidance*. 3rd ed. Boston: Houghton Mifflin, 1976.

> In Chapter 18, "Trends in Guidance," the authors predict future programs, preparation, and role. A valuable reading that projects an optimistic and realistic future.

Sinick, Daniel. "Guest Editor's Introduction," *Personnel and Guidance Journal* 55, no. 3 (1976), pp. 100–101.

> A special issue on "Counseling over the life span," which illustrates how this emphasis is beginning to have an impact on the profession.

Tyler, Leona E. "Counseling Girls and Women in the Year 2000." In *Counseling Girls and Women Over the Life Span*, edited by Edwin A. Whitfield and Alice Gustav, pp. 89–96. Washington, D.C.: National Vocational Guidance Association, 1972.

> One of the leaders in the field gives an illuminating glimpse into the role of counseling women in the 21st century.

Walz, Garry R. "Swinging into the Future." *Personnel and Guidance Journal* 53, no. 9 (1975), pp. 712–716.

> A provocative article about career guidance, touching on all aspects of life in the future and discussing implications for the counselor.

APPENDIX A

STANDARDS FOR
THE PREPARATION OF COUNSELORS
AND OTHER
PERSONNEL SERVICES SPECIALISTS

PREPARED BY THE ASSOCIATION
FOR COUNSELOR EDUCATION AND SUPERVISION

INTRODUCTION

These Standards are intended as guidelines for the graduate preparation of counselors and other personnel services specialists. They should be beneficial to college and university staff who are involved in initiating programs of preparation or in evaluating existing programs. The Standards can also be helpful to state, regional and national accrediting agencies. While the Standards are designed to serve as guidelines for minimum preparation, they are flexible enough to allow for creative approaches to counselor education. The Standards do not include guidelines for the preparation of support personnel or professional personnel at the doctoral level.

These Standards recognize that:

The faculty has developed a written statement of philosophy for the counselor education program and that this statement has been accepted by the institution.

The trend toward the development of competency based/performance based counselor education programs is likely to continue. However, whether or not a counselor education program is developed upon such a base, the standards reflect the concern that all programs should give to the assessment of demonstrated competencies by students during various stages of their development.

Students take varying rates of time to demonstrate the competencies and professional maturation demanded in the complexities of counseling and personnel services work. While the standards recommend minimum hours of study in certain areas, these stated minimum hours should be interpreted in the context that some students will demonstrate the desired competency and professional maturation levels in a shorter time than indicated while others may take substantially longer.

The need of counselors and other personnel services specialists for self-renewal and in-service education beyond minimum preparation or certification will increase. Therefore, the counselor education program should provide enriching experiences for those who have already completed the minimum program.

Minimum study in counselor education will increasingly extend beyond the one year program of graduate preparation. Such programs might include (1) a combination of an undergraduate major in guidance and a year of graduate study in counselor education, (2) two years of graduate study in counselor education, or (3) other models which include a minimum of one year of graduate study.

All counselor education programs are not expected to prepare counselors and other personnel services specialists for all the work settings encompassed by the Standards. Institutions should offer preparation programs only in those areas where sufficient qualified full-time staff and other resources are available.

The Standards reflect current thinking concerning the preparation of counselors and other personnel services specialists and combine the three existing statements on counselor preparation previously adopted by the Association for Counselor Education and Supervision (ACES): "Standards for the Preparation of Secondary School Counselors—1967"; "Standards for the Preparation of Elementary School Counselors," February, 1968; and "Guidelines for Graduate Programs in the Preparation of Student Personnel Workers in Higher Education—1969."

In addition to acknowledging the similarity of preparation among the various specialists, the Standards also provide for different goals which may exist in various work settings. While this single document has been developed for the entire profession, the respective divisions of the American Personnel and Guidance Association and other professional groups are encouraged to develop jointly, with ACES, specific statements concerning the specialized needs of counselors and other personnel services specialists who work in different settings. In this respect, attention is called to Section II, B.2 of the Standards, "Environmental and Specialized Studies."

Leadership for the development of these Standards was assumed by the ACES Commission on Standards and Accreditation, working under the supervision of the Executive Council of ACES. The Standards were adopted by the membership of ACES in 1973.

STANDARDS

SECTION I: OBJECTIVES

A. Objectives of the Program to Prepare Counselors and Other Personnel Services Specialists
   1. *The faculty has developed program objectives.*
       a. Objectives reflect a knowledge of studies and recommendations of local, state, regional, and national lay and professional groups concerned with counseling and personal services needs of society.
       b. Objectives reflect the needs in society which are represented by different ethnic and cultural groups served by counselors and other personnel services specialists.
       c. Objectives are reviewed and revised continuously through student as well as faculty participation.
       d. Objectives are developed and reviewed with the assistance of personnel in cooperating agencies.
       e. Objectives are written in such a way that evaluation of a student can be based on demonstrated competencies as he progresses through the program.
   2. *Objectives are implemented on a planned basis in all areas of the program including selection, retention and endorsement of students; curriculum; instructional methods; research activities; and administrative policies, procedures, and execution.*
   3. *Personnel in cooperating agencies and faculty members with primary assignments in other disciplines are aware of and are encouraged to work toward the objectives of the counselor education program.*
   4. *There is a planned procedure for a continuing evaluation of the outcomes of the program.*
       a. The program is evaluated in terms of demonstrated competencies of each student as he or she progresses through the program.
       b. Evaluation of the effectiveness of preparation is accomplished through evidence obtained from: (1) former students, (2) supervisors in agencies employing graduates of the program, and, (3) personnel in state and national licensing and accrediting agencies.

SECTION II: CURRICULUM — PROGRAM OF STUDIES AND SUPERVISED EXPERIENCES

A. General Program Characteristics
   1. *The institution provides a graduate program in counselor educa-*

tion designed for the preparation of counselors and other person-nel services specialists.

   a. The opportunity for full-time study throughout the academic year is provided and actively encouraged.

   b. Flexibility is provided within the curriculum to allow for individual differences in competencies and understandings developed before entering the program.

   c. Descriptions of the various program options and require-ments for graduate studies are published and distributed to prospective students.

   d. Concepts relating to differentiated staffing and preparation in counseling and personnel services are reflected in the pro-gram. The faculty is aware of lifetime opportunities for development and advancement in the field of counseling and personnel services. There is also an emphasis on the use of support personnel to free more professionally prepared per-sonnel for the performance of higher level functions.

2. *Continuing and/or in-service education offerings in counselor education meet all of the criteria in faculty qualifications, fac-ulty load, physical facilities, faculty-student ratios, etc. as de-scribed in these Standards.*

3. *There is evidence of high quality instruction in all aspects of the program.*

   a. Syllabi or other evidence of organized and coordinated in-structional units of the curriculum are available.

   b. Resource materials are provided.

   c. Responsibilities are assigned to, or assumed by faculty mem-bers only in those areas of the counselor education program for which they have demonstrated professional competency.

   d. Provisions are made for periodic evaluation by students and staff of all aspects of the program, i.e., course content, methods of instruction, and supervised experience, both on and off campus.

4. *Planned sequences of educational experiences are provided.*

   a. Within the minimum counselor education program a se-quence of basic and advanced graduate studies and other associated learning experiences is defined and provided.

   b. The program provides for the integration of didactic studies and supervised experiences.

   c. All prerequisite studies and other experiences are identified.

   d. Representatives of departments offering studies in related fields are regularly consulted regarding how related studies can be made more useful to counselor education majors.

   e. The faculty has identified performance indicators to determine whether the professional competencies to be developed by the sequence of educational experiences are achieved.

5. *A close relationship exists between the faculty of the counselor education program and the staff members in work settings.*
   a. The staff in the work settings is consulted in the design and implementation of all aspects of the program including practicum and internship experiences.
   b. The faculty of the preparation program is consulted in the design and implementation of in-service preparation of staff in work settings.

6. *Within the framework of the total program, there are opportunities for the student to develop understandings and skills beyond the minimum requirements of the program.*
   a. Elective courses and related experiences are available.
   b. Supervised individual study is available.
   c. Enrichment opportunities are provided and faculty encourage students to take part in them.

7. *The spirit of inquiry and the production and utilization of research data are encouraged among both faculty and students.*
   a. The statement of objectives of the program reflects an awareness of the role of research in the counseling and personnel services field.
   b. Instructional procedures make frequent use of, and reference to, research findings. Areas in which research is needed are identified.

8. *Opportunities for planned periodic self-evaluation and the development of greater self-understanding are provided for both students and faculty.*
   a. Self-analysis is encouraged through such activities as laboratory experiences, including audio and/or video tape recordings.
   b. Opportunities for improvement of interpersonal relationships are provided through small group activities.
   c. Counseling services for students are available and are provided by qualified persons other than counselor education faculty.

B. Program of Studies
   1. *Common core: The common core is composed of general areas considered to be necessary in the preparation of all counselors and other personnel services specialists.*
      a. Human growth and development: Includes studies that provide a broad understanding of the nature and needs of individuals at all developmental levels. Emphasis is placed

on psychological, sociological, and physiological approaches. Also included are such areas as human behavior (normal and abnormal), personality theory, and learning theory.

b. Social and cultural foundations: Includes studies of change, ethnic groups, sub-cultures, changing roles of women, sexism, urban and rural societies, population patterns, cultural mores, use of leisure time, and differing life patterns. Such disciplines as the behavioral sciences, economics, and political science are involved.

c. The helping relationship: Includes (a) philosophic bases of the helping relationship; (b) counseling theory, supervised practice, and application; (c) consultation theory, supervised practice, and application; and (d) an emphasis upon development of counselor and client (or consultee) self-awareness and self-understanding.

d. Groups: Includes theory and types of groups, as well as descriptions of group practices, methods, dynamics, and facilitative skills. It also includes supervised practice.

e. Life style and career development: Includes such areas as vocational choice theory, relationship between career choice and life style, sources of occupational and educational information, approaches to career decision-making processes, and career development exploration techniques.

f. Appraisal of the individual: Includes the development of a framework for understanding the individual including methods of data gathering and interpretation, individual and group testing, case study approaches, and the study of individual differences. Ethnic, cultural, and sex factors are also considered.

g. Research and evaluation: Includes such areas as statistics, research design, development of research and demonstration proposals. It also includes understanding legislation relating to the development of research, program development, and demonstration proposals, as well as the development and evaluation of program objectives.

h. Professional orientation: Includes goals and objectives of professional organizations, codes of ethics, legal considerations, standards of preparation, certification, licensing, and role identity of counselors and other personnel services specialists.

2. *Environmental and Specialized Studies: The counselor education program includes those specialized studies necessary for practice in different work settings. There is evidence that the*

faculty, in planning and evaluating the counselor education curriculum, has taken into consideration statements made by other professional groups relating to role, function, and preparation.

    a. Environmental studies: Includes the study of the environment in which the student is planning to practice. This includes history, philosophy, trends, purposes, ethics, legal aspects, standards, and roles within the institution or work setting where the student will practice.

    b. Specialized studies: Includes the specialized knowledge and skills needed to work effectively in the professional setting where the student plans to practice. For example, the student preparing to be an elementary school counselor may need to take, among other specialized courses, work in diagnosis of reading dysfunction; the student preparing to be a personnel services educator in higher education might need, among other specialized work, both course work and supervised experiences in student financial aid; or the student preparing to work in employment counseling may need additional information about employment trends as well as the sociology and psychology of work.

    The different professional associations jointly concerned with the preparation of counselors and other personnel services specialists are encouraged to develop statements concerning environmental and specialized studies, and make these statements available to the ACES Commission on Standards and Accreditation and to the profession in general.

C. Supervised Experiences

  1. *Appropriate supervised experiences provide for the integration and application of knowledge and skills gained in didactic study.*

    a. Students' supervised experiences are in settings which are compatible with their career goals.

    b. Supervised experiences include observation and direct work with individuals and groups within the appropriate work setting.

    c. Opportunities are provided for professional relationships with staff members in the work settings.

  2. *Supervised experiences include laboratory, practicum, and internship.*

    a. Laboratory experiences, providing both observation and participation in specific activities, are offered throughout the preparatory program. This might include role-playing, listening to tapes, viewing video tape playbacks, testing, organizing and using personnel records, interviews with field practitioners, preparing and examining case studies, and using career information materials.

b. Supervised counseling practicum experiences provide interaction with individuals and groups actually seeking services from counselors and other personnel services specialists. Some of these individuals and groups should come from the environments in which the counselor education student is preparing to work.

(1) Specific counseling practica have sufficient duration and continuity to assure optimum professional development. The minimum recommended amount of actual contact with individuals and groups is 60 clock hours extending over a minimum nine-month period.

(2) Supervision in consultation is also provided.

(3) The supervisor's role is clearly identified and sufficient time for supervision is allocated. The recommended weekly minimum of supervision is one hour of individual supervision and one hour of supervision in a group for the duration of the practicum experiences. Supervisory responsibilities include critiquing of counseling, either observed or recorded on audio or video tape.

c. Internship is a post-practicum experience that provides an actual on-the-job experience, and should be given central importance for each student.

(1) The internship placement is selected on the basis of the student's career goals.

(2) The internship includes all activities that a regularly employed staff member would be expected to perform. In the setting the intern is expected to behave as a professional and should be treated as one.

(3) For those students who have no prior work experience in their particular setting, an intensified or expanded internship is provided.

(4) The intern spends a minimum of 300 clock hours on the job. It is desirable that the internship be a paid experience.

(5) Supervision is performed by qualified staff in the field placement setting who have released time from other regular duties.

(6) The counselor education faculty provides these field supervisors opportunities for in-service education in counseling and personnel services supervision.

(7) There should be close cooperative working relationships

between staff in field placement setting and the counselor education faculty.

3. *A qualified faculty and staff with adequate time allocated to supervision is provided for laboratory, practicum, and internship experiences.*

    a. Members of the on-campus faculty responsible for supervision include those who:

        (1) have earned doctoral degrees, preferably in counselor education, from accredited institutions.

        (2) have had experience and demonstrate competencies in counseling and other personnel services at the level appropriate for the students supervised.

    b. Doctoral students serving as supervisors of practicum experiences are themselves supervised by qualified faculty.

    c. The practicum and internship experiences are tutorial forms of instruction; therefore, the supervision of five students is considered equivalent to the teaching of one three semester-hour course. Such a ratio is considered maximum.

4. *Facilities, equipment, and materials are provided for supervised experiences in both on- and off-campus settings. (See also Section IV.)*

D. Program Development Outreach

1. *The counselor education faculty assists individual counselors and other personnel services specialists in off-campus agencies providing supervised experiences in the program of preparation.*

    a. The institution encourages agency personnel to seek the counselor education faculty's assistance in planning and conducting in-service education and in developing program improvement models.

    b. The counselor education faculty is provided a teaching-work load recognition for their part in in-service and program development activities in cooperating agencies.

    c. The counselor education faculty involves advanced graduate students in programs of in-service education and in program development planning and implementation at the agency level.

2. *The counselor education faculty provides on-campus assistance to agency personnel in resolving unique problems or difficulties.*

    a. The faculty encourages agency personnel to seek assistance through the use of such techniques as personal appointments, telephone access programs, information storage and retrieval, position papers, and various audio and/or visual media.

3. *The counselor education faculty integrates the experiences of the*

outreach activity into its counselor education program by adapting or modifying the counselor education program as may be appropriate. Outreach activities are viewed as a significant function in the preparation program.

SECTION III: RESPONSIBILITIES CONCERNING STUDENTS IN THE PROGRAM

A. Information
    1. *Information concerning major aspects of the counselor education program and the faculty is available in a variety of media for prospective students.*
        a. The academic areas in which the program offers preparation and the degrees offered are clearly stated.
        b. Counselor education faculty are available to discuss the program of preparation.
        c. Personnel in various counseling and related job settings have been designated as referral sources for discussion of their areas of interest with prospective students.
B. Selection
    1. *Applicants accepted meet the institution's standards for admission to graduate study.*
        a. There is evidence that staff in cooperating agencies have been consulted relative to admission policies and procedures.
        b. Students in the program reflect an effort, on the part of the faculty, to select individuals who represent a variety of sub-cultures and sub-groups within our society.
        c. A committee of faculty members makes the decisions concerning admission of applicants to the program based upon established criteria such as:
            (1) Potential effectiveness in close interpersonal relationships.
            (2) Aptitude for counseling and related human development responsibilities.
            (3) Commitment to a career in counseling and personnel work.
            (4) Potential for establishing facilitative relationships with people at various levels of development.
            (5) Openness to self-examination and commitment to self-growth.
C. Retention
    1. *A continuing evaluation through systematic review is made of students as they progress through the program.*
    2. *In situations where evaluations of a student indicates an inappropriateness for the counseling field, faculty members assist in facilitating change to an area more appropriate for the student.*

D. Endorsement

1. *A statement of policy relating to the institution's procedure for formal endorsement has been adopted and approved by the faculty and administrative authorities.*

    a. Each candidate is informed of procedures of endorsement for certification, licensing, and employment.

    b. Insofar as possible, all faculty members acquainted with the student, including supervisors of practicum and internship experiences, should participate in the endorsement process.

2. *Endorsement is given by the counselor education faculty only for the particular job setting for which the student has been prepared.*

3. *Endorsement is given only on the basis of evidence of demonstrated proficiency. The candidate should have completed a substantial part of his graduate work in counselor education, including supervised counseling experience, at the endorsing institution.*

E. Placement

1. *The institution has a placement service with policies and procedures consistent with recognized placement practices.*

    a. The faculty assist the student with the preparation of placement papers and the selection and securing of a suitable position.

    b. Placement services are available to graduates of the program throughout their professional careers.

    c. Opportunities are provided for students to participate in local, state, and federal examinations for employment opportunities.

F. Research and Evaluation

1. *Policies and procedures relating to recruitment, selection, retention, and placement are continually studied through various research and evaluative methods.*

    a. Regular follow-up studies are made of former students, including dropouts, students removed from the program, and graduates.

    b. Evaluation is followed by appropriate revisions and improvements in the preparation program.

SECTION IV: SUPPORT FOR THE COUNSELOR EDUCATION PROGRAM, ADMINISTRATIVE RELATIONS, AND INSTITUTIONAL RESOURCES

1. *Administrative organization and procedures provide recognition and designated responsibilities for a counselor education program.*

a. The program is a clearly identified part of the institution's graduate program.

    (1) There is preferably only one unit directly responsible for the preparation of counselors and other personnel services specialists.

    (2) If more than one unit in the institution is directly involved in the preparation of counselors and other personnel services specialists, there is evidence of close cooperation and coordination.

b. Cooperative relationships exist between the counselor education program and other units of the institution related to the program.

    (1) Contributions of other units to the program are defined.

    (2) Channels of communication with faculty members in other units are identified and maintained.

c. Use is made of a wide range of professional and community resources. Evidence of positive working relationships exists with agencies off the campus that have the potential for contributing to the preparation of counselors and other personnel services specialists. They may be potential employers of graduates of the program.

2. *The institution provides for the professional development of the counselor education faculty as well as students in the counselor education program.*

a. Faculty are involved in professional activities on local, state, regional, and national levels.

b. Faculty participate in voluntary professional service capacities.

c. The institution provides encouragement and financial support for the faculty to participate in professional activities.

d. Faculty engage in programs of research and contribute to literature of the field.

e. Students participate in the activities of professional organizations.

3. *The institution provides adequate faculty and supporting staff for all aspects of the counselor education program.*

a. An individual is designated as the professional leader of the counselor education program.

    (1) This individual is an experienced counselor and possesses an earned doctorate in counselor education from an accredited institution.

    (2) This individual has full-time assignment to the counselor education program.

    (3) This individual is recognized for his leadership in the counseling profession.

(4) This individual is qualified by preparation and experience to conduct and to supervise research activities.

4. *In addition to the designated leader there are at least two full-time faculty members with comparable qualifications.*

    a. Additional faculty are provided at the ratio of one full-time staff member for every ten full-time graduate students or their equivalent in part-time graduate students. This ratio should be reduced in institutions where a large percentage of the counselor education students are enrolled on a part-time basis and/or when program changes create the need for the faculty to spend more time in the evaluation of each student.

5. *The full-time teaching load of faculty members is consistent with that of other graduate units in the institution which require intensive supervision as an integral part of professional preparation.*

    a. The faculty load is modified in proportion to assigned responsibilities for graduate advisement and research supervision on a formula that is consistent with established graduate school policy in the institution.

    b. Time is provided within the total faculty work load for cooperative interdisciplinary activities with teaching faculty in related fields.

    c. The total work load of faculty members includes a recognition of time needed for professional research.

6. *Faculty in closely related disciplines are qualified in their respective areas and also are informed about the objectives of the counselor education program.*

7. *Off-campus agency personnel who supervise students are qualified through academic preparation and professional experience.*

    a. Such staff members have two or more years of appropriate professional experience.

    b. These staff members have at least two years of graduate work in counselor education or can demonstrate equivalent preparation.

8. *Graduate assistantships are provided to assist the faculty and to provide additional experiences for students in the program.*

    a. Regular procedures are established for the identification and assignment of qualified students to assistantships.

    b. A minimum of one half-time graduate student is assigned to the counselor education program for each 30 full-time equivalent students.

    c. Assignments are made in such a way as to enrich the professional learning experiences of the graduate assistants.

9. *Secretarial, clerical, and other supportive staff are provided in the counselor education program.*

a. A minimum of one full-time secretary or equivalent is provided for the clerical work of the counselor education program.

b. Additional clerical service is provided at the ratio of one full-time clerical assistant for the equivalent of every three faculty members.

c. Responsibilities of secretarial, clerical and other supportive staff are defined and adequate supervision is provided.

10. *The institution provides facilities and a budget that insures continuous operation of all aspects of the counselor education program.*

a. The institution provides a designated headquarters for the counselor education program.

   (1) The headquarters is located near the classroom and laboratory facilities used in the counselor education program.

   (2) The headquarters area includes a private office for each faculty member.

   (3) The headquarters area includes office space for secretarial, clerical, and other supportive staff.

   (4) The headquarters provides appropriate work space, equipment, and supplies for graduate assistants.

b. Facilities for supervised experiences are provided in a coordinated laboratory setting on campus. Consideration is given to:

   (1) Facilities for individual counseling in rooms with assured privacy and adequate space for related equipment.

   (2) Facilities for small group work. The area provides for small group counseling, testing, staffing, meetings, and so forth.

   (3) Classroom and seminar meeting rooms.

   (4) Facilities appropriately equipped with the following:

      (a) recording and listening devices, both portable and permanent

      (b) one-way vision glass

      (c) video-tape recording and playing devices, both portable and permanent

   (5) Technical assistance for both operational and maintenance services.

   (6) Acoustical treatment throughout the facility.

   (7) Facilities that are conducive to modeling and demonstrating exemplary environments and practices in counseling and personnel services. The facilities should include a "model" counseling laboratory with related resource materials and audio-visual equipment. Included as resources in the "model" laboratory are:

(a) career occupational and educational information materials

(b) standardized tests and interpretation data

(c) a variety of media, equipment, and materials

(d) space for teaching and laboratory experiences

(8) Data processing assistance and equipment that are available for both teaching and research.

(9) Facilities that are located in close approximation to the counselor education faculty offices and away from centers of extreme noise and confusion.

c. Library facilities provide an appropriate supply of resource materials for study and research in counselor education.

(1) The facilities include basic resources, both books and periodicals, in areas in which the counselor education program provides preparation. Resources in related areas such as psychology, sociology, and economics are also available.

(2) Both current and historical materials are available.

(3) Library resources are available during evening and weekend hours.

(4) Inter-library loans, ERIC services, microfilm, and photocopy services are available.

(5) Multiple copies of frequently used publications are available.

11. *Research facilities are available to faculty and students in counselor education.*

a. Facilities include offices and laboratories equipped to provide opportunities for the collection, analysis, and synthesis of data.

b. Consultant services are available from research specialists on the institution's faculty.

c. Campus computer centers and other data-processing facilities are available.

d. Appropriate settings, for research both off and on campus, are provided.

12. *The institution recognizes the individual needs of graduate students and provides services for personal as well as professional development.*

a. Since full-time academic-year attendance is possible for most graduate students only if some form of financial assistance is available, efforts are made to develop financial assistance for students in the counselor education program.

(1) The counselor education program is assigned a proportionate share of the institution's funds for student assistance.

(2) Part-time work opportunities appropriate for students in the program are identified and efforts are made to secure assignments for those desiring such opportunities.

(3) Loan resources are available to students in counselor education.

(4) Prospective students are provided information about possible sources of financial assistance.

b. Personal counseling services are available to all counselor education students.

(1) A counseling service is available from professionals other than the members of the counselor education faculty.

(2) Procedures for referral are known by all faculty members.

APPENDIX B

COMMISSION POSITION ON
STATE LICENSURE OF COUNSELORS
PREPARED BY THE AMERICAN PERSONNEL
AND GUIDANCE ASSOCIATION

A. Background Statement

The Commission on Counselor Licensure and an official "Position Paper" on the Licensing of Counselors was approved by the APGA Senate at its annual meeting in New York City in March of 1975. Following that approval the Commission held two meetings at the Americana Hotel in New York where initial plans for the Commission's work were developed. The development of guidelines for state legislation for the licensure of counselors was considered of prime importance. At subsequent meetings in Washington rough drafts of a "Counselor Licensing Model" were completed. The present "Guidelines" (Draft #7) is the result of feedback received by the Commission and further meetings to revise the original legislative material.

At the present time all states regulate the practice of counseling in school settings through counselor certification or endorsement on a teaching certificate. Virginia has become the first state to provide for licensing as a Professional Counselor. Michigan regulates mental health counselors practicing in state institutions or agencies on the basis of emergency rules for the Michigan Mental Health Code. California provides for the licensing of marriage, family, and child (MFC) counselors under a Behavioral Science Board.

The APGA Licensure Commission has a basic responsibility to assist all fifty states and the District of Columbia in the development of licensure procedures to regulate the practice of counseling. The purpose of such legislation is solely and only to protect the public. This protection is uppermost in the minds of Commission members and should be the continuing concern of counselors and members of the American Personnel and Guidance Association. The Commission is also well aware of the need to provide licensure regulation in many states where counselors are not prohibited from "engaging in their lawful profession" in the private sector and where other acts of discrimination make employment in certain agencies or institutions almost impossible without licensure.

From time to time it is alleged that abuses are committed not only by persons of little or no training but also by counselors whose training included little if any supervised experience in counseling practice. If counseling is to be organized as a full-fledged profession and if the public is to be guaranteed reasonable protection then the profession of counseling must assume a responsible role in regulating its practice and protecting the title "Professional Counselor." Legislation is clearly needed to prevent charlatans and inadequately trained individuals who hold themselves out to be "counselors" from practicing as well as using the title "counselor" and offering their services to the public for a fee.

B. Mission of Licensure Commission

The APGA Licensure Commission as originally conceived in 1975 was created with several distinct purposes in mind. The first of these is to represent the association in dialogue with other professional organizations and government agencies which may have supportive or conflicting interests in the regulation of helping professionals using counseling as a basic skill. A second responsibility assumed by the Commission is to provide APGA Divisions and Branches in individual states with legislative assistance as changes are sought in present state laws which may deny counselors the right to practice and/or the public the right to their services. The Commission also functions as a clearinghouse for receiving and disseminating information on licensure, certification and registration practices among the various states. This function includes responsibility not only for leadership in promoting conferences and workshops but for the research, interpretation, and explanation of various aspects of professional quality control of counseling such as registry, third party payments, and legislative approaches to regulation. Commission resources here focus on suggested legislative language, plans for statutory changes and/or organizational action, and designs for field strategies to familiarize counselors with the basic issues in the licensure process. Finally, the Commission serves as a central clearance point within APGA for individual members who need assistance with licensure problems involving such concerns as legal suits, psychology board rejection and other forms of discrimination.

C. Licensure and Legislative Change

In recommending these guidelines for legislative action, the APGA Licensure Commission recognizes the many professional, political and social variables that influence legislative changes. Each state must work within the existing set of conditions as it seeks to meet the needs of the public, various groups of helping professionals, and the legislative system. Given these circumstances, any suggested set of guidelines should only be viewed as proposals for considerations, not final models for individual state action.

The guidelines are designed to indicate options for licensure, certification or registration depending upon state circumstances. As these options are considered commensurate titles, training qualifications and limited practices may be recommended. Likewise appropriate board structures, requirements, and exemptions will necessarily be proposed. It is practically impossible and politically naive to suggest a single model for all states, granting all the conditions involved in legislative change. These assumptions are compounded by the obvious fact that the helping process as a social phenomenon cannot be completely legislated, controlled, or prevented. Our primary task is to offer possible solutions to the problem of quality service and protection to society plus professional regulation of the title and practice of counseling as a human function.

D. Nature of Guidelines

APGA is committed, through the Commission on Licensure to helping states and individual groups effect changes in present legislation or regulatory board policies that limit services to the public. In this process APGA can only offer suggestions or recommendations which will give any group of concerned professionals a wide range of alternatives as to legal or policy changes that are possible and how such changes can be implemented. Regulatory practices stem both from statutory controls and policy interpretation of these laws. To maximize the options any state may want to consider, the guidelines identify a number of standard regulatory areas. However, the Commission felt that it was feasible only to set forth explicit legislative language in certain of these areas. In some instances suggested legislative language in standard form is recommended. However, in other instances, policies for general guidance or interpretative comments relative to that particular area are outlined in brief. These comments are designed to offer ideas on content or procedural issues that may face state groups seeking to propose counselor regulation laws. This format, while lacking internal consistency may be more applicable to the widely varying conditions in the various states.

GUIDELINES AND SUGGESTED LEGISLATIVE LANGUAGE FOR COUNSELOR LICENSURE LAWS

1. *Statement of Policy*

It is declared to be the policy of this state that the activities of those persons who render services to the public in the behavioral science (counseling) area and use the title licensed professional counselor be regulated to ensure the protection of the public health, safety and welfare.

2. *Enabling Clause*

Legislation shall provide for the regulation of the practice of counseling as well as the use of the title "licensed professional counselor" or "certified counselor" for those who offer services to the public for a fee.

Comment: While it is recognized that some professions are regulated through registration or certification acts, the Commission believes that the preferred legislative regulation is through licensing. Depending upon existing conditions and relevant factors in a state, certification or registration may be viewed as viable options.

Although there are exceptions, the general rule of thumb is that *registration* only regulates the use of the title. *Certification* not only regulates the use of the title but also specifies that the minimum amount of education, training and supervision needed by the individuals be so certified, i.e., Certified Professional Counselor.

Licensing regulates the use of the title (Licensed Professional Counselor) and requires minimum education, training and supervision. In addition, licensure specifies the particular acts or practices which are held to be the sole prerogative of the profession. While certification would afford some protection to the public, the Commission strongly believes that licensing can afford the maximum protection and recommends that whenever possible the legislation be drafted as a licensing statute.

3. *Establishment of Professional Counselor Licensing Board*

    a. *The board shall consist of seven members, residents of the state of _____ who shall be appointed by the governor to serve the following terms . . . .*
    b. *Five board members shall be licensed counselors under this chapter. Two members shall be from the public at large. The*

governor shall, through the appointments to the board, represent the differences in gender, racial, and ethnic origins, and the different levels of graduate and professional degrees and specialties, though not all such differences necessarily will be reflected at the same time in board membership.

When the term of each member of the board ends, the governor may appoint his/her successor for a term of three years from a list of eligible candidates. Any vacancy occurring on the board may be filled by the governor from a list of all eligible candidates. The governor may remove any board member for misconduct, incompetency, or neglect of duty after giving the board member a written statement of the charges and an opportunity to be heard thereon.

c. *At all times, the board shall have members who are engaged primarily in rendering counseling services and two members who are engaged primarily in teaching, training, or research in counseling.*

d. *No board member shall serve more than two full consecutive terms.*

e. *When the initial appointments are made to the board by the governor, there shall be staggered terms. One member from the public at large shall initially serve a one year term and the other member from the public at large shall initially serve a three year term. Of the remaining board members two shall initially serve one year terms, one shall initially serve a two year term and the remaining two board members shall initially serve three year terms.*

f. *The members of the board shall be reimbursed for the necessary expenses when engaged in performing their duties as members of the board.*

Principle: Counselor licensing legislation should contain provisions concerning the establishment, organization and administration of the professional counselor licensing board. All board members should have an equal voice and vote in the affairs of the board. In addition to the professional members, the board should also include at least two members from the general public.

Comment: Each state should study the feasibility of establishing an independent board versus the creation of a behavioral science board or the incorporation of a professional counselor licensing board within an existing board.

4. *Definitions*

    4.1   Licensed Professional Counselor

"Licensed professional counselor" means and is restricted to any person who holds himself/herself out to the public by any title or description of services incorporating the words "licensed professional counselor"; and who offers to render professional counseling services to individuals, groups, organizations, corporations, institutions, government agencies or the general public for a fee, monetary or otherwise, implying that he/she is licensed and trained, experienced, or expert in counseling, and who holds a current, valid license to practice counseling.

Comment: The difficulty in finding a suitable title for legislative purposes is surpassed only by the task of defining counseling to meet the same end. This is not unique to counseling, but no less troublesome. The Commission's recommendation is predicated on a belief that basic legislation would define the generic term "licensed professional counselor" while enabling provisions may be made to allow for specialties through board rules.

Each state association may want to consult with organized specialties within counseling to establish liaison and support for legislation which defines, delimits, or otherwise significantly affects the practice of counseling in their area (e.g., rehabilitation, school, marriage and family; see Section 507). The purpose of establishing the modifiers "licensed professional" or "limited licensed" counselor is to help distinguish between professionally trained, ethically concerned individuals and persons who may use the term "counselor" loosely to denote commercial or similar enterprises of a significantly different nature.

    4.2   Limited Licensed Counselor

"Limited licensed counselor" shall mean any person who has been granted a limited license by the board to offer counseling services as defined in this act while under the supervision of a licensed professional counselor.

    4.3   Practice of Counseling

The "practice of counseling" within the meaning of this act is defined as rendering, offering to render, or supervising those who render to individuals, groups, organizations, corporations, institutions, government agencies or the general public any service involving the application of counsel-

ing procedures and other related areas of the behavioral sciences to help in learning how to solve problems or make decisions related to careers, personal growth, marriage, family, or other interpersonal or intrapersonal concerns.

Comment: Each state association should consult with organized specialty counseling groups to determine their wish to be included and offer subsequent support of this legislation.

4.4 Counseling Procedures

"Counseling procedures" include but are not restricted to the use of counseling methods and psychological and psychotherapeutic techniques, both verbal and nonverbal, which require the application of principles, methods, of procedures of understanding, predicting and/or influencing behavior, such as principles pertaining to learning, conditioning, perception, motivation, thinking, or emotions; to methods of procedures of administering and/or interpreting tests of mental abilities, aptitudes, interests, achievement, attitudes, personality characteristics, emotions, or motivation; informational and community resources for career, personal, or social development; group and/or placement methods and techniques which serve to further the goals of counseling; and designing, conducting and interpreting research on human subjects or any consultation on any item above.

Comment: The definition of counseling procedures (4.4) is intended to provide a layman's description of the kinds of services familiar to the public. They incorporate both the preventive and remedial aspects of counseling services. Practically speaking, there will be overlap with other professions who use counseling procedures as a part of their intervention strategies. There is no intention by the Commission to suggest restriction of the use of counseling procedures to persons licensed as counselors. To do so would not only be undesirable but impractical. The purpose of the above definitions is to insure that counseling procedures may be used rightfully by persons trained, qualified and licensed to do so.

5. *Requirements for Licensure*

5.1 Professional Training

The board shall issue a license as a licensed professional counselor to each applicant who files an application upon a form and in such a man-

ner as the board prescribes, accompanied by such fee as is required by this act, and who furnishes satisfactory evidence of the following to the board that:

(a) *The applicant is at least nineteen (19) years of age;*
(b) *The applicant is a citizen of the United States or has declared his intention to become a citizen. A statement by the applicant under oath that he is a citizen or that he intends to apply for citizenship when he becomes eligible to make such application, is sufficient proof of compliance with the requirement;*
(c) *The applicant is of good moral character;*
(d) *The applicant resides in the state of _____;*
(e) *The applicant is not in violation of any of the provisions of this act and the rules and regulations adopted hereunder;*
(f) *The applicant has received a master's degree from a regionally accredited institution of higher learning which is primarily professional counseling in content based on not less than thirty (30) graduate semester hours and which meets the academic and training content standards established by the board, or the substantial equivalent in both subject matter and extent of training. The board shall use the* (Standards for the Preparation of Counselors and Other Personnel Specialties) *as approved by the association of counselor education and supervision and the American School Counselors Association as a guide in establishing the standards for counselor licensure;*
(g) *The applicant has four (4) years of supervised full-time experience in professional counseling acceptable to the board; one (1) year of which may be obtained prior to the granting of the master's degree. An applicant may subtract one (1) year of the required professional experience for every thirty (30) graduate semester hours obtained beyond the master's degree, provided that such hours are clearly related to the field of professional counseling and are acceptable to the board. However, in no case may the applicant have less than two (2) years of the required professional experience;*
(h) *The applicant demonstrates professional competence in specialty areas by passing an examination written and/or oral and/or situational, as the board will prescribe. Upon examination of credentials the board may, by a majority of the board members present and voting, consider such credentials adequate evidence of professional competence and recommend to the chairman of the board that a license be approved.*

Comment: The Commission members are aware that there are various training modes and settings for persons in counseling practice. At the present state of the profession's development, our history is based primarily upon experience in education and vocationally oriented employment institutions. This is rapidly and profoundly changing as societal needs for counseling services have shifted. While there is justification for questioning graduate level training as a minimal level for all persons who practice counseling with specific clientele (e.g., drug or alcohol), we must emphasize that independent practice or its equivalent in an institutional setting suggests a breadth of knowledge and experience which increasingly have both legal and ethical implications.

The Association of Counselor Education and Supervision (ACES) *Standard for the Preparation of Counselors and Other Personnel Service Specialists* recommend minimally a one-year master's degree program with an endorsement for two-year preparation programs. The Commission does not believe that it should recommend less than these standards for practitioners in the light of the great diversity of settings and clientele for whom counselors provide services. The ACES standards are now being used throughout the nation in the accreditation of programs. Equally important, counselor educators must be even more responsive in developing preservice and in-service experiences for counselors who are and will continue to be asked to expand the type and range of their services in schools, agencies, and private practice.

5.2   Supervised Experience

The Professional Counselor Licensing Board shall establish criteria for determining what constitutes supervised experience.

Comment: The Commission is aware that problems may develop in establishing acceptable criteria for supervised experience. The Commission recommends that the boards seek assistance from appropriate professional organizations for developing criteria generally uniform and accepted within the profession. Such criteria should be sufficiently broad in scope to accommodate a variety of experiences. The Commission believes that these experiences should not be limited only to formal practice or internships *per se.*

The Commission suggests that supervision require at least weekly face-to-face conferences with a licensed or licensable counselor having appropriate experience in the area supervised.

5.3   Examinations

The Professional Counselor Licensing Board shall make specific provisions for examination of applicants for licensure at least once each year.

Comment: The Commission believes that nationally standardized examinations in counseling should be established and required of all applicants for licensing. Such examinations would not be competency examinations as such, but rather demonstrate that the applicant has sufficient understanding of counseling to warrant the board's consideration for licensing. A uniform application of the examination would help to protect the board against charges of discrimination.

The board's evaluation of the applicant's credentials is a routine procedure. The Commission believes it wise for the Professional Counselor Licensing Board to establish and publish criteria for evaluation of the applicant's credentials.

The establishment of an oral and/or field (competency) examination is desirable.

An appeal procedure following the Professional Counselor Licensing Board's adverse ruling on the applicant's application for licensure may include examination. All such procedures must be clearly spelled out.

5.4   Professional Ethics

The Professional Counselor Licensing Board shall adopt the Code of Ethics of the American Personnel and Guidance Association and any revision or additions deemed appropriate by the board to govern appropriate practice or behavior as referred to in this act.

Comment: Since the only acceptable purpose of legislation to license the practice of counseling is to protect the public, it is absolutely essential that a code of ethics be given the force of law. This Commission strongly recommends that a Code of Ethics based on the American Personnel and Guidance Association's Code of Ethics be included as part of the licensing rules.

5.5   Limited License

The board shall issue a limited license to each applicant who files an application upon a form and in such manner as the board prescribes accompanied by such fees as are required by this act, and who furnishes satisfactory evidence of the following to the board that:

(a) *The applicant has received a master's degree from a regionally accredited institution of higher learning based on a program of studies which is primarily professional counseling in content which conforms to the Standards for the Preparation of Counselors and Other Personnel Specialists (ACES) and which meets the academic and training content standards established by the board, or the substan-*

tial equivalent in both subject matter and extent of training. The limited licensed counselor may not practice without direct supervision by a licensed professional counselor. The plan for supervision of the limited licensed counselor is to be approved by the board prior to any actual performance of counseling on the part of the limited licensed counselor;

(b) *The applicant demonstrates professional competence in counseling by passing an examination and/or written and/or oral, or situational, or all three (3), as the board will prescribe. Upon examination of credentials the board may, by a majority of the board members present and voting, consider such credentials adequate evidence of professional competence, and recommend to the chairman of the board that a limited license be approved;*

(c) *The applicant has complied with provisions outlined in section 5.1, (a), (b), (c), (d), and (e), of this act;*

(d) *Any limited licensed counselor after meeting the requirements specified in section 5.1 (g) may petition the board for licensure as a professional counselor.*

5.6 Certification for Counselors in Areas of Restricted Employment Settings

Any state association of counselors or any state organization affiliated with a nationally recognized association of counselors may petition the state professional counselor licensing board, in accordance with rules and procedures adopted by the board, to create an area of restricted employment settings within the field of counseling. The professional standards of the association shall accompany any such petition.

For such purpose, he may practice those arts, utilize those counseling procedures, and utilize those titles that are permitted within the standards and ethics of his area of restricted practice. No such person shall offer or render services as a counselor outside his area of restricted practice, or otherwise engage in the practice of counseling outside his area of restricted practice, for a compensation or other personal gain.

Comment: In many states there are concerned groups of persons in drug, alcohol, rehabilitation, and employment settings who may perceive licensure legislation as a means of displacing them from jobs that they now hold. Minorities also may experience further discrimination by such legislation if not properly considered. There is evidence to suggest that peer groups and paraprofessionals can be at least as effective as trained counselors in assisting persons of like background under certain circumstances. For these and similar reasons, the Commission believes consideration of alternative methods of professional identification is important.

Such efforts should clearly distinguish between the titles and relative autonomy of those persons licensed to practice counseling and those who are registered or certified. For example, there have been federally funded programs to prepare and establish state credentialing of drug workers and drug programs. The identification of persons as drug counselors to work in approved drug programs seems to lend itself well to a registry or certification process.

5.7 Specialty Designation

Comment: The Commission recommends that when desirable, state professional counselor licensing boards establish requirements for certifying or licensing persons of special competence for areas of practice within the field of counseling. In order for an area of special competence to be approved, the standards of the appropriate state or nationally recognized association of counselors must accompany the petition of a state affiliated organization in accordance with procedures established by the board. Requirements may include those contained in sections 5.1, 5.2, 5.3, and 5.4, providing they are in accord with the standards of the appropriate national association of special competence.

This recommendation is based upon the belief that there are areas of special competence in counseling which require more intensive or special training, experience, and evidence of expertise, than generalist training can permit. Unlike national association bodies which certify members, legislation carries legal as well as ethical implications for protecting the public against charlatans who identify themselves as counselors of various persuasions or specialty. Of similar practical importance, persons in search of marriage, career, or similar counseling services may prefer evidence and further assurance that persons listed in the telephone directory have the specialized assistance that they desire.

In point of fact, at least seven states now license or certify marriage and family counselors. A number of other groups are seeking various means of specialty identification. Allowed to proceed without leadership, non-legislative, quasi-professional "specialty" bodies could become unmanageable and self-defeating to the development of the profession.

One means of establishing an orderly identification of areas of special competence is for state professional counselor licensing board rules to recommend that where possible state representatives of national associations present evidence of their national standards for use by the board in considering a new specialty if such identity is requested. In this manner, only organized nationally affiliated groups of specialists could request special consideration.

6. *Renewal of License and Continuing Education*

Annual renewal of a license or certificate, as the case may be, shall require that every two years evidence of continuing professional educational experiences acceptable to the professional counselor licensing board be submitted.

Comment: Current social and political pressures are increasingly mandating continuing professional education experiences to insure that the licensed professional is maintaining his/her ability in his/her professional practice.

The Commission recognizes that state legislative activity, particularly in relation to medical malpractice problems has already established precedent for the above recommendation. In addition, federal regulations relating to professional care being provided individuals under Medicare, Medicaid, Social Security and other federal programs are requiring increasingly tighter control of the professional individual in his/her practice.

If counseling is to maintain professional status, Professional Counselor Licensing Boards will find it absolutely necessary to support continuing education for counselors. The Commission suggests that the necessity for continuing education be made part of the legislation with the more specific criteria and requirements being developed by the Professional Counselor Licensing Board. The Board is urged to seek assistance from appropriate professional organizations.

7. *Reciprocity*

Comment: Counselor licensing legislation should contain provisions which allow the counselor licensing board to waive any formal examination of a candidate for licensing provided such candidate is licensed or certified in another state, district or territory of the United States. Standards of other such boards must be deemed by the members of this board to be equivalent and like reciprocity extended to holders of licenses issued by this board.

8. *Privileged Communication*

Comment: Professional counselor licensing legislation should include statements which guarantee privileged communication between a licensed counselor and client recognized in the same manner as provided by the laws of that state protecting the relationship and communication between an attorney and a client. Provisions also should be made which guarantee that nothing in the legislation shall be construed to require any such privileged communication to be disclosed.

The Commission fully understands the responsibility which the above recommendation places on the counselor but believes that this protection for the counselee is absolutely necessary to guarantee the viability of the counseling relationship. While true in some states, this may be a difficult privilege to establish by counselor legislation. Field research should be done to develop data on other state practices before legal changes are sought.

The Commission also recognizes the possibility of the rare incident of a counselee divulging an intent to commit a dangerous act but believes that the ability of the licensed counselor to provide adequate help to the client would be severely diminished if the relationship was not held to be privileged. The Commission believes it is essential that the licensed counselor be professionally prepared to deal independently and privately with occasional difficult interpersonal situations.

9. Protection of the Public

9.1 Unlawful Practice

Any person who represents him/herself by the title "licensed professional counselor" or "certified counselor" or engages in the practice of counseling without having first complied with the provisions of this act shall be guilty of a felony and upon conviction thereof shall be punished by a fine of not less than $500 nor more than $1000 for each offense and in addition may be imprisoned for a term not to exceed twelve months. All client fees received for such services shall be refunded.

Comment: Counselor licensing legislation should contain provisions which provide the appropriate sanctions for the unlawful use of the title "Professional Counselor" or "Certified Counselor" and/or the unlawful practice of counseling as defined in the Counselor Licensing Act.

9.2 Power to Petition for Injunctions

The courts of this state are hereby vested with the jurisdiction and power to enjoin the unlawful practice of counseling and/or the false representation as a licensed professional counselor in a proceeding brought by the

Professional Counselor Licensing Board or any members thereof or by any citizen of said state.

Comment: Professional counselor licensing legislation should contain the provisions which allows the Counselor Licensing Board to petition appropriate courts to enjoin the unlawful use of the title "Licensed Professional Counselor" or "Certified Counselor" and/or to enjoin the unlawful practice of counseling as defined in the Counselor Licensing Act.

This provision provides the power to prevent continuing infractions of the Professional Counselor Licensing Act.

9.3   Ethical Violations

Comment: Suspension and/or revocation and/or other sanctions should be provided in case of a licensee being found guilty of violating ethical, moral or professional standards.

10.   *Fees*

Comment: Counselor Licensing Legislation should contain provisions for defining "fees" as used in the counselor licensing act.

The Commission suggests that a "fee for counseling services" be defined as the giving or offering to give money or anything else of value whether paid directly by the person or individual receiving the services or by any other individual or person whether on a pre-paid basis or by any other third party or corporation or insurance company or government funds or by any salary or any other form of compensation received for the practice of counseling.

11.   *Exemptions*

11.1   Exemptions of Other Professions

Comment: Nothing in a counselor licensing act should be construed to limit or prevent the practice of an individual's profession or to restrict a person from doing counseling provided that that person or individual does not hold themselves out to the public by title or description as being a licensed or certified professional counselor under this act, and that person is duly statutorily regulated to practice his/her profession.

The Commission believes that it is both fair and necessary to exempt other professionals or individuals from the control of the professional counselor licensing act when that individual has met the qualifications for licensing in another profession and is licensed in that profession.

11.2   Out-of-State Counselors

Comment: Counselor licensing legislation should contain provisions allowing counselors with out-of-state residence to practice within the state for no more than a total of thirty work days a year provided the counselor is authorized under the laws of his/her state or country of residence to perform these activities and services. Special requests for exemptions to this policy must be approved by the Licensing Board.

The Commission believes that it is reasonable and common practice to allow out-of-state counselors the privilege of limited practice within the state provided those counselors are authorized to do so in their state or country of residence.

11.3   Clergy

Comment: The activities of rabbis, priests, ministers or clergy of any religious denomination or sect should be exempt when their activities are within the scope of the performance of their regular or specialized ministerial duties, and for which no separate charge is made or when such activities are performed, whether with or without charge, for or under auspices or sponsorship of an established and legally recognizable church, denomination or sect, and when the person rendering services remains accountable to the established authority thereof.

11.4   License without Examination

Persons, who, in the judgment of the board, do not meet the appropriate criteria of this act shall be granted a temporary license for a period not to exceed five years during which time the persons must qualify themselves.

Comment: Counselor licensing legislation should contain provisions which allow the counselor licensing board to waive formal examination of candidates for licensure within a specific set time following enactment of the legislation provided such candidate is currently engaged in the practice of counseling in the state at the time of the enactment of the legislation and meets such other reasonable requirements as may be determined by the counselor licensing board.

"Grandfather Clauses" are generally a necessary provision in the enactment of any new legislation regulating a profession. Legislators frequently, if not almost universally, are very sensitive to passing any legislation which would deny a person or individual his or her right to earn a living, particularly if that person or individual has been gainfully employed in that activity prior to the enactment of the legislation. This frequently means that for a period of time following the enactment of the legislation some individuals will be licensed who do not necessarily meet the education, training or supervisory criteria which are required following the grandfathering period.

APPENDIX C

ETHICAL STANDARDS

PREPARED BY THE AMERICAN PERSONNEL AND GUIDANCE ASSOCIATION

PREAMBLE

The American Personnel and Guidance Association is an educational, scientific, and professional organization whose members are dedicated to the enhancement of the worth, dignity, potential, and uniqueness of each individual and thus to the service of society.

The Association recognizes that the role definitions and work settings of its members include a wide variety of academic disciplines, levels of academic preparation, and agency services. This diversity reflects the breadth of the Association's interest and influence. It also poses challenging complexities in efforts to set standards for the performance of members, desired requisite preparation or practice, and supporting social, legal, and ethical controls.

The specification of ethical standards enables the Association to clarify to present and future members and to those served by members the nature of ethical responsibilities held in common by its members.

The existence of such standards serves to stimulate greater concern by members for their own professional functioning and for the conduct of fellow professionals such as counselors, guidance and student personnel workers, and others in the helping professions. As the ethical code of the Association, this document establishes principles which define the ethical behavior of Association members.

SECTION A: GENERAL

1. The member influences the development of the profession by continuous efforts to improve professional practices, teaching, services,

and research. Professional growth is continuous throughout the member's career and is exemplified by the development of a philosophy that explains why and how a member functions in the helping relationship. Members are expected to gather data on their effectiveness and to be guided by the findings.

2. The member has a responsibility both to the individual who is served and to the institution within which the service is performed. The acceptance of employment in an institution implies that the member is in substantial agreement with the general policies and principles of the institution. Therefore the professional activities of the member are also in accord with the objectives of the institution. If, despite concerted efforts, the member cannot reach agreement with the employer as to acceptable standards of conduct that allow for changes in institutional policy conducive to the positive growth and development of counselees, then terminating the affiliation should be seriously considered.

3. Ethical behavior among professional associates, members and non-members, is expected at all times. When information is possessed which raises serious doubt as to the ethical behavior of professional colleagues, whether Association members or not, the member is obligated to take action to attempt to rectify such a condition. Such action shall utilize the institution's channels first and then utilize procedures established by the state, division, or Association.

   The member can take action in a variety of ways: conferring with the individual in question, gathering further information as to the allegation, conferring with local or national ethics committees, and so forth.

4. The member must not seek self-enhancement through expressing evaluations or comparisons that are damaging to others.

5. The member neither claims nor implies professional qualifications exceeding those possessed and is responsible for correcting any misrepresentations of these qualifications by others.

6. In establishing fees for professional services, members should take into consideration the fees charged by other professions delivering comparable services, as well as the ability of the counselee to pay. Members are willing to provide some services for which they receive little or no financial remuneration, or remuneration in food, lodging, and materials. When fees include charges for items other than professional services, that portion of the total which is for the professional services should be clearly indicated.

7. When members provide information to the public or to subordinates, peers, or supervisors, they have a clear responsibility to ensure that the content is accurate, unbiased, and consists of objective, factual data.

8. The member shall make a careful distinction between the offering of counseling services as opposed to public information services. Counseling may be offered only in the context of a reciprocal or face-to-face relationship. Information services may be offered through the media.

9. With regard to professional employment, members are expected to accept only positions that they are prepared to assume and then to comply with established practices of the particular type of employment setting in which they are employed in order to ensure the continuity of services.

SECTION B: COUNSELOR-COUNSELEE RELATIONSHIP

This section refers to practices involving individual and/or group counseling relationships, and it is not intended to be applicable to practices involving administrative relationships.

To the extent that the counselee's choice of action is not imminently self- or other-destructive, the counselee must retain freedom of choice. When the counselee does not have full autonomy for reasons of age, mental incompetency, criminal incarceration, or similar legal restrictions, the member may have to work with others who exercise significant control and direction over the counselee. Under these circumstances the member must apprise counselees of restrictions that may limit their freedom of choice.

1. The member's *primary* obligation is to respect the integrity and promote the welfare of the counselee(s), whether the counselee(s) is (are) assisted individually or in a group relationship. In a group setting, the member-leader is also responsible for protecting individuals from physical and/or psychological trauma resulting from interaction within the group.

2. The counseling relationship and information resulting therefrom must be kept confidential, consistent with the obligations of the member as a professional person. In a group counseling setting the member is expected to set a norm of confidentiality regarding all group participants' disclosures.

3. If an individual is already in a counseling/therapy relationship with another professional person, the member does not begin a counseling relationship without first contacting and receiving the approval of that other professional. If the member discovers that the counselee is in another counseling/therapy relationship after the counseling relationship begins, the member is obligated to gain the consent of the other professional or terminate the relationship, unless the counselee elects to terminate the other relationship.

4. When the counselee's condition indicates that there is clear and imminent danger to the counselee or others, the member is expected to take direct personal action or to inform responsible authorities. Consultation with other professionals should be utilized where possible. Direct interventions, especially the assumption of responsibility for the counselee, should be taken only after careful deliberation. The counselee should be involved in the resumption of responsibility for his actions as quickly as possible.

5. Records of the counseling relationship including interview notes, test data, correspondence, tape recordings, and other documents are to be considered professional information for use in counseling, and they are not part of the public or official records of the institution or agency in which the counselor is employed. Revelation to others of counseling material should occur only upon the express consent of the counselee.

6. Use of data derived from a counseling relationship for purposes of counselor training or research shall be confined to content that can be sufficiently disguised to ensure full protection of the identity of the counselee involved.

7. Counselees shall be informed of the conditions under which they may receive counseling assistance at or before the time when the counseling relationship is entered. This is particularly so when conditions exist of which the counselee would be unaware. In individual and group situations, particularly those oriented to self-understanding or growth, the member-leader is obligated to make clear the purposes, goals, techniques, rules of procedure, and limitations that may affect the continuance of the relationship.

8. The member has the responsibility to screen prospective group participants, especially when the emphasis is on self-understanding and growth through self-disclosure. The member should maintain an awareness of the group participants' compatibility throughout the life of the group.

9. The member reserves the right to consult with any other professionally competent person about a counselee. In choosing a consultant, the member avoids placing the consultant in a conflict of interest situation that would preclude the consultant's being a proper party to the member's efforts to help the counselee.

10. If the member is unable to be of professional assistance to the counselee, the member avoids initiating the counseling relationship or the member terminates it. In either event, the member is obligated to refer the counselee to an appropriate specialist. (It is incumbent upon the member to be knowledgable about referral resources so that a satisfactory referral can be initiated.) In the event the counselee de-

clines the suggested referral, the member is not obligated to continue the relationship.

11. When the member learns from counseling relationships of conditions that are likely to harm others, the member should report *the condition* to the responsible authority. This should be done in such a manner as to conceal the identity of the counselee.

12. When the member has other relationships, particularly of an administrative, supervisory, and/or evaluative nature, with an individual seeking counseling services, the member should not serve as the counselor but should refer the individual to another professional. Only in instances where such an alternative is unavailable and where the individual's condition definitely warrants counseling intervention should the member enter into and/or maintain a counseling relationship.

13. All experimental methods of treatment must be clearly indicated to prospective recipients, and safety precautions are to be adhered to by the member.

14. When the member is engaged in short-term group treatment/training programs, e.g., marathons and other encounter-type or growth groups, the member ensures that there is professional assistance available during and following the group experience.

15. Should the member be engaged in a work setting that calls for any variation from the above statements, the member is obligated to consult with other professionals whenever possible to consider justifiable alternatives. The variations that may be necessary should be clearly communicated to other professionals and prospective counselees.

SECTION C: MEASUREMENT AND EVALUATION

The primary purpose of educational and psychological testing is to provide descriptive measures that are objective and interpretable in either comparative or absolute terms. The member must recognize the need to interpret the statements that follow as applying to the whole range of appraisal techniques including tests and nontest data. Test results constitute only one of a variety of pertinent sources of information for personnel, guidance, and counseling decisions.

1. It is the member's responsibility to provide adequate orientation or information to the examinee(s) prior to and following the test administration so that the results of testing may be placed in proper perspective with other relevant factors. In so doing, the member must recognize the effects of socioeconomic, ethnic, and cultural factors on test scores. It is the member's professional responsibility to use additional unvalidated information cautiously in modifying interpretation of the test results.

2. In selecting tests for use in a given situation or with a particular counselee, the member must consider carefully the specific validity, reliability, and appropriateness of the test(s). "General" validity, reliability, and the like may be questioned legally as well as ethically when tests are used for vocational and educational selection, placement, or counseling.

3. When making any statements to the public about tests and testing, the member is expected to give accurate information and to avoid false claims or misconceptions. Special efforts are often required to avoid unwarranted connotations of such terms as IQ and grade equivalent scores.

4. Different tests demand different levels of competence for administration, scoring, and interpretation. Members have a responsibility to recognize the limits of their competence and to perform only those functions for which they are prepared.

5. Tests should be administered under the same conditions that were established in their standardization. When tests are not administered under standard conditions or when unusual behavior or irregularities occur during the testing session, those conditions should be noted and the results designated as invalid or of questionable validity. Unsupervised or inadequately supervised test-taking, such as the use of tests through the mails, is considered unethical. On the other hand, the use of instruments that are so designed or standardized to be self-administered and self-scored, such as interest inventories, is to be encouraged.

6. The meaningfulness of test results used in personnel, guidance, and counseling functions generally depends on the examinee's unfamiliarity with the specific items on the test. Any prior coaching or dissemination of the test materials can invalidate test results. Therefore, test security is one of the professional obligations of the member. Conditions that produce most favorable test results should be made known to the examinee.

7. The purpose of testing and the explicit use of the results should be made known to the examinee prior to testing. The counselor has a responsibility to ensure that instrument limitations are not exceeded and that periodic review and/or retesting are made to prevent counselee stereotyping.

8. The examinee's welfare and explicit prior understanding should be the criteria for determining the recipients of the test results. The member is obligated to see that adequate interpretation accompanies any release of individual or group test data. The interpretation of test data should be related to the examinee's particular concerns.

9. The member is expected to be cautious when interpreting the results of research instruments possessing insufficient technical data. The

specific purposes for the use of such instruments must be stated explicitly to examinees.

10. The member must proceed with extreme caution when attempting to evaluate and interpret the performance of minority group members or other persons who are not represented in the norm group on which the instrument was standardized.

11. The member is obligated to guard against the appropriation, reproduction, or modifications of published tests or parts thereof without the express permission and adequate recognition of the original author or publisher.

12. Regarding the preparation, publication, and distribution of tests, reference should be made to:

   a. *Standards for Educational and Psychological Tests and Manuals*, revised edition, 1973, published by the American Psychological Association on behalf of itself, the American Educational Research Association, and the National Council on Measurement in Education.

   b. "The Responsible Use of Tests: A Position Paper of AMEG, APGA, and NCME," published in *Measurement and Evaluation in Guidance* Vol. 5, No. 2, July 1972, pp. 385–388.

SECTION D: RESEARCH AND PUBLICATION

1. Current American Psychological Association guidelines on research with human subjects shall be adhered to (*Ethical Principles in the Conduct of Research with Human Participants*. Washington, D.C.: American Psychological Association, Inc., 1973).

2. In planning any research activity dealing with human subjects, the member is expected to be aware of and responsive to all pertinent ethical principles and to ensure that the research problem, design, and execution are in full compliance with them.

3. Responsibility for ethical research practice lies with the principal researcher, while others involved in the research activities share ethical obligation and full responsibility for their own actions.

4. In research with human subjects, researchers are responsible for their subjects' welfare throughout the experiment, and they must take all reasonable precautions to avoid causing injurious psychological, physical, or social effects on their subjects.

5. It is expected that all research subjects be informed of the purpose of the study except when withholding information or providing misinformation to them is essential to the investigation. In such research, the member is responsible for corrective action as soon as possible following the research.

6. Participation in research is expected to be voluntary. Involuntary participation is appropriate only when it can be demonstrated that participation will have no harmful effects on subjects.

7. When reporting research results, explicit mention must be made of all variables and conditions known to the investigator that might affect the outcome of the investigation or the interpretation of the data.
8. The member is responsible for conducting and reporting investigations in a manner that minimizes the possibility that results will be misleading.
9. The member has an obligation to make available sufficient original research data to qualified others who may wish to replicate the study.
10. When supplying data, aiding in the research of another person, reporting research results, or in making original data available, due care must be taken to disguise the identity of the subjects in the absence of specific authorization from such subjects to do otherwise.
11. When conducting and reporting research, the member is expected to be familiar with and to give recognition to previous work on the topic, as well as to observe all copyright laws and follow the principle of giving full credit to all to whom credit is due.
12. The member has the obligation to give due credit through joint authorship, acknowledgement, footnote statements, or other appropriate means to those who have contributed significantly to the research, in accordance with such contributions.
13. The member is expected to communicate to other members the results of any research judged to be of professional or scientific value. Results reflecting unfavorably on institutions, programs, services, or vested interests should not be withheld for such reasons.
14. If members agree to cooperate with another individual in research and/or publication, they incur an obligation to cooperate as promised in terms of punctuality of performance and with full regard to the completeness and accuracy of the information provided.

SECTION E: CONSULTING AND PRIVATE PRACTICE

Consulting refers to a voluntary relationship between a professional helper and help-needing social unity (industry, business, school, college, etc.) in which the consultant is attempting to give help to the client in the solution of some current or potential problem. When "client" is used in this section it refers to an individual, group, or organization served by the consultant. (This definition of "consulting" is adapted from "Dimensions of the Consultant's Job" by Ronald Lippitt, *Journal of Social Issues*, Vol. 15, No. 2, 1959.)

1. Members who act as consultants must have a high degree of self-awareness of their own values and needs in entering helping relationships that involve change in social units.
2. There should be understanding and agreement between consultant and client as to the task, the directions or goals, and the function of the consultant.

3. Members are expected to accept only those consulting roles for which they possess or have access to the necessary skills and resources for giving the kind of help that is needed.

4. The consulting relationship is defined as being one in which the client's adaptability and growth toward self-direction are encouraged and cultivated. For this reason, the consultant is obligated to maintain consistently the role of a consultant and to avoid becoming a decision maker for the client.

5. In announcing one's availability for professional services as a consultant, the member follows professional rather than commercial standards in describing services with accuracy, dignity, and caution.

6. For private practice in testing, counseling, or consulting, all ethical principles defined in this document are pertinent. In addition, any individual, agency, or institution offering educational, personal, or vocational counseling should meet the standards of the International Association of Counseling Services, Inc.

7. The member is expected to refuse a private fee or other remuneration for consultation with persons who are entitled to these services through the member's employing institution or agency. The policies of a particular agency may make explicit provisions for private practice with agency counselees by members of its staff. In such instances, the counselees must be apprised of other options open to them should they seek private counseling services.

8. It is unethical to use one's institutional affiliation to recruit counselees for one's private practice.

SECTION F: PERSONNEL ADMINISTRATION

It is recognized that most members are employed in public or quasi-public institutions. The functioning of a member within an institution must contribute to the goals of the institution and vice versa if either is to accomplish their respective goals or objectives. It is therefore essential that the member and the institution function in ways to: (a) make the institution's goals explicit and public; (b) make the member's contribution to institutional goals specific; and (c) foster mutual accountability for goal achievement.

To accomplish these objectives it is recognized that the member and the employer must share responsibilities in the formulation and implementation of personnel policies.

1. Members should define and describe the parameters and levels of their professional competency.

2. Members should establish interpersonal relations and working agreements with supervisors and subordinates regarding counseling or clinical relationships, confidentiality, distinction between public

and private material, maintenance and dissemination of recorded information, work load, and accountability. Working agreements in each instance should be specified and made known to those concerned.

3. Members are responsible for alerting their employers to conditions that may be potentially disruptive or damaging.
4. Members are responsible for informing employers of conditions that may limit their effectiveness.
5. Members are expected to submit regularly to review and evaluation.
6. Members are responsible for in-service development of self and/or staff.
7. Members are responsible for informing their staff of goals and programs.
8. Members are responsible for providing personnel practices that guarantee and enhance the rights and welfare of each recipient of their service.
9. Members are expected to select competent persons and assign responsibilities compatible with their skills and experiences.

SECTION G: PREPARATION STANDARDS

Members who are responsible for training others should be guided by the preparation standards of the Association and relevant division(s). The member who functions in the capacity of trainer assumes unique ethical responsibilities that frequently go beyond that of the member who does not function in a training capacity. These ethical responsibilities are outlined as follows:

1. Members are expected to orient trainees to program expectations, basic skills development, and employment prospects prior to admission to the program.
2. Members in charge of training are expected to establish programs that integrate academic study and supervised practice.
3. Members are expected to establish a program directed toward developing the trainees' skills, knowledge, and self-understanding, stated whenever possible in competency or performance terms.
4. Members are expected to identify the level of competency of their trainees. These levels of competency should accommodate the paraprofessional as well as the professional.
5. Members, through continual trainee evaluation and appraisal, are expected to be aware of the personal limitations of the trainee that might impede future performance. The trainer has the responsibility of not only assisting the trainee in securing remedial assistance, but also screening from the program those trainees who are unable to provide competent services.

6. Members are expected to provide a program that includes training in research commensurate with levels of role functioning. Paraprofessional and technician-level personnel should be trained as consumers of research. In addition, these personnel should learn how to evaluate their own and their program effectiveness. Advanced graduate training, especially at the doctoral level, should include preparation for original research by the member.

7. Members are expected to make trainees aware of the ethical responsibilities and standards of the profession.

8. Training programs are expected to encourage trainees to value the ideals of service to individuals and to society. In this regard, direct financial remuneration or lack thereof should not influence the quality of service rendered. Monetary considerations should not be allowed to overshadow professional and humanitarian needs.

9. Members responsible for training are expected to be skilled as teachers and practitioners.

10. Members are expected to present thoroughly varied theoretical positions so that trainees may make comparisons and have the opportunity to select a position.

11. Members are obligated to develop clear policies within their training institution regarding field placement and the roles of the trainee and the trainer in such placements.

12. Members are expected to ensure that forms of training focusing on self-understanding or growth are voluntary, or if required as part of the training program, are made known to prospective trainees prior to entering the program. When the training program offers a growth experience with an emphasis on self-disclosure or other relatively intimate or personal involvement, the member should have no administrative, supervisory, or evaluative authority regarding the participant.

13. Members are obligated to conduct a training program in keeping with the most current guidelines of the American Personnel and Guidance Association and its various divisions.

APPENDIX D

NATIONAL DIVISIONS OF
THE AMERICAN PERSONNEL AND
GUIDANCE ASSOCIATION

APGA has 12 special interest divisions that members may join. Each division publishes a journal and many publish newsletters. The divisions are described below:

Division 1: *American College Personnel Association* (ACPA)

ACPA is the collective voice of the college student profession—teachers, counselors, deans, department heads, researchers. It meets the demands of individual students who seek help to make their college experience personally significant. Publication: The Journal of College Student Personnel. Regular voting membership is open to APGA members employed in higher education with responsibilities in student personnel work including teaching, administration, counseling and/or research. Student voting membership is open to graduate students.

Division 2: *Association for Counselor Education and Supervision* (ACES)

ACES emphasizes the need for highly skilled guidance and personnel workers in efforts to improve counselor education and supervision at all levels of education, rehabilitation and employment settings. Publication: Counselor Education and Supervision; ACES Newsletter. Regular voting membership open to individuals in counselor education and supervisory positions. Applicants for regular membership must be either: a recipient of the doctoral degree based in part upon course work and providing preparation for performing duties indicated above; a recipient of a master's degree with the same appropriate course work and at least three years' employment in counseling and personnel activities.

Division 3: *National Vocational Guidance Association* (NVGA)

NVGA is concerned with the life-long use of people's knowledge, abilities and skills. NVGA seeks to gain recognition and status for the profession of counseling and to improve skills, systems and standards of service in counseling. Publications: The Vocational Guidance Quarterly; NVGA Newsletter. Regular voting membership requires professional employment in guidance or personnel work and a bachelor's degree.

Division 4: *Association for Humanistic Education and Development* (AHEAD) (formerly SPATE)

AHEAD seeks to provide a forum for the exchange of information about humanistically oriented educational practices and to promote changes in education which reflect the growing body of knowledge about human development and potential. Publication: The Humanist Educator. Regular voting membership is open to any person committed to the implementation of humanism whose primary responsibilities are in the field of education.

Division 5: *American School Counselor Association* (ASCA)

ASCA works to define and advance the role of the school counselor at all educational levels, elementary through post-secondary, and to achieve national recognition for this important function in education. Publications: The School Counselor; Elementary School Guidance and Counseling; ASCA Newsletter. Regular voting membership is open to those with a bachelor's degree, plus 15 more semester hours of graduate credit in courses pertinent to school guidance, counseling and testing, and who devote at least half their time to counseling and/or other guidance activities, or who work in a related field or institution. Professional voting, officeholding membership is available to persons with a master's degree of 30 or more semester hours of graduate credit in counseling, guidance and testing courses, who have had three years' experience, are now employed at least half-time in school guidance and counseling, and hold a valid certificate in school counseling or guidance if available in the state where employed.

Division 6: *American Rehabilitation Counseling Association* (ARCA)

The rehabilitation counselor works with physically, mentally or emotionally handicapped people. ARCA links the practitioner with a nationwide community of rehabilitation counselors. Publication: Rehabilitation Counseling Bulletin. Associate voting membership requires a bachelor's degree and at least half-time employment in some areas of rehabilitation counseling. Professional voting membership is open to those with a master's degree, and who have three years' experience in and who now devote at least half-time to some area of rehabilitation counseling.

Division 7: *Association for Measurement and Evaluation in Guidance* (AMEG)

AMEG members plan, administer and conduct testing programs; provide test scoring services; interpret and use test results; and develop evaluation instruments. They also teach college-level courses or conduct research in this area of interest. Publications: Measurement and Evaluation in Guidance; AMEG Newsnotes. Regular voting membership is open to those with a doctoral or master's degree, who have completed at least two courses in measurement or in closely related subjects such as statistics or research design. They must also have had at least one year of professional experience in measurement, evaluation or research in personnel and guidance.

Division 8: *National Employment Counselors Association* (NECA)

NECA offers professional leadership to people who counsel in an employment setting or to those employed in related areas of counselor education, research, administration or supervision in business and industry, colleges and universities and federal and state governments. Publication: Journal of Employment Counseling. Regular voting members are required to have a bachelor's degree and be employed in employment counseling settings. Professional voting membership is open to persons with a master's degree and five years' full-time experience or a doctoral degree and three years' full-time experience.

Division 9: *Association for Non-White Concerns in Personnel and Guidance* (ANWC)

By seeking to eliminate prejudice and discrimination and by defending those human and civil rights which have been secured by law, ANWC is dedicated to the insurance of equality as regards the treatment, advancement, qualification and status of non-white individuals in personnel and guidance work. ANWC programs emphasize all charitable, scientific and educational activities which are designed to assist and further the interests of non-whites. Association members represent all personnel and guidance settings. Publications: Journal of Non-White Concerns in Personnel and Guidance, ANWC Newsletter. Regular voting membership is open to all APGA members involved in personnel and guidance work. Associate nonvoting membership is open to persons interested in the general aims and purposes of the association.

Division 10: *National Catholic Guidance Conference* (NCGC)

Through a common interest in promoting counseling and guidance services in parochial and nonpublic schools, NCGC seeks to integrate values, theological and philosophical considerations and principles with current student-pupil personnel practices and to share this knowledge with colleagues in Catholic, private and public education. Publication:

Counseling and Values. Regular voting membership is open to persons who are engaged in or interested in guidance, counseling, personnel work or allied fields, and who are also interested in the purposes of the conference.

Division 11: *Association for Specialists in Group Work* (ASGW)

This is the division for workers in education, mental health, physical health, offender rehabilitation, religion and the human potential movement who share a common interest in group work. ASGW seeks to assist and further the interests of children, youth and adults by seeking to provide effective services through the group medium to prevent problems, to promote maximum development and to remediate disabling behaviors. Publication: Together.

Division 12: *Public Offender Counselor Association* (POCA)

POCA is concerned with the delivery of effective counseling services to public offenders and is committed to providing leadership in developing public offender counseling as a profession. The division will work to improve the standards of service to offenders and to improve national awareness of public offender counseling through information activities. Membership is open to offender counselors and to other professionals interested in this field. A division publication is planned.

APPENDIX E

CODE OF ETHICS

PREPARED BY THE AMERICAN SCHOOL COUNSELOR ASSOCIATION

Responsibilities of the school counselor stem from these basic premises and basic tenets in the counseling process.

A. Each person has the right to dignity as a human being
   1. without regard to race, sex, religion, color, socio-economic status.
   2. without regard to the nature and results of behavior, beliefs and inherent characteristics.

B. Each person has the right to individual self-development.

C. Each person has the right to self-direction and responsibility for making decisions.

D. The school counselor, equipped with professional competency, an understanding of the behavioral sciences and philosophical orientation to school and community, performs a unique, distinctive and highly specialized service within the context of the education purpose and structure of the school system. Performance of this rests upon acquired techniques and informed judgment which is an integral part of counseling. Punitive action is not a part of the counseling process. The school counselor shall use these skills in endeavoring constantly to insure that the counselee has the afore-mentioned rights and a reasonable amount of the counselor's time.

E. The ethical conduct of the school counselors will be consistent with the state regulations.

F. The school counselor may share information gained in the counseling process for essential consultation with those appropriate persons specifically concerned with the counselee. Confidential information may be released only with consent of the individual except when required by court order.

I. Principal responsibilities of the School Counselor to pupils

A. The school counselor
   1. has a principal obligation and loyalty to respect each person as an unique individual and to encourage that which permits individual growth and development.
   2. must not impose consciously his attitudes and values on the counselee though he is not obligated to keep his attitudes and values from being known.
   3. should respect at all times the confidences of the counselee; should the counselee's condition be such as to endanger the health, welfare, and/or safety of self or others, the counselor is expected to report this fact to an appropriate responsible person.
   4. shall be knowledgeable about the strengths and limitations of tests; will share and interpret test information with the counselee in an accurate, objective and understandable manner to assist the counselee in self-evaluation.
   5. shall assist the counselee in understanding the counseling process in order to insure that the persons counseled understand how information obtained in conferences with the counselor may be used.

II. Principal responsibilities of the School Counselor to parents

A. The school counselor
   1. shall work with parents so as to enhance the development of the counselee.
   2. shall treat information received from the parents of a counselee in a confidential manner.
   3. shall share, communicate and interpret pertinent data, and the counselee's academic progress, with his parents.
   4. shall share information about the counselee only with those persons properly authorized to receive this information.

III. Principal responsibilities of the School Counselor to faculty, administration and colleagues

A. The school counselor
   1. shall use discretion, within legal limits and requirements of the state, in releasing personal information about a counselee to maintain the confidences of the counselee.

2. shall contribute pertinent data to cumulative records and make it accessible to professional staff (except personal factors and problems which are highly confidential in nature).
3. shall cooperate with colleagues by making available as soon as possible requested reports which are accurate, objective, meaningful and concise.
4. shall cooperate with other pupil personnel workers by sharing information and/or obtaining recommendations which would benefit the counselee.
5. may share confidential information when working with the same counselee, with the counselee's knowledge and permission.
6. must maintain confidentiality even though others may have the same knowledge.
7. shall maintain high professional integrity regarding fellow workers when assisting in problem areas related to actions, attitudes and competencies of faculty or colleagues.

IV. *Principal responsibilities of the School Counselor to* school and community

A. The school counselor
1. shall support and protect the educational program against any infringement which indicates that it is not to the best interest of the counselee or program.
2. must assume responsibility in delineating his role and function, in developing educational procedure and program, and in assisting administration to assess accountability.
3. shall recommend to the administration any curricular changes necessary in meeting valid educational needs in the community.
4. shall work cooperatively with agencies, organizations and individuals in school and community which are interested in welfare of youth.
5. shall, with appropriate release, supply accurate information according to his professional judgment to community agencies, places of employment and institutions of higher learning.
6. should be knowledgeable on policies, laws and regulations as they relate to the community, and use educational facilities accordingly.
7. shall maintain open communication lines in all areas pertinent to the best interest of counselees.
8. shall not accept remuneration beyond contractual salary for counseling any pupil within the school district. The counselor

shall not promote or direct counselees into counseling or educational programs which would result in remuneration to the counselor.

9. shall delineate in advance his responsibilities in case of any confrontation and have an agreement which is supported by the administration and the bargaining agency.

V. *Principal responsibilities of the School Counselor to* self

A. The school counselor
   1. should continue to grow professionally by
      a. attending professional meetings.
      b. actively participating in professional organizations.
      c. being involved in research.
      d. keeping abreast of changes and new trends in the profession and showing a willingness to accept those which have proved to be effective.
   2. should be aware of and function within the boundaries of his professional competency.
   3. should see that his role is defined in mutual agreement among the employer, students to be served, and the counselor. Furthermore, this role should be continuously clarified to students, staff, parents and community.

VI. *Principal responsibilities of the School Counselor to the* profession

A. The school counselor
   1. should be cognizant of the developments in his profession and be an active contributing participant in his professional association—local, state and national.
   2. shall conduct himself in a responsible manner and participate in developing policies concerning guidance.
   3. should do research which will contribute to professional and personal growth as well as determine professional effectiveness.
   4. shall under no circumstances undertake any group encounter or sensitivity sessions, unless he has sufficient professional training.
   5. shall, in addition to being aware of unprofessional practices, also be accountable for taking appropriate action to eliminate these practices.

Accepted by the ASCA Governing Board in October 1972.

GLOSSARY

Accountability: Being responsible for achieving specified results. It involves the utilization of facilities, resources, and personnel to attain pre-established goals.

Accurate Empathy: See *Empathy*.

Affect, Affective, Affective Education: *Affect* refers to feeling and emotions as contrasted with cognition, which is thinking, knowing, and reasoning. *Affective education* deals with the emotional aspects of education, i.e., expressing, recognizing, and managing emotions. For example, an affective educational program may aim to help pupils feel good about themselves and express pleasure.

Assertiveness Training: Training or teaching, usually in groups, that helps individuals recognize their own points-of-view, stand up for themselves, and take positions of equality in dealing with others. Training sessions teach individuals to assert themselves, but not in a hostile, aggressive, or dominating way.

Attending Behavior: Behavior in which an individual pays close attention to verbal and non-verbal communication of another person. It may involve the physical position of the listener, eye contact, or a demonstrated understanding of the feeling expressed or implied.

Baseline, Baseline Data, Base Rate: Data that illustrate performance, attitudes, or characteristics at a particular time, usually before a change is made in a guidance program or technique. To detect changes, later assessments may be compared with baseline data. For example, a baseline of discipline problems referred to the principal could be established prior to instituting a program to improve human relations.

Behavioral Counseling: An approach in which specific behavioral objectives are established by counselor and counselee and reinforcement-type techniques are used to achieve them.

Behavior Modification: Techniques that use learning theories such as operant conditioning to change behavior. Usually, there are specific targets, such as fear of talking in class or information-seeking. Techniques are used in individual and group counseling and in the classroom setting.

Biofeedback: Techniques by which the individual, with the help of technological equipment, obtains immediate feedback on his or her involuntary physiological processes, e.g., muscle tension, heart beat. The objective is self-regulation.

Career Education: An approach to education in which elements like career awareness, exploration, choice, preparation, entry, or progress are the central, unifying theme.

Career Maturity: The individual's degree of success with career developmental tasks he or she faces. For example, the graduating high school pupil should have acquired information about educational or occupational options.

Classical Conditioning: See *Conditioning*.

Client-Centered Counseling: An approach based on the proposition that a positive growth force motivates the counselee. Counselor actions, attitudes, and relationships to free this force from conflicts and inhibitions lead to productive and satisfying behavior.

Cognitive: Having to do with thinking and knowing, e.g., knowledge of mathematics or requirements for entry into an occupation.

Concreteness: The counselor-facilitated condition in which the counselee deals with specific feelings and experiences instead of generalities. See also *Core Facilitative Conditions*.

Conditioning: A learning theory principle involving drive, response, and reward. A change in the individual is induced by either classical or operant techniques. In classical conditioning, a previously neutral stimulus becomes powerful enough to elicit a response. For example, if candy is given when a child follows the leader's previously ignored directions, the directions themselves may eventually elicit the response. The drive is the child's hunger for candy.

Operant conditioning, on the other hand, involves an individual being rewarded for a response. Suppose the child wants the candy but does not know what type of behavior will obtain it. Following directions, disruptive behavior, and other types of behavior may be tried until one is effective. The rewarded behavior will most likely be adopted.

Congruence: Agreement between feelings and behavior. Awareness of feelings is essential.

Consulting, Consultation: A process by which the counselor helps the counselee aid a third person. Newer uses of the concept involve teaching and training. See *Giving Counseling Away*.

Contingency, Contingency Managers: The systematic application of learning principles with individuals to reward desired behavior and discourage disruptive behavior. The manager keeps a record of behavior and provides rewards when appropriate.

Core Facilitative Conditions: The conditions generally considered essential for counselee progress in counseling. This concept was first suggested by Carl Rogers and then further developed and incorporated into scales by Carkhuff and Truax. The conditions include empathy, positive regard, and congruence. Additional conditions such as immediacy and concreteness have been identified as important helping characteristics. See *Concreteness, Congruence, Empathy, Genuineness,* and *Immediacy.*

Criterion Reference: Measurement in which the individual's performance is compared with a standard rather than scores of other performances as in norm referenced techniques. Success is measured in mastery of a prescribed amount of material rather than by comparison to others' accomplishments.

Decision-Making Counseling: Emphasizes a systematic approach to decision-making, typically incorporating concepts from decision theory.

Desensitization: The use of learning theory principles to remove or decrease a response of fear or anxiety. The unwanted response is replaced by one of relaxation. *Systematic desensitization* has the same meaning.

Development Counseling: An approach based on the point-of-view that individuals must deal with a series of tasks as they grow; therefore, effective behavior can be facilitated by counseling that helps individuals accomplish these developmental tasks.

Discriminant Bridge: See *Norm Bridge.*

Eclectic Counseling: An approach in which there is selective use of concepts and techniques from other counseling approaches.

Empathy: A characteristic of the helping relationship in which the counselor understands the feelings of the counselee and conveys this. The prefix *accurate* is sometimes used to emphasize that the counselor's perceptions of the counselee's emotions are correct.

Existential Counseling: More a philosophy of counseling than a systematic approach, it emphasizes the sharing of the counselee's world by the counselor, with both engaging in the process of becoming.

Exploration of Feelings: Activities in which the focus is on the feelings of participants. (For example, "How do you feel when you are happy? How does it make you feel to receive a compliment?")

Facilitative: Helping another accomplish something. Facilitative conditioning in counseling helps the counselee grow and resolve problems. See *Core Facilitative Conditions* for specific elements.

Feedback: A technique used in counseling and guidance in which one person is told how he or she appears to others, i.e., is given feedback. For example, "When you say that to me, it makes me feel good."

F test: A statistical test used to determine the likelihood of an observed distribution (e.g., attitudes about the value accorded career information by persons who use career centers differently) occurring by chance. In the preceding example, if the F test results were not significant, it could be concluded that visits to an information center were not related to an increased appreciation of the value of career information.

Genuineness: The counselor's honest presentation of himself or herself in the helping relationship, free of roles and facades.

Gestalt Therapy: A type of helping that emphasizes growth through openness to experience and willingness to interact with others. Motivating the counselee to deal with the here-and-now is a major feature.

Giving Counseling Away: Teaching others to use helping techniques which usually are the special devices of counselors. For example, teachers may be taught how to respond to students' feelings.

Hypnosis: Inducing in the individual a relaxed state of heightened suggestibility to the hypnotist.

Immediacy: A characteristic of counseling in which attention is on events and experiences of the moment.

Interpretation: A counseling technique in which the counselor compiles data about the counselee to explain causes of problems such as anxiety by using principles of personality development and counseling.

Magic Circle: A technique used primarily in elementary school. A group of pupils, seated in a circle, discuss topics of personal interest to develop awareness of feelings, build self-confidence, and learn how to interact with others.

Micro Counseling: A technique for building counseling skills in which specific skills are isolated and each is practiced until proficiency is reached. For example, attending behavior may be the desired skill, and bodily position may be one aspect that is practiced.

Modeling: A guidance procedure in which specific behavior of an individual, usually the counselor, is imitated by others (e.g., demonstrating how to discuss feelings or how to take turns in making comments). Peer models are frequently used. *Model reinforcement* and *social modeling* have the same meaning.

Model Reinforcement: See *Modeling*.

Modular Scheduling: A system for scheduling pupils in which the basic unit is usually 15 minutes. Modules rather than traditional class periods are used to permit greater flexibility.

Norm Bridge: A way of conveying test and inventory results to the individual. Others are the *regression bridge* and the *discriminant bridge*. In the *norm bridge*, scores that the individual makes are compared with those of a norm group (e.g., high school seniors) to determine relative standing. In the *regression bridge*, scores are used to predict performance (e.g., freshman grades). In the *discriminant bridge*, scores are used to determine the group which the individual most closely resembles. The terms were made popular by Leo Goldman in his discussions of test interpretation.

Norm Groups: See *Norms*.

Norm Reference: See *Norms*.

Norms: The scores of a specific group to whom a test has been given to determine levels of performance. The scores are arranged from low to high and serve as a basis of comparison to judge the performance of others taking the test. The norm group represents an identifiable group, e.g., high school seniors. A norm referenced measurement is one in which relative standing is based on comparison of the individual's scores with those of the norm group.

.001, .01 Levels: See *Significance Level*.

Operant Conditioning: See *Conditioning*.

Paraprofessionals: Individuals who have received less than the professional level of guidance training, but perform specific guidance functions under the supervision of a counselor.

Peer Counseling: Pupils serve as helpers to other pupils. They usually have been trained in a particular guidance function, e.g., leading discussion groups. Peer counselors are supervised by a counselor. The term *peer facilitator* denotes the same role.

Peer Facilitator: See *Peer Counseling*.

Percentiles: A system for organizing test results or other similar data in which a group of scores is divided into hundredths. Thus, if a pupil scores in the 75th percentile, the pupil's scores exceed the scores of 75 percent of those with whom the pupil is compared.

Positive Regard: One of the *core facilitative conditions* involving positive feelings toward the counselee and communication of these feelings.

Positive Reinforcement: See *Reinforcement-Type Activities*.

Practical Significance: Results are of practical value. Even though results may be statistically significant (see *Significance Level*), they may not have practical applicability. For example, a new guidance program may increase self-understanding, but the gain may be so slight that even though statistically significant, the new procedure cannot be justified in terms of cost and time required.

Preventative: A guidance approach with an emphasis on prevention of problems (e.g., preparing pupils to successfully cope with anticipated tasks). Often, changes may also be made in the environment to eliminate causes of problems.

Primal Therapy: Therapy based on the assumption that emotional problems are caused by infantile traumas, and the individual must reexperience the pain to eliminate the problem. In both individual and group sessions, screaming is a major method of releasing tension.

Psychoanalytic Therapy: An approach based on Freudian personality theory postulating biologically based stages of development and a personality structure that includes the ego, super-ego, and id.

Psychological Education: The use of one or more techniques to help individuals in self-understanding, effective communication, and expression of feelings. *Education* implies a planned program as part of the regular curriculum. The psychological educator, usually a counselor, is often the "teacher" in this type of program.

Rational Emotive Therapy (R.E.T.): An approach to counseling that attributes problems of the individual to irrational ideas that have become the basis of behavior.

Ratios: Test scores involving the relation of one quantity to another, e.g., some I.Q. scores are the relation of mental age to chronological age.

Reality Therapy (R.T.): An approach to counseling that emphasizes responsibility for one's own actions. An important strategy is helping the counselee learn more productive patterns of behavior.

Reflect: See *Reflection of Feeling.*

Reflection of Feelings: A counselor response in which awareness of the counselee's emotions is communicated. The counselee's feelings may be apparent or may be inferred by the counselor. The response may be verbal or non-verbal. The aim is to show the counselee that the counselor is aware of the feeling he or she is experiencing.

Regression Bridge: See *Norm Bridge.*

Reinforced: See *Reinforcement-Type Activities.*

Reinforcement: The process by which some behavior or attitude of the individual is strengthened by presentation of a reinforcer, i.e., a reward or satisfier. Negative reinforcement uses a stimulus that leads to an escape response.

Reinforcement-Type Activities: Activities that tend to strengthen a response by providing a reward, e.g., praise, material items, privileges. Both operant and classical conditioning use these types of activities. In positive reinforcement the rewards are designed to promote a specified behavior; negative reinforcement aim to inhibit behavior. Reinforcement can be arranged in a schedule in which specific rewards are given after designated periods of desirable behavior. See also *Conditioning* and *Reinforcement.*

Reliablity: A characteristic of tests, usually indicated by a correlation coefficient, that shows consistency of scores. Several types are used, e.g., giving two forms of the same test and comparing scores.

Scores: Quantitative data indicating test or inventory results. Raw scores are usually a simple count of items responded to correctly. It is necessary to compare them with a standard to determine the level of performance. See also *Norm Reference* and *Criterion Reference.*

Self-Actualization: Maslow's concept of an individual's achievement of his or her greatest potential in line with the ideals of humanity.

Self-Congruence: See *Congruence.*

Significance Level: A statistical expression of confidence that results are not chance differences. For example, significant at .05 level means that the results could have been obtained by chance 5 times in 100. Significance at the .01 level means that results could have been obtained by chance 1 time in 100.

Social Modeling, Social Models: See *Modeling.*

Sociometric, Sociometric Ratings: Measurements of social preferences. Respondents indicate choices and rejections of other individuals for various activities, tasks, or roles. For example, a question might be, "Choose three persons in the classroom with whom you would like to work on a project."

Staff Development: The process of improving a guidance staff's effectiveness. It may involve personal or professional growth, or a combination of both. Staff development is often conducted as in-service education.

Staffing Conference: A technique which involves a meeting of those concerned with the status and development of a pupil. Data are reviewed, diagnoses formulated, and plans developed to help the individual. The counselor is often the initiator and leader of the meeting.

Systematic Desensitization: See *Desensitization.*

Time-Out Procedure, Time-Outs: A guidance technique frequently used in behavior modification. The pupil is required to leave the room or other setting for a brief period because of undesirable behavior.

Token Economy: A procedure in which rewards (tokens) are given for desired behavior. Tokens may then be used to purchase items or privileges.

Trait-Factor Counseling: An approach that makes extensive use of measurement of psychological traits, enabling the counselee to compare personal attributes with requirements of work, education, or other environments.

Transactional Analysis (T.A.): The use of transactions between persons to clarify the roles they play and help them move toward more adult relationships.

Transcendental Meditation: Meditation in which the silent repetition of one word empties the mind of thoughts and relaxes the autonomic nervous system. Meditation is practiced at regular intervals, usually twice each day.

Validity: The degree to which an instrument successfully measures what it is supposed to measure. There are several types of validity, e.g., predictive validity indicates how well a test predicts future performance.

Values Clarification: Procedures designed to help individuals become aware of personal values and learn how to select them and use them in decision-making. Usually groups or classes are involved in the process.

BIBLIOGRAPHY

Abert, James G. 1974. "Wanted: Experiments in Reducing the Cost of Education." *Phi Delta Kappan* 55, no. 7, pp. 444–445.

Adams, Harold J. 1973. "The Progressive Heritage of Guidance: A View from the Left." *Personnel and Guidance Journal* 51, no. 8, pp. 531–538.

Agne, Russell M., and Nash, Robert J. 1973. "School Counselors: The Conscience of Career Education." *School Counselor* 21, no. 2, pp. 90–101.

Alexander, Jaclyn J., and Wall, Judy. 1975. "Righting the Wrongs of Writing: Copy Editors Speak Out." *Personnel and Guidance Journal* 53, no. 10, pp. 768–773.

Alford, Albert L. 1977. "The Education Amendments of 1976." *American Education* 13, no. 1, pp. 6–11.

American Personnel and Guidance Association. 1967a. "Standards for the Preparation of Secondary School Counselors—1967," *Personnel and Guidance Journal* 46, no. 1, pp. 96–106.

———. 1967b. "Support Personnel for the Counselor: Their Technical and Non-Technical Roles and Preparation." *Personnel and Guidance Journal* 45, no. 8, pp. 857–861.

———. 1973. *Standards for the Preparation of Counselors and Other Personnel Services Specialists.* Washington, D.C.: American Personnel and Guidance Association.

———. 1974. "Ethical Standards." *Guidepost* 17, 4 July, pp. 4–5.

American Psychological Association. 1967. *Casebook on Ethical Standards of Psychologists.* Washington, D.C.: American Psychological Association.

———. 1968. "Ethical Standards of Psychologists." *American Psychologist* 23, no. 5, pp. 357–361.

———. 1973. *Ethical Principles in the Conduct of Research with Human*

Participants. Washington, D.C.: American Psychological Association.

———. 1974. *Standards for Educational and Psychological Tests.* Washington, D.C.: American Psychological Association.

———. 1976. "A New Method of Testing Children." *APA Monitor* 7, no. 5, p. 13.

American School Counselor Association. 1965. "Statement of Policy for Secondary School Counselors," and "Guidelines for Implementation of the ASCA Statement of Policy for Secondary School Counselors." In *Counseling, A Growing Profession,* edited by John W. Loughary, pp. 93–106. Washington, D.C.: American Personnel and Guidance Association.

———. 1973. "ASCA Code of Ethics." *School Counselor* 21, no. 2, pp. 137–140.

———. 1974a. "The Role and Function of Post-Secondary Counseling." *School Counselor* 21, no. 5, pp. 387–390.

———. 1974b. "The Role of the Secondary School Counselor." *School Counselor* 21, no. 5, pp. 379–386.

———. 1974c. "The Unique Role of the Elementary School Counselor." *Elementary School Guidance and Counseling* 8, no. 3, pp. 219–223.

———. 1974d. "The Unique Role of the Middle/Junior High School Counselor." *Elementary School Guidance and Counseling* 8, no. 3, pp. 216–218.

Arbuckle, Dugald S. 1974. "The Practice of the Theories of Counseling." *Counseling Education and Supervision* 13, no. 3, pp. 214–222.

———. 1975. "An Existential-Humanistic Program of Counselor Education." *Counselor Education and Supervision* 14, no. 3, pp. 168–174.

Arnow, Betsy. 1977. "Meeting Parents' Needs." *1977 Convention Summaries, Abstracts, and Research Reports.* Washington, D.C.: American Personnel and Guidance Association, p. 201.

Asimov, Isaac. 1976. "His Own Particular Drummer." *Phi Delta Kappan* 58, no. 1, pp. 99–103.

Association for Counselor Education and Supervision. 1967. *Manual for Self-Study by a Counselor Education Staff.* Washington, D.C.: American Personnel and Guidance Association.

Association for Measurement and Evaluation in Guidance. 1973. AMEG Commission on Sex Bias in Interest Measurement. "AMEG Commission Report on Sex Bias in Interest Measurement." *Measurement and Evaluation in Guidance* 6, no. 3, pp. 171–177.

Aubrey, Roger F. 1969. "Misapplication of Therapy Models to School Counseling." *Personnel and Guidance Journal* 48, no. 4, pp. 273–278.

———. 1977. "Historical Developments of Guidance and Counseling and Implications for the Future." *Personnel and Guidance Journal* 55, no. 6, pp. 288–295.

Authier, Jerry; Gustafson, Kay; Guerney, Bernard, Jr.; and Dasdorf, Jerry A. 1975. "The Psychological Practitioner as Teacher: A Theoretical-Historical and Practical Review." *Counseling Psychologist* 5, no. 2, pp. 31–50.

Baker, Stanley B., and Hansen, James C. 1972. "School Counselor Attitudes on a Status-Quo-Change Agent Measurement Scale." *School Counselor* 19, no. 4, pp. 243–248.

Bale, Richard L.; Park, Donna R.; and McMeekin, Robert W., Jr. 1976. *Family-Centered Residential Career and the Rural Poor: A National Needs Assessment,* vol. 1. Washington, D.C.: National Institute of Education.

Banks, William. 1977. "Group Consciousness and the Helping Professions." *Personnel and Guidance Journal* 55, no. 6, pp. 319–322, 327–330.

Barclay, James R. 1969. "A Commentary on 'Counselee Participation in Test Selection.' " *Counseling Psychologist* 1, no. 3, pp. 77–78.

Bard, E. Ronald. 1977. "The Counselor and the Foster Child." *Elementary School Guidance and Counseling* 11, no. 3, pp. 215–222.

Bardon, Jack J. 1968. "School Psychology and School Psychologists." *American Psychologist* 23, no. 3, pp. 157–194.

Barnes, Melvin W. 1974. "Junior High School: Yesterday and Tomorrow." In *The American Intermediate School,* edited by Max E. Brough and Russell L. Hamm, pp. 147–158. Danville, Ill.: Interstate Printers and Publishers.

Baron, Bruce G. 1975. "Experience-Based Career Education: (Model II) Guidance Perspectives." *1975 Convention Summaries, Abstracts, and Research Reports.* Washington, D.C.: American Personnel and Guidance Association, pp. 210–212.

Barro, Stephen M. 1970. "An Approach to Developing Accountability Measures in the Public Schools." *Phi Delta Kappan* 52, no. 4, pp. 196–205.

Barry, Ruth, and Wolf, Beverly. 1957. *Modern Issues in Guidance-Personnel Work.* New York: Bureau of Publications, Teachers College, Columbia University.

Baymor, F. R., and Patterson, C. H. 1960. "A Comparison of Three Methods of Assisting Underachieving High School Students." *Journal of Counseling Psychology* 7, no. 2, pp. 83–89.

Beck, Carlton E. 1963. *Philosophical Foundations of Guidance.* Englewood Cliffs, N.J.: Prentice-Hall.

Becvar, Raphael J., and Dustin, Richard. 1974. "Counselor Education, Don't Tell Us/Show Us." *School Counselor* 21, no. 4, pp. 309–313.

Bell, Cynthia M. 1976. "Student Facilitators in the Guidance Process: Peer Counseling in an Urban Setting." *1976 Convention Summaries, Abstracts, and Research Reports.* Washington, D.C.: American Personnel and Guidance Association, p. 12.

Bell, T. H. 1975. "The Child's Right to Have a Trained Parent." *Elementary School Guidance and Counseling* 9, no. 4, pp. 271–276.

Benedict, David Speare. 1973. "A Generalist Counselor in Industry." *Personnel and Guidance Journal* 51, no. 10, pp. 717–722.

Benson, Arland N., and Blocher, Donald H. 1975. "The Change Process Applied to Career Development Programs." *Personnel and Guidance Journal* 53, no. 9, pp. 656–661.

Benson, Ronald L., and Blocher, Donald H. 1967. "Evaluation of Developmental Counseling with Low Achievers in a High School Setting." *School Counselor* 14, no. 4, pp. 215–220.

Berdie, Ralph F. 1972. "The 1980 Counselor: Applied Behavioral Scientist." *Personnel and Guidance Journal* 50, no. 6, pp. 451–456.

Bernstein, Bianca L., and LeComte, Conrad. 1976. "An Integrative Competency-Based Counselor Education Model." *Counselor Education and Supervision* 16, no. 1, pp. 26–36.

Bertotti, Joseph M.; Sweeney, Thomas J.; McIntire, Paul H.; and McManus, Vin. 1975. "G.E. Community-Based Programs: Educators in Industry." *1975 Convention Summaries, Abstracts, and Research Reports.* Washington, D.C.: American Personnel and Guidance Association, pp. 197–198.

Bettinghaus, Erwin P., and Miller, Gerald R. 1973. *Keeping the Public Informed: Accent on Accountability.* Denver, Colo.: Cooperative Accountability Project.

Biggs, Donald A. 1963. "An Historic Philosophy of Guidance." *Counselor Education and Supervision* 2, no. 4, pp. 201–203.

Blake, Richard. 1975a. "Counseling in Gerontology." *Personnel and Guidance Journal* 53, no. 10, pp. 733–737.

———. 1975b. "Counseling the Elderly: An Emerging Area for Counselor Education." *Counselor Education and Supervision* 15, no. 2, pp. 156–157.

Blocher, Donald H. 1974. "Toward an Ecology of Student Development." *Personnel and Guidance Journal* 52, no. 6, pp. 360–365.

———. 1977. "The Counselor's Impact on Learning Environments." *Personnel and Guidance Journal* 55, no. 6, pp. 352–355.

Blocher, Donald H., and Rapoza, Rita S. 1972. "A Systematic Eclectic Model for Counseling-Consulting." *Elementary School Guidance and Counseling* 7, no. 2, pp. 106–112.

Bluhm, Harry P., and Anderson, H. Reese. 1976. "Intervention in Elementary Guidance: One State's Approach." *Elementary School Guidance and Counseling* 10, no. 3, pp. 165–-170.

Boller, Jon D. 1973. "Counselor Educators and Administrators: What Do They Want from Each Other?" *Counselor Education and Supervision* 13, no. 1, pp. 2–7.

Borow, Henry. 1964. "Milestones of Notable Events in the History of

Vocational Guidance." In *Man in a World at Work*, edited by Henry Borow, pp. 45–64. Boston: Houghton Mifflin.

Bostwick, Willard P. 1972. "Cooperative Education: Vocational Guidance Implications." *Vocational Guidance Quarterly* 21, no. 2, pp. 120–124.

Bowlsbey, Jo Ann Harris. 1975. "Sex Bias and Computer-Based Guidance Systems." In *Issues of Sex Bias and Sex Fairness in Career*, edited by Esther E. Diamond, pp. 177–200. Washington, D.C.: U.S. Department of Health, Education and Welfare.

Bradley, Richard W. 1973. "Following the ACES Standards on Preparation of Secondary School Counselors in Career Guidance." *Counselor Education and Supervision* 13, no. 1, pp. 30–35.

Brammer, Lawrence M. 1968. "The Counselor Is a Psychologist." *Personnel and Guidance Journal* 47, no. 1, pp. 4–8.

———. 1969. "Eclecticism Revisited. " *Personnel and Guidance Journal* 48, no. 3, pp. 192–197.

Brasington, Jo. 1976. "Thoughts on Being a Paraprofessional: Some Personal Notes." In *Psychological and Vocational Counseling Center Monograph Series*, edited by Paul G. Schauble and Jacquelyn Liss Resnick, vol. 2, pp. 95–99.

Brewer, John M. 1942. *History of Vocational Guidance.* New York: Harper and Brothers.

Brigante, Thomas R. 1958. "Fromm's Marketing Orientation on the Values of the Counselor." *Journal of Counseling Psychology* 5, no. 2, pp. 83–88.

Briskin, Alan S., and Anderson, Donna M. 1973. "Students as Contingency Managers." *Elementary School Guidance and Counseling* 7, no. 4, pp. 262–268.

Brodsky, Stanley L. 1974. "Personal Commitment: Challenge for Change." *Personnel and Guidance Journal* 53, no. 2, pp. 163–165.

Brough, James R. 1968. "A Comparison of Self-Referral Counselees and Non-Counseled Junior High School Students." *Personnel and Guidance Journal* 47, no. 4, pp. 329–332.

Brough, Max E., and Hamm, Russell L., eds. 1974. *The American Intermediate School.* Danville, Ill.: Interstate Printers and Publishers.

Brown, Roger, and Herrnstein, Richard J. 1975. *Psychology.* Boston: Little, Brown.

Buckner, Eugene T. 1975. "Accountable to Whom? The Counselor's Dilemma." *Measurement and Evaluation in Guidance* 8, no. 3, pp. 187–192.

Bundy, Robert F. 1974. "Accountability: A New Disneyland Fantasy." *Phi Delta Kappan* 56, no. 3, pp. 176–180.

Burcky, William D., and Childers, John H., Jr. 1976. "Buckley Amendment: Focus of a Professional Dilemma." *School Counselor* 23, no. 3, pp. 162–164.

Burgum, Thomas, and Anderson, Scott. 1975. *The Counselor and the Law.* Washington, D.C.: American Personnel and Guidance Association.

Calia, Vincent F. 1974. "Systematic Human Relations Training: Appraisal and Status." *Counselor Education and Supervision* 14, no. 2, pp. 85–94.

Call, O. Dean. 1970. "Make Counselor Education Relevant." *Personnel and Guidance Journal* 48, no. 10, pp. 797–798.

Callis, Robert. 1976. *Ethical Standards Casebook.* 2d ed. Washington, D.C.: American Personnel and Guidance Association.

Campbell, Clyde M. 1972. "Contributions of the Mott Foundation to the Community Education Movement." *Phi Delta Kappan* 54, no. 3, pp. 195–197.

Campbell, David P. 1965. *The Results of Counseling: Twenty-Five Years Later.* Philadelphia, Pa.: W. B. Saunders.

Campbell, Donald T. 1969. "Reforms as Experiments." *American Psychologist* 24, no. 4, pp. 409–429.

Campbell, Robert E.; Walz, Garry R.; Miller, Juliet V.; and Kriger, Sara F. 1973. *Career Guidance.* Columbus, Ohio: Charles E. Merrill.

Cantrell, Jacqueline; Aubrey, Roger; and Graff, Franklyn. 1974. "A Dialogue: Where Do We Go from Here?" *School Counselor* 21, no. 4, pp. 266–279.

Caplan, Gerald. 1959. *Concepts of Mental Health and Consultation.* Washington, D.C.: U.S. Department of Health, Education and Welfare.

Career Counseling for Adults: An Overview of the Home-and-Community-Based Career Education Project. 1975. Washington, D.C.: U.S. Government Printing Office.

Career Education. 1971. Washington, D.C.: U.S. Government Printing Office.

Career Education Development Task Force. 1973. *Forward Plan for Career Education Research and Development.* Washington, D.C.: National Institute of Education.

Carey, Albert. 1968. "Test Interpretation: Verbal Versus Written Summaries." *School Counselor* 16, no. 2, pp. 120–124.

Carkuff, Robert R. 1969. *Helping and Human Relations,* vol 2. New York: Holt, Rinehart and Winston.

——. 1972. "New Directions in Training for the Helping Professions: Toward Technology for Human and Community Resource Development." *Counseling Psychologist* 3, no. 3, part 1, pp. 12–30.

——. 1973. *The Art of Helping.* Amherst, Mass.: Human Resources Development Press.

Carkhuff, Robert R., and Alexik, Mae. 1967. "Effect of Client Depth of Self-Exploration Upon High-and-Low Functioning Counselors." *Journal of Counseling Psychology* 14, no. 4, pp. 350–355.

Carkhuff, Robert R., and Berenson, Bernard G. 1969. "The Counselor Is a Man and a Woman." *Personnel and Guidance Journal* 48, no. 1, pp. 24–28.

Carlson, Jon. 1972. "Introduction." *Elementary School Guidance and Counseling* 7, no. 2, pp. 81–82.

Carlson, Jon; Cavins, David A.; and Dinkmeyer, Don. 1969. "Guidance for All Through Support Personnel." *School Counselor* 16, no. 5, pp. 360–366.

Carlson, Jon, and Pietrofesa, John J. 1971. "A Tri-Level Guidance Structure: An Answer to Our Apparent Ineffectiveness." *Elementary School Guidance and Counseling* 5, no. 3, pp. 190–195.

Carlson, Jon; Splete, Howard; and Kern, Roy, eds. 1975. *The Consulting Process.* Washington, D.C.: American Personnel and Guidance Association.

Carmical, La Verne, and Calvin, Leland, Jr. 1970. "Functions Selected by School Counselors." *School Counselor* 17, no. 4, pp. 280–285.

Carroll, Marguerite R. 1973a. "The Current Issue." *School Counselor* 21, no. 2, p. 89.

———. 1973b. "The Regeneration of Guidance." *School Counselor* 20, no. 5, pp. 355–360.

———. 1975a. "Social Issues and the School Counselor." *School Counselor* 22, no. 5, p. 309.

———. 1975b. "What Every Editor Knows (and Everyone Else Should Know)." *School Counselor* 23, no. 2, pp. 76–77.

Cassell, Russell N., and Mehail, Terry. 1973. "The Milwaukee Computerized Vocational Guidance System (VOCGUID)." *Vocational Guidance Quarterly* 21, no. 3, pp. 206–213.

Centers for Community Education Development. 1975. Flint, Mich.: C. S. Mott Foundation.

Chaffee, John, Jr. 1976. "This We Propose. . . ." In *New Dimensions for Educating Youth*, edited by John Chaffee, Jr. and James P. Clark, pp. 1–2. Reston, Virginia: National Association of Secondary School Principals.

Chaney, Reece; Linkenhoker, Dan; and Horne, Arthur. 1977. "The Counselor and Children of Imprisoned Parents." *Elementary School Guidance and Counseling* 11, no. 3, pp. 177–184.

Christensen, Edward W. 1975. "Counseling Puerto Ricans: Some Cultural Considerations." *Personnel and Guidance Journal* 53, no. 5, pp. 349–356.

Christie, Charles A. 1974. "From Canada. . . ." *Personnel and Guidance Journal* 53, no. 1, pp. 43–44.

Ciavarella, Michael A., and Doolittle, Lawrence W. 1970. "The Omsbudman: Relevant Role Model for the Counselor." *School Counselor* 17, no. 5, pp. 331–336.

Clapsaddle, David K. 1973. "Career Development and Teacher Inservice Preparation." *Elementary School Guidance and Counseling* 8, no. 2, pp. 92–97.

Clay, Vidal S. 1976. "Children Deal with Death." *School Counselor* 23, no. 3, pp. 175–184.

Cohen, Charles, and Drugo, John. 1976. "Test-Re-Test Reliability of the Singer Vocational Evaluation System." *Vocational Guidance Quarterly* 24, no. 3, pp. 267–270.

Cole, Robert W. 1975. "Apprenticeship Is the Answer." *Phi Delta Kappan* 56, no. 9, pp. 601–604.

Combs, Arthur W., and Soper, Daniel W. 1963. "The Perceptual Organization of Effective Counselors." *Journal of Counseling Psychology* 10, no. 3, pp. 222–226.

"Coming to the Defense of Children." 1975. *Carnegie Quarterly* 23, no. 3, pp. 1–31.

"Community Education Vignettes." 1972. *Phi Delta Kappan* 44, no. 3, pp. 182–191.

The Community Is the Teacher. 1975. Washington, D.C.: National Institute of Education.

Conyne, Robert K. 1975. "Environmental Assessment: Mapping for Counselor Action." *Personnel and Guidance Journal* 54, no. 3, pp. 151–154.

Conyne, Robert K., and Cochran, Donald. 1976. "From Seeker to Seer: The Odyssey of Robert Hoppock." *Personnel and Guidance Journal* 54, no. 5, pp. 273–279.

Cook, David R. 1972. "The Change Agent Counselor: A Conceptual Context." *School Counselor* 20, no. 1, pp. 9–15.

Cooker, Philip G. 1973. "Vocational Values of Children in Grades Four, Five, and Six." *Elementary School Guidance and Counseling* 8, no. 2, pp. 112–118.

Cooker, Philip G., and Cherchia, Peter J. 1976. "Effects of Communication Skill Training on High School Students' Ability to Function as Peer Group Facilitators." *Journal of Counseling Psychology* 23, no. 5, pp. 464–467.

Cooperative Accountability Project. 1975. *Accounting for Accountability.* Denver, Colo.

Cotler, Sherwin B. 1975. "Assertion Training: A Road Leading Where?" *Counseling Psychologist* 5, no. 4, pp. 20–29.

Cottingham, Harold F. 1969. "Conceptualizing the Guidance Function in the Elementary School." *Elementary School Guidance and Counseling* 4, no. 2, pp. 112–119.

———. 1975. "School Counselors Face the Question of Licensing." *School Counselor* 22, no. 4, pp. 255–258.

Cottingham, Harold F., and Swanson, Carl D. 1976. "Recent Licensure Developments: Implications for Counselor Education." *Counselor Education and Supervision* 16, no. 2, pp. 84–97.

"Counselors Want Elderly Care Role." 1975. *Guidepost* 18, no. 7, pp. 1–3.

Crabtree, Mary Frances. 1975. "Chicago's Metro High: Freedom, Choice, Responsibility." *Phi Delta Kappan* 56, no. 9, pp. 613–615.

Cramer, Stanley H. 1974. "Planned Utilization and Change of Environments." In *Vocational Guidance and Human Development*, edited by Edwin L. Herr, pp. 399–418. Boston: Houghton Mifflin.

Cramer, Stanley H.; Herr, Edwin L.; Morris, Charles N.; and Frantz, Thomas T. 1970. *Research and the School Counselor*. Boston: Houghton Mifflin.

Creange, Norman C. 1976. "Norm Creange Discusses ASCA and His Presidential Term." *ASCA Newsletter* 13, no. 5, p. 3.

Cremin, Lawrence A. 1965. "The Progressive Heritage of the Guidance Movement." In *Guidance, An Examination*, edited by Ralph L. Mosher, Richard F. Carle, and Chris D. Kehas, pp. 3–12.

Crites, John O. 1969. *Vocational Psychology*. New York: McGraw-Hill.

Cross, William C., and Maldonado, Bonnie. 1971. "The Counselor, the Mexican-American and the Stereotype." *Elementary School Guidance and Counseling* 6, no. 1, pp. 27–31.

Cunin, Bert. 1976. "Peer Counseling: A Dynamic Approach to Counseling." *1976 Convention Summaries, Abstracts, and Research Reports*. Washington, D.C.: American Personnel and Guidance Association, p. 34.

Danish, Steven J., and Brock, Gregory W. 1974. "The Current Status of Paraprofessional Training." *Personnel and Guidance Journal* 53, no. 4, pp. 299–303.

Danish, Steven J.; D'Augelli, Anthony R.; and Brock, Gregory W. 1976. "An Evaluation of Helping Skills Training: Effects on Helpers' Verbal Responses." *Journal of Counseling Psychology* 23, no. 3, pp. 259–266.

Dash, Edward F. 1969. "Comment." *Personnel and Guidance Journal* 47, no. 6, pp. 599–601.

DeBlassie, Richard R., and Cowan, Mary Ann. 1976. "Counseling with the Mentally Handicapped Child." *Elementary School Guidance and Counseling* 10, no. 4, pp. 246–253.

Deen, Nathan. 1974. "From The Netherlands. . . ." *Personnel and Guidance Journal* 53, no. 1, pp. 45–46.

———. 1977. "Counselor Education in the Netherlands." *1977 Convention Summaries, Abstracts, and Research Reports*. Washington, D.C.: American Personnel and Guidance Association, pp. 56–57.

Deffenbacher, Jerry L., and Kemper, Calvin C. 1974. "Counseling Test-

Anxious Sixth Graders." *Elementary School Guidance and Counseling* 9, no. 1, pp. 22–29.

Delworth, Ursula. 1974. "The Paraprofessionals Are Coming!" *Personnel and Guidance Journal* 53, no. 4, p. 250.

DeVoe, Marianne, and Sherman, Thomas M. 1975. "Microtechnology: A Tool for Elementary School Counselors." *Elementary School Guidance and Counseling* 10, no. 2, pp. 110–115.

Diamond, Esther E., ed. 1975. *Issues of Sex Bias and Sex Fairness in Careers Interest Measurement.* Washington, D.C.: U.S. Department of Health, Education, and Welfare, pp. xxiii–xxix.

Dickey, Frank G. 1968. "What is Accrediting and Why Is It Important for Professional Organizations?" *Counselor Education and Supervision* 7, no. 3, pp. 194–199.

Dinkmeyer, Don. 1971. "Developmental Counseling: Rationale and Relationship." *School Counselor* 18, no. 4, pp. 246–252.

———. 1971. "A Developmental Model for Counseling-Consulting." *Elementary School Guidance and Counseling* 6, no. 2, pp. 81–85.

———. 1973*a*. "Elementary School Counseling: Prospects and Potentials." *Personnel and Guidance Journal* 52, no. 3, pp. 171–174.

———. 1973*b*. "The Parent 'C' Group." *Personnel and Guidance Journal* 52, no. 4, pp. 252–256.

Dinkmeyer, Don, and McKay, Gary D. 1974. "Leading Effective Parent Study Groups." *Elementary School Guidance and Counseling* 9, no. 2, pp. 108–115.

———. 1976. *Systematic Training for Effective Parenting.* Circle Pines, Minn.: American Guidance Service.

"Discover, An Informational Manual for Decision Makers." n.d. Mimeographed. Westminster, Md.: Discover Foundation.

Dolliver, Robert H., and Nelson, Richard E. 1975. "Assumption Regarding Vocational Counseling." *Vocational Guidance Quarterly* 24, no. 1, pp. 12–19.

Donovan, Carey. 1974. "A Volunteer's View." *Personnel and Guidance Journal* 53, no. 4, p. 329.

Doverspike, James E. 1971. "GUICO: A Synthesized Group Approach." *Personnel and Guidance Journal* 50, no. 3, pp. 182–187.

Drapela, Victor J. 1974. "Counselors, Not Political Agitators." *Personnel and Guidance Journal* 52, no. 7, pp. 449–453.

———. 1975. "Comparative Guidance Through International Study." *Personnel and Guidance Journal* 53, no. 6, pp. 438–445.

———. 1977. "APGA International Education Committee." *Report.* 2 April.

Drum, Davis J., and Figger, Howard E. 1972. *Outreach in Counseling: Applying the Growth and Prevention Model in Schools and Colleges.* New York: Intext Educational Publishers.

Dudley, Gerald, and Ruff, Eldon E. 1970. "School Counselor Certification: A Study of Current Requirements." *School Counselor* 16, no. 4, pp. 304–311.

Dunn, James A. 1972. "Career Education and Guidance in the PLAN System of Individualized Education." In *Career Education and the Technology of Career Development*, pp. 81–116. Palo Alto: American Institutes for Research.

Dustin, Richard. 1974. "Training for Institutional Change." *Personnel and Guidance Journal* 52, no. 6, pp. 422–427.

Dye, Larry L., and Gluckstern, Norma B. 1974. "Counselors in Corrections: Surveying the Scene." *Personnel and Guidance Journal* 53, no. 2, pp. 128–129.

Dyer, Wayne W., and Vriend, John. 1975. *Counseling Techniques That Work! Applications to Individual and Group Counseling.* Washington, D.C.: APGA Press.

Easton, Robert, and Resnikoff, Arthur. 1969. "Who Decided What?" *Personnel and Guidance Journal* 47, no. 6, pp. 597–598.

"EBCE: A Design for Career Education." 1975. *Curriculum Report* 4, no. 3, pp. 1–11.

Ebel, Robert L. 1975. "Educational Tests: Valid? Biased? Useful?" *Phi Delta Kappan* 57, no. 2, pp. 83–88.

Eddy, William B., and Lubin, Bernard. 1971. "Laboratory Training and Encounter Groups." *Personnel and Guidance Journal* 49, no 8, pp. 625–635.

Edington, Everett D. 1976. "Evaluation of Methods of Using Resource People in Helping Kindergarten Students Become Aware of the World of Work." *Journal of Vocational Behavior* 8, no. 2, pp. 125–131.

Editors of British Journal of Guidance and Counselling. 1973. "Editorial." *British Journal of Guidance and Counselling* 1, no. 1, p. 2.

Editors of *The School Guidance Worker*. 1973. "Editorial." *The School Guidance Worker* 29, no. 1, pp. 2–3.

Education and Work Group. 1977. *Program Plan for Fiscal Years 1977–78.* Washington, D.C.: U.S. Department of Health, Education and Welfare.

Ehlert, Richard. 1975. "Kid Counselors." *School Counselor* 22, no. 4, pp. 260–262.

Elam, Stanley M. 1974. "Holding the Accountability Movement Accountable." *Phi Delta Kappan* 55, no. 10, pp. 657–674.

———. 1975. "The Future at Work." *Phi Delta Kappan* 57, no. 4, p. 226.

———. 1976. "Without Hope, the People Perish." *Phi Delta Kappan* 58, no. 1, p. 3.

Elkins, Kerry. 1975. "Student Evaluation and Experience." *1975 Convention Summaries, Abstracts, and Research Reports.* Washington, D.C.: American Personnel and Guidance Association.

Elleson, Vera J., and Onmink, Allen G. 1976. "Jobs Inc.-Inschool Career Education/Experience." *Elementary School Guidance and Counseling* 10, no 4, pp. 290–292.

Ellis, Albert. 1975. "A Commentary," *Personnel and Guidance Journal* 54, no. 2, pp. 92–93.

————. 1975. "Rational-Emotive Therapy and the School Counselor." *School Counselor* 22, no. 4, pp. 236–242.

Emener, William G., Jr. 1975. "Counselor Education Applied to Industry." *Counselor Education and Supervision* 15, no. 1, pp. 72–76.

Emerson, Patricia, and Smith, Edward W. L. 1974. "Contributions of Gestalt Psychology to Gestalt Therapy." *Counseling Psychologist* 4, no. 4, pp. 8–12.

Englehardt, Leah; Sulzer, Beth; and Alterkruse, Michael. 1971. "The Counselor as a Consultant in Eliminating Out-of-Seat Behavior." *Elementary School Guidance and Counseling* 5, no. 3, pp. 196–204.

English, Horace B., and English, Ava Champney. 1965. *A Comprehensive Dictionary of Psychological and Psychoanalytical Terms.* New York: David McKay.

Entine, Alan D. 1976. "Mid-Life Counseling: Prognosis and Potential." *Personnel and Guidance Journal* 55, no. 3, pp. 112–114.

"Ertl Machine Triggers Controversy." 1973. *Phi Delta Kappan* 54, no. 5, p. 360.

Ewing, Dorlesa Barmettler. 1977. "Twenty Approaches to Individual Change." *Personnel and Guidance Journal* 55, no. 6, pp. 331–338.

Eysenck, H. J. 1952. "The Effects of Psychotherapy: An Evaluation." *Journal of Consulting Psychology* 16, pp. 316–324.

Fagan, Joen; Lauver, David; Smith, Sally; Deloach, Stan; Katz, Michael; and Wood, Elaine. 1974. "Critical Incident in the Empty Chair." *Counseling Psychologist* 4, no. 4, pp. 33–42.

Fantaci, Anthony. 1973. "A Challenge Decade for Employment Counselors." *Personnel and Guidance Journal* 52, no. 3, pp. 161–166.

Faust, Verne. 1968. *History of Elementary School Counseling.* Boston: Houghton Mifflin.

Felix, Joseph L. 1968. "Who Decided *That*?" *Personnel and Guidance Journal* 47, pp. 9–11.

Fernald, Peter S., and Makarewicz, Joan F. 1967. "Use of Personal Validation." *Journal of Counseling Psychology* 14, no. 6, pp. 568–569.

Fiedler, F. E. 1950a. "A Comparison of the Therapeutic Relationships in Psychoanalytic, Non-Directive, and Adlerian Therapy." *Journal of Consulting Psychology* 14, pp. 436–445.

————. 1950b. "The Concept of an Ideal Therapeutic Relationship." *Journal of Consulting Psychology* 14, pp. 239–245.

Field, Hubert S., and Gatewood, Robert. 1976. "The Paraprofessional and the Organization." *Personnel and Guidance Journal* 55, no. 4, pp. 181–185.

Fisher, Thomas J.; Reardon, Robert C.; and Burck, Harman D. 1976. "Increasing Information-Seeking Behavior with a Model-Reinforced Videotape." *Journal of Counseling Psychology* 23, no. 3, pp. 234–238.

Flanagan, John C. 1973*a*. "The First Fifteen Years of Project Talent: Implications for Career Guidance." *Vocational Guidance Quarterly* 22, no. 1, pp. 8–14.

———. 1973*b*. "Some Pertinent Findings of Project Talent." *Vocational Guidance Quarterly* 22, no. 2, pp. 92–96.

———. 1977. "The PLAN System for Individualizing Education." *National Council on Measurement in Education* 2, no. 2, pp. 1–8.

Flanagan, John C.; Tiedeman, David V.; Willis, Mary B.; and McLaughlin, Donald H. 1973. *The Career Data Book.* Palo Alto, Calif.: American Institutes for Research.

Fletcher, Brady J. 1976. "Thoughts on Parental Involvement in the Guidance Program." *Elementary School Guidance and Counseling* 10, no. 3, pp. 210–213.

"Florida Facts and Figures." 1977. *Florida Vocational Journal* 2, no. 7, p. 34.

Forrer, Stephen E. 1975. "Battered Children and Counselor Responsibility." *School Counselor* 22, no. 3, pp. 161–165.

Foulds, Melvin L., and Hannigan, Patricia S. 1976. "Effects of Gestalt Marathon Workshops on Measured Self-Actualization: A Replication and Follow-Up Study." *Journal of Counseling Psychology* 23, no. 1, pp. 6–65.

Franklin, A. J. 1977. "Counseling Youth in Alternative Schools." *Personnel and Guidance Journal* 55, no. 7, pp. 419–421.

Frazier, Fred, and Mathes, William S. 1975. "Parent Education: A Comparison of Alderian and Behavioral Approaches." *Elementary School Guidance and Counseling* 10, no. 1, pp. 31–38.

Frey, David H. 1973. "Being Systematic When You Have But One Subject: Ideographic Method, N = 1, and All That." *Measurement and Evaluation in Education* 6, no. 1, pp. 35–43.

Gallup, George H. 1975. "Seventh Annual Gallup Poll of the Public's Attitudes Towards the Public Schools." *Phi Delta Kappan* 57, no. 4, pp. 227–241.

———. 1976. "Eighth Annual Gallup Poll of the Public's Attitudes Towards the Public Schools." *Phi Delta Kappan* 58, no. 2, pp. 187–200.

Gamsky, Neal R. 1970. "A Follow-Up Study of Pupil Personnel Services." *Journal of the International Association of Pupil Personnel Workers* 15, no. 3, pp. 130–134.

Gartner, Alan, and Riessman, Frank. 1974. "The Paraprofessional Movement in Perspective." *Personnel and Guidance Journal* 53, no. 4, pp. 253–256.

Gatewood, Thomas E., and Dilg, Charles A. 1975. *The Middle School We Need.* Washington, D.C.: Association for Supervision and Curriculum Development.

Geiwitz, James. 1976. *Looking at Ourselves.* Boston: Little, Brown.

Gelatt, H. B. 1962. "Decision-Making: A Conceptual Frame of Reference for Counseling." *Journal of Counseling Psychology* 9, no. 3, pp. 240–245.

———. 1967. "Information and Decision Theories Applied to College Choice and Planning." In *Preparing School Counselors in Educational Guidance*, pp. 101–114. New York: College Entrance Examination Board.

Gelatt, H. B.; Varenhorst, Barbara; and Carey, Richard. 1972. *Deciding.* New York: College Entrance Examination Board.

Gelatt, H. B.; Varenhorst, Barbara; Carey, Richard; and Miller, Gordon P. 1973. *Decisions and Outcomes.* New York: College Entrance Examination Board.

Gellman, William, and Murov, Herman. 1973. "The Broad Role of the Community Agency Counselor." *Personnel and Guidance Journal* 52, no. 3, pp. 157–159.

Gerler, Edwin R., Jr. 1976. "New Directions for School Counseling." *School Counselor* 23, no. 4, pp. 247–251.

Gibson, Robert L.; Mitchell, Marianne H.; and Higgins, Robert E. 1973. *The Development and Management of School Guidance Programs.* Dubuque: William C. Brown.

Giddan, Norman S., and Price, Mary K. 1975. "Whither Counseling?" *School Counselor* 22, no. 3, pp. 154–160.

Ginzberg, Eli. 1971. *Career Guidance.* New York: McGraw-Hill.

———. 1972. "Strategies for Educational Reform." Columbus, Ohio: Center for Vocational and Technical Education.

Glaser, Edward M., and Taylor, Samuel H. 1973. "Factors Affecting the Success of Applied Research." *American Psychologist* 28, no. 2, pp. 140–146.

Glass, Gene V. 1968. "Educational Piltdown Men." *Phi Delta Kappan* 50, no. 3, pp. 148–151.

Glasser, William, and Zunin, Leonard M. 1973. "Reality Therapy." In *Current Psychotherapies*, edited by Raymond Corsini, pp. 287–315. Itasca, Ill.: F. E. Peacock.

Glatthorn, Allan A. 1975. *Alternatives in Education: Schools and Programs.* New York: Dodd, Mead.

Glickman, L. Jane. 1975. "Federal Funds–Career Education." *American Education* 11, no. 10, pp. 26–27.

Gluckstern, Norma B., and Wenner, Kate. 1974a. "The Model Program at Berkshire." *Personnel and Guidance Journal* 53, no. 2, pp. 153–155.

———. 1974b. "The Program: A Discussion." *Personnel and Guidance Journal* 53, no. 2, pp. 160–162.

Goethals, George W., and Klos, Dennis S. 1976. *Experiencing Youth.* 2d ed. Boston: Little, Brown.

Goldman, Leo. 1971. *Using Tests in Counseling.* 2d ed. New York: Appleton-Century-Crofts.

———. 1972a. "It's Time to Put Up or Shut Up." *Measurement and Evaluation in Guidance* 5, no. 3, pp. 420–423.

———. 1972b. "Tests and Counseling: The Marriage That Failed." *Measurement and Evaluation in Guidance* 4, no. 4, pp. 213–220.

———. 1973. "Career Information for Ourselves." *Personnel and Guidance Journal* 52, no. 3, p. 139.

———. 1974. "Guidance U.S.A.: Views from Abroad." *Personnel and Guidance Journal* 53, no. 1, p. 40.

"Goodbye I.Q., Hello E.I." 1972. *Phi Delta Kappan* 54, no. 2, pp. 89–95.

Goodyear, Rodney K. 1976. "Counselors as Community Psychologists." *Personnel and Guidance Journal* 54, no. 10, pp. 513–516.

Gordon, Edmund W. 1974. "Vocational Guidance: Disadvantaged and Minority Populations." In *Vocational Guidance and Human Development*, edited by Edwin L. Herr, pp. 452–477. Boston: Houghton Mifflin.

Gordon, Thomas. 1970. *P.E.T.: Parent Effectiveness Training.* New York: Peter H. Wyden.

Graff, Robert W., and Warner, Richard W., Jr. 1968. "Attitude Toward School's Counseling Services as Seen By Administrators, Teachers, and Counselors." *Journal of Secondary Education* 43, no. 7, pp. 320–323.

Grala, Christopher, and McCauley, Clark. 1976. "Counseling Truants Back to School: Motivation Combined with a Program for Action." *Journal of Counseling Psychology* 23, no. 2, pp. 166–169.

Grant, W. Vance. 1975. "Estimates of School Dropouts." *American Education* 11, no. 4, back cover.

Gray, H. Dean, and Tindall, Judith. 1974. "Communications Training Study: A Model for Training Junior High School Peer Counselors." *School Counselor* 22, no. 2, pp. 107–112.

Griggs, Shirley A., and Gale, Patricia. 1977. "The Abused Child: Focus for Counselors." *Elementary School Guidance and Counseling* 11, no. 3, pp. 187–194.

Grubb, W. Norton, and Lazerson, Marvin. 1975. "Rally 'Round the Workplace: Continuities and Fallacies in Career Education." *Harvard Educational Review* 45, no. 4, pp. 451–474.

Grummon, Donald L. 1965. "Client-Centered Theory." In *Theories of Counseling*, edited by Buford Stefflre, pp. 30–90. New York: McGraw-Hill.

———. 1972. "Client-Centered Theory." In *Theories of Counseling*, edited by Buford Stefflre and W. Harold Grant, pp. 73–135. 2d ed. New York: McGraw-Hill.

Grzegorek, Alfred E. 1976. "On the Status of Paraprofessional Services." In *Psychological and Vocational Counseling Center Monograph Series*, edited by Paul G. Schauble and Jaquelyn Liss Resnick, vol. 2, pp. 112–115.

Gubser, M. N. 1974. "Performance-Based Counseling: Accountability or Liability?" *School Counselor* 21, no. 4, pp. 296–302.

Gumaer, Jim. 1973. "Peer-Facilitated Groups." *Elementary School Guidance and Counseling* 8, no. 1, pp. 4–11.

Gustad, John W., and Tuma, Abdul H. 1957. "The Effects of Different Methods of Test Introduction and Interpretation on Client Learning in Counseling." *Journal of Counseling Psychology* 4, no. 4, pp. 313–317.

Guzzetta, Roberta A. 1976. "Acquisition and Transfer of Empathy by the Parents of Early Adolescents Through Structured Learning Training." *Journal of Counseling Psychology* 23, no. 5, pp. 449–453.

Haase, Richard F. 1974. "Power Analysis of Research in Counselor Education." *Counselor Education and Supervision* 14, no. 2, pp. 124–132.

Haettenschwiller, Dustan L. 1969. "Style of Role Enactment Expected of Parent, Teacher, and Counselor." *Personnel and Guidance Journal* 47, no. 10, pp. 963–969.

Haettenschwiller, Dustan L., and Jabs, William. 1969. "The Counselor and the Instructional Program." *School Counselor* 17, no. 2, pp. 118–125.

Hambleton, R. K., and Novick, M. R. 1972. *Toward an Integration of Theory and Method for Criterion-Referenced Tests.* Iowa City, Iowa: The American College Testing Program.

Hamilton, Andrew. 1975. "Career Education: Working Model." *American Education* 11, no. 10, pp. 22–25.

Hampson, David H. 1975. "Focusing on the School to Work Transition: Problems and Elements to be Considered in Developing a Work Experience Program." In *Models of Career Education Programs: Work Experience, Career Guidance, Placement and Curriculum*, edited by Arthur F. Terry and Barbara M. Bednarz, pp. 3–13. Columbus, Ohio: Center for Vocational Education.

Handel, Linda. 1973. "Three Tips on Career Guidance Activities." *Elementary School Guidance and Counseling* 7, no. 4, pp. 290–291.

Hannaford, Mary Joe. 1974. "A TA Approach to Teacher Group Counseling." *Elementary School Guidance and Counseling* 9, no. 1, pp. 6–13.

Hansel, James D.; Niland, Thomas M.; and Zani, Leonard P. 1969. "Model Reinforcement in Group Counseling with Elementary School Children." *Personnel and Guidance Journal* 47, no. 8, pp. 741–744.

Hansen, John H., and Hearn, Arthur C. 1971. *The Middle School Program.* Chicago: Rand McNally.

Hansen, Lorraine Sundal. 1970. *Career Guidance Practices in School and Community.* Washington, D.C.: National Vocational Guidance Association.

———. 1972. "We are Furious (Female) But We Can Shape Our Own Development." *Personnel and Guidance Journal* 51, no. 2, pp. 87–93.

Hansen, Lorraine Sundal, and Gysbers, Norman C. 1975. "A Different Approach to Career Education." *Personnel and Guidance Journal* 53, no. 9, p. 636.

Harman, Robert L. 1975. "A Gestalt Point of View on Facilitating Growth in Counseling." *Personnel and Guidance Journal* 53, no. 5, pp. 363–366.

Harman, Robert L., and Franklin, Richard W. 1975. "Gestalt Interactional Groups." *Personnel and Guidance Journal* 54, no. 1, pp. 49–54.

Harman, Willis W. 1976. "'Seis-ing' of the Social Revolution," *Phi Delta Kappan* 58, no. 1, pp. 99–103.

Harris, Jo Ann. 1972a. *Computer Assisted Guidance Systems.* Washington, D.C.: National Vocational Guidance Association.

———. 1972b. "Willowbrook Computerized Vocational Information System." In *Career Education and the Technology of Career Development,* pp. 152–155. Palo Alto, Calif.: American Institutes for Research.

———. 1974. "The Computer: Guidance Tool of the Future." *Journal of Counseling Psychology* 21, no. 4, pp. 331–339.

Harris, Mary B., and Trujillo, Amaryllis E. 1975. "Improving Study Habits of Junior High School Students Through Self-Management Versus Group Discussion." *Journal of Counseling Psychology* 22, no. 6, pp. 513–517.

Harris, Philip R. 1968. "Guidance and Counseling in the Year 2000." *Counselor Education and Supervision* 7, no. 3, pp. 262–266.

Harris, Roy. 1974. "From England. . . ." *Personnel and Guidance Journal* 53, no. 1, pp. 47–49.

Harris, Sandra R. 1974. "Sex Typing in Girls' Career Choices: A Challenge to Counselors." *Vocational Guidance Quarterly* 23, no. 2, pp. 128–133.

Harris, Thomas A. 1969. *I'm O.K.—You're O.K.* New York: Harper and Row.

Harris-Bowlsbey, Jo Ann. 1975a. "Model of Career Guidance." In *Models of Career Education Programs*, pp. 15–25. Columbus, Ohio: The Center for Vocational Education.

———. 1975b. "Sex Bias and Computer-Based Guidance Systems." In *Issues of Sex Bias and Sex Fairness in Career Interest Measurement*, edited by Esther E. Diamond, pp. 177–200. Washington, D.C.: U.S. Department of Health, Education, and Welfare.

Hart, Darrell H., and Prince, Donald J. 1970. "Role Conflict for School Counselors: Training Versus Job Demands." *Personnel and Guidance Journal* 48, no. 5, pp. 374–380.

Hatch, Raymond N., and Stefflre, Buford. 1965. *Administration of Guidance Services*. 2d ed. Englewood Cliffs, N.J.: Prentice-Hall.

Havighurst, Robert J. 1952. *Developmental Tasks and Education*. New York: Longmans, Green.

Hawener, Rebecca M., and Phillips, Wallace. 1975. "The Grieving Child." *School Counselor* 22, no. 5, pp. 347–352.

Hays, Donald G. 1972. "Counselors—What Are You Worth?" *School Counselor* 19, no. 5, pp. 309–312.

Healy, Charles C. 1973. "Toward a Replicable Method of Group Career Counseling." *Vocational Guidance Quarterly* 21, no. 3, pp. 214–221.

———. 1974. "Evaluation of a Replicable Group Career Counseling Procedure." *Vocational Guidance Quarterly* 23, no. 1, pp. 34–40.

Heath, Earl J. 1970. *The Mentally Retarded Student and Guidance*. Boston: Houghton Mifflin.

Hecht, Murray. 1977. "A Cooperative Approach Toward Children from Alcoholic Families." *Elementary School Guidance and Counseling* 11, no. 3, pp. 197–203.

Heddesheimer, Janet C. 1975. *Managing Elementary School Guidance Programs*. Boston: Houghton Mifflin.

Heilfron, Marilyn. 1960. "The Function of Counseling as Perceived by High School Students." *Personnel and Guidance Journal* 39, no. 2, pp. 133–136.

Herr, Edwin L. 1974. "Manpower Policies, Vocational Guidance and Career Development." In *Vocational Guidance and Human Development*, edited by Edwin L. Herr, pp. 32–62. Boston: Houghton Mifflin.

Herr, Edwin L., and Cramer, Stanley H. 1972. *Vocational Guidance and Career Development in the Schools: Toward a Systems Approach*. Boston: Houghton Mifflin.

Hewett, Kathryn D. 1975. *Eleven Career Education Programs*. Cambridge, Mass.: ABT Publications.

Hilgard, Ernest R. 1973. "The Domain of Hypnosis." *American Psychologist* 28, no. 11, pp. 972–982.

Hill, George E. 1966. "The Evaluation of Occupational Literature." *Vocational Guidance Quarterly* 14, no. 4, pp. 271–277.

———. 1968. "Standards for the Preparation of Secondary School Counselors." *Counselor Education and Supervision* 7, no. 3, pp. 179–186.

———. 1974. *Management and Improvement of Guidance.* 2d ed. Englewood Cliffs, N.J.: Prentice-Hall.

Hillman, Bill W., and Shields, Frank L. 1975. "The Encouragement Process in Guidance: Its Effect on School Achievement and Attending Behavior." *School Counselor* 22, no. 3, pp. 166–173.

Hipple, John L., and Muto, Lee. 1974. "The TA Group for Adolescents." *Personnel and Guidance Journal* 52, no. 10, pp. 675–681.

Hoffman, S. David, and Rollin, Stephen A. 1972. "Implications of Future Shock for Vocational Guidance." *Vocational Guidance Quarterly* 21, no. 2, pp. 92–96.

Holland, Glen A. 1973. "Transactional Analysis." In *Current Psychotherapies*, edited by Raymond Corsini, pp. 353–399. Itasca, Ill.: F. E. Peacock.

Holland, John L. 1972. *Self-Directed Search, Professional Manual.* Palo Alto, Calif.: Consulting Psychologist Press.

———. 1973. *Making Vocational Choices.* Englewood Cliffs, N.J.: Prentice-Hall.

Holland, John L., and Nafziger, Dean H. 1975. "A Note on the Validity of the Self-Directed Search." *Measurement and Evaluation in Guidance* 7, no. 4, pp. 259–262.

Hollis, Joseph William, and Hollis, Lucille Ussery, 1965. *Organizing for Effective Guidance.* Chicago: Science Research Associates.

Holt, Fred D. 1975. *The Pupil Personnel Team in the Elementary School.* Boston: Houghton Mifflin.

Hopkins, Robert F. 1969. "Comment." *Personnel and Guidance Journal* 47, no. 6, pp. 598–599.

Hoppock, Robert. 1976. *Occupational Information.* 4th ed. New York: McGraw-Hill.

Hopson, Barrie. 1973. "Career Development in Industry: The Diary of an Experiment." *British Journal of Guidance and Counselling* 1, no. 1, pp. 51–61.

Hosford, Ray E. 1969. "Behavioral Counseling—A Contemporary Overview." *Counseling Psychologist* 1, no. 4, pp. 1–33.

Hosford, Ray E., and deVisser, Louis A. J. M. 1974. *Behavioral Approaches to Counseling: An Introduction.* Washington, D.C.: American Personnel and Guidance Association.

Hosford, Ray E., and Ryan, T. Antoinette. 1970. "Systems Design in the Development of Counseling and Guidance Programs." *Personnel and Guidance Journal* 49, no. 3, pp. 221–230.

House, Ernest R.; Rivers, Wendell; and Stufflebeam, Daniel L. 1974. "An Assessment of the Michigan Accountability System." *Phi Delta Kappan* 55, no. 10, pp. 663–669.

Howard, Alvin W., and Stoumbis, George C. 1970. *The Junior High School and the Middle School: Issues and Practices.* Scranton: Intext Educational Publishers.

Hoyt, Kenneth B. 1974. "Professional Preparation for Vocational Guidance." In *Vocational Guidance and Human Development,* edited by Edwin L. Herr, pp. 502–527. Boston: Houghton Mifflin.

———. 1975a. "Career Education: Challenges for Counselors." *Vocational Guidance Quarterly* 23, no. 4, pp. 303–310.

———. 1975b. "Career Education and Counselor Education." *Counselor Education and Supervision* 15, no. 1, pp. 6–11.

———. 1975c. *An Introduction to Career Education.* Washington, D.C.: U.S. Government Printing Office.

Humes, Charles W., Jr. 1972. "Accountability: A Boon to Guidance." *Personnel and Guidance Journal* 51, no. 1, pp. 21–26.

Humes, Charles W., Jr., and Kennedy, Thomas F., Jr. 1970. "The Counselor's Role in Collective Negotiation." *Personnel and Guidance Journal* 48, no. 6, pp. 449–455.

Innaccone, Laurence, and Lutz, Frank W. 1970. *Politics, Power, and Policy.* Columbus, Ohio: Charles E. Merrill.

Inniss, James. 1977. "Counseling the Culturally Disrupted Child." *Elementary School Guidance and Counseling* 11, no. 3, pp. 229–235.

Institute for Educational Development. 1963. *A Review of the Developmental Program Goals for the Comprehensive Career Education Model.* New York.

Ivey, Allen E. 1974a. "Adapting Systems to People." *Personnel and Guidance Journal* 53, no. 2, pp. 137–139.

———. 1974b. "Micro Counseling and Media Therapy: State of the Art." *Counselor Education and Supervision* 13, no. 3, pp. 172–183.

———. 1976. "Counseling Psychology, the Psychoeducator Model and the Future." *Counseling Psychologist* 6, no. 3, pp. 72–75.

Ivey, Allen E., and Alschuler, Alfred S. 1973a. "An Introduction to the Field." *Personnel and Guidance Journal* 51, no. 9, pp. 591–597.

———. 1973b. "Psychological Education Is. . . ." *Personnel and Guidance Journal* 51, no. 9, pp. 588–589.

Ivey, Allen E., and Gluckstern, Norma B. 1974. *Basic Attending Skills, Leader Manual.* North Amherst, Mass.: Microtraining Associates.

Ivey, Allen E., and Leppaluoto, Jean R. 1975. "Changes Ahead! Implications of the Vail Conference." *Personnel and Guidance Journal* 53, no. 10, pp. 747–752.

Jacobs, Margaret; Krogger, Albert H.; Lesar, David J.; and Redding, Arthur

J. 1971. "Parent Perception of the Role of Counselors in the Junior High School." *School Counselor* 18, no. 5, pp. 356–361.

Jacobson, Thomas J. 1972. "Career Guidance Centers." *Personnel and Guidance Journal* 50, no. 7, pp. 599–604.

———. 1975. "A Study of Career Centers in the State of California, Final Report." La Mesa, Calif.: Pupil Personnel Services, Grossmont Union High School District.

Jacobson, Thomas J., and Mitchell, Anita M. 1975. *Master Plan for Career Guidance and Counseling.* Grossmont, Calif.: Grossmont Union High School District.

Jeffries, Doris, and Spedding, Sally. 1974. "Education and the World of Work." *Elementary School Guidance and Counseling* 9, no. 1, pp. 49–51.

Jencks, Christopher. 1972. *Inequality: A Reassessment of the Effect of the Family and Schooling in America.* New York: Basic Books.

Jepsen, David A. 1974. "Vocational Decision-Making Strategy-Types: An Exploratory Study." *Vocational Guidance Quarterly* 23, no. 1, pp. 17–23.

———. 1975. "Occupational Decision Development Over the High School Years." *Journal of Vocational Behavior* 7, pp. 225–237.

Jersild, Arthur T.; Telford, Charles W.; and Sawrey, James M. 1975. *Child Psychology.* 7th ed. Englewood Cliffs, N.J.: Prentice-Hall.

Johansson, Charles B. 1975. "Technical Aspects: Problems of Scale Development, Norms, Item Differences by Sex, and the Rate of Change in Occupational and Group Characteristics." In *Issues of Sex Bias and Sex Fairness in Career Interest Measurement,* edited by Esther E. Diamond, pp. 65–88. Washington, D.C.: U.S. Department of Health, Education, and Welfare.

Johnson, David L., and Parker, Jackson V. 1965. "Walden III: An Alternative High School Survives Evaluation Quite Nicely, Thank You." *Phi Delta Kappan* 56, no. 9, pp. 624–628.

Johnson, Karen. 1977. "Meeting Teachers' Needs." *1977 Convention Summaries, Abstracts, and Research Reports.* Washington, D.C.: American Personnel Guidance Association, p. 201.

Johnson, Mauritz, Jr.; Busacker, William E.; and Bowman, Fred Q., Jr. 1961. *Junior High School Guidance.* New York: Harper and Brothers.

Johnson, William F.; Korn, Thomas A.; and Dunn, Dennis J. 1975. "Comparing Three Methods of Presenting Occupational Information." *Vocational Guidance Quarterly* 24, no. 1, pp. 62–66.

Jones, G. Brian; Tiedeman, David V.; Mitchell, Anita M.; Unruh, Waldemar R.; Helliwell, Carolyn B.; and Granschow, Laurie H. 1973. *Planning, Structuring, and Evaluating Practical Career Guidance for Integration by Non-College-Bound Youths.* Palo Alto, Calif.: American Institutes for Research.

Jones, Lawrence K. 1976. "A National Survey of the Program and Enrollment Characteristics of Counselor Education Programs." *Counselor Education and Supervision* 15, no. 3, pp. 166–176.

Jones, Wendell H. 1970. "Counselors in a Double-Bind." *Personnel and Guidance Journal* 48, no. 8, p. 606.

Kagiwada, George, and Fujimoto, Isao. 1973. "Asian-American Studies: Implications for Education." *Personnel and Guidance Journal* 51, no. 6, pp. 400–405.

Kaplan, Louis, and Stoughton, Robert W. 1974. *Pupil Personnel Services Guidelines for Introducing and Developing a Program of Accountability.* Princeton, N.J.: National Association of Pupil Personnel Administrators.

Kaplan, Marvin S.; Charin, Michael; and Clancy, Barbara. 1977. "Priority Roles for School Psychologists as Seen by Superintendents." *Journal of School Psychology* 15, no. 1, pp. 75–80.

Kater, Donna, and Spires, Jeannette. 1975. "Biofeedback: The Beat Goes On." *School Counselor* 23, no. 1, pp. 16–21.

Kearney, Annette G., and Clayton, Robert L. 1973. "Career Education and Blacks: Trick or Treat?" *School Counselor* 21, no. 2, pp. 102–108.

Kearney, C. Philip; Donovan, David L.; and Fisher, Thomas H. 1974. "In Defense of Michigan's Accountability Program." *Phi Delta Kappan* 56, no. 1, pp. 14–19.

Keebler, Nancy. 1976. "Family Therapy." *APA Monitor* 7, no. 5, pp. 4–5, 12.

Keefe, Joseph A. 1970. "The School Counselor as an Organizational Type." *Personnel and Guidance Journal* 48, no. 10, pp. 798–799.

Keller, F. J., and Viteles, M. S. 1937. *Vocational Guidance Throughout the World.* New York: Norton.

Kelly, F. Donald, and Dowd, E. Thomas. 1975. "The Staffing Conference: An Approach to Student Evaluation." *Counselor Education and Supervision* 15, no. 2, pp. 135–139.

Kemp, C. Gratton. 1971. "Existential Counseling." *Counseling Psychologist* 2, no. 3, pp. 2–30.

Kempler, Walter. 1973. "Gestalt Therapy." In *Current Psychotherapies*, edited by Raymond Corsini, pp. 251–286. Itasca, Ill.: F. E. Peacock.

Kennedy, Daniel A. 1976. "Some Impressions of Competency-Based Training Programs." *Counselor Education and Supervision* 15, no. 4, pp. 244–250.

Kimbrough, Ralph B. 1964. *Political Power and Educational Decision-Making.* Chicago: Rand McNally.

Kincaid, Marylou, and Kincaid, John. 1971. "Counseling for Peace." *Personnel and Guidance Journal* 49, no. 9, pp. 727–735.

Kirk, Barbara, A. 1969. " 'Counselee Participation' in Test Selection." *Counseling Psychologist* 1, no. 2, pp. 78–83.

Kirk, Jim, and Martin, Eileen. 1977. "Crisis Situations at the Middle/

Junior High Level: What Would You Do?" *Elementary School Guidance and Counseling* 11, no. 2, pp. 145–148.

Kohut, Sylvester, Jr. 1976. *The Middle School: A Bridge Between Elementary and Secondary Schools.* Washington, D.C.: National Education Association.

Kroll, Arthur M. 1976. "Career Education's Impact on Employability and Unemployment: Expectations and Realities." *Vocational Guidance Quarterly* 24, no. 3, pp. 209–218.

Krumboltz, John D. 1970. "Job Experience Kits." *Personnel and Guidance Journal* 49, no. 3, p. 233.

———. 1974. "An Accountability Model for Counselors." *Personnel and Guidance Journal* 52, no. 10, pp. 639–646.

Krumboltz, John D., and Baker, Ronald D. 1973. "Behavioral Counseling for Vocational Decision." In *Career Guidance for a New Age*, edited by Henry Borow, pp. 235–283. Boston: Houghton Mifflin.

Krumboltz, John D., and Schroeder, Wade W. 1965. "Promoting Career Planning Through Reinforcement." *Personnel and Guidance Journal* 44, no. 1, pp. 19–26.

Kunze, Karl R. 1973. "Business and Industry Look Out for Their Own." *Personnel and Guidance Journal* 52, no. 3, pp. 145–149.

Kurtz, Robert R. 1974. "Using a Transactional Analysis Format in Vocational Group Counseling." *Journal of College Student Personnel* 15, no. 6, pp. 447–451.

Kushel, Gerald. 1970. "The Counselor's Image and the Chameleon." *School Counselor* 17, no. 4, pp. 286–291.

Kuzniar, Joseph. 1973. "Teacher Consultation: A Case Study." *Personnel and Guidance Journal* 52, no. 2, pp. 108–111.

LaCrosse, Michael B., and Barak, Azy. 1976. "Differential Perception of Counselor Behavior." *Journal of Counseling Psychology* 23, no. 2, pp. 170–172.

Lane, David. 1970. "A Sterile Feud." *Personnel and Guidance Journal* 48, no. 6, p. 421.

Larson, William R., and Rice, Roger E. 1967. "The Differential Perception of the School Counselor by Deviant and Non-Deviant Students." *School Counselor* 15, no. 1, pp. 26–31.

Lauver, Philip J.; Gastellum, Richard M.; and Sheehey, Marilyn. 1975. "Bias in OOH Illustrations?" *Vocational Guidance Quarterly* 23, no. 4, pp. 335–340.

Lazarus, Richard S. 1975. "A Cognitively Oriented Psychologist Looks at Bio-Feed-Back." *American Psychologist* 30, no. 5, pp. 553–561.

Lechowicz, Joseph S. 1975. "Career Values Exploration Via Peer Group Counseling in High School." *1975 Convention Summaries, Abstracts, and Research Reports.* Washington, D.C.: American Personnel and Guidance Association, p. 137.

Leonard, George E.; Sather, Greg; Sheggrud, Darryl B.; and Handel, Linda.

1973. "Career Guidance in the Elementary School." *Elementary School Guidance and Counseling* 7, no. 4, pp. 287–291.

Leonard, George E., and Splete, Howard H. 1975. "Career Guidance in the Elementary School." *Elementary School Guidance and Counseling* 10, no. 1, pp. 50–56.

Leonard, George E., and Vriend, Thelma J. "Update: The Developmental Career Guidance Project." *Personnel and Guidance Journal* 53, no. 9, pp. 668–671.

Leviton, Harvey S. 1977. "Consumer Feedback on a Secondary School Guidance Program." *Personnel and Guidance Journal* 55, no. 5, pp. 242–244.

Lewis, Judy. 1972. "Introduction." *Personnel and Guidance Journal* 51, no. 2, p. 85.

Lewis, Michael D., and Lewis, Judith A. 1970. "The Counselor and Civil Liberties." *Personnel and Guidance Journal* 49, no. 1, pp. 9–13.

———. 1977. "The Counselor's Impact on Community Environments." *Personnel and Guidance Journal* 55, no. 6, pp. 356–358.

"The Licensing and Certification of Psychologists." *Counseling Psychologist* 5, no. 3, p. 135.

Liddle, Gordon P., and Ferguson, Donald G. 1968. *Pupil Personnel Development.* Washington, D.C.: Administrative Service.

Lifton, Walter M. 1969. "Making Mirror Images." *Personnel and Guidance Journal* 48, no. 2, pp. 133–134.

Lipsman, Clair K. 1969. "Revolution and Prophecy: Community Involvement for Counselors." *Personnel and Guidance Journal* 48, no. 2, pp. 97–100.

Lister, James L. 1969. "The Consultant to Counselors: A New Professional Role." *School Counselor* 16, no. 5, pp. 349–354.

Litwack, Lawrence. 1975. "Testimonial Privileged Communication: A Problem Reexamined." *School Counselor* 22, no. 3, pp. 194–196.

Lombana, Judy. 1977. *Perspectives on Secondary Guidance.* Tallahassee, Fla.: Department of Education.

Long, James D. 1971. "School Phobia and the Elementary Counselor." *Elementary School Guidance and Counseling* 5, no. 4, pp. 289–294.

Lounsbury, John H. 1974. "How the Junior High School Came to Be." In *The American Intermediate School*, edited by Max E. Brough and Russell L. Hamm, pp. 5–8. Danville, Ill.: Interstate Printers and Publishers.

Lounsbury, John H., and Douglass, Harl R. 1974. "Recent Trends in Junior High School Practice, 1954–1964." In *The American Intermediate School*, edited by Max E. Brough and Russell L. Hamm, pp. 168–178. Danville, Ill.: Interstate Printers and Publishers.

McCann, Barbara Goldman. 1975. "Peer Counseling: An Approach to Psychological Education." *Elementary School Guidance and Counseling* 9, no. 3, pp. 180–187.

McGehearty, Loyce. 1968. "The Case for Consultation." *Personnel and Guidance Journal* 47, no. 3, pp. 257–262.

McGlasson, Maurice. 1973. *The Middle School: Whence? What? Whither?* Bloomington, Ind.: Phi Delta Kappa Educational Foundation.

McKee, James B. 1969. *Introduction to Sociology.* New York: Holt, Rinehart and Winston.

McKinnon, Byron E., and Jones, G. Brian. 1975. "Field Testing a Comprehensive Career Guidance Program, K–12." *Personnel and Guidance Journal* 53, no. 9, pp. 663–667.

McLaughlin, Donald H. 1976. *Career Education in the Public Schools 1974–1975: A National Survey.* Washington, D.C.: U.S. Government Printing Office.

Macaluso, Lila. 1976. "Case Analysis: Consultation and Counseling." *Elementary School Guidance and Counseling* 10, no. 3, pp. 218–220.

Magoon, Thomas. 1973. "Outlook in Higher Education: Changing Functions." *Personnel and Guidance Journal* 52, no. 3, pp. 175–179.

Malcolm, David D. 1974. "The Center/Satellite Model: Grand Strategy for Change." *Personnel and Guidance Journal* 52, no. 5, pp. 303–308.

Mallory, Al. 1972. "IBM Educational and Career Exploration System (ECES)." In *Career Education and Technology for Career Development,* pp. 156–158, Palo Alto, Calif.: American Institutes for Research.

Mallory, Alva E., and Drake, Jeffrey W. 1973. *Final Report of the Educational and Career Exploration System (ECES) for 1972–73.* Flint, Mich.: Genesee Intermediate School District.

Marland, Sidney P., Jr. 1972. "Career Education. Now." *Vocational Guidance Quarterly* 20, no. 3, pp. 188–192.

———. 1974. *Career Education.* New York: McGraw-Hill.

Marland, Sidney P., Jr.; Lichtenwald, Harold; and Burke, Ralph. 1975. "Career Education, Texas Style! The Skyline Center in Dallas." *Phi Delta Kappan* 56, no. 9, pp. 616–620, 635.

Marple, Betty Lou W. 1972. "Guidance in 1995: The Possible Dream." *Personnel and Guidance Journal* 51, no. 3, pp. 191–194.

Martinson, William D., and Seay, Maurice F. 1974. "Counseling in Community Education." In *Community Education: A Developing Concept,* edited by Maurice F. Seay, pp. 261–281. Midland, Mich.: Pendell.

Maser, Arthur L. 1971. "Counselor Function in Secondary Schools." *School Counselor* 18, no. 5, pp. 367–372.

Masih, Lalit K. 1969. "Elementary School Teachers View Elementary Counseling." *School Counselor* 17, no. 2, pp. 105–107.

Matthews, Esther E. 1972. "Adolescence and Young Adulthood." In *Counseling Girls and Women Over the Life Span,* edited by Edwin H. Whitfield and Alice Gustav, pp. 23–33. Washington, D.C.: National Vocational Guidance Association.

Meador, Betty D., and Rogers, Carl R. 1973. "Client-Centered Therapy." In *Current Psychotherapies*, edited by Raymond Corsini, pp. 119–166. Itasca, Ill.: F. E. Peacock.

Mease, William, and Benson, Loren L. 1973. *Outcome Management Applied to Pupil Personnel Services.* St. Paul: Minnesota Department of Education.

Meltzoff, Julian, and Kornreich, Melvin. 1970. *Research in Psychotherapy.* New York: Atherton.

Menacker, Julius, 1975. "Inequality: Implications for Career Guidance." *Vocational Guidance Quarterly* 23, no. 3, pp. 243–249.

Mesa Public Schools. n.d.*a. Accountability for Counselors.* Mesa, Ariz.: Board of Education.

Mesa Public Schools. n.d.*b. Toward Accountability.* Mesa, Ariz.: Board of Education.

Meyer, Adolphe E. 1965. *An Educational History of the Western World.* New York: McGraw-Hill.

Michigan School Counselors Association. 1974. *Reaction to Action Guidance.* Kentwood: Executive Board, Michigan School Counselors Association.

Miller, Anna L., and Tiedeman, David V. 1974. "Technology and Guidance: The Challenge to More Elastic Existence Amid Accelerating Obsolescence." In *Vocational Guidance and Human Development*, edited by Edwin L. Herr, pp. 381–398. Boston: Houghton Mifflin.

Miller, Carroll H. 1961. *Foundations of Guidance.* New York: Harper and Brothers.

———. 1964. "Vocational Guidance in the Perspective of Cultural Change." In *Man in a World at Work*, edited by Henry Borow, pp. 3–23. Boston: Houghton Mifflin.

———. 1973. "Historical and Recent Perspectives on Work and Vocational Guidance." In *Career Guidance for a New Age*, edited by Henry Borow, pp. 3–39. Boston: Houghton Mifflin.

Miller, Delbert C., and Form, William H. 1951. *Industrial Sociology.* New York: Harper and Brothers.

Miller, Edith, and Warner, Richard W., Jr. 1975. "Single Subject Research and Evaluation." *Personnel and Guidance Journal* 54, no. 3, pp. 130–133.

Miller, George A. 1969. "Psychology as a Means of Promoting Human Welfare." *American Psychologist* 24, no. 12, pp. 1063–1075.

Miller, Juliet V., and Grisdale, George A. 1975. "Guidance Program Evaluation: What's Out There." *Measurement and Evaluation in Guidance* 8, no. 3, pp. 145–154.

"Millions of Adults Want Counseling." 1976. *Guidepost* 19, no. 1, p. 5.

Minzey, Jack. 1972. "Community Education: An Amalgam of Many Views." *Phi Delta Kappan* 54, no. 3, pp. 150–153.

Mitchell, Anita M., and Saum, James A., eds. 1972. *A Master Plan for*

Pupil Services. Fullerton: California Personnel and Guidance Association.

Mitchell, Dewayne W., and Crowell, Phyllis J. 1973. "Modifying Inappropriate Behavior in an Elementary Art Class." *Elementary School Guidance and Counseling* 8, no. 1, pp. 34–42.

Mobley, James Otis. 1976. "Occupational and Placement Specialists: A Survey and Status Report." *Florida Vocational Journal* 2, no. 1, pp. 20–22.

"Model Licensing Bill Written." 1976. *Guidepost* 18, no. 9, pp. 1–7.

Morgan, Lewis B. 1974. "Counseling for Future Shock." *Personnel and Guidance Journal* 52, no. 5, pp. 283–287.

Morrill, Weston H.; Oetting, Eugene R.; and Hurst, James C. 1974. "Dimensions of Counselor Functioning." *Personnel and Guidance Journal* 52, no. 6, pp. 354–359.

Mosher, Ralph L., and Sprinthall, Norman A. 1971. "Psychological Education: A Means to Promote Personal Development During Adolescence." *Counseling Psychologist* 2, no. 4, pp. 3–82.

Muro, James J. 1977. "New Services in Elementary School Counseling." *1977 Convention Summaries, Abstracts, and Research Reports.* Washington, D.C.: American Personnel and Guidance Association, p. 22.

Murray, Donald, and Schmuck, Richard. 1972. "The Counselor-Consultant as a Specialist in Organization Development." *Elementary School Guidance and Counseling* 7, no. 2, pp. 99–104.

Myrick, Robert D., and Wilkinson, Gary. 1976. "The Occupational Specialist: A Study of Guidance Support Personnel." *Vocational Guidance Quarterly* 24, no. 3, pp. 244–249.

Nasman, Daniel H. 1977. *Legal Concerns for Counselors.* Washington, D.C.: American School Counselor Association.

National Assessment of Educational Progress. 1976. "Classroom Benefits Seen in Assessment, Panelists Say." *NAEP Newsletter* 9, no. 4, pp. 1, 3–4.

National Commission on the Reform of Secondary Education. 1973. *The Reform of Secondary Education.* New York: McGraw-Hill.

National Forum on Educational Accountability. 1975. *Striving Toward Dialogue.* Denver, Colo.: Cooperative Accountability Project.

National Study of Secondary School Evaluation. 1969. *Evaluative Criteria, Section 7, Guidance Services.* 4th ed. Washington, D.C.: National Study of Secondary School Evaluation, pp. 289–300.

National Vocational Guidance Association. 1972. *Guidelines for the Preparation and Evaluation of Career Information Media.* Washington, D.C.: National Vocational Guidance Association.

——. 1973. "Career Development and Career Guidance." *NVGA Newsletter* 13, no. 1, pp. 5–8.

"Negotiations Survey." 1975. *ASCA Newsletter* 12, no. 3, p. 6.

"Negotiations Survey Results Show Need for More Membership Input." 1975. *ASCA Newsletter* 13, no. 1, p. 8b.

Neill, Shirley Ross. 1976. "Pasadena's Approach to the Classic School Debate." *American Education* 12, no. 3, pp. 6–10.

Nelson, Richard C., and Peterson, William D. 1975. "Challenging the Last Great Taboo: Death." *School Counselor* 22, no. 5, pp. 353–358.

Nierman, Wayne. 1972. "T. Wendell Williams Community Education Center for Coordination of Community Resources." *Community Educational Journal* (Feb., 1972).

Noeth, Richard J.; Roth, John D.; and Prediger, Dale J. 1975. "Student Career Development: Where Do We Stand?" *Vocational Guidance Quarterly* 23, no. 3, pp. 210–218.

Nordberg, Robert B. 1975. "Limitations of the Baseline Technique." *Personnel and Guidance Journal* 53, no. 7, p. 488.

Norris, Willa; Zeran, Franklin R.; Hatch, Raymond N.; and Engelkes, James R. 1972. *The Information Service in Guidance*. 3d ed. New York: Rand McNally.

O'Brien, Bernard A., and Lewis, Mel. 1975. "A Community Adolescent Self-Help Center." *Personnel and Guidance Journal* 54, no. 4, pp. 213–216.

O'Connor, James Robert. 1973. "Guidance Program Evaluation in 1970–71—A Follow-Up of Its Effectiveness and Value in Ohio Schools." Columbus, Ohio: Ohio State University (unpublished doctoral dissertation).

Odell, Charles E.; Pritchard, David H.; and Sinick, Daniel. 1974. "Whose Job Is Job Placement?" *Vocational Guidance Quarterly* 23, no. 2, pp. 138–145.

Odell, Louise M. 1975. "Secondary School Counseling: Past, Present, and Future." *Personnel and Guidance Journal* 52, no. 3, pp. 151–155.

Oetting, Eugene R., and Hawkes, James. 1974. "Training Professionals for Evaluative Research." *Personnel and Guidance Journal* 52, no. 6, pp. 434–438.

Ognibene, Gerald L., and Riccio, Anthony C. 1973. "Students' and Counselors' Knowledge of Drugs and Their Effects." *School Counselor* 20, no. 5, pp. 384–386.

O'Leary, K. Daniel, and Wilson, G. Terence. 1975. *Behavior Therapy*. Englewood Cliffs, N.J.: Prentice-Hall.

Omvig, Clayton P.; Tulloch, Rodney W.; and Thomas, Edward G. 1975. "The Effect of Career Education on Career Maturity." *Journal of Vocational Behavior* 7, no. 2, pp. 265–273.

Overs, Robert P. 1975. "Comment on 'Bias in OOH Illustrations?'" *Vocational Guidance Quarterly* 23, no. 4, pp. 340–341.

Palmo, Artis J., and Kuzniar, Joseph. 1972. "Modification of Behavior Through Group Counseling and Consultation." *Elementary School Guidance and Counseling* 6, no. 4, pp. 258–262.

Palomares, Uvaldo H. 1971*a*. "Introduction." *Personnel and Guidance Journal* 50, no. 2, p. 86.

———. 1971*b*. "Viva La Raza." *Personnel and Guidance Journal* 50, no. 2, pp. 119–129.

Panther, Edward W. 1972. "Counselors and Legislators: A Case History." *Personnel and Guidance Journal* 50, no. 8, pp. 667–671.

Passons, William R. 1976. "Community Mental Health Consultants in Schools." *School Counselor* 23, no. 4, pp. 275–280.

Paterson, Donald G. 1938. "The Genesis of Modern Guidance." *The Educational Record* 19, pp. 36–46.

Patouillet, Raymond; Drapela, Victor J.; and Karayanni, Mousa. 1975. "International Perspective on Vocational Guidance." *1975 Convention Summaries, Abstracts, and Research Reports.* Washington, D.C.: American Personnel and Guidance Association, pp. 43–44.

Patterson, C. H. 1969*a*. "The Counselor in the Elementary School." *Personnel and Guidance Journal* 47, no. 10, pp. 979–987.

———. 1969*b*. "A Current View of Client-Centered or Relationship Therapy." *Counseling Psychologist* 1, no. 2, pp. 2–25.

———. 1973. *Theories of Counseling and Psychotherapy.* 2d ed. New York: Harper and Row.

Patterson, Lewis E.; Hayes, Robert W.; and McIntire, Paul R. 1974. "Careers in Operation: Industry as a Laboratory for Counselor Development." *Counselor Education and Supervision* 14, no. 1, pp. 64–70.

Penney, James F. 1969. "Student Personnel Work: A Profession Stillborn." *Personnel and Guidance Journal* 47, no. 10, pp. 958–962.

Perrone, Philip A. 1973. "A Longitudinal Study of Occupational Values in Adolescents." *Vocational Guidance Quarterly* 22, no. 2, pp. 116–123.

Perrone, Philip A., and Kyle, Gene W. 1975. "Evaluating the Effectiveness of a Grade 7–9 Career Development Program." *Vocational Guidance Quarterly* 23, no. 4, pp. 317–323.

Perrone, Philip A.; Weiking, Mary C.; and Nagel, Elwyn H. 1965. "The Counseling Function as Seen by Students, Parents, and Teachers." *Journal of Counseling Psychology* 12, no. 2, pp. 148–152.

Peters, Herman J. 1970. *The Guidance Process.* Itasca, Ill.: F. E. Peacock.

Peterson, James A., and Park, Dick. 1975. "Values in Career Education: Some Pitfalls." *Phi Delta Kappan* 56, no. 9, pp. 621–623.

Pierce, Wendell. 1975. "Education's Evolving Role." *American Education* 11, no. 4, pp. 16–17, 22–24, 28–29.

Pietrofesa, John J.; Leonard, George E.; and Giroux, Roy F., eds. 1975. *Career Education and the Counselor.* Washington, D.C.: American Personnel and Guidance Association.

Pine, Gerald J. 1974. "Let's Give Away School Counseling." *School Counselor* 22, no. 2, pp. 94–99.

————. 1975. "Evaluating School Counseling Programs: Retrospect and Prospect." *Measurement and Evaluation in Guidance* 8, no. 3, pp. 136–144.

Piotrowski, Low J. 1975. "The Third Century Educational Process." Reprint V-6-13 from *Community Education Journal* Nov./Dec.

Ponzo, Zander. 1976. "Integrating Techniques from Five Counseling Theories." *Personnel and Guidance Journal* 54, no. 8, pp. 414–419.

Popham, W. James. 1976. "Normative Data for Criterion-Referenced Tests?" *Phi Delta Kappan* 57, no. 9, pp. 594.

Poppem, William A., and Thompson, Charles L. 1974. *School Counseling–Theories and Concepts*. Lincoln, Neb.: Professional Educators.

Potter, Micki. 1974. "Career Education and Counseling." *Personnel and Guidance Journal* 53, no. 4, pp. 328–329.

Prediger, Dale J. 1971. *Converting Test Data to Counseling Information*. Iowa City: The American College Testing Program.

————. 1972. "Test and Developmental Career Guidance: The Untried Relationship." *Measurement and Evaluation in Guidance* 5, no. 3, pp. 426–429.

Prediger, Dale J.; Roth, John D.; and Noeth, Richard J. 1973. *Nationwide Study of Career Development: Summary of Results*. ACT Research Report 61. Iowa City: American College Testing Program.

Protinsky, Howard, Jr. 1976. "Rational Counseling with Adolescents." *School Counselor* 23, no. 4, pp. 240–246.

Quesada-Fulgado, Carmencita. 1975. "Paraprofessionals' Need to Work." *Vocational Guidance Quarterly* 23, no. 3, pp. 263–266.

Quirk, Daniel A. 1976. "Life-Span Opportunities for the Older Adult." *Personnel and Guidance Journal* 55, no. 3, pp. 140–142.

Rabush, Carol M. 1976. "CVIS Catalogue." Mimeographed. Westminster, Md.: Western Maryland College.

Ralston, Lee. 1974. "Using TV to Promote Career Awareness Among Preschoolers." *Vocational Guidance Quarterly* 21, no. 3, pp. 73–76.

Raming, Henry E., and Frey, David H. 1974. "A Taxonomic Approach to the Gestalt Theory of Perls." *Journal of Counseling Psychology* 21, no. 3, pp. 179–184.

Randolph, Daniel Lee, and Saba, Robert G. 1973. "Changing Behavior Through Modeling and Consultation." *Elementary School Guidance and Counseling* 8, no. 2, pp. 98–106.

Raney, Barbara. 1975. "Helping Students Understand the World of Work." *Florida Vocational Journal* 1, no. 1, pp. 14–17.

Rathus, Spencer. 1975. "Principles and Practices of Assertive Training: An Eclectic Overview." *Counseling Psychologist* 5, no. 4, pp. 9–20.

Riccio, Anthony C., and Barnes, Keith D. 1973. "Counselor Preferences of Senior High School Students." *Counselor Education and Supervision* 13, no. 1, pp. 36–40.

Richardson, Lewis, Jr. 1976. "Implications of Peer Counseling for Urban Schools." *1976 Convention Summaries, Abstracts, and Research Reports.* Washington, D.C.: American Personnel and Guidance Association, p. 13.

Riese, Harlan C., and Stoner, William G. 1969. "Perceptions of the Role and Function of the School Counselor." *School Counselor* 17, no. 2, pp. 126–130.

Riles, Wilson C. 1975. "ECE in California Passes Its First Tests." *Phi Delta Kappan* 57, no. 1, pp. 3–7.

Ringness, Thomas A. 1975. *The Affective Domain in Education.* Boston: Little, Brown.

———. 1976 "The Educational Psychologist as a School Psychologist." *Educational Psychologist* 12, no. 1, pp. 89–90.

Robinson, Donald W. 1970. "Accountability for Whom? For What?" *Phi Delta Kappan* 52, no. 4, p. 193.

———. 1972. "An Interview with Christopher Jencks." *Phi Delta Kappan* 54, no. 4, pp. 255–257.

Rockwell, Perry J., and Rothney, John W. M. 1961. "Some Social Ideas of Pioneers in the Guidance Movement." *Personnel and Guidance Journal* 40, no. 4, pp. 349–354.

Rogers, Carl R. 1942. *Counseling and Psychotherapy.* Boston: Houghton Mifflin.

———. 1951. *Client-Centered Therapy.* Boston: Houghton Mifflin.

———. 1954. "An Overview of the Research and Some Questions for the Future." In *Psychotherapy and Personality*, edited by Carl R. Rogers and Rosalind F. Dymond, pp. 413–434. Chicago: University of Chicago Press.

———. 1975. "Empathic: An Unappreciated Way of Being." *Counseling Psychologist* 5, no. 2, pp. 2–10.

Rogers, Carl R., and Wallen, John L. 1946. *Counseling with Returned Servicemen.* New York: McGraw-Hill.

Roney, Anne M. 1975. "TA and Sex Stereotypes." *Personnel and Guidance Journal* 54, no. 3, pp. 165–170.

Rosen, Albert. 1967. "Client Preferences: An Overview of the Literature. *Personnel and Guidance Journal* 45, no. 8, pp. 785–789.

Rosen, Gerald M. 1976. "The Development and Use of Nonprescription Behavior Therapies." *American Psychologist* 31, no. 2, pp. 139–141.

Ross, Doris, 1976. "Compulsory Education, Not Compulsory Attendance." In *New Dimensions for Educating Youth,* edited by John Chaffee, Jr. and James P. Clark, pp. 19–20. Reston, Va.: National Association of Secondary School Principals.

Rossi, Robert J.; Bartlett, Wendy B.; Campbell, Emily A.; Wise, Lauress L.; and McLaughlin, Donald H. 1975. *Using the Talent Profiles in Counseling.* Palo Alto, Calif.: American Institutes for Research.

Rothney, John W. M. 1958. *Guidance Practices and Results*. New York: Harper and Brothers.

———. 1970. "Some Not-So-Sacred Cows." *Personnel and Guidance Journal* 48, no. 10, pp. 803–808.

Rothney, John W. M., and Roens, Bert A. 1952. *Guidance of American Youth*. Cambridge, Mass.: Harvard University Press.

Rotter, Joe, and Crunk, Bill. 1975. "It's a Child's Right." *Elementary School Guidance and Counseling* 9, no. 4, pp. 263–269.

Ruiz, Rene A., and Padilla, Amado M. 1977. "Counseling Latinos." *Personnel and Guidance Journal* 55, no. 7, pp. 401–408.

Russell Sage Foundation. 1970. "Proposed Principles for the Management of School Records: Excerpts." *Personnel and Guidance Journal* 49, no. 1, pp. 21–23.

Ryerson, Margaret S. 1977. "Death Education and Counseling for Children." *Elementary School Guidance and Counseling* 11, no. 3, pp. 165–174.

Salisbury, Hal. 1975. "Counseling the Elderly: A Neglected Area in Counselor Education." *Counselor Education and Supervision* 14, no. 3, pp. 237–238.

Sarason, Irwin G. 1968. "Verbal Learning, Modeling, and Juvenile Delinquency." *American Psychologist* 23, no. 4, pp. 254–266.

Sauber, S. Richard. 1975. "Multiple-Family Group Counseling." In *The Consulting Process*, edited by Jon Carlson, Howard Splete, and Roy Kern, pp. 310–316. Washington, D.C.: American Personnel and Guidance Association.

Schlossberg, Nancy K. 1975. "Programs for Adults." *Personnel and Guidance Journal* 53, no. 9, pp. 681–685.

Scholz, Nelle Tumlin; Prince, Judith Sosebee; and Miller, Gordon Porter. 1975. *How to Decide*. New York: College Entrance Examination Board.

"School Consolidation: Is Bigger Always Better?" 1976. *NIE Information*, Winter, pp. 1, 8.

Schwartz, Gary E. 1973. "Biofeedback as Therapy." *American Psychologist* 28, no. 8, pp. 666–673.

Schweisheimer, William, and Walberg, Herbert J. 1976. "A Peer Counseling Experiment: High School Students as Small-Group Leaders." *Journal of Counseling Psychology* 23, no. 4, pp. 398–401.

Seay, Maurice F. 1974. "The Community Education Concept—A Definition." In *Community Education: A Developing Concept*, edited by Maurice F. Seay and Associates, pp. 3–15. Midland, Mich.: Pendell.

Seidman, E., et al. 1970. "The Child Development Consultant: An Experiment." *Personnel and Guidance Journal* 49, no. 1, pp. 29–34.

Sessions, John A. 1975. "Misdirecting Career Education: A Union View." *Vocational Guidance Quarterly* 23, no. 4, pp. 311–316.

Shane, Harold G. 1976. "America's Next 25 Years: Some Implications for Education." *Phi Delta Kappan* 58, no. 1, pp. 78–83.

Shapiro, Michelle, and Asher, William. 1972. "Students Who Seldom Discuss Their Post High School Plans." *School Counselor* 20, no. 2, pp. 103–108.

Sharf, Richard S. 1974. "Interest Inventory Interpretation: Implications for Research and Practice." *Measurement and Evaluation in Guidance* 7, no. 1, pp. 16–23.

Shaw, Merville C. 1968a. "The Feasibility of Parent Group Counseling in Elementary Schools." *Elementary School Guidance and Counseling* 2, no. 4, pp. 276–285.

———. 1968b. *The Function of Theory in Guidance Programs.* Boston: Houghton Mifflin.

———. 1973. *School Guidance Systems.* Boston: Houghton Mifflin.

———. 1977. "The Development of Counseling Programs: Priorities, Progress, and Professionalism." *Personnel and Guidance Journal* 55, no. 6, pp. 339–345.

Shertzer, Bruce, and Stone, Shelley C. 1974. *Fundamentals of Counseling.* Boston: Houghton Mifflin.

———. 1976. *Fundamentals of Guidance.* 3d ed. Boston: Houghton Mifflin.

Shoben, Edward Joseph, Jr. 1962. "The Counselor's Theory as a Personal Trait." *Personnel and Guidance Journal* 40, no. 7, pp. 617–621.

———. 1969. "Stray Thoughts on Revisited Eclecticism." *Personnel and Guidance Journal* 48, no. 3, pp. 198–200.

Shoemaker, James T., and Splitter, Jackie L. 1976. "A Competency-Based Model for Counselor Certification." *Counselor Education and Supervision* 15, no. 4, pp. 267–274.

Siegel, Adelaide. 1972. "1921 to 1971: 50 Years of the *P & G.*" *Personnel and Guidance Journal* 50, no. 6, pp. 513–521.

Simon, Sidney B. 1973. "Values Clarification." *Personnel and Guidance Journal* 51, no. 9, pp. 614–618.

Sinick, Daniel. 1973. "Rehabilitation Counselors on the Move." *Personnel and Guidance Journal* 52, no. 3, pp. 167–170.

———. 1976. "Guest Editor's Introduction." *Personnel and Guidance Journal* 55, no. 3, pp. 100–101.

Smith, Darrell, and Peterson, James A. 1977. "Counseling and Values in a Time Perspective." *Personnel and Guidance Journal* 55, no. 6, pp. 309–318.

Smith, Elsie J. 1977. "Counseling Black Individuals: Some Stereotypes." *Personnel and Guidance Journal* 55, no. 7, pp. 390–396.

Smith, Gloria S.; Barnes, Edward; and Scales, Alice. 1974. "Counseling the Black Child." *Elementary School Guidance and Counseling* 8, no. 4, pp. 245–253.

Smith, Margaret Ruth. 1976. "The Voyage of Esther Lloyd-Jones: Travels with a Pioneer." *Personnel and Guidance Journal* 54, no. 9, pp. 474–480.

Smith, Vernon H. 1973. "Options in Public Education: The Quiet Revolution." *Phi Delta Kappan* 54, no. 7, pp. 434–437.

————. 1974. *Alternative Schools.* Lincoln, Nebr.: Professional Educators Publications.

Smith, Vernon H.; Burke, Daniel J.; and Barr, Robert D. 1974. *Optional Alternative Public Schools.* Bloomington, Ind.: Phi Delta Kappa.

Spang, Alonzo T., Jr. 1971. "Understanding the Indian." *Personnel and Guidance Journal* 50, no. 2, pp. 97–102.

Sparks, Dennis. 1977. "Involvement: Counseling in an Alternative School." *School Counselor* 24, no. 4, pp. 253–260.

Spence, Donald P. 1973. "Analog and Digital Descriptions of Behavior." *American Psychologist* 28, no. 6, pp. 479–488.

Splete, Howard. 1971. "The Elementary School Counselor: An Effective Consultant with Classroom Teachers." *Elementary School Guidance and Counseling* 5, no. 3, pp. 165–172.

Splete, Howard, and Rasmussen, Jeanette. 1977. "Aiding the Mobile Child." *Elementary School Guidance and Counseling* 11, no. 3, pp. 225–228.

Sporakowski, Michael J., and Eubanks, Janet M. 1976. "Parent-Adolescent Communication and School Adjustment." *School Counselor* 23, no. 3, pp. 185–190.

Sprinthall, Norman A., and Erickson, V. Lois. 1974. "Learning Psychology by Doing Psychology: Guidance Through the Curriculum." *Personnel and Guidance Journal* 52, no. 6, pp. 396–405.

"Standardized Tests: Sexy, Sexless, or Sexist?" 1975. *1975 Convention Summaries, Abstracts, and Research Reports.* Washington, D.C.: American Personnel and Guidance Association, pp. 253–254.

Staudenmeier, James J. 1967. "Student Perceptions of Counselor Behavior Contributing to a Helping Relationship." *School Counselor* 15, no. 2, pp. 113–117.

Stefflre, Buford, ed. 1965. *Theories of Counseling.* New York: McGraw-Hill.

Stefflre, Buford, and Grant, W. Harold, eds. 1972. *Theories of Counseling.* 2d ed. New York: McGraw-Hill.

Stephens, W. Richard. 1970. *Social Reform and the Origins of Vocational Guidance.* Washington, D.C.: National Vocational Guidance Association.

————. 1974. "New Light on Junior High School History." In *The American Intermediate School*, edited by Max E. Brough and Russell L. Hamm, pp. 9–18. Danville, Ill.: Interstate Printers and Publishers.

Stern, Barry E. 1975. "The Occupational Information Systems Grants

Program of the U.S. Department of Labor." *Vocational Guidance Quarterly* 23, no. 3, pp. 202–209.

Stiller, Alfred. 1974. "Presenting: The Consultant to Counselors." *School Counselor* 21, no. 5, pp. 342–349.

Stillwell, Larry, and Collison, Brooke B. 1974. "A Career Development Program for a Small School." *Vocational Guidance Quarterly* 23, no. 2, pp. 174–177.

Stilwell, William E. 1976. "A Systems Approach for Implementing an Affective Education Program." *Counselor Education and Supervision* 15, no. 3, pp. 200–210.

Stilwell, William E., and Santoro, David A. 1976. "A Training Model for the 1980s." *Personnel and Guidance Journal* 54, no. 6, pp. 323–326.

Stinzi, Vernon L., and Hutcheson, William R. 1972. "We Have a Problem—Can You Help Us?" *School Counselor* 19, no. 5, pp. 329–334.

Stolz, Stephanie B.; Wienckowski, Louis A.; and Brown, Bertram S. 1975. "Behavior Modification." *American Psychologist* 30, no. 11, pp. 1027–1048.

Strickland, Ben. 1969. "The Philosophy-Theory-Practice Continuum: A Point-of-View." *Counselor Education and Supervision* 8, no. 3, pp. 165–175.

Stubbins, Joseph. 1970. "The Politics of Counseling." *Personnel and Guidance Journal* 48, no. 8, pp. 611–618.

Stude, E. W., and Goodyear, Don L. 1975. *Ethics and the Counselor.* Fullerton: California Personnel and Guidance Association.

Stufflebeam, D. L. 1968. "Evaluation as Enlightenment for Decision-Making." Address sponsored by the Commission on Assessment of Educational Outcomes and Association for Supervision and Curriculum Development, Sarasota, Florida, January 1968.

Sue, Derald Wing. 1975a. "New Directions." *Personnel and Guidance Journal* 53, no. 8, p. 550.

———. 1975b. "What Do We Stand For?" *Personnel and Guidance Journal* 54, no. 1, p. 6.

———. 1977. "Counseling the Culturally Different: A Conceptual Analysis." *Personnel and Guidance Journal* 55, no. 7, pp. 422–425.

Sue, Derald Wing, and Sue, David. 1973. "An Overview." *Personnel and Guidance Journal* 51, no. 6, pp. 387–389.

Sue, Stanley. 1977. "Psychological Theory and Implications for Asian Americans." *Personnel and Guidance Journal* 55, no. 7, pp. 381–389.

Sullivan, Howard J., and O'Hare, Robert W., eds. 1971. *Accountability in Pupil Personnel Services: A Process Guide for the Development of Objectives.* Fullerton: California Personnel and Guidance Assn.

Super, Donald E. 1969. "Vocational Development Theory: Persons, Positions, and Processes." *Counseling Psychologist* 1, no. 1, pp. 2–9.

———. 1970. *Computer-Assisted Counseling.* New York: Teachers College Press.

Super, Donald E., and Bohn, Martin J., Jr. 1970. *Occupational Psychology.* Belmont, Calif.: Wadsworth.

Sweeney, T. J. 1966. "The School Counselor as Perceived by School Counselors and Their Principals." *Personnel and Guidance Journal* 44, no. 8, pp. 844–849.

Sweeney, Thomas J., and Sturdevant, Alan D. 1974. "Licensure in the Helping Professions: Anatomy of an Issue." *Personnel and Guidance Journal* 52, no. 9, pp. 575–580.

Tanney, Mary Faith. 1975. "Face Validity of Interest Measures: Sex Role Stereotyping." In *Issues of Sex Bias and Sex Fairness in Career Interest Measurement,* edited by Esther E. Diamond, pp. 89–99. Washington, D.C.: U.S. Department of Health, Education, and Welfare.

Thoresen, Carl E.; Hosford, Ray E.; and Krumboltz, John D. 1970. "Determining Effective Models for Counseling Clients of Varying Competencies." *Journal of Counseling Psychology* 17, no. 4, pp. 369–375.

Thorne, Frederick C. 1973. "Eclectic Psychotherapy." In *Current Psychotherapies,* edited by Raymond Corsini, pp. 445–486. Itasca, Ill.: F. E. Peacock.

Tindall, Judy. 1976. "Middle/Junior High Counseling." *ASCA Newsletter* 14, no. 1, pp. 5–8.

Toews, Jay M. 1969. "The Counselor as a Contingency Manager." *Personnel and Guidance Journal* 48, no. 2, pp. 127–134.

Tolbert, E. L. 1947. "An Evaluation of the Guidance Service of South High School, Columbus, Ohio." Master's thesis, Ohio State University.

———. 1959. *Introduction to Counseling.* New York: McGraw-Hill.

———. 1971. "A Prognosis for the Consultant as a Counseling Role." Mimeographed.

———. 1972. *Introduction to Counseling.* 2d ed. New York: McGraw-Hill.

———. 1974. *Counseling for Career Development.* Boston: Houghton Mifflin.

———. 1976. "Guest Editor's Introduction." *Vocational Guidance Quarterly* 24, no. 4, pp. 294–297.

Tolsma, Robert J.; Menne, John W.; and Hopper, Gordon. 1976. "The High School Characteristics Index as an Individual and Aggregate Response Measure." *Measurement and Evaluation in Guidance* 9, no. 1, pp. 5–14.

Trotzer, James P., and Kassera, Wayne J. 1971. "Do Counselors Do What They Are Taught?" *School Counselor* 18, no. 5, pp. 335–341.

Truax, Charles B. 1963. "Effective Ingredients in Psychotherapy: An Approach to Unraveling the Patient-Therapist Interaction." *Journal of Counseling Psychology* 10, no. 3, pp. 256–263.

Tseng, Michael, and Thompson, Donald L. 1968. "Differences Between

Adolescents Who Seek Counseling and Those Who Do Not." *Personnel and Guidance Journal* 47, no. 4, pp. 333–336.

Tuma, Abdul H., and Gustad, John W. 1957. "The Effects of Client and Counselor Personality Characteristics on Client Learning in Counseling." *Journal of Counseling Psychology* 4, no. 2, pp. 136–141.

Tuma, Margaret R. 1974. "Implementing a Program in Developmental Guidance and Counseling." *Personnel and Guidance Journal* 52, no. 6, pp. 376–381.

Tyler, Leona E. 1958. "Theoretical Principles Underlying the Counseling Process." *Journal of Counseling Psychology* 5, no. 1, pp. 3–8.

———. 1960. "Minimum Change Therapy." *Personnel and Guidance Journal* 38, no. 6, pp. 475–479.

———. 1969. *The Work of the Counselor.* 3d ed. New York: Appleton-Century-Crofts.

Tyler, Ralph W. 1975a. "Reconstructing the Total Educational Environment." *Phi Delta Kappan* 57, no. 1, pp. 12–13.

———. 1975b. "Tomorrow's Education." *American Education* 11, no. 7, pp. 16–19, 22–23.

Update, Experience-Based Career Education News. 1976. Volume 1, no. 1, p. 2.

U.S. Department of Health, Education, and Welfare. 1971. *Career Education.* Washington, D.C.: U.S. Government Printing Office.

U.S. Department of Labor. 1976. *Occupational Outlook Handbook.* Washington, D.C.: U.S. Government Printing Office.

———. 1977. *Dictionary of Occupational Titles.* 4th ed. Washington, D.C.: U.S. Government Printing Office.

Van Hoose, William H. 1975. "Children's Rights and the School Counselor." *Elementary School Guidance and Counseling* 9, no. 4, pp. 279–286.

Vannote, Vance G. 1974. "A Practical Approach to Behavior Modification Programs." *School Counselor* 21, no. 5, pp. 350–355.

Varenhorst, Barbara B. 1974. "Training Adolescents as Peer Counselors." *Personnel and Guidance Journal* 53, no. 4, pp. 271–275.

Veterans Administration. 1976. "Licensing Board Created." *Guidepost* 18, no. 15, p. 1.

Wall, Judy. 1974. "Getting into Print in *P & G:* How It's Done." *Personnel and Guidance Journal* 52, no. 9, pp. 594–602.

Walz, Garry R. 1975. "Swinging into the Future." *Personnel and Guidance Journal* 53, no. 9, pp. 712–716.

Walz, Garry R., and Benjamin, Libby. 1974. "The Life Career Development System." In *A Comprehensive View of Career Development,* edited by Garry R. Walz, Robert L. Smith, and Libby Benjamin, pp. 71–79. Washington, D.C.: American Personnel and Guidance Association.

Walz, Garry R., and Miller, Juliet. 1969. "School Climate and Student Behavior: Implications for Counselor Role." *Personnel and Guidance Journal* 47, no. 9, pp. 859–866.

Wandt, Edwin A. 1965. *A Cross-Section of Educational Research.* New York: David McKay.

Ward, Patricia, and Rouzer, David L. 1974. "The Nature of Pathological Functioning from a Gestalt Perspective." *Counseling Psychologist* 4, no. 4, pp. 24–27.

Ware, Martha L. 1971. "The Law and Counselor Ethics." *Personnel and Guidance Journal* 50, no. 4, pp. 305–317.

Warman, R. E. 1960*a*. "Differential Perceptions of Counseling Role." *Journal of Counseling Psychology* 7, no. 4, pp. 269–274.

———. 1960*b*. "The School Counselor's Counseling Role as Seen by Counselor and Administrator." Paper presented at the American Personnel and Guidance Association Meeting.

———. 1961. "The Counseling Role of College and University Counseling Centers." *Journal of Counseling Psychology* 8, no. 3, pp. 231–237.

Warnath, Charles F., ed. 1973*a*. *New Directions of College Counselors.* San Francisco: Jossey-Bass.

———. 1973*b*. "The School Counselors as Institutional Agent." *School Counselor* 20, no. 3, pp. 202–208.

Warner, Richard W. 1974. "Consulting with Parents." *Personnel and Guidance Journal* 53, no. 1, pp. 68–70.

———. 1975. "Research in Counseling." *Personnel and Guidance Journal* 53, no. 10, pp. 792–794.

Washburn, George, and Schmaljohn, Phyllis. 1975. "What Do You Want to Be When You Grow Up? A Pilot Project in Career Awareness." *Elementary School Guidance and Counseling* 10, no. 2, pp. 142–147.

Wasson, Robert M., and Strowig, R. Wray. 1965. "Counselor Isolation and Some Concomitant Perceptions." *Journal of Counseling Psychology* 12, no. 2, pp. 133–140.

Watts, A. G. 1973. "Counseling and Career Education in the United States: A Visitor's View." *Vocational Guidance Quarterly* 21, no. 4, pp. 254–261.

Weinrach, Stephen G. 1974. "How to Evaluate Career Information Materials." *School Counselor* 22, no. 1, pp. 53–57.

———. 1975. "How Effective Am I? Five Easy Steps to Self-Evaluation." *School Counselor* 22, no. 3, pp. 202–205.

Welbourne, Ann K. 1975. "A Peer Approach to Adolescent Sexual Information and Help." *Counseling Psychologist* 5, no. 1, pp. 77–80.

Wellman, Frank. 1967. "The Assessment of Counseling Outcomes: A Conceptual Framework." In *Research in Counseling: Evaluation and Refocus,* ed. J. M. Whiteley, pp. 153–174. Columbus, Ohio: Merrill.

Wesman, Alexander G. 1968. "Intelligent Testing." *American Psychologist* 23, no. 4, pp. 267–274.

————. 1972. "Testing and Counseling: Fact and Fancy." *Measurement and Evaluation in Guidance* 5, no. 3, pp. 397–402.

Westbrook, Bert W. 1974. "Content Analysis of Six Career Development Tests." *Measurement and Evaluation in Guidance* 7, no. 3, pp. 172–180.

Whitely, John, and Whitely, Rita. 1977. "California Court Expands Privilege Debate." *APA Monitor* 8, no. 2, pp. 5–6, 18.

Wilhelm, Charles D., and Case, Madelyn. 1975. "Telling It Like It Is— Improving School Records." *School Counselor* 23, no. 2, pp. 84–90.

Wilkinson, Gary S., and Bleck, Robert T. 1977. "Children's Divorce Groups." *Elementary School Guidance and Counseling* 11, no. 3, pp. 205–213.

Williams, John M. 1976. "Peer Career Advising Program." *1976 Convention Abstracts, Summaries, and Research Reports,* p. 350. Washington, D.C.: American Personnel and Guidance Association.

Williams, Robert I. 1970. "Black Pride, Academic Relevance and Individual Achievement." *The Counseling Psychologist* 2, no. 1, pp. 18–22.

Williamson, E. G. 1961. *Student Personnel Services in Colleges and Universities.* New York: McGraw-Hill.

————. 1965. *Vocational Counseling: Some Historical, Philosophical, and Theoretical Perspectives.* New York: McGraw-Hill.

Williamson, E. G., and Biggs, Donald A. 1975. *Student Personnel Work.* New York: John Wiley and Sons.

Wilson, Sandra Reitz, and Wise, Lauress L. 1975. *The American Citizen: 11 Years After High School.* Palo Alto, Calif.: American Institutes for Research.

Winter, Jeanne, and Schmidt, Jerry A. 1974. "A Replicable Career Program for Junior High." *Vocational Guidance Quarterly* 23, no. 2, pp. 177–179.

Wirtz, Willard. 1976. "Education/Work Policy: A New Imperative, a New Prospect." *Phi Delta Kappan* 58, no. 1, pp. 99–103.

Witmer, J. Melvin, and Cottingham, Harold F. 1970. "The Teacher's Role and Guidance Functions as Reported by Elementary Teachers." *Elementary School Guidance and Counseling* 5, no. 1, pp. 12–21.

Wittmer, Joe; Lanier, James E.; and Parker, Max. 1976. "Race Relations Training with Correctional Officers." *Personnel and Guidance Journal* 54, no. 6, pp. 302–306.

Woody, Robert H. 1968. "Vocational Counseling with Behavioral Techniques." *Vocational Guidance Quarterly* 17, no. 2, pp. 97–103.

Worthington, Robert M. 1974. *Career Education in the United States Today: What It Is, Where, and the Results So Far.* Flagstaff: Northern Arizona University.

Wortman, Paul M. 1975. "Evaluation Research." *American Psychologist* 30, no. 5, pp. 562–575.

Worzbyt, John C. 1976. "Pupil Records: A Crisis in Perspective." *School Counselor* 23, no. 5, pp. 358–361.

Wrenn, C. Gilbert. 1970. "The Three Worlds of the Counselor." *Personnel and Guidance Journal* 49, no. 2, pp. 91–96.

———. 1976. "Values and Counseling in Different Countries and Cultures." *School Counselor* 24, no. 1, pp. 6–14.

Wubbolding, Robert E. 1975. "Practicing Reality Therapy." *Personnel and Guidance Journal* 54, no. 3, pp. 164–165.

Wubbolding, Robert E., and Osborne, Lynda Byrd. 1976. "Increasing Success Identity Through Career Awareness: A Sequential Model." *Elementary School Guidance and Counseling* 10, no. 3, pp. 214–217.

Wyatt, Ouida L. 1969. "Comment." *Personnel and Guidance Journal* 47, no. 6, p. 599.

Wysong, H. Eugene. 1974. *Objectives of a Guidance Program.* Columbus, Ohio: Ohio Department of Education.

Zifferblatt, Steven M. 1972. "Analysis and Design of Counselor Training Systems: An Operant and Operations Research Perspective." *Counseling Psychologist* 3, no. 4, part 2, pp. 12–31.

Zimpfer, David; Frederickson, Ronald; Salim, Mitchell; and Sanford, Alpheus. 1971. *Support Personnel in School Guidance Programs.* Washington, D.C.: American Personnel and Guidance Association.

Ziv, Avner. 1974. "From Israel." *Personnel and Guidance Journal* 53, no. 1, pp. 55–56.

Zytowski, Donald G. 1967. "Some Notes on the History of Vocational Counseling." *Vocational Guidance Quarterly* 16, no. 1, pp. 53–55.

———. 1972. "Four Hundred Years Before Parsons." *Personnel and Guidance Journal* 50, no. 6, pp. 443–450.

———. 1975. "Editor's Page." *Measurement and Evaluation in Guidance* 8, no. 3, pp. 132–133.

ACKNOWLEDGMENTS *(Continued from page iv)*

The definition of consultation on page 207 is from Loyce McGehearty, "The Case for Consultation," *Personnel and Guidance Journal* 47, no. 3, pp. 259–260. Copyright 1968 by the American Personnel and Guidance Association. Reprinted by permission.

The table on page 209 is based on material in E. R. Gerler, Jr., "New Directions for School Counseling," *School Counselor* 23, no. 4, pp. 249–250. Copyright 1976 by the American Personnel and Guidance Association. Reprinted by permission.

The list on pages 243–244 and table on page 245 are adapted from page 42 and page 30 in *Support Personnel in School Guidance Programs* by D. Zimpfer, R. Frederickson, M. Salim, and A. Sanford. Copyright 1971 by the American Personnel and Guidance Association. Reprinted by permission.

The table on page 246 is from S. J. Danish, A. R. D'Augelli, and G. W. Brock, "An Evaluation of Helping Skills Training: Effects on Helpers' Verbal Responses," *Journal of Counseling Psychology* 23, no. 3, p. 263. Copyright 1976 by the American Psychological Association. Reprinted by permission.

The table on page 252 is from P. G. Cooker and P. J. Cherchia, "Effects of Communication Skill Training on High School Students' Ability to Function as Peer Group Facilitators," *Journal of Counseling Psychology* 23, no. 5, p. 466. Copyright 1976 by the American Psychological Association. Reprinted by permission.

The evaluation on page 253 is from James Otis Mobley, "Occupational and Placement Specialists: A Survey and Status Report," *Florida Vocational Journal* 2, no. 1. (1976), pp. 20–22. Reprinted by permission.

Survey results on pages 261–262 are from "Eighth Annual Gallup Poll of the Public's Attitudes Toward the Public Schools," *Phi Delta Kappan* 58, no. 2 (October 1976), pp. 189–190. Reprinted by permission.

The table on page 267 is taken in part from E. D. Edington, "Evaluation of Methods of Using Resource People in Helping Kindergarten Students Become Aware of the World of Work," *Journal of Vocational Behavior* 8, no. 2 (1976), p. 129. Reprinted by permission.

The table on page 268 is excerpted from one in C. P. Omvig, R. W. Tulloch, and E. G. Thomas, "The Effects of Career Education on Career Maturity," *Journal of Vocational Behavior* 7, no. 2 (1975), p. 270. Reprinted by permission.

On pages 294–296, the material from *Ethics and the Counselor* by E. W. Stude and D. L. Goodyear, pp. 26–28, is reprinted by permission. Copyright © 1975 by the California Personnel and Guidance Association.

The table on page 325 is from *A Cross-Section of Educational Research* by Edwin Wandt, p. 5. Copyright © 1965 by David McKay Company, Inc., © 1977 by Longman, Inc. Reprinted by permission of Longman, Inc.

Appendix A on page 351, *Standards for the Preparation of Counselors and Other Personnel Services Specialists*, is reprinted by permission of the American Personnel and Guidance Association and its Division 2, Association for Counselor Education and Supervision.

Appendix B on page 367, *Commission Position on State Licensure of Counselors*, is from the American Personnel and Guidance Licensure Commission Action Packet (February 1977).

Appendix C on page 384, *Ethical Standards*, copyright 1974 by the American Personnel and Guidance Association, is reprinted by permission.

Appendix D on page 397, *National Divisions of the American Personnel and Guidance Association*, is from American Personnel and Guidance Association, *Counseling Resource—1977* (Washington, D.C.), p. 21.

Appendix E on page 401, *Code of Ethics*, is reprinted with permission from *School Counselor* 21, no. 2, 1973, pp. 137–140, copyright 1973 by American Personnel and Guidance Association.

NAME INDEX

SUBJECT INDEX